剑桥应用语言学年度评论 2010
Annual Review of Applied Linguistics

应用语言学专题
A Survey of Selected Topics in Applied Linguistics

主编 〔美〕Charlene Polio

导读 郑萱

2016年·北京

Originally published by Cambridge University Press in 2010. This reprint edition is published with the permission of the Syndicate of the Press of the University of Cambridge, Cambridge, England.
原书由英国剑桥大学出版社于 2010 年出版。
本版经英国剑桥大学出版社授权出版。

This edition is licensed for sale in the People's Republic of China only (excluding Hong Kong SAR, Macao SAR and Taiwan Province). No part of this publication may be reproduced or distributed by any means, or stored in a database or retrieval system, without the prior written permission of the publisher.
本版仅限在中华人民共和国境内（不包括香港特别行政区、澳门特别行政区及台湾）销售。未经出版者书面许可，不得以任何方式复制或发行本书的任何部分。

剑桥应用语言学年度评论
专家委员会

主　任　胡壮麟

副主任　田贵森　朱永生

委　员　曹　进　何　伟　靳　琰　赖良涛　李战子
　　　　　彭宣维　齐振海　孙迎晖　王振华　辛志英
　　　　　杨信彰　于　晖　张　辉　张　琳　张　薇
　　　　　郑　萱

CONTENTS

总序 ··· 胡壮麟　1
导读 ··· 郑　萱　11
Editor's Introduction ·· Charlene Polio　i

SECTION A: HERITAGE LANGUAGE LEARNING

Current Issues in Heritage Language Acquisition
·· Silvina Montrul　3
Curriculum Development for Advancing Heritage Language Competence:
　Recent Research, Current Practices, and a Future Agenda
·· Kimi Kondo-Brown　31
International Comparative Perspectives on Heritage
　Language Education Policy Research
·· Jeffrey Bale　57
The Heart of Heritage: Sociocultural Dimensions of
　Heritage Language Learning
·· Agnes Weiyun He　89

SECTION B: RESEARCH METHODS AND TECHNIQUES

Meta-analysis in Second Language Research:
　Choices and Challenges
·· Frederick L. Oswald and Luke Plonsky　115
Concurrent Verbal Reports in Second Language
　Acquisition Research
·· Melissa A. Bowles　150

Qualitative Interviews in Applied Linguistics: From
Research Instrument to Social Practice
.... Steven Talmy 173

Uses of Eye-Tracking Data in Second Language
Sentence Processing Research
.... Paola E. Dussias 201

SECTION C: LANGUAGE SOCIALIZATION

Language Socialization into Academic Discourse Communities
.... Patricia A. Duff 229

Becoming National: Classroom Language Socialization and
Political Identities in the Age of Globalization
.... Debra A. Friedman 262

Language Socialization in the Workplace
.... Celia Roberts 286

SECTION D: LINGUISTIC THEORY AND SECOND LANGUAGE ACQUISITION

Semantic Theory and Second Language Acquisition
.... Roumyana Slabakova 313

Second Language Acquisition and Syntactic Theory
in the 21st Century
.... Juana M. Liceras 335

Usage-Based Approaches to Language and Their
Applications to Second Language Learning
.... Andrea Tyler 365

CONTRIBUTOR BIODATA

总　　序

自 2013 年 8 月起，商务印书馆与剑桥大学出版社开始商洽在大陆出版《应用语言学年度评论》(Annual Review of Applied Linguistics) 事宜，至 2014 年春末签约。此后，商务印书馆英语编辑室领导栾奇和马浩岚并责任编辑杨子辉博士先后来访，约我办三件事，一是代为组织国内学者为各卷写导读，二是承担导读的审稿任务，三是为商务版《应用语言学年度评论》写一个总序。作为对我的照顾，同意我邀请复旦大学朱永生教授[①]和北京师范大学田贵森教授[②]参加导读审定工作。就总序而言，多次思考之后，想谈以下四个方面。

一、刊物方针

《应用语言学年度评论》(以下简称《年度评论》) 是美国应用语言

[①] 朱永生：复旦大学教授、博导，杭州师范大学钱塘学者，高校功能语言学研究会副会长，高校语篇分析研究会副会长，Linguistics and Human Sciences 编委及《中国外语》等杂志编委。曾任苏州大学外语系主任、复旦大学外文系主任和国际文化交流学院院长、国际系统功能语言学研究会执委、国务院学科评议组成员、全国高校外语教学指导委员会委员等职务。著有《系统功能语言学多维思考》《系统功能语言学再思考》《语境动态研究》《系统功能语言学概论》等。

[②] 田贵森：北京师范大学外文学院教授、博导，中国功能语言学学会常务理事、中国社会语言学学会理事。1976 年河北师范大学外语系毕业后留校任教，1987 年北京外国语大学硕士，1991 年纽约市立大学硕士，1997 年北京大学博士。曾任河北师大外国语学院院长，河北省高校外语教学研究会会长，中国教育学会外语教学专业委员会副理事长。著有《禁忌语的功能研究》《英语专业毕业论文写作教程》《新编英语词汇学教程》等。

学学会（American Association for Applied Linguistics，简称 AAAL）主办的一部书刊结合的出版物，自 1980 年起每年一卷，至 2014 年已出版 34 卷。该刊最初由 Newbury House 出版社出版，自第 5 卷起改为剑桥大学出版社出版，延续至今。美国南加州大学美国语言研究所主任 Robert B. Kaplan 教授筹划第 1 卷《年度评论》时，邀请犹他州布里格姆-扬大学日耳曼语系 Randall L. Jones 教授和华盛顿大学应用语言学中心主任 G. Richard Tucker 教授三人合作主编。在他们领导下的编委会对办刊宗旨确定这样一个基本认识：尽管 1941 年美国密执安大学率先成立了将语言学理论应用于语言教育的英语学院，1956 年英国爱丁堡大学成立了应用语言学系，1959 年美国华盛顿大学建立了应用语言学中心，1966 年 *TESOL Quarterly* 出版，1977 年美国应用语言学学会成立，《年度评论》编委会无意选定其中之一作为应用语言学界共同遵循的蓝图，而是决定走自己的路。在此基础上编委会确定的方针有如下特点：（1）《年度评论》不是杂志，因为它一年只出一本；它又被看作是一本杂志，因为它由出版社的杂志部负责编辑、发行事务。[①]（2）该出版物不对应用语言学做面面俱到的报道，而是对应用语言学学科的现状进行专题评论、综述和文献式的归纳。（3）应用语言学具有高度的跨学科性，因此该刊重点结合双语教育、语言教育学、心理语言学和社会语言学四个方面进行选题。考虑到这四个学科枝叶蔓生，年刊会对一个学科的某一领域做全面的综述和评论。（4）即使上述四个学科也不是应用语言学的唯一研究领域，因为该刊遵循美国应用语言学学会所倡导的功能导向，着眼于具体应用更甚于理论。（5）所有的文章由编委会组织某一领域的专家撰写，不转载已在其他刊物上发表的文章，也不采用在某个学术会议上已经宣读的论文，更不对某一部具体的学术著作进行评论。因此，《年度评论》的主要任务是收集和突出被学术界很少报道或研究的领域，不重复已有工作，更不企图贬低某一

[①] 《应用语言学年度评论》问世后，受到国际学术界的高度重视，被权威的《社会科学引文索引》（SSCI）、《艺术和人文科学引文索引》（AHCI）和《科学引文索引》（SCI）所收录。

个方面,或对本学科内某项研究的价值进行排队。这样,《年度评论》对二语习得和语言干扰等内容谈得不多,因为这方面的研究成果已经发表很多。反之,微语言学、符号语言学、计算机辅助教学等受到重视。(6)《年度评论》本身应当正确面对来自不同领域实践者的认同或挑战。①② 鉴于上述情况,《年度评论》每卷都有一个主题,如"语言和语言教育政策"(卷 2)、"书面话语"(卷 3)、"读写教育"(卷 4)等。这些选题均具有学术性、实用性、时代性和独特性。与此同时,该刊每隔四五年会有一卷就应用语言学的整体研究从不同方面进行总结式的调研和讨论,内容涉及语言学习和教学、话语分析、教学创新、二语习得、计算机辅助教学、职场语境下的语言用途、社会语言学、语言政策和语言评估(如卷 1、5、10、15、19 等)。每年向读者提供 500 多个新的文献,以帮助本学科教学科研人员能深入掌握情况,点面结合。《年度评论》原计划的第 1 卷在 1980 年出版,由于组稿和印刷的原因,实际上在 1981 年问世。这一脱节现象直到 1994 年第 14 卷才得到扭转,即每卷标明的年度与出版年度取得一致。③

二、主编更迭

三十多年来,《年度评论》的总主编大约十年更换一次。美国南加利福尼亚大学美国语言研究所主任 Robert B. Kaplan 教授从创刊起任总主编,连续十年。Kaplan 曾任美国应用语言学会会长、英语作为第二语言教

---

① Rota, A. (1982). ANNUAL REVIEW OF APPLIED LINGUISTICS (ARAL). Robert B. Kaplan (Gen. Ed.); Randall L. Jones and G. Richard Tucker (Co-Eds.). *TESOL Quarterly*, 16, 398–404.

② Kaplan, Robert B. (1980). Introduction. *Annual Review of Applied Linguistics*, 1, vii–xi.

③ Kaplan, Robert B. and William Grabe. (2000). Applied Linguistics and the Annual Review of Applied Linguistics. in *Annual Review of Applied Linguistics*, 20, 3–17. Cambridge University Press.

学学会会长、《牛津应用语言学手册》总主编、《国际语言学百科全书》编委等。① 在 Kaplan 主编的《牛津应用语言学手册》中,他认为应用语言学家至少应该具备以下领域的一些知识:人类学、社会学、经济学、政治学、教育学、老年人学、历史学、国际关系、语言学习和教学、词典编纂学、政策研究、心理学和神经科学、公共管理、教师培训和文本生成等。此外,每一位应用语言学家都应精于计算机使用,能够对数据进行统计分析。②③

自第 11 卷起,William Grabe 任主编。Grabe 是美国北亚利桑那州大学负责科研的副校长,曾先后在该校英语系和应用语言学系任教。Grabe 认为应用语言学的核心是"试图解决人们在日常生活中遇到的与语言相关的问题",是一种"研究现实世界语言问题的、实践驱动的学科"。④ 鉴于这个原因,应用语言学必然是一个交叉学科,涉及许多其他领域。这可见之于他对每卷的选题,如"读写教育"(卷 12)、"二语教学"(卷 13)、"语言政策和规划"(卷 14)、"技术和语言"(卷 16)、"多语现象"(卷 17)、"二语教育基础"(卷 18)、"应用语言学的学科性"(卷 19、20)。Grabe 任总主编至 2000 年卸任。在他最后一次负责的第 20 卷,他和 Robert Kaplan 合写了一篇回顾应用语言学和《年度评论》发展历程的总结性文章。

自 2001 年起任总主编的是北亚利桑那大学英语系的 Mary McGroarty 教授。她主要研究双语现象、语言政策、语言教育和课堂研究、社会语言学、二语教学的文化影响等。由于第一次出任主编,McGroarty 邀请了美

---

① Bruthiaux, Paul, Dwight Atkinson, William G. Egginton, William Grabe, Viadehi Ramanathan. Eds. (2005). *Directions in Applied Linguistics in Honour of Robert B. Kaplan.* Clevedon: Multilingual Matters Ltd.
② Kaplan, Robert B. (1999). *The Oxford Handbook of Applied Linguistics.* Edinburgh: Edinburgh University Press.
③ 刘海涛. 从比较中看应用语言学. 北华大学学报(社会科学版), 2007, 8(2): 4.
④ Grabe, William. (2000). Introduction. *Annual Review of Applied Linguistics*, 20, 1–2. Cambridge University Press.

国著名外语教学法专家Wilga M. Rivers为第21卷"语言和心理学"写序,题为"沿着记忆巷道的漫长旅程"。此后,McGroarty在她任期内主编了"话语和对话"(卷22)、"语言接触和演变"(卷23)、"语言教育学的进展"(卷24)和"通用语语言"(卷26)。《年度评论》第27和28卷的主题分别为"语言与科技"和"神经语言学和认知语言处理",但未见到这两卷本应由总主编执笔的引言,在目录中也未出现,原因不详。作为总主编的McGroarty在第29卷"语言政策和语言评估"中再次出现,不过她邀请了著名学者Bernard Spolsky作为客座主编。Spolsky教授长期在以色列的Bar-Ilan大学任教,曾任该校人文学院院长,并创建语言政策研究中心。在编辑业务方面,他曾任国际刊物 *Language Policy* (《语言政策》)的总主编,*Asia TEFL*(《亚洲英语作为外语教学》)杂志的出版部主任和总编辑。Spolsky的专著都与语言政策和语言教育有关,如《教育语言学导论》(1978)、《二语学习的条件》(1991)、《社会语言学》(1998)、《以色列诸语言:政策、意识和实践》(1999)、《语言政策》(2004)、《语言管理》(2009)等。[①] 由此看来,Spolsky无力全心投入《年度评论》的编辑工作,这次只是扮演一次客串角色而已。

自第30卷起,总主编一职由美国密执安州立大学的Charlene Polio教授担任。Polio的主要研究领域为二语写作、二语习得、外语课堂话语、新技术和有经验教师之间的行为差异。她在编辑工作上有较多经验,除接受《年度评论》的总主编任务外,也是 *Modern Language Journal*(《现代语言杂志》)的编辑,此前曾为 *Journal of Second Language Writing*(《二语写作杂志》)和 *TESOL Quarterly* 杂志编委会委员。[②]Polio为《年度评论》各卷确定的选题为"应用语言学专题"(卷30)、"第二语言教育研究"(卷31)、"公式化语言研究"(卷32)、"多语现象研究"(卷33)、"研究方法专题"(卷34)。这体现了她作为总主编延续了该刊创办时的主导思

---

① Spolsky, Bernard. Homepage. http://www.biu.ac.il/faculty/spolsky/. 2015.1.3.
② Polio, Charlene. http://www.wsu.edu/~oikui/. 2015.1.5.

想,即每卷的稿子都是就某一领域的特定问题而精选的。

为《年度评论》写稿的作者中不乏名人,如 Henry G. Widdowson、James R. Martin、Bernard Spolsky、Alan Davies 等都是国际著名语言学家。

三、国人参与

我国大陆、港台地区和国际华人圈对《应用语言学年度评论》很为重视。台湾学者郑锦全(Chan-chuan Cheng)在第 7 卷上发表"语言和计算机"一文。郑当时任台湾师范大学华语文教学研究所讲座教授、台湾地区研究院语言所研究员和人文社会科学研究中心通信研究员(Cheng,2014)。[①] 另一位是台湾清华大学培养的许静芬(Ching-fen Hsu)博士,现在台湾华梵大学人文学院师资培养研究中心工作,专攻威廉姆斯综合征(Williams Syndrome)发育障碍的语言习得研究,是第 28 卷"威廉姆斯综合征:基因型和认知表型描述"一文的第一作者。[②] 香港教育学院语言教学研究中心主任的李楚成(David C. S. Li)教授在第 26 卷上发表"作为大中华通用语的汉语"一文。[③] 在《年度评论》第 30 卷独立发表有关传承语学习的社会文化维度一文的何纬芸(Agnes Weiyun He)教授,早期毕业于北京外国语大学,现为 Stony Brook 大学应用语言学和亚洲研究专业的教授,筹建了该校多语和跨文化交际中心。何纬芸主要研究语言语境和语篇的结合,人们如何通过日常互动逐步构建和重构概念、社团和文化。近十年来,她专门研究不同时期和不同背景下汉语作为传承语的社会化。[④] 在《年度评论》第 27 卷与 John Flowerdew 联名发表"多语制和二语写作在电

[①] Cheng, Chan-chuan(郑锦全). http://doc88.com/P-795557797523.html. 2014.12.9.
[②] Hsu, Ching-fen(许静芬). http://www.docin.com/p-2898691.html & key. 2015.1.5.
[③] Li, David, C. S.(李楚成). http://dfl.shufe.edu.cn/structure/xueshu-com-142410-1.htm. 2014.12.9.
[④] He, Agnes Weiyun(何纬芸). http://www.stonybrook.edu/commcms/asian/PROGRAMS.html. 2014.12.9.

子时代的关系"一文的李咏燕博士(Yongyan Li)任教于香港大学教育学院英语教育系,其研究范围包括专业写作、多语学者的研究和发表实践、言而有据的写作、科学文章的整篇抄袭现象、在职教育等。① 令人瞩目的是,上述学者与大陆高校和研究单位保持良好的学术联系,如郑锦全教授曾担任四川大学文学与新闻学院兼职教授、厦门大学嘉庚学院中文系兼职教授、北京大学汉语语言学研究中心兼职研究员;李楚成教授曾在上海财经大学举行关于中国外语学习者和使用者常见错误的纠正讲座;何纬芸教授与上海交通大学苗瑞琴副教授合作编写了"继承语之习得及其社会化"一文。②

大陆学者对《年度评论》也做出了应有的反应和贡献。早在1981年《年度评论》第1卷问世后,我国学者左焕琪教授便在国内语言学权威刊物《当代语言学》上作了报道,既介绍了编者Kaplan的背景,也对该卷四个部分作了近似导读的介绍。作者当时就以敏锐的眼光指出这是"近年来美国应用语言学领域引人瞩目的新刊物"。③ 较近的可举2012年方秀才的"程式语面面观介绍"一文,对《年度评论》第32卷从认知视角、教学应用、社会学进展和未来展望四个部分深入介绍。作者特别注意到,为了从多种视角讨论程式语这一主题,总主编没有限定程式语的定义、内涵,也没有统一术语,让每篇文章的作者采用自己认同的术语和定义,④ 这表明《年度评论》并没有因为总主编的变动而放弃原有的风格。

行文至此,有必要提一下以Charlene Polio为首的新编委会所作的一个重大决定,那就是她代表编委会聘请了我国广东外语外贸大学王初明教授从第31卷起任《年度评论》顾问委员会的委员。这是对我国应用语言

---

① Li, Yongyan(李咏燕). http://www_researchgate.net/profile/Yongyan_Li/publications. 2014.12.9.
② 何纬芸,苗瑞琴.继承语之习得及其社会化.载姬建国,蒋楠主编:应用语言学(西方人文社会科学前沿述评).北京:中国人民大学出版社,2007.239–255.
③ 左焕琪.应用语言学年度评述(1980).《国外语言学》,1983,(3):46–49.
④ 方秀才.《程式语面面观》介绍.《当代语言学》,2013,15(4):492–495.

学研究发展和水平的肯定。我与王初明教授结识于1995年9月,当时我是香港中文大学的访问学者,他是英语系的博士生。我们经常一起讨论学术问题。长江后浪推前浪,2011年我从北京外国语大学中国外语教育研究中心学术委员会主任退下后,他接替了此职。王初明教授现在的学术兼职有国务院学位委员会外国语言文学学科评议组成员、中国高等教育学会外语教学研究分会副会长。他的主要研究方向为第二语言习得研究及其在外语教学中的应用,主要学术创见有外语写长法、语境补缺假说、外语语音学习假设、外语学习的学伴用随原则、读后续写的理论和应用价值。

四、"商务"特色

除保留剑桥版《应用语言学年度评论》的原有特色外,商务版《应用语言学年度评论》有它自己的特色。

商务版《年度评论》从第20卷开始,而不是从第1卷开始。我认为商务印书馆此举着眼于让读者以更多的精力把握应用语言学在新世纪的发展,急读者之所急。我们还应该看到,《年度评论》第20卷实际上起到承前启后的作用。在该卷中,为上世纪创刊时立下汗马功劳的Robert Kaplan、William Grabe 和 G. Richard Tucker 分别对应用语言学和《年度评论》在二十年中的发展作了系统的总结,帮助读者对前二十年有个总体了解,又寄厚望于这门新学科在新世纪、新千年的发展,把握前进的方向。其次,商务版《年度评论》增加了满足中国读者需求的新内容,那就是每卷都有一篇1.5万字左右的中文导读。这便于帮助读者掌握每卷的基本内容和背景材料,特别是汉语界的教师、研究者和学生。

参与此任务的导读作者有国内外语界著名学者,也有新生代的中青年学者。这些专家学者对自己撰写的内容比较熟悉。作为此项目的组织者,我没有向他们摊派任务,而是让各位学者根据自己熟悉的领域自由选题。对各位作者的努力我在此谨表谢意。如前所述,导读初稿完成后均由上海复旦大学朱永生教授和北京师范大学田贵森教授分别先行审读。对两位教授退休后仍能不辞辛苦、鼎力相助的感激之情,难以言表。

由于《年度评论》涉及多个学科和领域,各卷原版的体例不全相同,而各位导读作者的学术生涯也不尽相同,我们对导读编写体例上只作大致要求,不强调绝对统一。总的印象是,每位导读作者对本卷各章内容都能做提纲挈领的介绍和解释,帮助读者理解和抓住要点,这是共同的优点。导读作者各自的特色则表现在:(1)能在正文之前对本卷的总主编、客座编辑做介绍,并对总主编的引言深入分析,起到画龙点睛的作用;(2)对本卷主题进行了解释;(3)对有关主题在20世纪的研究状况或《年度评论》已经发表过的专辑作必要回顾;(4)对每卷论文内容进行归纳,指出其特点;(5)坦率指出某卷内容的不足之处;(6)结合国内现状进行讨论,并进行反思;(7)在讨论中,引入当代先进理论;(8)向我国学界和领导部门提出今后有待深入展开研究的问题。

在结束本序之际,再次感谢各位导读作者,以及永生教授和贵森教授的共同努力,使本项艰巨任务得以顺利完成;祝贺商务版《应用语言学年度评论》正式出版;祝愿商务印书馆今后在应用语言学和理论语言学等领域为外语教育界和学术界做出更多更大贡献!

北京大学蓝旗营寓所

2015年元月

导　读

郑　萱[①]

一、引言

　　由剑桥大学出版社出版的《应用语言学年度评论》(*Annual Review of Applied Linguistics*，简称 ARAL)是美国应用语言学学会(American Association for Applied Linguistics，简称 AAAL)的定期出版物。该刊每年都针对一个特别的主题，每 5 年左右出一卷特刊，将一系列不相关的主题放在一起论述。第 30 卷就是这样一卷特刊。这一卷的主编，密歇根州立大学语言学系教授 Charlene Polio 第一次接手此任务。这卷特刊选择了四个议题：传承语学习、研究方法和技术、语言社会化、语言学理论和二语习得。

　　事实上，这些看似"毫不相干"的议题正反映了应用语言学这个宽广领域的多种理论和方法视角。应邀的撰稿人来自不同的学科背景：语言学、教育学、心理学和人类学。本卷既有二语习得的形式语言学理论的部分，又有语言社会化的部分。在这两个领域中活跃的研究者持有非常不同的语言观，之所以将它们放在一起，是因为 Charlene Polio 认为社会和认知这两大流派对语言学习和运用的研究都有益处，只是它们关注的研究问题不同。为了给关键概念和术语提供语境，以便不同读者理解，此卷的各

[①] 郑萱，北京大学外国语学院语言学与应用语言学研究所讲师。美国华盛顿大学英语系英语教学硕士，语言与修辞方向博士。研究方向为外语教育、跨文化交际。

位作者先回溯了过去的相关研究，然后综述了各领域的最新研究进展，有的还选取了尚未发表的会议论文和博士论文。丰富的视角和内容是本卷的一大特色。

二、内容介绍

第一部分　传承语学习

第一部分选取了四篇文章。四位学者从不同的视角探讨了传承语学习（heritage language learning）的相关研究。

1. 传承语习得中的现有问题

本文作者 Silvina Montrul 是美国伊利诺伊大学香槟分校西班牙、意大利、葡萄牙语系的系主任，同时也是该校语言学系的教授。她在阿根廷出生，接受了本科教育，又分别在美国辛辛那提大学和加拿大麦吉尔大学获得了英语专业硕士学位和语言学博士学位。她的研究通常依据语言学理论和心理语言学的方法探索二语习得、双语发展和传承语学习中语言层面的问题。

传承语这个概念于20世纪70年代中期由加拿大学者首次提出（Cummins, 2005），90年代开始在美国被采用。在美国具有代表性的传承语有西班牙语、东亚语、俄语和阿拉伯语。传承语学习通常指的是那些讲少数语言的移民家庭的孩子。例如，在美国的华侨家庭长大的孩子，家里接触的是汉语，外面接触的是英语，那么汉语就是他们的传承语和家庭语言。有的学者也用这个词指原住民语言，例如美国的印第安语。有时候也被称为"来源国语言"、"家庭语言"、"移民母语"。随着美国的外国移民日益增加，语言文化日趋多元化，对传承语语言教育、语言学习者的研究已成为应用语言学一个重要研究领域。

本文的主要目的是探讨传承语使用者从童年到成年语言知识的发展，以及传承语学习在什么条件下发生。作者赞同传承语习得应该区别于外语学习的观点，并指出如果要使传承语习得成为一个独立的研究领域，必须把传承语语言习得的过程理论化。尽管目前对传承语学习者文化认同、语言政策的研究有所增加,对传承语学习所做的理论化研究依然缺乏。为了弥补这个缺陷,作者从认知和语言学理论的视角探讨了对传承语学习的研究。

为了描述传承语语言系统,作者综述了语音与音系、词汇、形态句法、句法四个层面的研究。她首先指出传承语语法的许多方面体现了语言接触情形下的语言简化过程,然后比较了母语、二语、传承语习得的异同。她用一张对比表格清晰地表明了母语与二语习得的区别,而标黑的部分是传承语习得也具有的特点。可见,因为是在双语的环境下,传承语习得既有一部分母语习得的特点(在读写能力开始之前),也有一部分二语习得的特点,但与二者又不完全相同。理论上说,传承语习得者也可以达到他们所用语言的完整的语言水平,可事实上多种因素影响了语言的发展:父母的话语策略,传承语在当地社区的地位,除了家庭之外的传承语言语社区是否存在,语言态度和通过传承语传授的教育。因为这种教育的缺失,许多传承语使用者都没有学到正式用语或是书面语中复杂的词汇和句法。

之后,作者概括了现有的解释语言习得的三种理论视角:生成语言学,认知/神经语言学和突现论(emergentism)。这三种视角分别强调了语言学习过程的不同方面:与生俱来的语言知识,总体的学习过程和语言输入。本文指出这三种视角应被视为是相互补充的,可以用来共同解释传承语语言习得。

最后,Montrul 提出,最新的实证研究主要针对以下问题:1)不完全习得的本质(哪些语法特点得到了发展,哪些没有?);2)二语习得者与传承语习得者的比较(语音、形态句法知识等);3)习得的方式、知识的种类和任务(传承语使用者通常听说能力强而缺失读写能力,而通过接受显性外语教育的二语学习者正好相反);4)课堂教学的作用和最终获得语言的程度。Montrul 还提出,未来的研究需要做到以下三点:①更多地将理论研究应用于课堂教学;②研究成人传承语使用者如何吸收语言输入,并历时研究追踪学龄儿童从上学到青春期阶段,探索他们是如何由于接受主流语言的教育而失去家庭语言的;③研究父母给孩子的语言输入和传承语使用者一生中接受的语言输入。

2. 为提高传承语能力的课程设置:最近的研究、现在的实践和未来计划

本文作者 Kimi Kondo-Brown 是美国夏威夷大学马诺阿分校语言、语言学和文学学院副院长,东亚语言和文学系(日本语言和语言学)教授。她出生在日本,在那里接受本科教育之后来到美国,获得语言学硕士(犹他大学)和教育学博士(夏威夷大学)。从 1988 年执教以来,她讲授的课程和研究的领域包括日语教学法、语言测试和传承语教育。

本文主要关注美国有关传承语的课程设计和教学。作者首先描述了美国传承语教学的情况:在美国的正式教育系统中,传承语教育非常普及。在多种传承语中,西班牙语是使用人数最多的传承语,对西班牙语的教学法和课程研究也领先于其他语种。她认为传承语教学与外语教学不同。外语教学的目的是给学习者提供丰富的接触、使用语言的机会;而传承语教学则是基于学生本来就有的语言和文化技能的基础之上。全文由三个部分组成:1)传承语课程发展的概述;2)大学以前的传承语能力发展的教学和评估问题;3)高中以后的传承语教学。

传承语课程发展的概述谈到了几种课程发展的重要流派,主要参照点有三类:学习者导向,内容导向,成果导向。学习者导向的课程设计从学生自身的需要出发,此类研究发现学生和老师的相互协商对课程设置是至关重要的。内容导向的课程将内容教学与语言技能教学相结合,例如增加文化的内容可以帮助学生增加归属感;另外,鼓励以项目为中心的课堂活动。成果导向的研究与语言测试联系紧密;近年来成果导向的课程越来越热,美国外语教学委员会(ACTFL)设计的口语水平测试也被越来越多的传承语教学采用。今后的研究方向是对档案袋评估法(portfolio assessment)效果的探究。大学以前的传承语能力发展的教学和评估问题综述了两种学习传承语课程的渠道:一种是双向浸入式课程,一种是基于社区的学校。对双向浸入式课程(用两种语言传授学科知识)的研究发现

这类课程通常有利于学生学习学科知识,但对该学生传承语的保持和发展有何作用需要更多的研究。另一方面,教传承语课程的社区学校多种多样,效果各有差异,父母和孩子对课程通常分别持积极和抵触的态度。作者提出了今后研究需要修改完善的地方。高中以后的传承语教学主要综述了四个方面的问题:学生以什么标准分班,口语和书面语水平差异非常大的学生怎么办,个人差异的问题以及解决会流利使用非正式、地位低的语言变体但不会使用正式、地位高的语言变体的问题。文章的最后对教育机构提出了提高传承语能力的九点建议。

3. 国际比较视角:传承语教育政策研究

本文作者 Jeffrey Bale 是多伦多大学安大略教育研究院课程与教学系副教授。他获得了德语本科学位(德保尔大学),德语文学和语言学硕士(乔治城大学),教育领导和政策研究的博士学位(亚利桑那州立大学)。他的研究植根于他在美国城市公立学校(中学)中积累的丰富的二语教学经验,研究方向是二语教育、应用语言学和多语言、教师教育和发展、语言政策等。

本文综述了世界不同地区对传承语语言政策的研究。这些地区包括:非洲、中国香港、马来西亚、新加坡、印度、北美、大洋洲、爱尔兰和英国。作者首先辨析了传承语的不同定义,指出这一概念在文献中实际上包括了许多完全不同的语言、历史、文化和社会语境。他建议采用更宽泛的定义,并告诫研究者应当重视这些不同。本文采取的是一种生态学视角(ecological approach),既关注传承语学习者本人的主观能动性,也关注环境对他们的制约。

在明确了适合语言政策研究的"传承语"定义以后,作者依据 Ricento 和 Hornberger1996 年报道的分析框架,综述了不同地区传承语语言政策的相关研究,分析了语言政策在不同层次的作用。这些研究采用了不同的方法,因为语言政策不仅是正式文本,也是话语、意识形态、合法化的过程,还有教师和学生对语言教育的实践。研究方法也不局限于语言和内容层面的分析,还包括定量社会语言学分析(quantitative sociolinguistic analyses)、史学方法(historiography)、质的研究方法(qualitative research methods)、对政策转型过程的民族志研究(ethnography)。

最后,作者提出了传承语语言政策研究的共同议题,指出了该研究未来的发展方向。他总结了语言政策和规划文献中存在两个冲突:1)随着语言政策和规划逐渐成为应用语言学中的一个研究领域,语言决策通常被新独立的国家看成是解决"语言问题"的手段。这种"语言即是问题"的立场与解决语言能够,或者说应该在建立、维持和扩大国家权力中起到什么作用的问题有深刻的联系。随着批判理论和后现代理论视角的流行,不再只从国家层面对权力和权力冲突进行分析,而是更多地把它放到地方层面来考虑。2)另一个是传承语与英语之间相互竞争的关系。英语究竟是对传承语的威胁,还是融入全球化世界的赋权工具?这在不同的地区答案大相径庭。作者认为有效的传承语语言政策应当因地制宜,没有放之四海而皆准的政策。

4.传承的核心:传承语学习的社会文化维度

本文作者 Agnes Weiyun He 是纽约大学石溪分校应用语言学和亚洲研究的教授,多语言、跨文化交际中心的奠基人、主任。她本科毕业于北京外国语大学英语系,于新加坡国立教育学院获教育学士,亚利桑那大学获英语作为第二语言硕士,加州大学洛杉矶分校获应用语言学博士。她的研究主要涉及语言交流如何建构身份认同、社区和文化。过去十年中,她一直致力于研究不同情境下中文作为传承语的社会化过程。

本文是从社会文化角度对传承语研究的综述,包括两大类:相关性研究和社会建构视角。相关性研究是二语研究中的一个主要流派。对传承语的相关性研究通常考查多重变量之间的关系,研究结果展示了影响传承语学习的社会文化变量之间紧密的联系。这类研究的问题在于它们将复杂变化的建构概念,如动机、态度、身份认同、语言水平和读写能力等量化,让人觉得这些社会文化特质是本质的、与生俱来的、永恒不变的。而社会建构视角不再将传承语看成独立的变量。人的身份不是预先设置好的、固定不变的,而是多重的、在社会交互中产生和维持的。语言是自我发展、心智发展、社会发展的必要部分。在这个视角下，语言使用者被视为某种语言、国家、种族、职业共同体的一员，并主动地建构和重构他们自己的身份。

作者认为社会建构视角重新回答了有关传承语发展的问题：1）会一种传承语意味着什么？ 2）传承语文化与传承语如何相连？ 3）学生学习到传承语的证据在哪里？ 4）传承语是如何被获得和被社会化的？她认为该视角的优势在于不再将研究结果概括化，也不再预设传承语使用者的"必要特征"，而是将社会和语言行为真实地展现出来。该视角对传承语使用者发展的多重社会文化维度更敏感，她用了 Atkinson 在 2002 年提出的比喻，认为语言学习的过程就像茂盛的"雨林"一样多姿多彩。

最后，作者总结了传承语学习的社会文化复杂性，再次强调语言学习应该被视为学习者参与社会实践、逐渐建构身份认同的过程。社会化不是单向的，而是辩证的、对话的、生态的、双向的。这意味着学习者本人也促进了帮助他们社会化的那些人的社会化过程。传承语学习者改变了社会化过程中所有的参与者。社会建构的视角给我们提供了丰富的土壤，让我们重新反思有关传承语学习的双重对立的概念（如母语与目的语的对立，内部动机与外部动机的对立），有助于我们在时间和空间的变化过程中重新审视传承语学习的轨迹。

第二部分 研究方法和技术

本部分的第 5 篇到第 8 篇文章综述了当今二语研究中比较热门的几种方法和技术：元分析、有声报告、质性访谈和眼球运动追踪技术。

5. 二语研究的元分析：选择和挑战

本文由两位作者，Frederick L. Oswald 和 Luke Plonsky 合写，前者是美国莱斯大学心理学系教授，后者是北亚利桑那州大学应用语言学系助理教授。他们在本文中综述了元分析（meta analysis）方法在二语研究中的选择和挑战。

从统计学的角度来说，元分析是指将多个研究结果整合在一起的统计方法。就用途而言，它是文献回顾的新方法。文献回顾的传统方法是叙事式的，由作者自行挑选觉得重要的前人研究，当各种研究结论冲突时，由作者自行判断哪一种结论较有价值。而元分析采用系统化的资料收集和数值分析，使文献回顾更加客观、有更多的证据支撑，有助于以更加全面的证据来支持或否定某一假设，发现该主题迄今研究的不足之处。

应用语言学家正在越来越多地探索元分析方法的应用领域，认为这种量化平均效应幅度（effect size）的方法，比传统的定性方法更系统、更可复制。其他优势还有：增加统计功效，调节变量分析和模型试验。该文描述了在第二语言习得研究中元分析的基本步骤：1）确定研究问题；2）编制可靠的编码方案；3）分析数据；4）解释结果。每个步骤都要做大量的合理的决策。这些决策将影响元分析的进行、结果的性质和二语习得研究成果的意义。本文强调了这些决策带来的优势和挑战。一般来说，如果元分析计划得周密，采用了合理的统计方法，并基于对相关理论的深入理解，那么它可以为理论、未来研究、实践和政策提供关键信息。

文章的结论和建议如下：

元分析通常可以改善传统描述性的综述，通过系统地识别、编码权衡、平均量化的效果，与证据的量化优势保持一致。元分析也对没有提供的结果提供了线索，为今后的研究暗示了未来的方向。

鉴于二语习得元分析方法应用的增多，作者提出了三条建议：1）鼓励在一组研究中寻找主要的、量化的证据，这些证据可以说明在论著中故意造成统计结果的偏移（publication bias）。专业期刊倾向于拒绝无显著效果的研究报告，元分析若仅仅依据专业期刊"显著作用"的发表要求，可能会高估总体效应幅度的大小。从独立的元分析结果来看，元分析中的一些方法学研究至少可以扩展专业期刊的发表空间，或通过在线补充材料，读者可以直观地检查自己潜在的发表性偏倚或其他可能不会透露的独特模式。二语习得元分析将更容易获得研究资源，从而减少研究方向的偏差。2）二语习得研究者的元分析研究应该尽可能透明，以便读者能够更好地理解元分析的过程和解释结果。透明度包括公开元分析决策因素，如编码表清单或图表,列出研究和分析中涉及的所有数据(如样本大小、效应幅度、人口统计学因素和可靠性系数)。3)元分析应当强调结果的现实意义,但根据问题改进科恩基准(Cohen's benchmark),依据是二语习得分支领域研究中独立变量的处理、现实意义和理论完善。本文在二语习得的 27 项元分析研究基础上,提供了一种不同的标尺来解释效应幅度估量(effect size estimates)。

本文强调,二语习得研究需要好的第一手资料研究,尽量去满足教科书理想的代表性取样、细致的实验设计和可靠的心理统计测量。因此,第一手资料研究和元分析一样有希望回答具有挑战性的理论和实践研究问题。元分析常常有利于第一手资料研究,告诉我们哪些理论领域更有发展潜力,哪些类型的研究更有令人信服的结果,指明了今后的研究方向。元分析对总结应用语言学的研究历史、并指导它的未来拥有巨大的潜力。

6. 二语习得中的口头报告法

本文作者 Melissa A. Bowles 博士是美国伊利诺伊大学西班牙语和葡萄牙语系的副教授。她在本文中概述了口头报告(又称有声思维)在二语习得认知流派研究中的应用。

口头报告是指学习者在完成一项任务时(或之后)将其思维过程表述出来的过程。如果表述和任务是同时,就叫作同时报告或有声思维;如果表述是在任务完成之后,就叫作回顾报告或刺激回忆。

口头报告的效度有两个问题:反应性(reactivity)和真实性(veridicality)。如果口头表达过程本身改变了任务完成的效果,那么这个口头报告就具有反应性;如果口头表达如实反映了被试的认知过程,那么它就具有真实性。作者针对这两个问题,评述了二语习得中口头报告的效度检测研究。她对比较沉默和有声思维的两组研究结果进行了元分析,建议进一步关注有声语言的研究和效度问题。

根据二语习得反应性研究,本文的结论是元分析的结果具有重要的影响,可以整合各种不同的研究理论观点。至关重要的是,各种因素似乎都在影响口头报告在应用于某一任务时是否有反应。

基于资料的有效证据，某些情况下的口头报告的确是学习发生的一个来源。至少接受性测试（receptive test）的研究结果表明，语言表达本身可以促进学习过程。同样，无声学习和有声学习两组的后测差异很小，研究发现口头报告可以用作数据收集工具。

二语习得的反应性研究至今仅有十年时间，因此还有许多问题亟须解决。这就促使研究人员继续探索是否是口头表达本身造成了任务完成时两组之间的显著差异，以确定在什么情境下口头表达可以准确地反映语言加工过程。

7. 应用语言学中的质性访谈：从研究工具到社会实践

本文作者 Steven Talmy 是加拿大温哥华英属哥伦比亚大学副教授。

几十年来，访谈法应用于实证调查，已成为社会科学生成数据的主要手段之一。在应用语言学研究领域，访谈研究近几年急剧增长，尤其是用于探讨被研究对象的质性研究上，如研究对各种现象的身份认同、经验、信念问题。然而，对如何将访谈理论化的问题依然存在巨大的分歧。本文评述了过去五年间部分应用语言学研究，包括案例研究、民族志、叙事、传记（自传）和相关的质性研究框架，重点分析这些研究中的语言意识形态、交流和访谈本身。

通过对比将访谈作为研究工具与将访谈作为社会实践的两种取向，本文提出应用语言学家在质性研究中应当对访谈法、访谈数据如何被定位、分析和呈现等问题进行更多的反思。

作者指出，撰写此文的初衷并不是一定要将访谈理论化为社会实践，只是想对似乎已经自然化（naturalized）的访谈理论加以质疑，让研究者认真思考访谈中的语言意识形态、沟通和访谈本身。否则，就像 Briggs（2007）所说，"访谈就像'黑匣子'（black boxes），研究者往里填进问题，然后就引用产出的语言，却毫不在意这些话语是如何产出的。这样的意识形态限制了我们的访谈过程，也限制了我们反思自己和他人的访谈。"所以无论访谈是作为研究工具还是社会实践，作者都呼吁研究者认真反思他们所采用的研究方法、选取访谈数据时研究者的作用以及数据是如何被定位、分析和呈现的。

8. 二语句子处理研究中眼球运动追踪数据的应用

本文作者 Paola E.Dussias 是美国宾夕法尼亚大学西班牙语、意大利语和葡萄牙语系的副教授,心理学系的兼职教授。

当我们听到或读到二语单词和句子时,我们不确定所指的人和物是如何相互联系的。相对熟练的二语使用者在理解词汇、句子和计划说话的时候都能使用两种语言,而近年来的研究表明,这两种语言系统并不完全独立。因此,一个关键问题就是两种语言的知识如何影响语言加工过程。本文综述了如何应用眼球运动跟踪法解决这一问题。首先讨论的是为什么眼球运动是一个有用的语言加工研究方法。作者描述了一个实验范式来开发探索阅读的眼球运动,并综述了二语使用者语言处理的眼球运动跟踪研究新进展。文章还强调使用多种测量研究方法的重要性,如在线句子加工过程的结果讨论,使用移动窗口任务和眼球运动跟踪仪记录二语使用者阅读语法上含糊不清的关系从句。最后讨论的是二语使用者处理混合语言的句法加工方面的研究调查,由此提出了未来的研究方向和建议。

作者强调,会使用两种语言的人不等同于两个只会一种语言的人的简单相加;同一个大脑中的两种语言是相互作用的,而这些交互作用影响了二语使用者分别用两种语言阅读和进行听力理解。因此,眼球运动跟踪技术可以给我们带来很有趣的发现。这一部分首先综述了在词汇层面的语言处理。眼球运动技术的研究发现二语听者在单一的英语环境中似乎并没有关闭他们的母语词汇,这说明当双语者处理非母语时,其母语都处于活跃状态,不过反之则不完全成立,即处理母语时非母语不一定处于活跃状态。之后,本文综述了眼球运动研究在以下方面的运用:二语句子处理、二语模糊性的解决以及二语口语理解。

二语句子理解领域研究已达到一个令人兴奋的阶段。涉及不同的句法结构类型研究和发现迅速增多,焦点是二语学习者和母语学习者的语言加工过程质量上的异同。目前的研究表明,大量的语言变量影响二语学习者的阅读加工;学习者的特征如语言熟练程度和语言经验,经常与输入的语言层面有交互作用，产生解析的结果。研究问题的性质变得更精细，需要更复杂的在线行为测量已成为中心议题。这些方法的使用为研究日益精细的问题拓展了前景。

进一步研究需要探索不同的网上测量方法。视觉世界范式带来了一种新的令人兴奋的可能性，即研究实时口语的语言理解。此外，二语理解的研究需要更多的参照和语用信息。依靠多种研究方法可以使各种方法取长补短。最后，很重要的一个研究方向是使用眼球运动跟踪方法，探讨二语使用者语言加工的各个发展阶段，以发现在逐渐成为更精通的二语使用者过程中阅读能力的发展轨迹。这些方法的优势在于稳定的结果能够拓展该领域的理论研究范围。

第三部分　语言社会化

这个部分包括三篇文章（第9—11篇），包含了不同言语社区的语言社会化研究。

9. 学术话语社区中的语言社会化

本文作者 Patricia A. Duff 是加拿大英属哥伦比亚大学语言及读写教育教授，中文及读写教育中心的共同负责人，讲授英语作为第二语言教学及现代语言教育研究生课程，目前致力于跨语言的语言社会化相关研究、应用语言学质性研究方法、民族志及补修（remedial）教学。此外，她也关注中文、英文和外语教学、第二语言学习者在学校及社会的融合、职场与语言多元化以及教育中言语的社会文化、语言、政治层面等议题。

学术话语社会化研究主要关注如何帮助新手有效参与学术话语社区（academic discourse community）的实践。本文为读者详尽地回溯了学术话语中语言社会化的研究发展，以及口语、写作、网络交流及社会实践中的社会化研究。作者强调有些学习者遵从并且复制学术话语中的既定规范，而另一些学习者却与规范争论和抵抗。作者还对学术出版物中的社会化以及文字身份认同等相关研究做了全面的综述。最后，她总结了种族、文化、性别对学术言语社会化的影响，指出社会定位（自我定位或被他人定位)能影响学习者在他们所在的多种学习共同体中的参与度和表现。

作者指出,在过去的20年里,和学术言语相关的理论研究,尤其是英语方面,已有全方位的探讨,但有关学术话语社会化,尤其是对母语读写能力、后习得的语言读写能力、或新的话语社区社会化研究相对较少。学术话语社会化是动态的、基于社会情境的过程,通常以多模态、多语言混用及互文形式出现。其特点有:存在不同程度的示范、反馈及回应(uptake);学习者有不同程度的投资和能动性;权力与身份认同的协商;对于某些参与者来说,还会经历重大的个人转变。然而,作者认为,无论是短期或是长远来看,学术话语社会化的结果都难以预测。

未来的研究需要更多地关注学术活动参与者主体间性(intersubjectivity)的发展过程,以及学习共同体通过中介(mediation)和支架式教学(scaffolding)发展新知识、能力和文本身份的过程。作者强调了教师、学生和社会人士共同肩负促进社会化过程的责任。认为学校和学术话语社会化的其他场所也需要增强对学生和教师的元话语支持,以使新加入的成员能更顺利地融入话语社区。

10. 成为民族的:全球化时代的课堂语言社会化和政治认同

本文作者 Debra A. Friedman 于 2006 年取得加州大学洛杉矶分校应用语言学及英语教学博士学位,现为美国印第安纳大学助理教授,专业方向为第二语言及多语言的语言社会化、第二语言教学、社会政治及意识形态、第二语言教学、传承语教育及质性研究方法等。

长久以来,学校被视为现代民族国家培养公民的主要场所。然而,传统的社会同化主义者和排他主义者主张的国家认同近来却受到了多元文化、族群混合及跨国主义(transnationalism)等挑战。本文综述了近年来以课堂为研究场所的语言社会化研究,探索如何使新手通过社会化从政治上认同自己是某一国家或跨国界社区的成员。本文探讨了五个主题:1)国家语言中的社会化;2)移民者的社会化;3)新形式国家认同的社会化;4)政治认同的少数群体在国内的社会化;5)跨国认同的社会化。本文最后总结了从语言社会化的角度研究上述议题的贡献,并为未来相关研究提出了建议。

作者在文献综述中揭示了两个要点：第一，课堂不是真空，而是处在一张文化、社会、意识形态和社会实践相互交织的网中，因此，课堂的日常活动和对课堂活动的解释均受到这张网的制约。第二，研究通常发现学生抵制本质化的、排他的政治认同，而在社会化过程中发挥自己的主观能动性，产生了另外形式的认同，例如将文化认同与民族国家认同分开，表明语言社会化具有改变社会和重塑社会的潜力。

作者最后提出了此类研究的欠缺之处：1）关于政治认同形成的语言社会化研究仍然有限，未来需要进一步拓展。比如，虽然关于移民学生的第二语言社会化研究已大幅增加，但很少直接涉及语言课堂是如何将新手社会化，使他们认同与讲民族语言相联系的意识形态和主体性的。2）由于中后期的童年阶段被视为身份认同形成的重要阶段，需要更多对青少年及大龄儿童的社会化研究。3）如 Kulick 和 Schieffelin 指出（2004：350）的那样，需要展现某种语言和文化实践是如何随着时间增长、地点变化而慢慢习得的。因此，需要更多纵向研究，长期跟踪观察学生在课内课外不同场所的政治身份认同的表现。

11. 职场的语言社会化

本文作者 Celia Roberts 是伦敦国王学院应用语言学教授，研究领域为跨文化交际和第二语言社会化、话语分析、语言与文化研究。过去 10 年间，她在非英语母语者的有效练习、医疗对话、求职面谈和民族语言劣势等领域取得了卓越的成果。

本文首先关注在全球化经济之下职场对用人要求的变化。新的职场秩序创造了新的话语秩序，"劳动力"（workforce）变成了"语言力"（word force），出现了新的语言和交际体裁。全球化下的人群流动从缺乏财富和安全感的社会进入稳定富足的社会，也创造了多语言的工作环境。这两者的改变同时对传统定义上的语言社会化提出了挑战。本文接下来探讨了这些挑战。复杂多变的职场会使移民经历双重社会化，除了在工作场合中所使用的混合话语之外，这些新住民们还会面临不同文化风俗语言表达的差异及挑战等问题。

职场筛选过程所需的语言要求往往大于工作本身的语言要求,因而对移民劳工及移民白领们产生了额外的语言惩罚。而其中地位较低的移民劳工所处的多语言环境和国际化组织的员工所处的共同语交流环境之间有着鲜明的对比,因此本文最后重点讨论了多语言场所的语言社会化,包括强势语言下的语言社会化。最后用一个例子说明了复杂的语言及高科技技术环境下能产生与以往极为不同的语言社会化条件。鉴于越来越多国际化及多语言全球组织的兴起,21世纪的语言社会化研究将面临新的挑战。

第四部分 语言学理论和二语习得

这个部分的三篇文章(第12—14篇)综述了语言学理论在二语习得研究领域的应用。

12. 语义学理论和二语习得

本文作者 Roumyana Slabakova 是英国南安普顿大学应用语言学系主任与语言学、语言教育和习得研究中心(CLLEAR)的主任。她在保加利亚出生,获得学士学位,并在保加利亚索菲亚大学讲授学术英语,之后在加拿大麦吉尔大学获得博士学位,研究保加利亚人对英语体(aspect)的习得。

本文辨析了语言的不同构成模块的四种语义类型。这种模块化语言结构的视角表明,不同层面的习得难点不同。研究者认为二语语义的习得涉及第一语言和第二语言在句法-语义连接上的解释不匹配。在获得语义方面,学习者面临着两种类型的学习情境。一种学习情境是句法简单,但语义复杂,另一种学习情境是句法复杂,但语义简单。本文综述了这些学习情境的代表性研究,论述了有关解释性显性教学的重要性以及母语对习得二语的影响,还探讨了习得特定语言话语属性与普遍语用学的一些问题。这些具有代表性的研究和许多其他二语习得语义的研究表明,通往语义和语用习得最终的成功之路是没有明显障碍的。

作者指出，语言习得的难点在于将语言形式与意义相匹配。她首先举了四种类型的意义：词汇意义、句子意义、语法意义和语用意义，并解释了这四个不同层面的语法与它们所含语义的对应关系，并借用 Reinhart（2006）的图表非常直观地展现了作者所指的语言的不同模块以及各模块之间的关系。正文部分通过七个例句阐释了二语习得中由于句法与语义的不匹配给学习者造成的困难。接着，作者还用例句分别阐述了句法-话语的连接，以及句法-语用的连接。一个重要发现是二语学习者在获得语言的中期就开始遵循格莱斯合作准则，甚至比母语者还要严格。

作者的结语强调，将语法形式与词汇、语法意义相对应是语言习得中重要也是最困难的部分。而句子和话语-语用意义，是通过普遍计算机制（universal computation mechanism）算出的。一旦学习了词汇屈折规则，学习者就知道对应的语义变化。甚至在语用层面，学习者也能学习到母语中没有的语用属性。因此，形态学成了习得的瓶颈。一旦打破这个瓶颈，其他层面的意义就不难掌握了。

作者指出，将来需要进一步探讨的是不同语言中意义与形式的不匹配现象以及同样的意义在不同语言中的表现形式。例如，如果母语只用词汇形式标注主题和焦点，而二语用不同的形式标注（如语调，语序），会给二语习得带来困难吗？对此类问题的探讨将帮助我们加深对二语意义习得的理解。

13. 二十一世纪的二语习得和句法理论

本文作者 Juana M. Liceras 是加拿大渥太华大学现代语言和语言学系教授，其研究方向有语言学理论与母语／二语习得、比较语法、语言接触和双语现象之间的关系等。

本文以乔姆斯基的内部语言／外部语言为框架，综述了二语习得研究的进展。作者指出，自 20 世纪 80 年代初以来，句法理论在二语习得研究中发挥了重要作用。有关"功能参数化假说"（functional parameterization hypothesis）以及有关二语学习者是激活了语言新特征还是转换了特征实质的争论，推动了对不同非母语语法句法属性的细致而深入的分析。

近 10 年来，以乔姆斯基最简方案为背景的分析已经越来越偏离这些用来证明或者证伪不同版本普遍语法的句法属性。最近的研究焦点是认知科学领域的非母语语法的地位。因此，分析以特征（性别、格、动词和限定词）为基本单位，并特别注意语言输入的质量、加工原则与限制，将非母语语法与语言接触的范式进行比较。语言接触的范式是基于后续双语现象、儿童二语习得、混合语形成和历时变化的研究。

作者指出，虽然对句法特征的属性和地位仍有许多悬而未决的问题，用特征这个概念来探讨语言接触和二语习得有着明显的优势，有助于探讨以往忽略的现象，并提出新的研究课题。比如，句法特征有助于将语言接触情境下的语言产出作为内部语言进行分析。今后的研究需要强调以下几点：

（1）建立句法特征清单和定义；

（2）确定句法特征的内部语法内容和建立结构关系；

（3）确定如何将句法特征进行分类；

（4）建立特征之间的联系。

14. 基于使用的语言流派与二语学习

本文作者 Andrea Tyler 是美国乔治城大学语言学系的教授，其研究方向包括认知语言学、跨文化语用学和话语分析、语言和法律、阅读理论和写作理论。

本文指出，在过去二十年中，二语学习和教学领域提出了许多语言模型，强调语言的交际性。这些模型通常是基于使用的，因为它们强调语言的实际使用，认为语言的使用塑造了语言形式。这些模型的支持者还认为，意义的制造是塑造语言的核心。基于使用的模型还包含其他一些假设。虽然模型之间有相同之处，但它们还是生成了一些非常不同的语言流派。这些观点常用相似的术语，如认知和隐喻，但所提供的解释却随着模型的不同而不同。结果是，没有广泛的阅读，就不清楚这些模型的不同和它们独特的贡献。本文试图解决这个问题，评述了三个主要的基于使用的模型：系统功能语言学、语篇功能主义和认知语言学。作者先论述了三种模型共同的基本原理，然后辨析了这些语言流派的理论基础和关注点的不同之处，最后论述了如何将模型应用于二语学习的问题。由于认知语言学流派最近开始成为热门，也是二语研究中比较新的流派，作者花了最大的篇幅加以讨论。

结语指出，这三种语言学流派最大的差别在于对语言形成的关键因素持有不同看法。系统功能语言学几乎完全依靠社会交际因素来进行语言分析；语篇功能主义认识到社会交际功能，同时也添加了认知加工的一般原理；认知语言学则突出人体的神经生理解剖学和人与物理环境的互动。

三、特点与评价

本卷"年度评论"的特别之处有两点。第一，内容丰富，涉及传承语学习、研究方法、语言社会化和二语习得等四个应用语言学的重要议题。第二，针对这些议题选择了来自不同学科背景的供稿人，因而涵盖了通常处在对立位置的不同理论流派、方法和观点，例如社会文化与认知流派，量的研究方法与质的研究方法，二语学习/习得的不同语言观（结构、功能、交际）。在不同声音的呈现和碰撞中，读者对相关的核心概念有了更丰富、立体、深刻的认识。

由于作者来自不同背景，文中对关键概念的定义有时也各不相同。以第一部分有关传承语研究的文章为例。四篇文章就传承语这一概念定义的争论，就代表了不同理论视域的声音。对"传承语"定义的主要分歧在于大部分文献都是取以语言熟练程度为基础的定义。例如，Silvina Montrul 和 Kimi Kondo-Brown 都强调传承语学习者有一定的使用该语言的能力。Silvina Montrul 定义传承语学习者为"讲少数语言的移民家庭的孩子和成人，他们在家里接触到传承语，并希望学习、重新学习或提高他们现有的语言水平。"她认为传承语的使用者有一个共同点：他们的家庭语言达到了一定的水平，但是不如他们的父母和在来源国长大的同龄人，尤其是读写能力。他们的传承语水平通常弱于主流语。Kimi Kondo-

Brown 的定义则是:"他们在家庭社会化过程中作为母语习得了该语言,有一定的语言能力,但由于需要转换到当地社会的强势语言(dominant language)环境,并没有完全掌握该语言。"

另一部分文献考虑了语言的社会文化政治因素,认为以语言水平为标准的定义不能反映复杂的语言实际:许多在只说英语的环境中成长的"传承语学习者",虽然完全不能使用该语言,却对她父母的来源国有着很强的归属感,并希望重拾这种语言能力。如果采用语言水平的定义,她却不能算成是传承语学习者。有学者提出,研究者对研究对象贴上的标签(如传承语学习者)通常并不符合这些人群自己的语言身份认同。例如,Jeffrey Bale 采用 Hornberger and Wang 2008 年的宽泛定义:考虑个人主观能动性,即传承语学习者自己的认同,以及传承语和其使用者在社会、政治、和经济话语中的位置。有些学者考虑到这两种观点。例如,Agnes Weiyun He 认为传承语既是交流的工具,也是社会文化团体认同和转型的方式。她的定义既包括了语言水平的涵义,也包括了传承语的社会文化功能:"传承语学习者是指那些与传承语有一种民族语言联系,有一定的说和/或者读写能力的人。当从非正式的口语环境转换到正式或书面语境时,他们的语言需要一些调整,也需要发展,除了和家庭、朋友沟通之外,能适应不同语域、语体、听众和目的的语言能力。"

除了第一部分之外,其他三部分也为研究方法、语言社会化、二语习得等问题提供了不同理论视域,为我们认识问题提供了更丰富的视角。而将不同流派的声音集合起来,也代表了美国应用语言学领域近年来的发展方向。在 2013 年美国应用语言学学会年会中,数位著名学者就如何在应用语言学中的认知科学和社会语言学两个流派之间"架桥"展开了一场专题研讨,内容包括"哲学和理论建构"、"数据和研究方法"和"尚待解决的问题",他们的发言发表在 2014 年的《二语习得研究》期刊上(Hulstijn and Young, 2014)。年会的新动向表明,应用语言学各流派中的研究者都开始意识到各自的局限,并努力使理论和方法更丰富,从而对研究问题提供更完整的答案。在架桥的过程中,研究者开始探索这些问题：流派之间的差异是在"我们应该研究的现象是什么？"的问题层面，还是"我们应该如何开展研究？"，或是两者都有？而本卷选取的文章就已经开始呈现这些问题和争论了。

尽管第30卷内容丰富，四个议题中仍有不少问题有待展开。

首先，有关传承语的四篇文章并没有详细讨论传承语学习者自己的视角。在美国应用语言学学会2013年的年会上，给本卷撰文的作者之一，Agnes Weiyun He作为大会主旨发言人，讲述了一个将她过去10年研究的不同传承语学习者合成的人物Jason的故事，提出传承语研究应该以身份认同为核心，考虑时间跨度、多样的语境和复杂的交流模式。传承语学习者的声音可以让我们更深入地了解传承语的发展与学习者身份认同的联系。

第二，传承语教育在美国为什么难以展开，对一些孩子（尤其是读写说的能力）效果不佳？这与美国主流文化、意识形态和英语的强势地位是否有关系？是怎样的关系？除了家庭和移民社团，美国的主流文化中是否有提供传承语社会化的场所？传承语教育和外语教育能否相互支持，对美国开展开放、多元、包容的教育起到促进作用？学习者对传承语的态度是否会随着传承语来源国经济实力的提升而变化？

第三，对这些问题的探究或许对中国情境下如何促进和完善母语教育、外语教育的问题也有借鉴意义。在以汉语为主导的语境中，哪些语言算作"传承语"，传承语概念的涵义和范围是什么，对传承语使用者又该如何提供语言教育和社会支持，都是值得思考和探索的问题。

第四，有关语言社会化的议题，所选的三篇文章分别讨论了学术话语社区、课堂话语和职场话语，但没有涉及其他情境。而网络社区作为新兴的话语社区，不受时间、空间的限制，也是如今大多数人参与的话语社区。网络社区中的语言社会化有怎样的特点？给身份认同提供了怎样的资源？对这些问题的探索可以给现有的语言社会化研究提供很好的补充。

最后，有关语言学理论和二语习得的议题，西方二语学习的模式在国内的教学和研究中是否适用？在国际化进程发展迅速的当代中国，二语、外语的界限如何划分？英语教育是否遵循英语国家二语习得的模式？这些问题都值得国内国外的学者共同探究。

综上所述，这本精心选题、"野心勃勃"的特刊能帮助读者全方位了解当今西方、尤其是美国应用语言学领域的重要研究议题，给读者提供多重视角和方法。其中的许多议题，例如传承语研究、语言社会化和国家身份认同等，对我国的应用语言学研究具有重要参考价值。

参考文献

Atkinson, D., (2002). "Toward a Sociocognitive Approach to Second Language Acquisition," *The Modern Language Journal*, 86(4), 525–545.

Briggs, C. L., (2007). "Anthropology, Interviewing, and Communicability in Contemporary Society," *Current Anthropology*, 48(4), 551–580.

Cummins, J., (2005). "A Proposal for Action: Strategies for Recognizing Heritage Language Competence as a Learning Resource within the Mainstream Classroom," *Modern Language Journal*, 585–592.

He, Agnes. "Language of the Heart and Heritage: A Tangled Tale." Dallas Ballroom BC. Dallas, Texas. American Association for Applied Linguistics Conference. 19 March 2013. Plenary Session.

Hornberger, N. H., & Wang, S. C. (2008). "Who Are Our Heritage Language Learners? Identity and Biliteracy in Heritage Language Education in the United States," In D. M. Brinton, O. Kagan, & S. Bauckus (eds.), *Heritage Language Education: A New Field Emerging*, New York & London: Routledge, 3–35.

Hulstijn, Jan H., et al. (2014). "Cognitive and Social Approaches to Research in Second Language Learning and Teaching," *Studies in Second Language Acquisition*, 36, 361–421.

Kulick, D., & Schieffelin, B. B. (2004). "Language Socialization," In A. Duranti (ed.), *A Companion to Linguistic Anthropology*, Malden, MA: Blackwell, 349–368.

Reinhart, T. (2006). *Interface Strategies*. Cambridge, MA: MIT Press.

Ricento, T. K., & Hornberger, N. H. (1996). "Unpeeling the Onion: Language Planning and Policy and the ELT Professional," *Tesol Quarterly*, 30(3), 401–427.

Editor's Introduction

Charlene Polio

This issue is my first edited volume of the *Annual Review of Applied Linguistics* (*ARAL*). Each year *ARAL* focuses on a specific theme, but about every five years it covers a range of mostly unrelated topics in a survey issue. Volume 30 was scheduled to be a survey issue, and after some discussion with the editorial directors, I decided to keep this tradition. Thus, I had the daunting task of choosing four broad topics, and then within each broad topic, a few narrow topics on which to invite scholars to write review articles. I chose a wide range of areas as a statement that I see the field of applied linguistics as not only being broad but as also representing a range of perspectives on theory and research methods. For example, I have included sections both on language socialization and on linguistic theory (mostly formal) in second language acquisition. I felt that these two areas were quite far apart with regard to the view that researchers in those areas held, but in my mind, both social and cognitive approaches to language learning and use are valid and simply seek to answer different questions. In the section on research methods, the articles focus on using both cognitive and social approaches, as well as quantitative and qualitative methods. The articles on heritage language learning focus on acquisition, policy, pedagogy, and sociocultural issues.

Generally review articles in *ARAL* cover fairly recent research, and the authors have indeed tried to keep their coverage of their respective topics recent. Because the reviews need to be accessible to a range of readers, however, the authors usually had to include older research in order to contextualize the current research and to explain concepts and terms that might not be familiar to all readers. In addition, because of the range of topics, some variation exists in the level of detail reported about the reviewed research and the length of the articles. For example, it is difficult to summarize the results of some of the semantic research without carefully explaining the studies and terminology. Furthermore, in some areas, such as eye tracking in second language learning, much of the research is new, and the authors had to cite unpublished studies including conference papers and dissertations. You will also note that authors used different definitions of certain concepts, such as *heritage learner*. In this case, however, all four authors carefully addressed the problems of and issues related to defining the term.

Although the articles in this volume were invited, each was reviewed by a member of the board and/or outside reviewers. I was extremely pleased with the willingness of my colleagues to accept this important job. They responded cheerfully and promptly. In particular, I thank Christine Casanave, Debra Friedman, Debra Hardison, Kathy Howard, Shaofeng Li, Kim Potowski, Jason Rothman, Irina Sekerina, Paula Winke, Eve Zyzik, and two anonymous reviewers. All of their reviews improved the final versions of the articles.

In addition, I would like to thank Morrell Gillette and Robert Dreesen from Cambridge University Press for answering all my questions; my graduate student, Sally Behrenwald, for her help in editing; my colleague, Debra Friedman, for our lengthy discussions about editing dilemmas; the editorial directors for their careful reviewing and for their suggestions of topics and contributors; and most of all, Mary McGroarty, the past editor of *ARAL*, for all her help with this first issue.

I will end by mentioning one of the vexing challenges in editing this issue. Applied linguistics is a diverse field with researchers coming from areas such as linguistics, education, psychology, and anthropology. The contributors to this volume are no exception. I made the choice to follow the conventions of the American Psychological Association (APA) style guidelines, as a large majority of journals in applied linguistics do. What was difficult was forcing authors to change conventions that were not standard in their areas. For example, those working in the area of formal syntax tend to capitalize certain syntactic operations and the titles of theories. I chose not to do this because I felt it privileged certain concepts. Furthermore, most terms in applied linguistics are in a state of flux; capitalizing them makes them seem static. Another problem was the issue of scare quotes, that is, the use of quotation marks when not citing a specific source. APA guidelines suggest avoiding them except to show irony. I found that those researchers coming from a more qualitative or anthropological background tended to use them, while those from a more quantitative or psychological background did not. My personal opinion is that they cause confusion: Is the author quoting a source or making a comment on someone else's use of the term? I tried to keep them to a minimum, but again, it was difficult to force everyone to write "like a psychologist". Irony intended.

SECTION A: HERITAGE LANGUAGE LEARNING

Current Issues in Heritage Language Acquisition

Silvina Montrul

An increasing trend in many postsecondary foreign language classes in North America is the presence of heritage language learners. Heritage language learners are speakers of ethnolinguistically minority languages who were exposed to the language in the family since childhood and as adults wish to learn, relearn, or improve their current level of linguistic proficiency in their family language. This article discusses the development of the linguistic and grammatical knowledge of heritage language speakers from childhood to adulthood and the conditions under which language learning does or does not occur. Placing heritage language acquisition within current and viable cognitive and linguistic theories of acquisition, I discuss what most recent basic research has so far uncovered about heritage speakers of different languages and their language learning process. I conclude with directions for future research.

INTRODUCTION

An increasing trend in many postsecondary foreign language classes in North America is the presence of heritage language learners. In its broadest sense, heritage language learners are the children of families who speak an ethnolinguistically minority language, but in this article I only discuss the case of immigrants. As adults, these children of immigrant families wish to learn, relearn, or improve their current level of linguistic proficiency in their family language. In language programs such as Spanish, Russian, East Asian languages, Hindi-Urdu, Turkish, Arabic, and others, heritage language learners attend classes initially geared to second language (L2) learners with no previous knowledge of the language. Alternatively, and depending on the institution, heritage speakers can also enroll in classes specifically designed for students with cultural and linguistic ties to the language. Although the presence of heritage speakers in language classes is not new,[1] what is new is the recognition that heritage language learners are a different breed of language learners whose partial knowledge of the language presents a unique set of challenges to language practitioners. What is also new is the growing sense that minority languages are worth preserving and maintaining, rather than suppressing or ignoring.[2] Indeed, among certain political circles, heritage language learners represent a unique and valuable national resource, as they can potentially fulfill the need for advanced and competent speakers of critical languages (Campbell & Rosenthal, 2000).

Today, the upcoming field of heritage language education has found a place and a voice of its own within applied linguistics. As a field that emerged out of necessity, driven primarily by demographic changes, heritage language education has been strongly concerned with issues of cultural identity (i.e., who exactly are heritage speakers?) as well as pedagogical and practical questions, including what to teach and how to best instruct heritage language learners so that their personal, cultural, and linguistic needs can be properly met (Brinton, Kagan, & Bauckus, 2008). Nonetheless, Valdés (1997, 2005) and Lynch (2003) have raised concerns about the atheoretical character of the field and its blind appropriation and adaptation of foreign language methods (Valdés, Fishman, Chávez, & Pérez, 2006). The implication of claims such as these seems to be that if heritage language education wants to move forward as a field of inquiry, it must develop a theory of heritage language acquisition. Although there is a growing body of descriptive studies (large-scale and single case-studies) of heritage speakers' profiles, there is very little systematic theoretically driven research on heritage language learners, heritage acquisition, and the psycholinguistic processes involved in this type of learning. This situation is rapidly changing. Although there is a substantial body of work on language policy and identity related to heritage speakers (see the special issue of *The Modern Language Journal 2005*, volume 89, number 4), my purpose in this article is to discuss the development of linguistic knowledge of heritage language speakers from childhood to adulthood and the conditions under which language learning does or does not occur. Placing heritage language acquisition within current and viable cognitive and linguistic theories of acquisition, I discuss what most recent basic research has so far uncovered about heritage speakers of different languages and their language learning process. I conclude by establishing directions for future research.

HERITAGE LANGUAGE LINGUISTIC SYSTEMS

The term *heritage speaker* was first introduced in Canada in the mid-1970s (see Cummins, 2005) but has been gaining ground in the United States since the 1990s. Broadly defined, heritage speakers are child and adult members of a linguistic minority who grew up exposed to their home language and the majority language. For some researchers, this definition also includes indigenous languages, not just immigrant languages (Fishman, 2006). Representative minorities are Spanish, East Asian, Russian, and Arabic heritage speakers.

Despite different language backgrounds, cultures, educational and social classes, and exposure to different varieties and registers of their home language, heritage speakers share a common characteristic: They have achieved partial command of the family language, short of the native speaker level of their parents and of peers raised in their home countries. Heritage speakers are a special case of child bilingualism. Because the home or family language is a minority language, not all heritage language children have access to education in their heritage language. Consequently, the vast majority of adult heritage speakers typically have very strong command of the majority language, while proficiency and literacy in the family language varies considerably. Although one can certainly find some heritage speakers with very advanced or even nativelike proficiency in the two languages (e.g., some Spanish heritage speakers studied by Montrul, 2006), for most heritage speakers, the home language is the weaker language. Proficiency in the weaker language can range from mere receptive skills (most often listening) to intermediate and advanced oral and written skills, depending on the language, the community, and a host of other sociolinguistic circumstances.

Recent linguistic, psycholinguistic, sociolinguistic, and pedagogical research has identified a series of grammatical areas that are affected in heritage language grammars. These linguistic areas include vocabulary, morphosyntax (case, verbal and nominal agreement, tense, aspect, and mood), pronominal reference, article semantics, word order, relative clauses, and conjunctions, among many others. Yet the fact that heritage speakers display gaps in their linguistic knowledge does not mean they have acquired a rogue grammar or that their knowledge is somehow chaotic. Linguistically oriented studies of heritage language systems show that in many respects heritage language grammars reveal processes of simplification attested in language contact situations, the emergence of new linguistic varieties, and diachronic language change. Let us examine some specific characteristics of heritage language grammars as revealed by most recent linguistic research.

Phonetics and Phonology

Although the language of heritage speakers is usually perceived as having nonnative and nonstandard features, pronunciation is the linguistic domain most spared from this impression. Heritage speakers are typically described as having good phonology, especially when they are compared to adult L2 learners of similar morphosyntactic proficiency. For example, Au, Knightly, Jun, and Oh (2002) and Oh, Jun, Knightly, and Au (2003) studied the phonetic perception and production abilities of Korean and Spanish heritage speakers of very low productive proficiency in the languages (*overhearers*). Tests of pronunciation and voice onset time (VOT) measurements for Spanish voiceless stops (labial /p/, dental /t/, velar /k/) and for the denti-alveolar Korean stops (aspirated /t^h/, plain /t/, tense and /t'/) revealed that the heritage speakers were significantly more nativelike than comparison groups of L2 learners who had not been exposed to Korean or Spanish since childhood. Nonetheless, the heritage speakers also differed significantly from the Spanish and Korean native speaker control groups, suggesting that heritage speakers also display some nonnative phonological features.

Similar measurable nonnative effects in pronunciation of Korean as a heritage language are reported by Yeni-Komshian, Flege, and Liu (2000). Other evidence comes from a study of the vowels system of Western Armenian conducted by Godson (2004). Godson found that the vowel quality of the heritage speakers showed some transfer from English in some Western Armenian vowels, but the quality of other vowels was also different from the quality of the same vowels in monolingual and fluent bilingual Western Armenian speakers. To date, the pronunciation of heritage speakers remains an understudied area, but the few available studies suggest that there are measurable systematic differences between monolinguals and heritage speakers worth investigating in future research, especially to address theoretical debates on the role of early input for phonological abilities in bilinguals.

Vocabulary

The acquisition of vocabulary is context specific and depends largely on experience. Heritage language speakers know many words in their heritage language, but most often these are words related to common objects used in the home and childhood vocabulary. In fact, heritage language speakers also have significant gaps in their vocabulary and find it difficult to retrieve words they do not use very frequently. Polinsky (1997, 2007) found that vocabulary proficiency correlated positively with structural accuracy in Russian heritage speakers: Those speakers who knew more basic words from a list of 200 items exhibited better control of agreement, case markers, and subordination in spontaneous speech. In a more recent study, Polinsky (2005) investigated knowledge of word classes in heritage speakers of very low proficiency in Russian. Polinsky found that heritage speakers had better command of verbs (as measured in word recognition and translation accuracy) than of nouns and adjectives. These findings are not surprising, given the fact that in language attrition situations nouns are more frequently used in code switching and borrowings than verbs and adjectives (Poplack, 1980). Furthermore, as Polinsky explained, verbs are semantically more dense and heavier than nouns (containing both lexical and structural information), and hence more costly to lose.

To date, there are very few studies of lexical knowledge in this population. In particular, the relationship between grammar and the lexicon needs to be explored more closely in future psycholinguistic research, especially if, as several authors suggested, this relationship has pedagogical and assessment potential for both L2 learners and heritage language learners (Fairclough, 2008; Lam, Pérez-Leroux, & Ramírez, 2003).

Morphosyntax

Perhaps the linguistic area most noticeably affected in heritage language grammars is inflectional morphology. In the nominal domain, many languages mark number, gender, and case. Heritage speakers of languages with overt gender, number, and case marking produce a significant number of errors as compared to native speakers or even their own parents (first generation immigrants). For example, Russian has a three-way gender system (masculine, feminine, neuter), and Spanish has a two-way system (masculine, feminine). Although monolingual Russian and Spanish-speaking children control gender marking by age 4 or earlier with almost 100% accuracy (with the exception of most irregular, less frequent, and marked forms), Polinsky (2008a) and Montrul, Foote, and Perpiñán (2008a) have independently shown that heritage speakers display very high error rates with gender marking (ranging from 5% to 25%). In Russian, the neuter and feminine genders are the most affected in heritage speakers. Indeed, Polinsky (2008a) found that while higher-proficiency Russian heritage speakers still displayed a three-way gender system, lower-proficiency speakers had a two-way distinction, consisting of only masculine and feminine, and no neuter. Similarly, Montrul et al. found that when Spanish heritage speakers made gender errors, these were most frequent with feminine nouns and with nouns with noncanonical or nontransparent word endings. If masculine gender is considered the default in Spanish and feminine is the marked form, clearly Spanish heritage language grammars also show simplification of marked forms and retention of the default.

Agreement in noun phrases has also been studied in Arabic as a heritage language. Arabic is a language with a very complex system of gender and plural morphology: There are different endings for masculine and feminine plural nouns and adjectives. Furthermore, Arabic makes an important distinction between nouns for people (human) and nouns for things (nonhuman). The feminine human ending-*aat* is the most frequent ending, and the masculine human ending is *-uun/-iin* (*mudarris* "teacher," *mudarrisun* "teachers"), but there are numerous exceptions to these patterns. Arabic has what is called the broken plural, which is a very productive process involving a change of root rather than simply suffixation (similar but not identical to ablaut verbs in English, such as *bring-brought*). Examples of broken plurals are *kitaab* "book" *-kutub* "books" and *film* "film" *-?aflaam* "films." Benmamoun, Albirini, Saadah, and Montrul (2008) investigated productive control of plural agreement patterns in heritage speakers of Egyptian Arabic, heritage speakers of Palestinian-Jordanian Arabic, and native speakers of the two dialects in spontaneous oral production and elicited oral production tasks. Benmamoun et al. found that the native speakers performed at 99–100% accuracy; but the heritage speakers produced up to 30% error rates with some words. While heritage speakers retained knowledge of broken plurals and Semitic roots in general, they tended to use the wrong pattern. Heritage speakers also made the same types of errors attested in monolingual Arabic speaking children during the stage of early language development: They overextended the plural feminine suffix -*aat* to masculine contexts.

Case marking is another candidate for erosion and imperfect mastery in heritage language grammars. Full Russian has a six-way distinction in nouns: nominative, accusative, dative, instrumental, oblique, and genitive. According to Polinsky (2007, 2008b), the case system is severely reduced in heritage speakers: Dative is replaced by accusative, and accusative by nominative, in many constructions with subjects, direct, and indirect objects. Thus, while native speakers of Russian use the six-case markings, heritage speakers tend to use two: nominative and accusative. Similar omission patterns have been reported in Korean by Song, O'Grady, Cho, and Lee (1997). Although nominative and accusative case markers are typically dropped in Korean, monolingual children and adults gain full control of the case system, including the discourse-pragmatic conditions under which case markers can be dropped or retained. Song et al. found that while 5- to 8-year-old monolingual Korean children were 86% accurate at comprehending OVS sentences in Korean with nominative and accusative case markers, 5- to 8-year-old Korean heritage speakers performed at less than 34% accuracy. They tended to interpret OVS sentences as SOV sentences, ignoring the case markers. Similar omission of case markers and reliance on a more fixed SVO nominative-accusative order has been documented in Spanish heritage speakers and in heritage speakers of South Asian languages (Moag, 1995). Montrul and Bowles (2009) showed that adult Spanish heritage speakers omit the dative preposition "a" with dative experiencer subjects with gustar-type verbs (**Juan le gusta la música* instead of *A Juan le gusta la música* "Juan likes music"), and they omit the same preposition when it appears with animate direct objects (*Juan vio María instead of *Juan vio a María* "Juan saw Maria").

The verbal domain exhibits similar morphological problems in heritage language speakers, especially problems with subject-verb agreement (see Moag, 1995, for South Asian languages) and with tense paradigms. Heritage speakers of Spanish and Russian seem to control regular forms of the present and past tenses but confuse aspectual distinctions between perfective and imperfective forms (Montrul,

2002; Polinsky, 2007; Silva-Corvalán, 1994). The subjunctive mood (in both present and past) is poorly controlled by Spanish heritage speakers in production and in comprehension (Montrul, 2007; Silva-Corvalán, 1994), and so is the conditional (Silva-Corvalán). These types of errors are not common in speakers who have full control of their native language (first generation immigrants and monolingual native speakers). Rothman (2007) also found that Brazilian Portuguese heritage speakers do not develop knowledge of inflected infinitives, a feature that is learned at school by exposure to written registers.

Syntax

The erosion of case and agreement morphology characteristic of many heritage language grammars has consequences for the basic clause structure and for pronominal reference. In languages with flexible word order, case markers allow the speaker and hearer to keep track of the participants (and grammatical relations). As a result, Russian and Spanish heritage speakers tend to rely on SVO word order, while Korean speakers prefer SOV order (Song et al., 1997). Montrul (2010) found that while Spanish heritage speakers accepted and comprehended SVO sentences accurately, they were much less accurate with sentences with preverbal objects. A typical consequence of the loss of agreement and more rigid word order relates to the licensing of null and overt subjects, especially in null subject languages such as Russian and Spanish. In these languages, both null and overt pronouns are grammatical because the person and number information is recoverable from the agreement morphology. However, the distribution of null and overt subjects is licensed by discourse-pragmatic factors, such as topic continuation, topic shift, or switch reference. Studies have found that Spanish and Russian heritage speakers tend to overuse overt subjects in topic shift and switch reference contexts where null subjects would be pragmatically more appropriate (Montrul, 2004; Polinsky, 2007; Silva-Corvalán, 1994).

Another vulnerable domain in heritage language grammars is long-distance dependencies, including pronominal reference within and beyond the sentence, as with reflexive pronouns (anaphors like English *himself*). Korean has three reflexives—*caki, casin*, and *caki-casin*—which differ in their distribution and interpretation. *Caki* is subject oriented and prefers long-distance antecedents (beyond the clause). *Caki-casin* requires a local antecedent (within the clause).

Casin can take local or long-distance antecedents. In English, reflexive pronouns (*himself* or *herself*) are typically subject oriented and take local antecedents (i.e., in *Paul said that Peter hurt himself, himself* refers to *Peter*, the subject of its own clause, but in a language like Korean, it could refer to *Paul*, the subject of the more distant main clause). Kim, Montrul, and Yoon (2009) found that long-distance preferences were affected in adult Korean heritage speakers. Heritage speakers preferred local binding for *caki* and seemed to treat *casin* and *caki-casin* indistinguishably, as if they had a two-anaphor system. Their interpretations differed sharply from those of monolingual Korean speakers. Other problems with reflexive pronouns are reported by Polinsky and Kagan (2007) in Russian heritage speakers.

Finally, heritage speakers have been shown to have problems with more complex structures, like relative clauses. Polinsky (2008c) tested comprehension of subject and object relative clauses in Russian heritage speakers, and so did O'Grady, Lee, and Choo (2001). They both found that heritage speakers had significant difficulty with object relative clauses (*the cat that the dog is chasing*) as opposed to subject relative clauses (*the dog that is chasing the cat*). Thus, in terms of relativization, there is an advantage for subjects as opposed to objects in heritage language grammars, as in many languages of the world (e.g., Malagasy).

To summarize, under reduced input and output conditions, heritage speakers seem to develop some core aspects of their family language, but their grammatical systems show a marked tendency toward simplification and overregularization of complex morphological patterns and restricted word order. It is also possible that many of these effects could also be triggered by transfer from English, the dominant language in most of the empirical studies conducted to date. After all, English has strict SVO order and does not have overt case markers, null subjects, subjunctive morphology, complex plural morphology, gender, or different types of reflexive pronouns. Ideally, studies of the same heritage language with different contact languages should be undertaken to investigate the extent to which transfer from the dominant language influences the degree of incomplete acquisition found in heritage language grammars. A study of this sort is Kim (2007), who investigated the local and long-distance properties of the three Korean reflexives *caki, casin*, and *caki-casin* in Korean heritage speakers residing in the United States (dominant language English) and Korean heritage speakers residing in China (dominant language Mandarin). Although Korean and Chinese have long-distance binding and

English does not, Kim found that the Korean heritage speakers still preferred more local binding than long-distance binding regardless of the contact language. Kim's results indicate that the contact language is not always the main cause behind the preferences observed with binding, but this is something that should be investigated in more detail.

Contrasting First, Second, and Heritage Language Acquisition

To understand the grammatical competence of adult heritage speakers whose language presents many of the characteristics described in the previous section, it is instructive to review how language acquisition may have taken place in their childhood, and how their acquisition path differs from that of normally developing children brought up in a predominantly monolingual environment. Normally developing monolingual children eventually acquire full grammatical competence in their native language. Early first language (L1) acquisition happens through the aural medium and takes place in a naturalistic setting by means of interaction with caregivers. Language acquisition is said to be uniform because children exposed to the same language or dialect reach the same level of linguistic development (and competence) despite variations in input. Eventually, children converge on the grammar of other adult members of their speech community. The outcome of normal L1 acquisition is successful, although this does not mean it is entirely error free.

Although it is common to read in the acquisition literature that by the age of 3–4, normally developing children have acquired the basic structural system of their language (Guasti, 2002; O'Grady, 1997); a great deal of vocabulary learning; and the acquisition of complex syntax, semantics, and pragmatics, as well as command of different spoken and written registers and pragmatic conventions take place during the school-age period (Chomsky, 1969; Menyuk & Brisk, 2005; Nippold, 1998). (In fact, vocabulary learning takes place throughout the life span.) Around age 4, children's metalinguistic ability develops through emergent literacy and continues at school, where children learn to read and write. At the end of the process, children become educated adult native speakers capable of functioning in different social and professional contexts.

In principle, children growing up in bilingual and multilingual environments — like heritage speakers—also have the potential to develop full linguistic competence in one, two or all the languages they are exposed to. However, the actual realization of such potential ultimately depends on many factors, including parental discourse strategies, status of the languages in the community, availability of a speech community beyond the family, attitudes toward the language, access to education in the language, and so on (Montrul, 2008). The precise situation of many heritage languages is that they are minority languages, spoken primarily at home in an informal context. Like monolingual children, heritage language children acquire the language naturalistically, from interaction with the family. Some heritage language children are simultaneous bilinguals: They were exposed to the heritage language and the majority language since birth, either because one or the two parents also speak the majority language, or because the child received child care in the majority language. Other heritage language children are sequential bilinguals or heritage language-dominant, at least up to age 5 (preschool). In these cases, perhaps the two parents speak the minority language and the language is used almost exclusively in the home. Other children immigrate with their parents in mid-childhood (ages 7–9). These children acquire the majority language predominantly at school, after the foundations of the heritage language are in place. If there are siblings in the family, the typical pattern is that the older siblings in the family have stronger command of the home language than the younger children in the family. In most heritage language families, siblings tend to speak in the majority language with each other and with other heritage language children. Highlighting the effect of age in incomplete acquisition and L1 attrition, Montrul (2008) showed that the extent of incomplete acquisition is greater in heritage speakers who are simultaneous bilinguals than in heritage language speakers who are sequential bilinguals and have had a longer period of sustained exposure to the heritage language before intense exposure to the majority language began.

In general, most heritage language children receive schooling in the majority language (English in the United States). Organized instruction in the heritage language is available for some children depending on the language, the community, and parental effort. East Asian families, for example, have been particularly proactive in organizing community-based schools to promote their language and culture, but similar schools are not available for many other heritage languages.

Restricted daily access to the language (in terms of frequency of exposure and use) in limited contexts (primarily home and possibly church) during the age of primary linguistic development (from birth to puberty, according to the critical period hypothesis) is one of the main reasons behind the incomplete patterns of acquisition, and perhaps attrition, as observed in many adult heritage language grammars.[3] Unlike monolingual children who reach full development of their native language, heritage language speakers have distinctive gaps in their linguistic knowledge, as we have seen. Lack of formal schooling in the heritage language makes the problem even worse for some language groups: As children, heritage speakers miss the chance to learn formal registers along with the vocabulary and complex structures that are typical of written language (Polinsky & Kagan, 2007; Rothman, 2007).

Descriptively, heritage language acquisition has some features of early L1 acquisition, but not all. Heritage language acquisition is incomplete L1 acquisition that takes place in a bilingual environment rather than a monolingual one. As such, heritage language acquisition also exhibits characteristics of adult L2 acquisition, which, due to its variable outcome, is typically described as *not uniform*, *not universal*, and *unsuccessful* (i.e., nonconvergent; see Bley-Vroman, 1989, 2009). Because L2 learners also bring solid knowledge of a mature linguistic system, they make both developmental errors, like L1 learners, and transfer errors due to influence from their L1, especially at early stages. A key difference between L1 and L2 acquisition, however, is that while child L1 learners overcome developmental errors without need for instruction, L2 learners continue to make many errors even after receiving instruction, practice, and correction. Although some researchers argue that attainment of full linguistic competence in the L2 is in principle possible, it is by no means guaranteed. Fossilization can occur at any point in L2 development.

Table 1 summarizes the main features of these three types of acquisition: L1, L2, and heritage language acquisition. Characteristics in italic bold font represent the intersecting subset between L1 and L2 acquisition that mark heritage language acquisition.

As can be seen in Table 1, heritage language learners like L1 learners are exposed to the language in early childhood through the aural medium in a naturalistic context (family), before the emergence of literacy. This is the period during which the essence of native speaker competence develops. Heritage language learners may command basic structures of the language if they received appropriate input and used (produced) the language, or only a subset of those structures, if the input and output were less abundant. Because heritage language acquisition takes place in a bilingual environment, as heritage language learners develop command of the majority language, they also make transfer errors. The outcome of heritage language acquisition is also variable and often incomplete, as in L2 acquisition, due to reduction of input and use of the target language in restricted contexts. Fossilization, so typical of L2 acquisition but undocumented in L1 acquisition, is also frequent in incomplete heritage language acquisition. Like L2 learners, heritage language learners need strong motivation to maintain and learn the heritage language, and issues of identity are very important. However, a key difference between heritage speakers and L2 learners has to do with context of acquisition and literacy. L2 acquisition typically occurs in a classroom setting, with heavy emphasis on reading and writing, and grammatical explanations, practice, feedback, and assessment of the developing L2 skills. If instructed, L2 learners are very literate in the L2 and have highly developed metalinguistic awareness of the language, while heritage language learners can be illiterate or have less developed literacy skills in the heritage language than in the majority language.

Table 1. Characteristics of L1, L2, and Heritage Language Acquisition

L1 Acquisition	L2 Acquisition
Early exposure to the language.	Late exposure to the language.
Abundant input in a naturalistic setting (aural input).	Varying amount of input in instructed and/or naturalistic setting (aural and written input).
Control of features of language acquired very early in life (phonology, some vocabulary, some linguistic structures).	Grammar may be incomplete (no chance to develop other structures and vocabulary).
Developmental errors.	*Developmental and transfer errors.*
Outcome is successful and complete.	*Outcome is variable proficiency. It is typically incomplete.*
Fossilization does not occur.	*Fossilization is typical.*
No clear role for motivation and affective factors to develop linguistic competence.	*Motivation and affective factors play a role in language development.*
More complex structures and vocabulary developed at school after age 5, when metalinguistic skills develop.	Experience with literacy and formal instruction.

THREE THEORETICAL PERSPECTIVES: FORMAL LINGUISTIC, COGNITIVE, AND EMERGENTIST

Existing theoretical perspectives on language acquisition have been applied to explain monolingual acquisition by children and L2 acquisition by adults. Bilingual acquisition can also be accommodated within these perspectives. For example, it has been hypothesized that L1 and L2 acquisition utilize very different learning mechanisms, as spelled out in Bley-Vroman's (1989, 2009) fundamental difference hypothesis (FDH). According to Bley-Vroman (and other generative linguists), child L1 acquisition is largely guided by innate mechanisms that are assumed to be part of Universal Grammar (Chomsky, 1986). That is, at the outset of language acquisition, children are guided by the inventory of principles and constraints subsumed under Universal Grammar. To explain the apparent differences between L1 and L2 acquisition in terms of outcome (successful and complete in L1 acquisition, variable and incomplete in L2 acquisition), the main claim of the FDH is that access to Universal Grammar is subject to a critical period. Postpuberty L2 learners can no longer use the same domain-specific (i.e., purely linguistic) mechanisms used by L1 learners. When learning a second language, L2 learners can only rely on their L1 knowledge (a particular instantiation of Universal Grammar, but not the full spectrum of linguistic options) and the principles and parameters active in their language. Consequently, in addition to L1 knowledge, L2 learners must resort to domain-general problem-solving skills, like analogy or pattern matching.[4]

This particular position within generative linguistics is echoed within cognitive and neurolinguistic perspectives on L2 acquisition, which do not necessarily view language and language learning by children as innate, but as part of general cognition, and take into account the distinction between procedural and declarative knowledge and implicit and explicit language learning (DeKeyser, 2003; Paradis, 2004, 2009). Implicit knowledge refers to that learned without awareness of what is being learned, and it is learned incidentally or not (depending on the author). Implicit knowledge is stored in procedural memory, and when this knowledge is accessed or recalled, it is executed automatically and quickly. By contrast, explicit knowledge is acquired with awareness of what is being learned and with conscious effort. Because explicit knowledge is learned explicitly, individuals can verbalize this knowledge on demand. It is stored in declarative or episodic memory, where our world knowledge is stored.

Adult educated native speakers have both systems of learning available and use them as needed. According to Paradis (2004), when young children speak or comprehend language, they use implicit competence (or knowledge) only. This is also true of adults who are illiterate. By contrast, incipient L2 learners use explicit knowledge of the L2 when producing or understanding the L2 and steadily and in tandem develop implicit competence of it. In agreement with Bley-Vroman's (1989) position, DeKeyser (2000, 2003) also contended that adult L2 learners use a different cognitive system to learn an L2 because maturational constraints apply to implicit linguistic competence acquired early in childhood. The decline of procedural memory and loss of implicit cognitive mechanisms for language somewhere in childhood — what Bley-Vroman took to be Universal Grammar and domain-specific mechanisms — forces late L2 learners to rely on explicit learning.

Another approach to language acquisition is emergentism (O'Grady, 2005). Like the cognitive and neurolinguistic approach, emergentism stands in contrast to the nativist approach that posits an innate Universal Grammar. The essence of emergentism is that language is an epiphenomenon, emerging from the interaction of general purpose cognitive abilities with each other and with the environment. For the theory of Universal Grammar, input underdetermines knowledge of language; however, for emergentism, it shapes it: General learning principles extract inductive generalizations and statistical regularities from the input. The key question for this approach is what the emergent linguistic knowledge looks like, and on this question answers vary. For N. C. Ellis (2002, 2009), the emergent linguistic knowledge consists of local associations and memorized chunks; for Goldberg (1999) and Tomasello (2003), it is constructions; and for O'Grady (2005), it is memorized processing routines. Although emergentism has extensively been applied to the problem of L2 acquisition (N. C. Ellis, 2002; MacWhinney, 1987; O'Grady, Lee, & Kwak, 2009), it is not clear how with respect to the outcome of the acquisition process the "fundamental" differences between child L1 and adult L2 learners are captured by this approach if the two populations use the same general learning mechanisms. One possibility is to say that the main differences between L1 and L2 acquisition are in the amount of input exposure and in the influence from the L1. Another possibility is that children and adults vary on how they parse and process input and the units they operate on (the less is more hypothesis of Johnson & Newport, 1989).

To summarize, the three perspectives described—Universal Grammar, cognitive approaches, and emergentism—emphasize different components of the language learning process: innate linguistic knowledge, general learning processes, and input, respectively, all of which are relevant in heritage language acquisition. While the three approaches often present themselves as competitors in confronting challenges of linguistic analysis and acquisition (nativism vs. emergentism, or cognitive approaches vs. Universal Grammar), they could actually be seen as complementary, were it not for the fact that they start from very different sets of assumptions about grammar, knowledge, and learning. I believe that the three approaches, or perhaps a combination of the three, are suitable to extend to heritage language acquisition.

RECENT EMPIRICAL FINDINGS

The Nature of Incomplete Acquisition

If some cases of heritage language acquisition are partial, incomplete, or interrupted L1 acquisition in a bilingual environment, one theoretical prediction is that heritage language learners' knowledge of the language (prior to instruction in a classroom) has been acquired as in L1 acquisition: implicitly and through access to Universal Grammar in childhood, before closure of the critical period. (See the weaker language as L1 hypothesis as spelled out by Montrul, 2008.) That is, heritage language learners should have implicit knowledge of aspects of phonology and morphosyntax that emerge or are acquired very early in childhood and that are not overly dependent on a heavy amount of continuous input (e.g., word order, pronominal reference, clitic pronouns). If a great deal of complex grammatical knowledge is underdetermined by input as the theory of Universal Grammar assumes, then heritage language speakers should also demonstrate knowledge of structures and constructions that are not frequent or obvious from the input, such as binding constraints, wh-movement, aspects of lexical semantics, and other poverty of the stimulus phenomenon. Kim et al. (2009) found that heritage speakers had basic knowledge of anaphor binding in Korean. Montrul, Foote, and Perpiñán (2008b) found that Spanish heritage speakers had robust knowledge of wh-movement in Spanish, and Montrul (2006) found that even heritage speakers of low proficiency in Spanish made a syntactic distinction between unaccusative and unergative verbs.

In turn, if other aspects of language need more input and sustained exposure and use, as the emergentist approach maintains, then inflectional morphology and other aspects of language that are context-dependent, acquired after age 4 or 5, and reinforced through reading and formal instruction at school will not be fully developed. For example, specialized vocabulary, forms of address and honorifics in East Asian languages, complex structures like relative clauses, and semantically and pragmatically conditioned uses of the subjunctive in Spanish and Russian should either be missing in heritage language learners or remain imperfectly acquired, depending on the amount of input received. Although many of the characteristics of heritage language grammars described earlier seem to match these theoretical predictions, few studies conducted to date have been carried out with these theoretical approaches in mind. Therefore, if one wants to tease apart which available language learning theory best applies to heritage language grammars, more basic and theory-driven empirical research should be pursued. It is also important to continue investigating heritage language grammars and heritage language competence in their own right, and to compare heritage speakers with speakers with full command of the language, or even monolingual children in the process of development. Not only is this research design important, but it is also suitable to pinpoint more precisely which grammatical features heritage language learners manage to develop under reduced input and output conditions and which others remain underdeveloped into adulthood at all levels of structural analysis.

Comparisons of L2 Learners and Heritage Language Learners

Since the field of heritage language education is primarily concerned with how to teach heritage language learners and how to help them regain aspects of language they lost or to help them acquire those that they never developed, it is also instructive to make predictions on how heritage language learners may approach the learning process as compared with L2 learners with no previous knowledge of the language. Here again, theoretical approaches that apply to these two learning conditions are very suitable to extend to heritage language acquisition: heritage language learners fall in between L1 and L2 acquisition, as shown in Table 1.

If early age of acquisition is particularly important for phonology, heritage language learners should have better pronunciation and perceptual discrimination than L2 learners. Although early age of acquisition should also bring advantages for heritage language learners in morphosyntax, the existing literature on critical periods for language indicate that phonology is more affected by age effects than morphosyntax. Nonetheless, both L2 learners and heritage language learners are expected to exhibit transfer from the dominant language, which is the L1 in the case of L2 learners but the majority language in the case of heritage language learners.

If timing of input is crucial for developing the essence of native speaker competence, heritage language learners should benefit from having received exposure to the heritage language, even if minimal, in early childhood. According to theoretical models that assume the critical period hypothesis, like some positions within Universal Grammar (Bley-Vroman, 1989, 2009) and cognitive and neurolinguistic approaches to L2 acquisition (DeKeyser, 2003; Paradis, 2004), heritage language learners should have more nativelike knowledge than L2 learners of comparable proficiency in the language. This hypothesis has been confirmed in the realm of phonology and pronunciation. As mentioned earlier, studies of Korean and Spanish heritage speakers and L2 learners by Au et al. (2002); Knightly, Jun, Oh, and Au (2003); and Oh et al. (2003) support this prediction. These studies found that heritage speakers with very low proficiency in the language performed significantly better than L2 learners on perception and production of VOTs in the two languages and in overall accent. Their findings on morphosyntax broadly defined, however, did not show differences between the groups. Similarly, Bruhn de Garavito's (2002) study of verb movement in Spanish and O'Grady et al.'s (2001) study of case markers and relative clauses in Korean found no differences between L2 learners and heritage language learners, echoing the findings of Au et al. (2002) and Knightly et al. (2003).

By contrast, Montrul's (2005) study of unaccusativity in Spanish found advantages for heritage language learners over L2 learners of low proficiency. Yet, other recent studies report mixed results. Håkansson (1995) found that heritage speakers of Swedish were significantly more nativelike with the verb second (V2) phenomenon than L2 learners of Swedish, but the two groups were equally nonnativelike on gender, number, and definiteness in noun phrases. Montrul (2010) found no differences between Spanish heritage speakers and Spanish L2 learners with knowledge of object clitic placement in a written grammaticality judgment task, but while the heritage speakers outperformed the L2 learners in their acceptance of sentences with alternative word order (topicalizations), the L2 learners were more nativelike than the heritage speakers at rejecting ungrammatical sentences without differential object marking in Spanish. Hence, it is not yet clear whether heritage speakers and L2 learners differ significantly from each other in their morphosyntactic knowledge.

Mode of Acquisition, Types of Knowledge and Tasks

Other hypotheses can be made if we take into account how age and mode of acquisition impinge on different types of knowledge. However, how the languages are tested and the types of tasks used to measure linguistic competence in the two types of learners become very significant. Since heritage language learners are primarily naturalistic and very often illiterate learners, and L2 learners are instructed and literate learners, heritage language learners should do better than L2 learners on grammatical areas tested through oral production and aural comprehension tasks. By contrast, L2 learners may outperform heritage language learners in untimed written tasks that maximize the use of metalinguistic and explicit knowledge of the language.

There is also the possibility that because heritage language learners are less literate in the heritage language than L2 learners are in their L2, many strict comparisons between the two groups are hard to interpret (or at least existing comparisons may say much less about actual grammatical competence than on language processing as a function of experience.) Because heritage language learners are primarily naturalistic learners, they are better at processing the language aurally. Furthermore, they have little metalinguistic competence and awareness. L2 learners acquire the language primarily through literacy, and oral skills tend to be less emphasized in the classroom. R. Ellis (2005) and R. Ellis, Loewen, and Erlam (2006) have discussed how different written and oral tasks used in typical L2 acquisition studies can indirectly tap more implicit or explicit knowledge of the language. It is thus not surprising to find that heritage language learners tend to outperform L2 learners in oral tasks that minimize metalinguistic knowledge (and conscious memorization of rules), while L2 learners outperform heritage language learners on written tasks that require high levels of metalinguistic awareness. Montrul et al. (2008a) found that Spanish heritage speakers were significantly more accurate than L2 learners on gender agreement in an oral picture naming task, but much less accurate on a written recognition task and a written comprehension task. It would be fruitful to expand this line of research to investigate how heritage language learners of different levels of proficiency in their different abilities (listening, speaking, reading, and writing) perform on different types of tasks, and how they compare with L2 learners of similar proficiency in the same skills. In addition to investigating grammatical knowledge, it is also crucial to investigate how heritage language learners process the heritage language during listening and reading.

Reactivity to Classroom Instruction, Type of Feedback, and Ultimate Attainment

Finally, let us consider the issue of whether pedagogical methods used with typical L2 learners can be applied with heritage language learners. Although Valdés et al. (2006) have voiced concerns about extending blindly pedagogies from L2 learning to heritage language classroom, it is time to evaluate the extent to which those methods work. In this respect, L2 classroom research has much to offer to the heritage language classroom, whether it involves classes developed exclusively for heritage language learners or mixed classes that cater to both types of learners.

Perhaps the biggest question is how heritage language learners react to classroom instruction, if they have implicit knowledge of the heritage language acquired in childhood. Once in the classroom, will they continue to learn the heritage language implicitly as L1-acquiring children, or will they now rely on explicit learning, like adult L2 learners? Can they eventually catch up with the missing explicit and metalinguistic knowledge that they did not get at school through reading and writing instruction?

There is no doubt that heritage language learners have high levels of communicative competence in the heritage language, but need to expand vocabulary, develop literacy skills in different genres, and improve grammatical accuracy. One possibility is that the implicit learning of the language heritage learners bring to the classroom may reactivate, facilitate, and speed up learning and relearning of the heritage language. The other possibility is that because they are adults, heritage language learners can only now rely on explicit learning, like L2 learners, and their acquisition of the heritage language will be as successful as that of L2 learners, but not necessarily nativelike in all domains. For the latter, research shows that occasional focus on form is beneficial for L2 learners (Carroll & Swain, 1993; R. Ellis et al., 2006). If L2 learners do not receive explicit instruction as to how or in which contexts something is correct or incorrect in the target language, they are not likely to notice it, especially if their native language interferes. Since interference from the majority language is also at play in heritage language learners, the same question applies to them.

Classroom research with heritage language learners is quite scant at the moment, but it is certainly an area that deserves more detailed investigation. A recent study by Montrul and Bowles (2009) found that Spanish heritage speakers omit the preposition "a" required with animate direct objects in Spanish and wanted to find out whether explicit instruction with feedback would help heritage language learners notice this gap in their linguistic knowledge. Montrul and Bowles (2010) tested two groups of adult Spanish heritage speakers using a pretest-posttest design with instruction intervention. Bowles and Montrul (2009) did the same with Spanish L2 learners. Results of both studies showed improvement and reactivity to instruction in the L2 learners and heritage language learners as measured by written production and a written grammaticality judgment task. Because the L2 learners and heritage language learners were of different proficiency level, it was not possible to compare the results of the two studies directly. Nonetheless, the magnitude of the improvement from pretest to posttest was much higher in heritage language learners than in the L2 learners, but this could have been due to the fact that the heritage language learners' were of higher proficiency than the L2 learners. Another recent study that compared L2 learners and heritage language learners' interpretations of imperfect subjunctive in written tasks and two types of instruction is Potowski, Jegerski, and Morgan-Short (2009). They found no differences between the groups by instruction type, but they did find differences between the groups on improvement on imperfect subjunctive after instruction. The L2 learners were more reactive to explicit instruction with subjunctive than the heritage language learners.

In summary, if heritage language learners received some crucial input during the critical period, given optimal amounts of input and time to develop the underdeveloped skills through instruction, they should be able to catch up with educated native speakers if that is what their linguistic goal is. According to the theoretical models discussed, heritage language learners have the cognitive and linguistic potential to reach nativelike competence in the heritage language at the grammatical level. Whether this potential is realized may not only depend on more optimal input and output conditions but also on motivation and specific needs.

TOWARD THE FUTURE

In conclusion, heritage language acquisition is a complex process with a host of linguistic, affective, political, educational, social, and cultural variables affecting its outcome. A great deal of existing studies have investigated the sociolinguistic situation of minority languages and have provided comprehensive profiles of the linguistic and academic abilities of some heritage language learners. While linguistic and acquisition-oriented research has offered a more nuanced perspective on the language and development of heritage language systems, far more needs to be done to make more direct contributions to the heritage language classroom. On the one hand, we need more psycholinguistically oriented studies of adult heritage speakers to find out how they process input in the heritage language and in different skills. On the other hand, we need to carry out more longitudinal studies of children at the onset of the school-age period and until adolescence, to trace more precisely the demise of home language skills as a result of schooling in the majority language. These types of studies are likely to give us a more precise picture of what exactly adult heritage language speakers are missing in terms of academic language and how lack of academic support affects later language development. Finally, if quality and quantity of input are crucial in heritage language development and form the bases of the theory of emergentism, then we definitely also need controlled studies of parental input and of input throughout the life span. Most studies to date rely on estimates of input frequency from self-reports or analyses of corpora. But estimates are not measurements. Studies of input will also help us understand more directly the role of the family and community in the shaping of heritage language grammars.

NOTES

1 Postsecondary heritage language classes and programs can be traced back to the mid-1970s, at least for Spanish in California (see Valdés et al., 2006).

2 See Tucker (2008) and Fishman (2006), among many others, for discussion of "English-only" policies in the United States.

3 The term *incomplete acquisition* (Montrul, 2002, 2008; Polinsky, 2007) has been used to describe the ultimate attainment of many adult heritage language speakers and is not intended as a value judgment. Other less felicitous terms used by different researchers to describe the imperfect language abilities of heritage speakers include *reduced, partial, truncated, deficient,* and *atrophied language acquisition.*

4 Other researchers consider that L2 learners have full access to Universal Grammar, like L1 learners, and deny the implication of maturational constraints (see White, 2003). An elaboration of this position is not relevant for this article.

REFERENCES

Au, T., Knightly, L., Jun, S., & Oh, J. (2002). Overhearing a language during childhood. *Psychological Science, 13,* 238–243.

Benmamoun, E., Albirini, A., Saadah, E., & Montrul, S. (2008, June). *Agreement and plural features in heritage Arabic speakers.* Paper presented at the Second Heritage Language Summer Institute, Harvard University, Cambridge, MA.

Bley-Vroman, R. (1989). The logical problem of second language learning. In S. Gass & J. Schachter (Eds.), *Linguistic perspectives on second language acquisition* (pp. 41–68). Cambridge, UK: Cambridge University Press.

Bley-Vroman, R. (2009). The evolving context of the fundamental difference hypothesis. *Studies in Second Language Acquisition, 31,* 175–198.

Bowles, M., & Montrul, S. (2009). Instructed L2 acquisition of differential object marking in Spanish. In R. Leow, H. Campos, & D. Lardiere (Eds.), *Little words. Their history, phonology, syntax, semantics, pragmatics, and acquisition* (pp. 199–210). Georgetown University Round Table. Washington, DC: Georgetown University Press.

Brinton, D., Kagan, O., & Bauckus, S. (2008). *Heritage language education: A new field emerging.* New York: Routledge.

Bruhn de Garavito, J. (2002). Verb-raising in Spanish, a comparison of early and late bilinguals. *Proceedings of the 26th Annual Boston University Conference on Language Development* (pp. 84–94). Somerville, MA: Cascadilla Press.

Campbell, R., & Rosenthal, J. (2000). Heritage languages. In J. Rosenthal (Ed.), *Handbook of undergraduate second language education* (pp. 165–184). Mahwah, NJ: Erlbaum.

Carroll, S., & Swain, M. (1993). Explicit and implicit negative feedback: An empirical study of the learning of linguistic generalizations. *Studies in Second Language Acquisition, 15*,357–386.

Chomsky, C. (1969). *The acquisition of syntax in children 5 to 10.* Cambridge, MA: MIT Press.

Chomsky, N. (1986). *Knowledge of language.* New York: Praeger.

Cummins, J. (2005). A proposal for action: Strategies for recognizing language competence as a learning resource within the mainstream classroom. *Modern Language Journal, 89*,585–591.

DeKeyser, R. (2003). Implicit and explicit learning. In C. Doughty & M. Long (Eds.), *The handbook of second language acquisition* (pp. 313–348). Malden, MA: Blackwell.

DeKeyser, R. (2000). The robustness of critical period effects in second language acquisition. *Studies in Second Language Acquisition, 22*, 499–534.

Ellis, N. C. (2002). Frequency effects in language processing: A review with implications for theories of implicit and explicit learning. *Studies in Second Language Acquisition, 23*,143–188.

Ellis, N. (2009). Optimizing the input: Frequency and sampling in usage-based and form-focused learning. In C. Doughty & M. Long (Eds.), *The handbook of language teaching* (pp. 139–159). Malden, MA: Blackwell.

Ellis, R. (2005). Measuring implicit and explicit knowledge of a second language: A psychometric study. *Studies in Second Language Acquisition, 27*, 141–172.

Ellis, R., Loewen, S., & Erlam, R. (2006). Implicit and explicit corrective feedback and the acquisition of L2 grammar. *Studies in Second Language Acquisition, 28*, 339–368.

Fairclough, M. (2008). La prueba de decisión léxica como herramienta para ubicar al estudiante bilingüe en los programas universitarios de español [The lexical decision task as tool to place the bilingual student in university language programs]. Unpublished manuscript, University of Houston, TX.

Fishman, J. (2006). Acquisition, maintenance and recovery of heritage languages. In G. Valdés, J. Fishman, R. Chávez, & W. Pérez (Eds.), *Developing minority language resources: The case of Spanish in California* (pp. 12–22). Clevedon, UK: Multilingual Matters.

Godson, L. (2004). Vowel production in the speech of Western Armenian heritage speakers. *Heritage Language Journal, 2*, 1–26.

Goldberg, A. (1999). The emergence of the semantics of argument structure constructions. In B. MacWhinney (Ed.), *The emergence of language* (pp. 197–212). Mahwah, NJ: Erlbaum.

Guasti, M. T. (2002). *Language acquisition. The growth of grammar.* Cambridge, MA: MIT Press.

Håkansson, G. (1995). Syntax and morphology in language attrition. A study of five bilingual expatriate Swedes. *International Journal of Applied Linguistics, 5*, 153–171.

Johnson, J., & Newport, E. (1989). Critical period effects in second language learning. The influence of maturational state on the acquisition of English as a second language. *Cognitive Psychology, 21*, 60–99.

Kim, J.-H. (2007). *Binding interpretations in adult bilingualism: A study of language transfer in L2 learners and heritage speakers of Korean.* Unpublished doctoral dissertation, University of Illinois, Urbana-Champaign.

Kim, J.-H., Montrul, S., & Yoon, J. (2009). Binding interpretation of anaphors in Korean heritage speakers. *Language Acquisition, 16*, 3–35.

Knightly, L., Jun, S., Oh, J., & Au, T. (2003). Production benefits of childhood overhearing. *Journal of the Acoustic Society of America, 114*, 465–474.

Lam, Y., Pérez-Leroux, A. T., & Ramírez, C. (2003, March). *Using lexical decision for Spanish language placement testing.* Paper presented at the American Association for Applied Linguistics Conference, Washington, DC.

Lynch, A. (2003). The relationship between second and heritage language acquisition: Notes on research and theory building. *Heritage Language Journal, 1*, 1–18. Retrieved February 13, 2010, from http://www.heritagelanguages.org.

MacWhinney, B. (1987). Applying the competition model to bilingualism. *Applied Psycholinguistics, 8*, 315–327.

Menyuk, P., & Brisk, M. E. (2005). *Language development and education. Children with varying language experience.* New York: Palgrave.

Moag, R. (1995). Semi-native speakers: How to hold and mold them. In V. Gambhir (Ed.), *The teaching and acquisition of South Asian languages* (pp. 168–181). Philadelphia: University of Pennsylvania Press.

Montrul, S. (2002). Incomplete acquisition and attrition of Spanish tense/aspect distinctions in adult bilinguals. *Bilingualism: Language and Cognition, 5*, 39–68.

Montrul, S. (2004). Subject and object expression in Spanish heritage speakers: A case of morpho-syntactic convergence. *Bilingualism: Language and Cognition, 7*, 1–18.

Montrul, S. (2005). Second language acquisition and first language loss in adult early bilinguals: Exploring some differences and similarities. *Second Language Research, 21*, 199–249.

Montrul, S. (2006). On the bilingual competence of Spanish heritage speakers: Syntax, lexical-semantics and processing. *International Journal of Bilingualism, 10*, 37–69.

Montrul, S. (2007). Interpreting mood distinctions in Spanish as a heritage language. In K. Potowski & R. Cameron (Eds.), *Spanish in contact: Policy, social and linguistic inquiries* (pp. 23–40). Amsterdam: John Benjamins.

Montrul, S. (2008). *Incomplete acquisition in bilingualism. Re-examining the age factor.* Amsterdam: John Benjamins.

Montrul, S. (2010). How similar are L2 learners and heritage speakers? Spanish clitics and word order. *Applied Psycholinguistics, 31*, 167–207.

Montrul, S., & Bowles, M. (2009). Back to basics: Differential object marking under incomplete acquisition in Spanish heritage speakers. *Bilingualism: Language and Cognition,12*, 363–383.

Montrul, S., & Bowles, M. (2010). Is grammar instruction beneficial for heritage language learners? Dative case marking in Spanish. *Heritage Language Journal 7*(1), 47–73. Retrieved February 13, 2010, from http://www.heritagelanguages.org/.

Montrul, S., Foote, R., & Perpiñán, S. (2008a). Gender agreement in adult second language learners and Spanish heritage speakers: The effects of age and context of acquisition. *Language Learning, 58*, 503–553.

Montrul, S., Foote, R., & Perpiñán, S. (2008b). Knowledge of wh-movement in Spanish L2 learners and heritage speakers. In M. Almazán, J. Bruhn de Garavito, & E. Valenzuela (Eds.), *Selected papers from the Eighth Hispanic Linguistics Symposium* (pp. 93–106). Somerville, MA: Cascadilla Press.

Nippold, M. (1998). *Later language development. The school-age and adolescent years.* Austin, TX: Pro-Ed.

O'Grady, W. (1997). *Syntactic development.* Chicago: University of Chicago Press.

O'Grady, W. (2005). *Syntactic carpentry: An emergentist approach to syntax.* Mahwah, NJ: Erlbaum.

O'Grady, W., Lee, M., & Choo, M. (2001). The acquisition of relative clauses by heritage and non-heritage learners of Korean as a second language. A comparative study. *Journal of Korean Language Education, 12*, 283–294.

O'Grady, W., Lee, M., & Kwak, H. (2009). Emergentism and second language acquisition. In W. Ritchie & T. Bhatia (Eds.), *Handbook of Second Language Acquisition* (pp. 68–88). Emerald Press, Bingley, UK.

Oh, J., Jun, S., Knightly, L., & Au, T. (2003). Holding on to childhood language memory. *Cognition*, 86, B53–B64.

Paradis, M. (2004). *A neurolinguistic theory of bilingualism.* Amsterdam: John Benjamins.

Paradis, M. (2009). *Declarative and procedural determinants of second languages.* Amsterdam: John Benjamins.

Polinsky, M. (1997). American Russian. Language loss meets language acquisition. *Proceedings of the Annual Workshop on Formal Approaches to Slavic Linguistics* (pp. 370–406). Ann Arbor, MI: Michigan Slavic.

Polinsky, M. (2005). Word class distinctions in an incomplete grammar. In D. Ravid & H. Bat-Zeev Shyldkrot (Eds.), *Perspectives on language and language development* (pp. 419–436).

Dordrecht, Netherlands: Kluwer.

Polinsky, M. (2007). Incomplete acquisition: American Russian. *Journal of Slavic Linguistics*, *14*, 191–262.

Polinsky, M. (2008a). Russian gender under incomplete acquisition. *Heritage Language Journal*, 5, 2007.

Polinsky, M. (2008b). Heritage language narratives. In D. Brinton, O. Kagan, & S. Bauckus (Eds.), *Heritage language education. A new field emerging* (pp. 149–164). New York: Routledge.

Polinsky, M. (2008c). Relative clauses in heritage Russian: Fossilization or divergent grammar? In A. Angtonenko, J. Bailyn, and C. Bethin (Eds.), *Annual Workshop on Formal Approaches to Slavic Linguistics* (pp. 333–358). Ann Arbor, MI: Michigan Slavic.

Polinsky, M., & Kagan, O. (2007). Heritage languages in the "wild" and in the classroom. *Language and Linguistic Compass*, *1*, 368–395.

Poplack, S. (1980). Sometimes I'll start a sentence in English y termino en espagnol: Toward a typology of code-switching. *Linguistics*, *18*, 581–618.

Potowski, K., Jegerski, J., & Morgan-Short, K. (2009). The effects of instruction on linguistic development in Spanish heritage language speakers. *Language Learning*, *59*, 537–579.

Rothman, J. (2007) Heritage speaker competence differences, language change and input type: Inflected infinitives in heritage Brazilian Portuguese. *International Journal of Bilingualism*, *11*, 359–389.

Silva-Corvalán, C. (1994). *Language contact and change. Spanish in Los Angeles.* Oxford, UK: Oxford University Press.

Song, M., O'Grady, W., Cho, S., & Lee, M. (1997). The learning and teaching of Korean in community schools. In Y.-H. Kim (Ed.), *Korean language in America* (Vol. 2, pp. 111–127). Manoa, HI: American Association of Teachers of Korean.

Tomasello, M. (2003). *Constructing a language: A usage-based theory of language acquisition.* Cambridge, MA: Harvard University Press.

Tucker, R. (2008). Learning other languages: The case of promoting bilingualism within our educational system. In Brinton D., Kagan, O., & Bauckus, S. (Eds.), *Heritage language education. A new field emerging* (pp. 39–52). New York: Routledge.

Valdés, G. (1997). The teaching of Spanish to bilingual Spanish-speaking students: Outstanding issues and unanswered questions [The teaching of Spanish to Spanish speakers]. In M. C. Colombi & F. Alarcón (Eds.), *La enseñanza del español a hispanoh-ablantes* (pp. 8–44). Boston, MA: Houghton Mifflin.

Valdés, G. (2005). Bilingualism, heritage language learners and SLA research: Opportunities lost or seized? *Modern Language Journal*, *89*, 410–426.

Valdés, G., Fishman, J., Chávez, R., & Pérez, W. (2006). *Developing minority language resources: The case of Spanish in California.* Clevedon, UK: Multilingual Matters.

White, L. (2003). *Second language acquisition and universal grammar.* Cambridge, UK: Cambridge University Press.

Yeni-Komshian, G. H., Flege, J. E., & Liu, S. (2000). Pronunciation proficiency in the first and second languages of Korean-English bilinguals. *Bilingualism: Language and Cognition, 3,* 131–149.

Curriculum Development for Advancing Heritage Language Competence: Recent Research, Current Practices, and a Future Agenda

Kimi Kondo-Brown

In the last few decades, research on teaching heritage language (HL) learners has expanded enormously and encouraged language professionals to work toward responsible curriculum development for this specific type of learners. This article suggests ways to expand current curriculum research and practices with the goal of advancing the HL competence of learners. To this end, this article examines the scope, trends, and issues in recent theoretical and practical studies concerning curriculum development for HL learners from various language backgrounds, especially those in the United States. A definition of HL learners is presented first, which is followed by a discussion of general second language curriculum development frameworks with specific reference to HL instruction. Then, the article examines the contexts, challenges, and possibilities for teaching HLs to school-age children in precollegiate programs. Next, it turns to a discussion of issues and recommendations for teaching postsecondary HL students. The article concludes by discussing curricular and pedagogical recommendations for HL professionals as well as a future research agenda that could promote the advancement of HL competence in all educational institutions.

In the wider applied linguistics literature, the phrase *heritage language* (*HL*) *learner* is used in various ways that refer to a highly heterogeneous population with diverse historical, linguistic, and cultural backgrounds (for discussions on this subject, see Hornberger & Wang, 2008; Kondo-Brown, 2003). However, in the literature that specifically deals with HL acquisition and pedagogy issues, the term *HL learners* usually refer to those who have acquired some competence in a nondominant language as their first language (L1) mainly through socialization at home, but did not achieve full-control over it due to a switch to the dominant language (Kim, 2008; Polinsky, 2008; Valdés, 1995).[1] The reported or demonstrated proficiency levels of HL learners differ widely because of at least three main factors: their diverse L1 backgrounds, degree of HL use and contact, and related sociopsychological factors (such as identity, attitudes, and motivation; Kondo-Brown, 2006a).

Heritage language instruction in the United States is extensively available within and outside the formal education system.[2] As the nation's most widely spoken immigrant language, Spanish seems to lead in pedagogy and curriculum studies on HL instruction, which is commonly known as *Spanish for native speakers*. At the same time, the work on other HLs taught in American schools and universities (many of which are what we call *less commonly taught languages*) is growing rapidly (e.g., Kondo-Brown, 2008). Behind the expansion of HL pedagogy and curriculum studies is a national interest in promoting advanced-level competence using approaches that go beyond the traditional foreign language (FL) instruction (Malone, Rifkin, Christian, & Johnson, 2005; Robinson, Rivers, & Brecht, 2006).[3] One of the challenges for FL teachers in promoting advanced-level competence through traditional FL instruction is to provide the students with sufficient opportunities for exposure to and use of the target language in naturalistic, contextualized settings inside and outside classrooms (Omaggio Hadley, 2001). In contrast, HL teachers are primarily concerned with how best to provide adequate instruction that builds on the students' HL backgrounds or their rich linguistic and cultural repertoires.

The goal of this article therefore is to make curricular and pedagogical recommendations as well as to suggest a future research agenda that will better serve HL learners in advancing their HL competence. To this end, this article first discusses selected second language (L2) curriculum development frameworks with specific reference to HL instruction. Second, a number of curricular, pedagogical, and assessment issues are examined concerning the advancement of HL competence during precollegiate period. Third, the same issues focusing on HL instruction offered at postsecondary institutions are explored.

CURRICULUM DEVELOPMENT FOR HERITAGE LANGUAGE STUDENTS

In the last 30 years, approaches to L2 curriculum development have been recommended from various perspectives. While a comprehensive discussion of these approaches is beyond the scope of the present article, it will review some of the key approaches with specific references to HL curriculum development, namely learner-centered, content-based, and outcomes-based.[4]

With learner-centered curriculum, "it is the learners themselves who should be taken as the central reference point for decision-making regarding both the content and the form of language teaching, and ... this goal should be realized interactively by a process of consultation and negotiation between the participants in the learning situation" (Tudor, 1996, p. 23). Because of the unique backgrounds and features of HL students, the notion of learner-centeredness is important and useful in teaching these students (Douglas, 2005; Webb & Miller, 2000; Wu, 2008). From this perspective, the teacher first needs to determine what the students already know or what they want or need to know, and if there is a discrepancy between teachers' and students' expectations, it should be resolved in negotiations between the teacher and students (Nunan, 1988).

Recent survey research that examined HL students' motivations for and preferences in learning an HL suggested that negotiations between the teacher and students are necessary and helpful in curriculum development (e.g., Ducar, 2008; Husseinali, 2006; Jensen, 2007; Lee & Kim, 2008). For example, Ducar's (2008) survey of Spanish HL students ($N = 152$) suggested that, while HL researchers and educators generally emphasize the importance of advancing HL students' knowledge and skills in the formal, academic variety (see the last section on postsecondary HL instruction), the acquisition of academic Spanish may not be very interesting to the students. In this study, the majority of the students were not Spanish majors and had little interest in pursuing a career in academics. Instead, they were more interested in working on nonstandard varieties of Spanish (such as Mexican or Mexican American varieties), because they were more relevant to their lives and career goals. Based on this finding, Ducar recommended the inclusion of sociolinguistic projects where the students critically examine nonstandard varieties of Spanish, for example, linguistic autobiographies, language use surveys in the community, and so forth.

Content-based curriculum aims at advancing the students' language competence by integrating particular content with the teaching of language skills. The focus for the students is on acquiring information in the L2, and in the process, they develop academic language skills in the L2 (Brinton, Snow, & Wesche, 2003). In the United States, content-based instruction in an HL is available to precollegiate HL students via two-way immersion or in some FLES (Foreign Language in the Elementary Schools) programs, where positive effects on HL development have been reported (see, e.g., Potowski, Berne, Clark, & Hammerand, 2008; also see the next section on precollegiate HL instruction). Recently, the potential benefits of content-based curriculum for postsecondary HL students have also been proposed (e.g. *Curriculum Guidelines*, 2003; Kagan & Dillon, 2001, 2003; Lee & Kim, 2008; Morioka, Takakura, & Ushida, 2008). For example, the survey results reported in Lee and Kim (2008) indicated that Korean HL students have a strong desire to connect with their Korean heritage and identity. Accordingly, they recommended content-based instruction that uses Korean culture as an organizing principle for the course content for such HL learners.

While interest in content-based curriculum for postsecondary HL students is growing, there seems to be a general lack of research on the effects of content-based instruction on postsecondary HL students. Future research should perhaps investigate these issues. For example, the potential for incorporating project-based activities, especially in mixed-level abilities HL programs might be examined (e.g., see Ilieva, 2008). Project-based activities can be highly adaptable in terms of degrees of student ownership, purposes, data collection methods, products, classroom interactions, assessment procedures, and so forth (Beckett & Miller, 2006). In Ilieva's (2008) study, project work not only provided HL students an opportunity to integrate their cumulative language abilities and cultural knowledge through individualized, project-based learning but also allowed the students to engage in community-based as well as literature-based projects that dealt with specific cultural, linguistic, and sociolinguistic issues of interest to them.

Recently, outcomes-based curriculum has received considerable attention in the FL literature (e.g., Glisan & Foltz, 1998; Mathews & Hansen, 2004; Norris & Pfeiffer, 2003; Rifkin, 2003). This is partly due to an increasing public awareness of accountability and assessment issues for all educational programs including FL programs. In the midst of the current outcomes-based curriculum movement, the integration of good assessment practices is increasingly demanded for any language program offered within a formal educational system (Norris, 2006). For example, assessment is a key component of curriculum development frameworks recommended for school-based two-way immersion programs, where learners of both languages are in the program, usually English L1 speakers learning the HL and HL speakers learning English (e.g., Howard, Sugarman, Christian, Lindholm-Leary, & Rogers, 2007).

As the national interest in outcomes-based curriculum and assessment grows, the use of standardized assessment instruments such as the American Council on the Teaching of Foreign Languages (ACTFL) oral proficiency test (OPI) may become more prevalent for HL instruction (see Ricardo-Osorio, 2008). While validity and reliability issues concerning the ACTFL OPI seem to remain controversial,[5] this instrument is likely to continue influencing FL and HL education in the United States. For example, the use of ACTFL OPI has recently been recommended by the National Council for the Accreditation of Teacher Education (NCATE) for teacher training accreditation purposes (Pearson, Fonseca-Greber, & Foell, 2006).[6] In the past, the appropriateness of using the ACTFL guidelines with HL students was examined, but it was mainly in the context of making placement decisions (see the last section on postsecondary HL instruction), and little is known about the degree to which the ACTFL guidelines will work for program assessment or evaluation purposes. For example, we do not know if the ACTFL guidelines can effectively measure the progress of postsecondary HL students, some of whom are believed to have advanced-level oral proficiency when they start the program (Campbell & Rosenthal, 2000). Future research on this issue is recommended. Also, future research could explore the possibility of using portfolios as an assessment option for HL students. Previous HL research has suggested that portfolio assessment has potential for use with HL students (e.g., Schwarzer & Petrón, 2005), but the benefits of portfolios have not been adequately investigated.[7]

PRECOLLEGIATE HERITAGE LANGUAGE INSTRUCTION

For precollegiate students, HL instruction is usually offered either as two-way immersion programs within the formal education system (largely for Spanish speakers) or as HL programs at community-based schools. This section examines issues concerning precollegiate HL instruction in these two settings, starting with the review of research on two-way immersion programs and followed by a discussion of community-based schools.

Two-way immersion programs, where the students are given content instruction in two languages, are rapidly expanding in the United States. According to the Center for Applied Linguistics online *Directory of Two-Way Bilingual Immersion Programs in the U.S.* (http://www.cal.org/twi/directory/), as of June 2009, 346 two-way immersion programs existed in the nation. Most of them are offered at elementary schools (85%), and the vast majority are operated in Spanish and English (92%). In some programs, the proportion of time taught in an HL gradually decreases from about 90% to 50%, but in others, an approximately equal amount of time is spent in the two languages from the beginning (Christian, 2008). There is a vast amount of literature on two-way immersion programs, but the primary interest of the investigation seems to be its impact on the students' overall academic achievement in the mainstream school, not HL maintenance or development per se. Unfortunately, in the United States bilingual education politics seems to have contributed biases to the procedures and interpretations of research investigating this issue (Crawford, 1992).

Research on two-way immersion programs that has a focus on HL maintenance and development is, however, expanding (e.g., Christian, 2008; Hayashi, 2006; Potowski, 2007; Sohn & Merrill, 2008). In these studies, the students attending a two-way immersion program in the United States are mostly English-dominant students, and their HL proficiency levels appear to vary considerably depending on their language use, attitudes, and identity constructions (e.g., Hayashi, 2006; Potowski, 2007). Despite individual differences, recent research generally suggests that attendance in a two-way immersion program is an effective approach to HL maintenance and development (Montrul & Potowski, 2007; Sohn & Merrill, 2008).[8] Future studies could continue to analyze the impact of a two-way immersion program on HL development, and in the process, one area that could be improved is the development of assessment instruments and procedures (Payton, 2008; Tucker, 2005). For example, the Center for Applied Linguistics Web site mentioned earlier provides a comprehensive list of Spanish-language assessments for dual language programs. Assessment instruments and procedures for students of different HL backgrounds have also been developed, but the reliability and validity of these instruments do not seem to be adequately investigated (see Hasegawa, 2008).

Community-based after-school or weekend HL programs are widely available for different language groups (see Kondo-Brown, 2006a; Lee & Shin, 2008; McGinnis, 2008; Payton, 2008). The students attending these schools come from diverse socioeconomic backgrounds, and the schools are operated and supported largely by the community leaders and volunteer parents. Community-based HL programs in the United States seem to differ widely in terms of curriculum (e.g., some use the target L2 as the main tool of communication, and others use it sparsely) as well as in terms of the resources available. Therefore, any generalization about these programs should be interpreted cautiously. However, one consistent finding across different studies is that parents usually have positive perceptions of community-based HL schools: They generally believe that attendance to HL schools helps their children maintain their ethnic identity and culture (Kondo-Brown, 2006a).

Despite the benefits perceived by the parents, many students who are attending HL schools experience a sense of burden as the demands for academic work and extracurricular activities in the mainstream school increase (Kondo, 1998). Also, previous quantitative studies that investigated the effect of HL instruction at community-based schools were not able to find a positive correlation between proficiency levels and length of instruction at community-based HL schools (see Kondo-Brown, 2006a). A number of pedagogical and situational problems associated with HL schools, whose operation largely relies on the parents, seem to explain the lack of relationship between the length of attendance in these schools and the demonstrated proficiency levels (e.g., Kataoka, Furuyama, & Koshiyama, 2000; Lee & Shin, 2008; Li, 2005; Wang, 2003).[9] Clearly, many community-based HL schools need substantial support for professional development, especially assistance in curriculum and materials development.

Among the variety of HL programs offered outside the formal education system in the United States, one of the most thoroughly researched types of HL programs is perhaps the set of immersion programs offered at *nihongo hoshuu jugyookoo* (Japanese language supplementary instruction schools), which are commonly referred to in the literature by the abbreviated form *hoshuukoo*. The hoshuukoo offer after-school or weekend immersion programs (usually from kindergarten to ninth grade) for Japanese L1 and HL children, which are supported from afar by the Japanese government as well as the local Japanese community.[10] Research suggested that the *hoshuukoo* plays a critical role not only for HL maintenance and development but also ethnic identity development (e.g., Chinen & Tucker, 2006). Research also suggested that attendance at *hoshuukoo* can help HL students advance their proficiency in Japanese (e.g., Kanno, Hasegawa, Ikeda, Ito, & Long, 2008; Nagasawa, 1995). For example, in Kanno et al.'s (2008) study, among HL and non-HL students who demonstrated Japanese proficiency at the advanced or superior levels on the ACTFL OPI, HL students who attended a *hoshuukoo* also showed superior performances on other kinds of spoken and written Japanese proficiency tests.

As in the case of two-way immersion programs, factors such as age of arrival, amount and quality of study in Japanese, and exposure to Japanese at home seem to directly affect the Japanese proficiency levels of *hoshuukoo* students (Kataoka, Koshiyama, & Shibata, 2008). Kataoka et al.'s (2008) large-scale study ($N = 1,591$) in fact revealed sizable individual differences in Japanese proficiency development among *hoshuukoo* students, and based on this finding, the authors suggested that the existing *hoshuukoo* curriculum, which requires the use of Japanese textbooks designed for Japanese L1 speakers, may need to be modified.

POSTSECONDARY HERITAGE LANGUAGE INSTRUCTION

This section examines issues raised in recent research on the teaching of HL students in postsecondary institutions: issues concerning the placement of these students; work on a subgroup of HL students whose proficiency levels in spoken and written language skills are critically unbalanced; issues of individual differences in HL proficiency levels among postsecondary HL students; and finally, work that deals with discrepancy between HL learners' advanced levels of informal, nonprestigious language varieties and their low levels of formal, prestigious language varieties.

Beginning with placement issues, recent national survey study suggested that most university FL programs in the United States use locally or internally developed tests and self-ratings, but certain commercial or externally developed tests are also widely used (e.g., AP subject tests, SAT II subject tests, Spanish-Computer-Adaptive Placement Exam [S-CAPE], OPI, etc.; Brown, Hudson, & Clark, 2004). The receptive skills (e.g., reading comprehension and grammatical knowledge) are much more commonly assessed than production skills. To date, no national survey has specifically examined the use of placement tests for HL learners. Most of the published studies concerning the placement of HL students are case studies conducted at the authors' home institutions. These studies suggested that the most useful placement tools for HL students are (a) autobiographic questionnaires that include self-reported language use and ratings (Domingo, 2008; Kagan, 2005; Ranjan, 2008) and (b) faculty-made performance tests such as oral tests, which were mostly based on the ACTFL guidelines (e.g., Dolgova, 2008; Takahashi, 2008; Zamar & Robotham, 2008).

The HL placement case studies are largely descriptive, but empirical studies that provided HL student placement data are also emerging (e.g., Fairclough, 2006; Kagan & Friedman, 2003; Kondo-Brown, 2004, 2005). For example, as discussed earlier, some placement test procedures for HL students were developed based on the ACTFL guidelines. Kagan and Friedman (2003) examined the degree to which this procedure is appropriate based on their data collected from university HL students of Russian.[11] Their study suggested that the ACTFL proficiency guidelines work as well for Russian HL learners as they do for their FL equivalents, while noting that, if they are at the same level on the ACTFL rating scale, an HL learner in Russian will have "better pronunciation, higher fluency, and a wider vocabulary range" than an FL learner (p. 543). Based on this study, they recommended the use of an OPI based on the ACTFL guidelines as part of the placement procedures for HL students.

Kondo-Brown (2004, 2005), on the other hand, suggested that the multiple-choice placement tests intended to measure the students' receptive skills may effectively place non-HL students as well as less proficient HL students into various courses, but the same placement procedures may not be effective for more proficient HL students.[12] With more proficient HL students, Kondo-Brown's (2004) study additionally suggested that a simple essay test can serve as an effective placement procedure for discriminating proficiency levels of all incoming HL and non-HL students, including those at the higher levels.[13] Likewise, the Sohn and Shin (2007) study of university Korean students indicated that their multiple-choice tests (listening, reading, and usage) have less discrimination power than a composition test. They also observed that the correlation between the multiple-choice tests scores was high, but the correlation between the multiple-choice and a composition test was relatively low. Based on this finding, they suggested the inappropriateness of making placement decisions for HL students based on a single test. They recommended the use of (a) a writing task that requires the use of formal academic language and (b) a diagnostic oral interview test on the first day of class for HL students, especially those whose performances on the multiple-choice test and composition tests are unbalanced in order to avoid possible misplacement of these students.

A second major issue for postsecondary HL instruction (especially in lower-division, i.e., first-and second-year courses) is how to deal with HL students who have acquired native-like fluency in their HLs at home but had received little or no formal instruction in literacy skills (Kondo-Brown, 2003). The unbalanced development of spoken and written language is a concern for teaching any HL, but this issue seems more central in teaching HLs with other than Roman-alphabet orthographies. For example, research suggested that there are notable differences in literacy skills among university HL students of East Asian and Slavic languages depending on the quality and length of previous formal instruction or schooling in the target HL (e.g., Friedman & Kagan, 2008; Kondo-Brown, 2004). In the case of Chinese HL instruction, the situation is a bit more complicated than other languages because one important pedagogical consideration for Chinese classrooms is whether the learners prefer traditional or simplified characters (Wiley, 2008).[14]

Many postsecondary institutions seem to offer special courses for HL students with highly unbalanced spoken and written language abilities (Kondo-Brown, 2003). Although little is known about how such classes are designed, implemented, and evaluated, one study suggested that a homogeneous accelerated class for HL students of Chinese offers more effective literacy instruction than a regular Chinese class where both HL and non-HL students study together (Shen, 2003). Some recent case studies also reported on the development of an online program for HL students who need special help with literacy skills (e.g., Wu, 2008; Zhang & Davis, 2008). For example, Wu (2008) reported on the development of an online literacy program specifically designed for a subgroup of Mandarin-speaking HL students who had not received formal instruction in Chinese. The program was developed based on a needs analysis as well as the *National Standards for Foreign Language Learning in the 21st Century* (ACTFL, 1999), and it required students to work on assignments and projects where they regularly interacted with their family and community. This line of research should continue in the future.

Individual learner differences in HL proficiency levels are another major concern. In some university programs, FL and HL students may study together in the same classroom from the very beginning (e.g., Gambhir, 2008; Ilieva, 2008; Yu, 2008), but in others, the FL and HL students study in separate courses initially but later merge into the same classes (e.g., Angelelli & Kagan, 2002; Sohn & Shin, 2007). In either context, the teacher more or less needs to deal with the issue of individual differences. In teaching less commonly taught languages such as Hindi, dealing with proficiency differences seems to be a serious matter (Gambhir, 2008).[15] As discussed earlier, one recommended model for individualized instruction is project-based learning (Ilieva, 2008). However, the dynamics and outcomes of mixed-abilities classrooms are largely unknown, and future research could continue to investigate the use of project work as a strategy to deal with large individual differences. Some researchers have proposed a differentiated instruction model for HL students because it allows students to work toward their learning goals at their own pace (e.g., Carreira, 2007). Another recommended model is computer-assisted instruction (e.g., Douglas, 2008; Meskill & Anthony, 2008). For example, Douglas (2008) examined the effect of using computer-assisted tools for a group of advanced-level Japanese HL students whose demonstrated Japanese proficiency levels were considerably different, especially literacy skills, including the ability to read and write *kanji*. The program provided individualized instruction on *kanji* and vocabulary learning as well as *kanji* learning strategy activities. The results of the pretest-posttest tests on *kanji* knowledge and kanji learning strategies indicated significant gains.

Some recent studies have revealed sizable intragroup differences in demonstrated or perceived knowledge and skills within each of the advanced-level

HL and non-HL student groups (Kanno et al., 2008; Kim, 2008; Kondo-Brown, 2009; Kondo-Brown & Fukuda, 2008; Rubio, 2003).[16] Clearly, some degree of individualized instruction is necessary in teaching HL students, especially when they study together with non-HL students in the same class. Future curriculum development studies that specifically address the issue of individual differences would be helpful in this regard. In doing so, researchers should especially consider the students' views on the presence of both HL and non-HL students in the same classroom. Research has suggested that some non-HL students may view the presence of HL students positively as language models, while other non-HL students may find the presence of HL students intimidating and also have concern about grading issues (e.g., Lee & Kim, 2008).

Finally, learning academic language is an important matter for HL learners. Postsecondary HL students who have acquired informal, vernacular varieties at home experience challenges in learning the standard variety, which is valued for academic learning (e.g., Jo, 2001; Parodi, 2008). Some researchers have suggested that HL students should improve their knowledge and skills in formal academic language by (a) having more opportunities to interact with speakers of the formal variety, (b) receiving explicit instruction on the notion of registers, and (c) engaging in classroom activities focusing on the high-level registers (Ducar, 2008; Valdés & Geoffrion-Vinci, 1998). Additionally, this process should be viewed as complementary to, not as a replacement for, the students' abilities to speak and write nonstandard varieties in informal, colloquial contexts (Ducar, 2008; Lacorte, 2005; Parodi, 2008).

A second issue is how best to teach academic vocabulary that goes beyond the domain of immediate personal use (e.g., Angelelli & Kagan, 2002; Campbell & Rosenthal, 2000; Kanno et al., 2008; Parodi, 2008). Unfortunately, to date, little research has examined the effectiveness of academic vocabulary instruction for HL students. One notable exception is McQuillan's (1996) quasi-experimental study that examined the effect of extensive free reading on HL students' academic vocabulary learning.[17] Without a control group, this study may not accurately measure the actual effect of the experiment, but it is notable that the HL students made significant gains in vocabulary knowledge. Given that reading authentic texts for authentic purposes is often recommended for HL learners (Schwarzer & Petrón, 2005), the option of teaching academic vocabulary to HL learners via extensive reading academic texts should be further examined in future HL study.[18]

A third issue that is often raised specifically for advanced-level HL students is to how to help them acquire the meta-language necessary for success in advanced-level academic courses (e.g., Angelelli & Kagan, 2002; Valdés & Geoffrion-Vinci, 1998). Earlier studies suggested that HL students placed in advanced-level courses may produce grammatically correct utterances, but have difficulty in describing and analyzing them due to their lack of metalinguistic knowledge (Kondo, 1999; Valdés, 1995). Angelelli and Kagan (2002) reported on the development of a university Spanish course that specifically aimed at helping advanced-and superior-level HL students acquire the meta-language for academic Spanish. The course, which "reflects the latest research available in the field of HL teaching" (Angelelli & Kagan, 2002, p. 207), included reading, speaking, and writing assignments that required students to analyze certain aspects of Spanish grammar (e.g., the use of past tenses in literary narratives) and report their analyses verbally and in writing. The end-of-course evaluations indicated that the students expressed satisfaction with their improved understanding of the Spanish linguistic system and their ability to discuss it using terminology appropriate for academic contexts.

CONCLUSION

This article examined recent theoretical and practical studies on HL pedagogy and curriculum development conducted mainly in the United States in order to suggest ways to expand the current curriculum research and practices, with the goal of helping students advance their HL competence. The following nine points summarize my curricular and pedagogical recommendations for HL professionals as well as provide a research agenda to promote the advancement of HL competence at educational institutions:

(1) To better serve the needs and interests of HL students, the notion of learner-centeredness is particularly important and useful in teaching. Future investigations on the process of teacher-student negotiation toward learner-centered curriculum as well as the outcomes of such efforts on the development of HL competence would be useful.

(2) There is growing interest in content-based instruction for HL students, especially at the postsecondary level. However, it is not clear how this approach can actually be implemented in HL settings, or how content-based instruction can help students advance their HL competence. Future work on content-based HL learning could address these issues. For example, future content-based HL research could examine how the integration of project-based activities might help students improve their HL competence.

(3) Little has been reported on the impact of the ongoing outcomes-based curriculum movements on HL curriculum development, especially at the postsecondary level. Future research could examine assessment issues concerning postsecondary HL students such as the appropriateness of using the ACTFL proficiency guidelines or portfolio procedures for program assessment or evaluation purposes.

(4) Evaluative studies on two-way immersion programs have indicated the positive effect of this approach on HL maintenance and development. Future research may continue to analyze the impact of two-way immersion programs on HL development. In doing so, the discussion on the reliability, validity, and appropriateness of the adopted assessment instruments and procedures is recommended.

(5) Research on community-based HL schools has indicated that they play an important role in maintaining HL students' culture and ethnic identity. However, at the same time, research has indicated that a number of pedagogical and situational problems associated with HL schools prevent them from providing effective HL instruction for the students. Clearly, many community-based HL schools need substantial support to improve their effectiveness in teaching the HL. The *hoshuukoo* model, a community-based immersion program that receives support from the Japanese government, may serve as a good model for other HL schools.

(6) The unbalanced development of spoken and written language is a major concern for HL instruction at the postsecondary level, especially when teaching an HL with other than Roman-alphabet orthographies. Program models such as accelerated special classes and special online programs seem to provide effective training for HL students' literacy skills. Fu-

ture research may continue to examine how these approaches can help HL students advance their HL competence. Also, in order to avoid the misplacement of HL students, especially those with unbalanced language skills, multiple placement procedures that include autobiographical data and performance-based tests (e.g., OPI or an essay writing test) are recommended.

(7) Postsecondary HL students, including those who are enrolled in advanced-level courses, are not a homogeneous group in terms of their HL proficiency levels, needs, and interests. In teaching less commonly taught languages, dealing with proficiency differences seems to be an especially serious matter. Future research may continue to investigate the effect of such approaches as project-based learning and computer-assessed instruction in dealing with large individual differences observed at this level.

(8) Postsecondary HL students who have acquired informal varieties at home experience considerable challenges in learning the standard variety, which is valued for academic learning. Future research may examine the degree to which instructional approaches that can help students enhance their ability to understand and critically analyze the standard and nonstandard varieties of their HLs are effective. Also, future research may examine how corrective feedback, academic vocabulary learning, and instruction on meta-language can meet the needs and interests of postsecondary HL students enrolled in advanced-level courses.

(9) Although the article did not address the issue of HL teacher training, such opportunities are clearly lacking (Potowski & Carreira, 2004). As we expand future HL research on various curriculum and pedagogical issues such as those discussed here, new practices, innovations, and workshops may become available and be widely disseminated among K–12 and postsecondary HL teachers via Web sites.[19]

NOTES

1 Using this definition, the present article primarily examines literature related to the curriculum development and instruction for HL students who are mostly

from immigrant backgrounds. Therefore, the literature focusing on students of other types of minority languages, for example, indigenous or colonial languages, will not be reviewed here.

2 Although there seem to be no comprehensive data that compile available HL programs in the nation, the official Web site for *Heritage Languages in America* (www.cal.org/heritage/profiles/view.html) lists some of these courses by language groups.

3 The challenges and limitations of promoting advanced-level competence by means of traditional FL instruction have been discussed in the literature (e.g., Glisan & Foltz, 1998; Liskin-Gasparro, 1982; Rifkin, 2003, 2005).

4 In the L2 curriculum literature, there are broader and narrower accounts of what curriculum is (Stern, 1984). In this article, *curriculum* is used as a general term that encompasses the entire process of and resources for planning, implementing, and evaluating language teaching and learning for a group of students participating in a given educational setting at local and national levels (Nunan, 1988).

5 Since the ACTFL proficiency guidelines did not emerge from a particular L2 acquisition or testing theory, their validity has been questioned by L2 researchers and testing specialists (Lantolf & Frawley, 1985; Malone, 2003; Salaberry, 2000). For example, Lantolf and Frawley questioned the rationale for using the construct "the educated native speaker" as the reference point. However, to date, no alternative that adequately replaces the ACTFL guides has been proposed.

6 Some online assessment instruments commercially available for national use, such as STAMP (Standards-Measurement of Proficiency), have also been developed based on the ACTFL guidelines.

7 Portfolios are much more than folders containing student work; the language exemplars that students choose to include must be carefully selected, revised, and presented by the student, who comes to an increased understanding of his or her own language development in the process of working on the portfolio (Delett, Barnhardt, & Kevorkian, 2001).

8 For example, Sohn and Merrill's (2008) study compared four-skill Korean proficiency test scores as well as standardized English test scores among fourth-and fifth-grade Korean HL students who had attended three different educational settings: (a) an English immersion program (no support for Korean HL maintenance), (b) a "modified bilingual program" where Korean-speaking teachers

are allowed the minimum use of Korean only to support instruction conducted primarily in English, and (c) the Korean/English Dual Language Program (KDLP). The results indicated that Korean HL students in the KDLP group not only performed significantly better than the other groups in Korean but also performed significantly better than or equally well to other groups in English.

9 For example, Wang (2003) observed two Chinese after-school HL programs and reported that the active and supporting roles that parents play are critical for the success of the programs, the teachers did not generally receive adequate professional training in teaching methodology, and the students used English predominantly.

10 When they were first funded, *hoshuukoo* were primarily intended to serve Japanese children abroad who were planning to return to Japan after a short stay, but a growing number of the *hoshuukoo* students today are citizens or permanent residents of the host country. According to the Ministry of Foreign Affairs of Japan, as of April 2009, there were 201 *hoshuukoo* in 51 countries, 88 of which were located in the United States. Some variations in the *hoshuukoo* curriculum exist, but the majority of the schools teach *kokugo* (language arts or Japanese language), mathematics, and/or social science in Japanese for 100 – 200 hours a year following the same national academic curriculum guidelines (called *gakushuu shidoo yooryoo*) used in public schools in Japan. The Japanese government not only supplies all *hoshuukoo* with board-certified textbooks but also sends Japanese public elementary and lower secondary school teachers to selected *hoshuukoo*, including 31 *hoshuukoo* in North America.

11 Earlier, Valdés (1989) argued against the use of the ACTFL guidelines for placing HL students because they were developed based on the norm of an "educated native speaker" who speaks the standard variety, not the nonstandard varieties spoken by the HL speakers of Spanish.

12 In Kondo-Brown's (2005) study, correlations between the three sections of multiple-choice test scores (listening, reading, and grammar knowledge) were very high. The analyses indicated that the total placement test score distributions for the HL group were negatively skewed (i.e., most had higher scores), while the score distributions for non-HL groups were more or less evenly distributed over the range of possible scores.

13 In Kondo-Brown's (2004) study, each essay collected from 225 students

received three ratings independently given by three judges. Average scores based on the three ratings were used as essay test scores for individual students (the interrater reliabilities ranging from .93 to .95). The scores on the essay test were evenly distributed over the range of possible scores for both groups.

14 Not surprising, research suggests that Chinese HL students' preference between the two different script systems is closely related to their countries of origin (Li & Duff, 2008).

15 According to Gambhir (2008), 8 out of the 10 universities surveyed reported that Hindi was taught in mixed-abilities classes, where English L1 students who have zero functionality may study together with HL speakers of Hindi or other cognate languages such as Gujarati and Punjabi at home.

16 For example, Kondo-Brown (2009) indicated that there were considerable individual differences in reading ability self-ratings and motivation profiles within each of the HL and non-HL student groups, and that overall, students in both groups were strongly motivated to read for extrinsic reasons (e.g., knowledge-based and instrumental values), but those who gave themselves higher self-ratings were also intrinsically involved in reading in the target language, in this case, Chinese, Japanese, or Korean.

17 In the McQuillan (1996) study, 20 HL learners of Spanish enrolled in a lower-division HL class and received a 10-week treatment where they were required to survey various genres of popular and classic literature and also participate in self-selected literature circles.

18 Research on L2 reading has suggested that L2 readers frequently infer the meanings of unknown words when they read (Paribakht & Wesche, 1999) and that this mental activity of lexical inferencing is a major source of L2 vocabulary acquisition through reading (Day, Omura, & Hiramatsu, 1991). Kondo-Brown's (2006b) study found considerable individual differences within each of the HL and non-HL groups in reading comprehension ability as well as in *kanji* vocabulary inferencing ability.

19 For example, see the National Heritage Language Resource Center's Web site (http://www.international.ucla.edu/languages/nhlrc/).

REFERENCES

American Council on the Teaching of Foreign Languages (ACTFL). (1999). *National Stan-*

dards for foreign language learning in the 21st century. Lawrence, KS: Allen.

Angelelli, C., & Kagan, O. (2002). Heritage speakers as learners at the superior level: Differences and similarities between Spanish and Russian student populations. In B. L. Leaver & B. Shekhtman (Eds.), *Developing professional-level language proficiency* (pp. 119–140). Cambridge, UK: Cambridge University Press.

Beckett, G. H., & Miller, P. C. (Eds.). (2006). *Project-based second and foreign language education: Past, present, and future.* Greenwich, CT: Information Age.

Brinton, D. M., Snow, M. A., & Wesche, M. (2003). *Content-based second language instruction.* Ann Arbor: University of Michigan Press.

Brown, J. D., Hudson, T., & Clark, M. (2004). Issues in placement survey (Networks #40). Honolulu: University of Hawaii, National Foreign Language Resource Center. Retrieved December 15, 2008, from http://nflrc.hawaii.edu/NetWorks/NW40/SurveyResults.html.

Campbell, R. N., & Rosenthal, J. W. (2000). Heritage languages. In J. W. Rosenthal (Ed.), *Handbook of undergraduate second language education* (pp. 165–184). Mahwah, NJ: Erlbaum.

Carreira, M. (2007). Teaching Spanish in the U.S.: Beyond the one-size-fits-all paradigm. In K. Potowski & R. Cameron (Eds.), *Spanish in contact: Policy, social and linguistic inquiries* (pp. 81–99). Amsterdam/Philadelphia: John Benjamins.

Chinen, K., & Tucker, G. R. (2006). Heritage language development: Understanding the roles of ethnic identity, schooling and community. In K. Kondo-Brown (Ed.), *Heritage language development: Focus on East Asian immigrants* (pp. 89–126). Amsterdam: John Benjamins.

Christian, D. (2008). School-based programs for heritage language learners: Two-way immersion. In D. M. Brinton, O. Kagan, & S. Bauckus (Eds.), *Heritage language education: A new field emerging* (pp. 257–268). New York: Routledge.

Crawford, J. (1992). *Hold your tongue: Bilingualism and the politics of "English only."* Massachusetts, MA: Addison-Wesley.

Curriculum guidelines for heritage language classrooms at the University of California (National Heritage Language Focus Group Report). (2003). Retrieved March 1, 2008, from http://www.international.ucla.edu/article.asp?parentid=24734.

Day, R. R., Omura, C., & Hiramatsu, M. (1991). Incidental EFL vocabulary learning and reading. *Reading in a Foreign Language, 7,* 541–551.

Delett, J. S., Barnhardt, S., & Kevorkian, J. A. (2001). A framework for portfolio assessment in the foreign language classroom. *Foreign Language Annals, 34,* 559–568.

Dolgova, I. (2008). Placement examination for a heterogeneous group of Russian heritage learners. In T. Hudson & M. Clark (Eds.), *Case studies in foreign language placement: Practices and possibilities* (pp. 99–104). Honolulu, HI: University of Hawaii, National Foreign Language Resource Center.

Domingo, N. P. (2008). Towards a heritage-learner-sensitive Filipino placement test at UCLA. In T. Hudson & M. Clark (Eds.), *Case studies in foreign language placement: Practices and possibilities* (pp. 17–28). Honolulu: University of Hawaii, National Foreign Language Resource Center.

Douglas, M. O. (2005). Pedagogical theories and approaches to teach young learners of Japanese as a heritage language. *Heritage Language Journal, 3*. Retrieved March 1, 2006, from http://www.heritagelanguages.org/.

Douglas, M. O. (2008). A profile of Japanese heritage learners and individualized curriculum. In D. M. Brinton, O. Kagan, & S. Bauckus (Eds.), *Heritage language education: A new field emerging* (pp. 215–228). Mahwah, NJ: Erlbaum.

Ducar, C. M. (2008). Student voices: The missing link in the Spanish heritage language debate. *Foreign Language Annals, 41*, 415–433.

Fairclough, M. (2006). Language placement exams for heritage speakers of Spanish: Learning from students' mistakes. *Foreign Language Annals, 39*, 595–604.

Friedman, D., & Kagan, O. (2008). Academic writing proficiency of Russian heritage speakers. In D. M. Brinton, O. Kagan, & S. Bauckus (Eds.), *Heritage language education: A new field emerging* (pp. 181–198). Mahwah, NJ: Erlbaum.

Gambhir, V. (2008). The rich tapestry of heritage learners of Hindi. *South Asia Language Pedagogy and Technology, 1.* 2007. Retrieved May 15, 2008, from http://salpat.uchicago.edu/index.php/salpat/index.

Glisan, E. W., & Foltz, D. A. (1998). Assessing students' oral proficiency in an outcome-based curriculum: Student performance and teacher intuitions. *Modern Language Journal, 82*, 1–18.

Hasegawa, T. (2008). Measuring the Japanese proficiency of heritage language children. In K. Kondo-Brown & J. D. Brown (Eds.), *Teaching Chinese, Japanese and Korean heritage language students: Curriculum needs, materials, and assessment* (pp. 77–98). New York: Erlbaum.

Hayashi, A. (2006). Japanese English bilingual children in three different educational environments. In K. Kondo-Brown (Ed.), *Heritage language development: Focus on East Asian immigrants* (pp. 145–171). Amsterdam: John Benjamins.

Hornberger, N. H., & Wang, S. C. (2008). Who are our heritage language learners? Identity and biliteracy in heritage language education in the United States. In D. M. Brinton, O. Kagan, & S. Bauckus (Eds.), *Heritage language education: A new field emerging* (pp. 3–35). New York: Routledge.

Howard, E. R., Sugarman, J., Christian, D., Lindholm-Leary, K. J., & Rogers, D. (2007). *Guiding principles for dual language education* (2nd ed.). Washington, DC: Center for Applied Linguistics.

Husseinali, G. (2006). Who is studying Arabic and why? A survey of Arabic students' orientations at a major university. *Foreign Language Annals, 39*, 395–412.

Ilieva, G. N. (2008). Project-based learning of Hindi: Managing the mixed-abilities classroom. *South Asia Language Pedagogy and Technology, 1*. Retrieved May 15, 2008 from http://salpat.uchicago.edu/index.php/salpat/index.

Jensen, L. (2007). Heritage language reading in the university: A survey of students' experiences, strategies, and preferences. *Heritage Language Journal, 5*. Retrieved March 1, 2008, from http://www.heritagelanguages.org/.

Jo, H.-Y. (2001). "Heritage" language learning and ethnic identity: Korean Americans' struggle with language authorities. *Language, Culture, and Curriculum, 14*, 26–41.

Kagan, O. (2005). In support of a proficiency-based definition of heritage language learners: The case of Russian. *The International Journal of Bilingual Education and Bilingualism, 8*, 213–221.

Kagan, O., & Dillon, K. (2001). A new perspective on teaching Russian: Focus on the heritage learner. *Slavic and East European Journal, 45*, 507–518.

Kagan, O., & Dillon, K. (2003). Heritage speakers' potential for high-level language proficiency. In H. Byrones & H. Maxim (Eds.), *Advanced foreign language learning: A challenge to college programs* (pp. 99–112). Boston, MA: Thomson & Heinle.

Kagan, O., & Friedman, D. (2003). Using the OPI to place heritage speakers of Russian. *Foreign Language Annals, 36*, 536–545.

Kanno, K., Hasegawa, T., Ikeda, K., Ito, Y., & Long, M. H. (2008). Prior language-learning experience and variation in the linguistic profiles of advanced English-speaking learners of Japanese. In D. M. Brinton, O. Kagan, & S. Bauckus (Eds.), *Heritage language education: A new field emerging* (pp. 215–228). New York: Routledge.

Kataoka, H., Furuyama, H., & Koshiyama, Y. (2000). Minami kariforunia nihongo gakuen kyooshi ankeeto kekka bunseki hookokusho [Report on the Southern California Japanese language school teacher survey results]. Retrieved May 15, 2005, from http://www.jflalc.org/teaching/jflc/fclty_rpt/jpz_kyoushi/heritage2.html.

Kataoka, H., Koshiyama, Y., & Shibata, S. (2008). Japanese and English language ability of students at supplementary Japanese schools in the United Status. In K. Kondo-Brown & J. D. Brown (Eds.), *Teaching Chinese, Japanese and Korean heritage language students: Curriculum needs, materials, and assessment* (pp. 47–76). New York: Erlbaum.

Kim, H. H.-S. (2008). Heritage and nonheritage learners of Korean: Sentence processing differences and their pedagogical implications. In K. Kondo-Brown & J. D. Brown (Eds.), *Teaching Chinese, Japanese and Korean heritage language students: Curriculum needs, Materials, and assessment* (pp. 99–134). New York: Erlbaum.

Kondo, K. (1998). Social-psychological factors affecting language maintenance: Interviews with Shin Nisei university students. *Linguistics and Education, 9*, 369–408.

Kondo, K. (1999). Motivating bilingual and semibilingual university students of Japanese: An analysis of language learning persistence and intensity among students from immigrant backgrounds. *Foreign Language Annals, 32*, 77–88.

Kondo-Brown, K. (2003). Heritage language instruction for post-secondary students from immigrant backgrounds. *Heritage Language Journal, 1*. Retrieved December 30, 2003, from http://www.heritagelanguages.org/.

Kondo-Brown, K. (2004). Do background variables predict students' scores on a proficiency test?: Implications for placing heritage language learners. *Journal of the National Council of Less Commonly Taught Languages, 1*, 1–19.

Kondo-Brown, K. (2005). Differences in language skills: Heritage language learner subgroups and foreign language learners. *Modern Language Journal, 89*, 563–581.

Kondo-Brown, K. (2006a). East Asian heritage language proficiency development. In K. Kondo-Brown (Ed.), *Heritage language development: Focus on East Asian immigrants* (pp. 243–258). Amsterdam: John Benjamins.

Kondo-Brown, K. (2006b). How do English L1 learners of advanced Japanese infer unknown kanji words in authentic texts? *Language Learning, 56*, 109–153.

Kondo-Brown, K. (2008). Issues and future agenda for teaching Chinese, Japanese, and Korean heritage students. In K. Kondo-Brown & J. D. Brown (Eds.), *Teaching Chinese, Japanese and Korean heritage language students: Curriculum needs, materials, and assessment* (pp. 17–44). New York: Erlbaum.

Kondo-Brown, K. (2009). Background, motivation, and reading ability of students in university upper-level Chinese, Japanese, and Korean courses. *Reading in a Foreign Language, 21*, 179–197.

Kondo-Brown, K., & Fukuda, C. (2008). A separate track for advanced heritage language students?: Japanese intersentential referencing. In K. Kondo-Brown & J. D. Brown (Eds.), *Teaching Chinese, Japanese and Korean heritage language students: Curriculum needs, materials, and assessment* (pp. 135–156). New York: Erlbaum.

Lacorte, M. (2005). Teacher beliefs and practices in advanced Spanish classrooms. *Heritage Language Journal, 3*. Retrieved May 15, 2008, from http://www. heritagelanguages.org/.

Lantolf, J. P., & Frawley, W. (1985). Oral-proficiency testing: A critical analysis. *Modern Language Journal, 69*, 337–345.

Lee, J. S., & Kim, H.-Y. (2008). Heritage language learners' attitudes, motivations and instructional needs: The case of postsecondary Korean language learners. In K. Kondo-Brown & J. D. Brown (Eds.), *Teaching Chinese, Japanese and Korean heritage language students: Curriculum needs, materials, and assessment* (pp. 159–186). New York: Erlbaum.

Lee, J. S., & Shin, S. (2008). Korean heritage language education in the United States: The current state, opportunities, and possibilities. *Heritage Language Journal, 6.* Retrieved March 1, 2009, from http://www.heritagelanguages.org/.

Li, D., & Duff, P. (2008). Issues in Chinese heritage language education and research at the postsecondary level. In A. W. He & Y. Xiao, (Eds.), *Chinese as a heritage language: Fostering rooted world citizenry* (pp. 13–36). Honolulu: University of Hawaii, National Foreign Resource Center.

Li, M. (2005). The role of parents in Chinese heritage-language schools. *Bilingual Research Journal 29, 1.* Retrieved May 1, 2006, from http://brj.asu.edu/archive.html.

Liskin-Gasparro, J. E. (1982). *ETS oral proficiency testing manual.* Princeton, NJ: Educational Testing Service.

Malone, M. E. (2003). Research on the oral proficiency interview: Analysis, synthesis, and future directions. *Foreign Language Annals, 36,* 491–497.

Malone, M. E., Rifkin, B., Christian, D., & Johnson, D. (2005). Attaining high levels of proficiency: Challenges for foreign language education in the United States. *Center for Applied Linguistics Online Digest.* Retrieved January 15, 2006, from http://www.cal.org/resources/digest/attain.html.

Mathews, T. J., & Hansen, C. M. (2004). Ongoing assessment of a university foreign language program. *Foreign Language Annals, 37,* 630–639.

McGinnis, S. (2008). From mirror to compass: The Chinese heritage language education sector in the United Sates. In D. M. Brinton, O. Kagan, & S. Bauckus (Eds.), *Heritage language education: A new field emerging* (pp. 215–228). New York: Routledge.

McQuillan, J. (1996). How should heritage languages be taught? The effects of a free voluntary reading program. *Foreign Language Annals, 29,* 56–72.

Meskill, C., & Anthony, N. (2008). Computer mediated communication: Tools for instructing Russian heritage language learners. *Heritage Language Journal, 6.* Retrieved March 15, 2008, from http://www.heritagelanguages.org/.

Montrul, S., & Potowski, K. (2007). Command of gender agreement in school-age Spanish-English bilingual children. *International Journal of Bilingualism, 11,* 301–328.

Morioka, A., Takakura, A. H., & Ushida, E. (2008). Developing Web-based multi-level materials for Japanese content-based instruction. *Japanese Language and Literature, 42,* 361–388.

Nagasawa, F. (1995). L1, L2, bairingaru no nihongo bunpoo nooryoku [Comparative grammatical competence among L1, L2, and bilingual speakers of Japanese]. *Nohongo kyooiku, 86,* 173–189.

Norris, J. M. (2006). The why (and how) of assessing student learning outcomes in college foreign language programs. *Modern Language Journal, 90,* 576–583.

Norris, J. M., & Pfeiffer, P. C. (2003). Exploring the uses and usefulness of ACTFL oral proficiency ratings and standards in college foreign language departments. *Foreign Language Annals*, *36*, 572–581.

Nunan, D. (1988). *The learner-centered curriculum*. Cambridge, UK: Cambridge University Press.

Omaggio Hardley, A. (2001). *Teaching language in context* (3rd ed.). Boston, MA: Heinle & Heinle.

Paribakht, T. S. & Wesche, M. (1999). Reading and "incidental" L2 vocabulary acquisition. *Studies in Second Language Acquisition*, *21*, 195–224.

Parodi, C. (2008). Stigmatized Spanish inside the classroom and out: A model of language teaching to heritage speakers. In D. M. Brinton, O. Kagan, & S. Bauckus (Eds.), *Heritage language education: A new field emerging* (pp. 199–214). New York: Routledge.

Payton, J. K. (2008). Spanish for native speakers' education: The state of the field. In D. M. Brinton, O. Kagan, & S. Bauckus (Eds.), *Heritage language education: A new field emerging* (pp. 243–256). New York: Routledge.

Pearson, L., Fonseca-Greber, B., Foell, K. (2006). Educating foreign language teacher candidates to achieve advanced proficiency. *Foreign Language Annals*, *39*(3), 507–519.

Polinsky, M. (2008). Heritage language narratives. In D. M. Brinton, O. Kagan, & S. Bauckus (Eds.), *Heritage language education: A new field emerging* (pp. 149–164). New York: Routledge.

Potowski, K. (2007). *Language and identity in a dual immersion school*. Clevedon, UK: Multilingual Matters.

Potowski, K., Berne, J., Clark, A. and Hammerand, A. (2008). Spanish for K–8 heritage speakers: A standards-based curriculum project. *Hispania*, *91*, 25–41.

Potowski, K., & Carreira, M. (2004). Towards teacher development and national standards for Spanish as a heritage language. *Foreign Language Annals*, *37*, 421–431.

Ranjan, R. (2008). The challenge of placing Hindi heritage students. In T. Hudson & M. Clark (Eds.), *Case studies in foreign language placement: Practices and possibilities* (pp. 177–186). Honolulu: University of Hawaii, National Foreign Language Resource Center.

Ricardo-Osorio, J. (2008). A study of foreign language learning outcomes assessment in U.S. undergraduate education. *Foreign Language Annals*, *41*, 590–610.

Rifkin, B. (2003). Oral proficiency learning outcomes and curricular design. *Foreign Language Annals*, *36*, 582–588.

Rifkin, B. (2005). A ceiling effect in traditional classroom foreign language instruction: Data from Russian. *Modern Language Journal*, *89*, 3–18.

Robinson, J. P., Rivers, W., & Brecht, R. D. (2006). Speaking foreign languages in the United States: Correlates, trends, and possible consequences. *Modern Language Journal*, *90*, 457–472.

Rubio, F. (2003). Structure and complexity of oral narratives in advanced-level Spanish: A comparison of three learning backgrounds. *Foreign Language Annals, 36,* 546–554.

Salaberry, R. (2000). Revising the revised format of the ACTFL oral proficiency interview. *Language Testing, 17,* 289–310.

Schwarzer, D., & Petrón, M. (2005). Heritage language instruction at the college level: Reality and possibilities. *Foreign Language Annals, 38,* 568–578.

Shen, H. H. (2003). A comparison of written Chinese achievement among heritage learners in homogeneous and heterogeneous groups. *Foreign Language Annals, 36,* 258–266.

Sohn, S.-O., & Merrill, C. (2008). The Korean/English dual language program in the Los Angeles unified school district. In D. M. Brinton, O. Kagan, & S. Bauckus (Eds.), *Heritage language education: A new field emerging* (pp. 269–288). New York: Routledge.

Sohn, S.-O., & Shin, S.-K. (2007). True beginners, false beginners, and fake beginners: Placement strategies for Korean heritage speakers. *Foreign Language Annals, 40,* 407–418.

Takahashi, C. Y. (2008). A case study of Thai language program placement testing: Incorporating news articles into the Thai placement process. In T. Hudson & M. Clark (Eds.), *Case studies in foreign language placement: Practices and possibilities* (pp. 187–197). Honolulu: University of Hawaii, National Foreign Language Resource Center.

Tucker, G. R. (2005). Innovative language education programmes for heritage language students: The special case of Puerto Ricans? *The International Journal of Bilingual Education and Bilingualism, 8,* 188–195.

Tudor, I. (1996). *Learner-centeredness as language education.* Cambridge, UK: Cambridge University Press.

Valdés, G. (1989). Teaching Spanish to Hispanic bilinguals: A Look at oral proficiency testing the proficiency movement. *Hispania, 72,* 392–401.

Valdés, G. (1995). The teaching of minority languages as academic subjects: Pedagogical and theoretical challenges. *Modern Language Journal, 79,* 299–328.

Valdés, G., & Geoffrion-Vinci, M. (1998). Chicano Spanish: The problem of the "underdeveloped" code in bilingual repertoires. *Modern Language Journal, 82,* 473–501.

Yu, W. H. (2008). Developing a "compromise curriculum" for Korean heritage and non-heritage learners. Issues and future agenda for teaching Chinese, Japanese, and Korean heritage students. In K. Kondo-Brown & J. D. Brown (Eds.), *Teaching Chinese, Japanese and Korean heritage language students: Curriculum needs, materials, and assessment* (pp. 187–210). New York: Erlbaum.

Wang, M. (2003). An ethnographic study of Chinese heritage language education and technological innovations. *Journal of National Council of Less Commonly Taught Languages, 1,* 69–94.

Webb, J., & Miller, B. (Eds.). (2000). *Teaching heritage language learners: Voices from the classroom.* Yonkers, NY: ACTFL.

Wiley, T. G. (2008). Chinese "dialect" speakers as heritage language learners: A case study. In D. M. Brinton, O. Kagan, & S. Bauckus (Eds.), *Heritage language education: A new field emerging* (pp. 91–106). New York: Routledge.

Wu, S.-M. (2008). Robust learning for Chinese heritage learners: Motivation, linguistics, and technology. In K. Kondo-Brown & J. D. Brown (Eds.), *Teaching Chinese, Japanese and Korean heritage language students: Curriculum needs, materials, and assessment* (pp. 271–298). New York: Erlbaum.

Zamar, S., & Robotham, L. (2008). Placement test and course objectives: The case of the Filipino program at the University of Hawaii at Manoa. In T. Hudson & M. Clark (Eds.), *Case studies in foreign language placement: Practices and possibilities* (pp. 29–38). Honolulu, HI: University of Hawaii, National Foreign Language Resource Center.

Zhang, D., & Davis, N. (2008). Online chat for heritage learners of Chinese. In K. Kondo-Brown & J. D. Brown (Eds.), *Teaching Chinese, Japanese and Korean heritage language students: Curriculum needs, materials, and assessment* (pp. 299–328). New York: Erlbaum.

International Comparative Perspectives on Heritage Language Education Policy Research

Jeffrey Bale

As awareness of the unique abilities and needs of heritage language learners has grown, so too has recent research deepened our understanding of the dynamic between language policy and heritage language education (HLE). In this article, I review HLE policy research conducted in various international contexts. I begin by reviewing ongoing debates in the policy literature over definitions and adopt a broad understanding of the term so that we can glean as much insight as possible from the comparison of international contexts. I then turn to six international regions and countries that have been the focus of recent HLE policy research. Within each region, I apply the analytic framework proposed by Ricento and Hornberger (1996) to differentiate the multiple levels at which language policy functions. Finally, I identify common themes emerging across the research in these varied contexts and conclude with suggestions for future policy-oriented HLE research.

INTRODUCTION

As awareness of the unique abilities and needs of heritage language learners has grown, so too has recent research deepened our understanding of the dynamic between language policy and heritage language education (HLE). In this article, I review HLE policy research conducted in various international contexts. I begin by reviewing ongoing debates in the policy literature over definitions and adopt a broad understanding of the term so that we can glean as much insight as possible from the comparison of international contexts. I then turn to six international regions and countries that have been the focus of recent HLE policy research. Within each region, I apply the analytic framework proposed by Ricento and Hornberger (1996) to differentiate the multiple levels at which language policy functions. Finally, I identify common themes emerging across the research in these varied contexts and conclude with suggestions for future policy-oriented HLE research.

DEFINITIONS

Complicating the investigation of HLE policy are the multiple definitions of the term *heritage language* that operate in the literature. Even when restricted to the research included in this review, we encounter a formidable list of terms often positioned as synonymous with heritage: aboriginal, ancestral, autochthonous, (ex-)colonial, community, critical, diasporic, endoglossic, ethnic, foreign, geopolitical, home, immigrant, indigenous, language other than English, local, migrant, minority, mother tongue, refugee, regional, and strategic.[1] Certainly, no single term can (or perhaps should) encompass the widely divergent histories, contexts, and perspectives that such a list indexes. In their discussion of the applicability of heritage language to the African context, Brutt-Griffler and Makoni (2005) identified two inherent risks in labeling such a wide array of language and language contexts: Either a term misconstrues the specific local dynamics at play, or it is so broad that it loses any meaning. The work of Wiley (2005) reminds us that at the heart of this terminological debate is the ethical tension between researcher and researched; that is, the terms that applied linguists assign to languages are often not in concert with how speakers of those languages identify or perceive their own language(s).

In the United States, heritage language can refer to all languages other than English (Hornberger & Wang, 2008). Fishman (2001, 2006) categorized heritage languages in the United States as indigenous, colonial, or immigrant languages. The primary example of this typology is Spanish: It was introduced to the western hemisphere as a colonial language; thereafter, it was indigenous to territories annexed by the United States in the 19th century; and of course it constitutes the largest immigrant language in the country. Cummins (2005) and Wiley (2005) added to this typology the category of refugee languages as well.

However broadly heritage language is defined, the term has evoked a number of criticisms. The most persistent is that the term implies, even romanticizes, past language use, rather than focusing on actual and future language practice (e.g., García, 2005; McCarty, 2008; Wiley, 2005). García (2005) juxtaposed the emergence of HLE as a field of study with the constriction of social space for the practice of bilingual education. García argued:

> I believe the use of the term *heritage languages* in the United States signals a losing of ground for language minorities that was gained during the civil rights era. And yet, I agree with Cummins [2005] that the use of the term *heritage languages in education* ... provides a way to "crack" today's homogeneous monolingual schooling of very different children in the United States, providing a space for the use of languages other than English in educating children (2005, p. 602, emphasis in original).

Based on an international comparison of terms used to describe minority languages, Wiley (2005) suggested that *heritage and community languages* more accurately reflect contemporary language practice, while McCarty (2008) preferred *heritage mother tongue* to refer to indigenous languages.

The implications of labeling are even more acute in deliberations over *who* counts as a heritage language speaker or learner. In general, the debate has centered on the question of proficiency in the language. One approach defines heritage language speakers in terms of their individual or collective affiliation with a specific ethnolinguistic group (Fishman, 2001; McCarty, 2008). Another defines heritage language speakers in terms of their ability to speak or understand the language, no matter how limited that proficiency may be (Valdés, 2001). One example of how this distinction operates is to consider the example of an African American student in the United States in an introductory-level course in Hausa at university. An identity-based definition of *heritage language learner* might include such a student, assuming her studies were part of the student's efforts to rediscover and cultivate ancestral ties to western Africa. Assuming this student was born in the United States and raised with English only, a proficiency-based definition of *heritage language learner* would exclude the student for having no experience in the language at all.

The implications of this distinction are not insignificant. Certainly, a proficiency-based definition of heritage language learner has more immediate pedagogical consequences for the language education classroom. In fact, the vast majority of the studies reviewed here tacitly or explicitly adopted a proficiency-based definition of heritage language vis-à-vis HLE policy. Conversely, insisting on proficiency in defining heritage language speakers risks excluding those individuals and communities who maintain salient ethnolinguistic identities, especially when the ancestral language(s) experiences language shift or even extinction. Hornberger (2005) considered this position in terms of agency, that heritage learners decide for themselves whether or not they belong to a given heritage language community. This article does not take a position in this debate, other than to recognize, as mentioned earlier, that most of the HLE policy research reviewed implied or adopted a proficiency-based definition of heritage language speaker or learner.

The final definitional consideration of heritage language concerns the context in which such languages are used and taught. Thus far, I have used the United States as the touchstone for elaborating terminological definitions and debates. However, the origin of the term has been ascribed to Canada (Hornberger & Wang, 2008; Wiley, 2005). In a recent overview of HLE in Canada, Duff (2008) stated that *heritage* in fact refers to a category of languages distinct from Canada's official languages (i.e., French and English) and aboriginal languages. In both Australia and the United Kingdom, the term *community language* is used more frequently (Wiley, 2005), although not without its own problems. Mercurio and Scarino (2005) challenged the breadth of the term and whether it indeed fits disparate sociolinguistic profiles in Australia. They also recognized that speakers of Aboriginal languages in Australia tend to prefer terms such as *Australian indigenous languages or Australian languages*.

Beyond these contexts, uses of the term *heritage* in reference to language tend to be in the colloquial sense of the word, rather than in relation to a defined body of applied linguistic research or to a model of language education. Instead, a number of labels are ascribed to languages to distinguish between dominant, ex-colonial, official, and national languages on the one hand, and minoritized,[2] indeed perhaps threatened, indigenous, diasporic, regional, and/or immigrant languages on the other. In the African context, for example, Brutt-Griffler and Makoni (2005) stated that terms such as *home, ancestral,* and *indigenous* are more frequently employed to refer to languages other than colonial languages. De Bot and Gorter (2005) maintained that *heritage language* has little currency in Europe, where instead reference is made to *regional* and *immigrant minority languages*.[3] In addition, *mother tongue* is a term widely used in the sub-Saharan African, South Asian, and Southeast Asian contexts. It is also worth noting that much literature simply does not engage the terminological complexities, referring instead only to the languages in question by name. This is particularly true in HLE policy research on Irish, Scottish Gaelic, and Welsh in the Republic of Ireland and the United Kingdom.

Following Hornberger and Wang (2008), I adopt a broad definition of heritage languages to review recent HLE policy research. Their definition is based on an ecological approach to HLE that considers an individual's ancestral ties to the heritage language; individual agency in identifying as a heritage language learner or speaker; and how the heritage language and its speakers are positioned in social, political, and economic terms. Specifically, this review includes research that investigates HLE policy in contexts where English is the dominant, official, national, or ex-colonial language. The decision to limit the research to English-dominant contexts was driven solely by the logistical constraints of a single article; similar reviews in contexts with other dominant and ex-colonial languages are certainly needed. To be clear, my intention here is not to insist that such a broad conceptualization of heritage language define the field. Instead, because the purpose of research reviews is to synthesize a broad base of literature, we stand to gain by comparing the contexts, no matter how varied, in which HLE policies unfold.

APPROACHES TO ANALYSIS

This article makes two assumptions in discussing recent HLE policy research. The first recalls the onion metaphor proposed by Ricento and Hornberger (1996). This metaphor understands language policy not simply as legislative processes or formal policy texts operating at the national or supranational level. Rather, language policy at this formalized level is merely the outer layer of a much more complicated process in which policy actors not only implement a given policy but also appropriate it in ways that make the policy their own. This appropriation process assumes policy to be less about formal documents established by governing authorities, instead focusing of policy as social practice (Levinson & Sutton, 2001). The inner layers of the onion include institutional and interpersonal levels of policy formation and appropriation. Ricento and Hornberger identified many institutions in which language policy is made. However, for the purposes of this review, the focus is limited to educational institutions, for example, government-sponsored schools, community language programs, and nongovernmental organizations. Interpersonal policy processes refer to teachers, their interactions with students, and practices that reflect policymaking in a more localized context.

These layers of the onion are not merely markers of where language policy is made and contested but also suggest that the notion of policy has expanded greatly in the field of language planning and policy (LPP). A full discussion of such is beyond the scope of this article (see Ricento, 2006, for a comprehensive overview). However, the HLE policy research reviewed here includes studies of policy as formal texts, as discourse, as ideology, as a process of legitimacy, and less frequently as specific educator and student practices of language education. These varied policy domains also reflect that methods of HLE policy scholarship have expanded far beyond content or discourse analysis of formal texts to include quantitative sociolinguistic analyses, historiography, conventional qualitative research methods, and full-scale ethnographies of the policy appropriation process. As much as possible, discussion of the research reviewed the following sections identifies both the level of and the approach to HLE policy analysis.

The second organizational principle for this review is geographical. As mentioned earlier, this review encompasses HLE policy research in English-dominant contexts, or where English is the ex-colonial language. To honor the differences in how non-English languages are labeled across these contexts, and to acknowledge that there does seem to be consensus within specific regions as to how label non-English languages, the review is organized by geographical region and country. The discussion includes Africa (Botswana, Kenya, Malawi, Nigeria, Uganda, and Zimbabwe); Hong Kong, Malaysia and Singapore; India; North America (Canada and the United States); Oceania (Aotearoa/New Zealand and Australia); the Republic of Ireland, and the United Kingdom. With respect to terminology, the article will use *HLE policy* throughout, but to refer to specific languages, it will adopt the term employed by the study at hand.

THE AFRICAN CONTEXT

Bamgbose (2004) and Djité (2008, especially chap. 2) presented two comprehensive overviews of language-in-education policy in postcolonial Africa, including the role that heritage languages play in each country. They reported a language-in-education scheme, fairly consistent across Africa, which implements a 1953 UNESCO policy statement in which an African language is the medium of instruction at the primary level, generally in grades 1 to 3. Thereafter, English becomes the medium, and the African language(s) is taught as a subject. In general, HLE policy in the African context tends to reflect conflicts over which language(s) should be the media of instruction in formal, government-sponsored schooling; which should be taught as subjects; and which should be taught or maintained elsewhere in society. This is an instance in which the research assumes a proficiency-based definition of heritage language (HL) learners: the issue is not so much language maintenance (i.e., using language-in-education policy to revitalize a heritage language) as it is about aligning linguistic practices at school with those at home and in the community.

The work of Kamwendo and Mooko (2006) is fairly representative of much of the HLE policy research included in this discussion in terms of the structure of their analysis. After situating contemporary language policies against the history of colonial language practices in Botswana and Malawi, Kamwendo and Mooko conducted a comparative review of HLE policy at the national level in each country, identifying divergences in how indigenous medium-of-instruction policies have been legislated. They found that the dominance of English in official domains beyond education has been a major negative factor impacting HLE policies governing indigenous media of instruction in school. In an exhaustive overview of historical and contemporary language planning in Nigeria, Adegbija (2004) traced the history of three HLE policies initiated in the 1970s. The author enumerated a series of factors that have inhibited their success: lack of coordinated planning between national and local authorities, lack of suitable curricular materials in the indigenous language(s), lack of educators trained to teach the language(s), and no systematic assessment of the programs or student achievement. Similar inhibiting factors were reported in research in the contemporary Nigerian context (Iyamu & Aduwa Ogiegbaen, 2007), as well as in Kenya (Musau, 2003).

More often, however, HLE policy research in the African context explains the challenges facing indigenous medium-of-instruction policies in historical, sociopolitical, or ideological terms. For example, in a study focused on supranational levels of policymaking, Omoniyi (2003) enumerated a series of political, economic, and cultural forces at work across Africa and globally that have functioned to negatively impact the realization of HLE policies. Omoniyi tied these global forces to an analysis of how they have prevented the acquisition of indigenous literacy and argued, "The liberation of the continent from mass ignorance will require that the indigenous languages be equipped to convey the bodies of knowledge that exist in modes and media that are presently inaccessible to a vast majority of people" (p. 148). Similarly, Matiki (2006) argued that HLE policies regarding indigenous languages taught in the primary grades in Malawi should be assessed in terms of the extent to which they foster literacy and socioeconomic development of the country. However, he drew a different conclusion than Omoniyi. Especially considering that Malawian HLE policy has begun to incorporate additional indigenous languages beyond Chichewa, Matiki questioned whether instruction in these languages would indeed lead to successful literacy and socioeconomic development given Malawi's linguistic diversity. He justified this question in relation to Malawian attitudes: "While Malawians accept that literacy empowers, they contend that it is only literacy in English that pays" (p. 251).

In fact, policy stakeholders' attitudes and ideologies were cited most often in discussions of the challenges in realizing HLE policy for African languages as media of instruction. Musau (2003) was unique in exploring these attitudes at the national level. Adopting a framework of linguistic human rights, Musau reviewed general language policy in Kenya, as well as HLE policies in Kenyan schools. He stated, "Negative attitudes toward indigenous languages by the African élite are also a major obstacle in the implementation of linguistic justice" (p. 162) in the form of indigenous medium-of-instruction policies in Kenyan schools. He specified that these negative attitudes have framed indigenous medium-of-instruction programs as too expensive to implement or consider the languages themselves as not scientific, international, or neutral enough to be of valid use. Most HLE policy research on attitudes and ideologies of policy stakeholders, however, focuses on the institutional or interpersonal level. For example, Iyamu and Aduwa Ogiegbaen (2007) surveyed 1,000 literate parents and 1,500 primary school teachers in Nigeria about their attitude toward mother tongue policies for Hausa-, Yoruba- and Igbo-medium primary school programs. They found that parents and teachers indeed understood the value of mother tongue instruction in terms of promoting cultural heritage. However, parents reported more frequently than teachers that mother tongue education would not lead to improved learning overall. The authors concluded, "While mother-tongue medium policy is viewed as a major revolution in the history of education in Nigeria, opinions remain divided on its wisdom" (p. 99). Tembe and Norton (2008) explored attitudes among community stakeholders in rural and urban Uganda with respect to a 1992 HLE policy. The policy calls for the medium in grades 1 through 4 to be a relevant local language, switching to English from grade 5 and adding Kiswahili as a subject from grade 4. The authors conducted interviews and focus groups to assess the extent of (dis)agreement among rural and urban community members over the policy. They found that although members in both communities were aware of the policy shift, in general they expressed a desire for students to learn English as early as possible. In fact, some rural participants found the policy a "regressive step toward the past" (p. 50).

Importantly, recent HLE policy research in Africa highlights that power imbalances, whether perceived or lived, implicate African languages, not just ex-colonial languages, as the dominant, threatening language. While the focus of analysis in Makoni, Dube, and Mashiri (2006) is much broader than HLE policy as defined in this article, their overview of language planning in Zimbabwe is the most comprehensive in interrogating the indigenous-colonial language binary that frames much HLE policy analysis in the African context. Their exhaustive monograph documented the extent to which colonization and missionary work led to the artificial demarcation of one African language from another, and how this process privileged some newly "created" Zimbabwean languages, such as Shona and Ndebele, over others. Makoni, Makoni, and Nyika (2008) applied this type of analysis in their description of successful bottom-up language planning among the Tonga in Zimbabwe. The study analyzed efforts by Tonga leaders to reposition their language not as a minority but as an indigenous language in Zimbabwe, and the impact this reclassification would have on medium-of-instruction practices in local schools. The authors reported that Tonga concerns over the status of their language in Zimbabwe relate less to its status against English as against Shona and Ndebele. Igboanusi and Peter (2004) analyzed a similar dynamic in Nigeria. As with Makoni et al. (2006), their analysis is a broader sociolinguistic analysis: The study reported survey data collected among northern and southern minorities and their attitudes toward Hausa, the dominant national language in northern Nigeria, and English. Their data indicated that participants were as concerned with Hausa as with English as the cause of minority language loss.

The final note about HLE policy research in Africa concerns the prominence of nongovernmental organizations in the promotion of indigenous medium-of-instruction policies. Kamwendo (2005) recounted the role played by the Chitumbuka Language and Culture Association (CLACA) in raising the status of Chitumbuka in northern Malawi. Although the analysis of CLACA's advocacy goes beyond school-based HLE policy advocacy, Kamwendo identified the group's efforts to standardize Chitumbuka orthography and create textbooks as an essential step in implementing the language as the medium of instruction in northern Malawi schools. The study of Tonga as medium of instruction in Zimbabwe schools (Makoni et al., 2008) focused on the critical role played by the Tonga Language and Cultural Association. The organization focused its advocacy to change the status of Tonga from a minority to an indigenous language. This had the effect of positioning Tonga for use as medium of instruction in primary grades rather than simply a subject to be studied alongside a national language and English. Both studies labeled this sort of advocacy bottom-up language planning; however, both describe the language and cultural associations involved as representing the elite and/or elder members of each community. The elite status ascribed to each organization calls into question the researchers' classification of bottom-up, that is, whether this status obtains in relation to national institutions and authorities, or to the local community.

HONG KONG, MALAYSIA, AND SINGAPORE

A considerable amount of language policy research in recent years has addressed Southeast Asian contexts in which English is dominant or an ex-colonial language. Recent research on Malaysian language and language-in-education policy has tended to focus on the ideological and practical consequences of a 2002 policy mandating English as medium of instruction for science and math instruction at all levels (cf. David & Govindasamy, 2007; Gill, 2005; Martin, 2005). In Singapore, although medium-of-instruction policy is officially labeled as bilingual, it in fact centers on English with one of three official mother tongues (e.g., Malay, Mandarin, or Tamil) taught in addition as a subject. However, only in the case of Malay students does the official mother tongue policy correspond to the home language. In other words, Mandarin is not the home language for the majority of Chinese students in Singapore, nor is Tamil the home language for the majority of Indian students. In fact, recent language policy research in Singapore has tended to focus on initiatives such as the Speak Mandarin and Speak Good English campaigns (cf. Chew, 2007; Dixon, 2009; Rubdy, 2005). In both cases, because the focus of the policy research is more on English than the heritage language per se, this body of research falls somewhat outside the purview of this article.

Recent research about Hong Kong HLE policy has focused on various aspects of the region's formal language policy of trilingualism (in Cantonese, English, and Mandarin or Putonghua) and biliteracy (in Chinese and English). This policy emerged after the British "transfer" of Hong Kong to China in 1997, at which point Hong Kong was declared a Special Administrative Region (SAR). Hopkins (2006) reported 2001 census data citing 7 million residents of Hong Kong, 95% of whom were ethnically Southern Chinese and who claimed to use only Cantonese on a daily basis. In 1998 the government implemented a mother tongue education policy, which mandated that hitherto English-medium schools must switch to Cantonese as medium unless they could meet three criteria: 85% of their students must be in the top quintile academically; teachers must demonstrate sufficient proficiency in English; and the school must demonstrate that it has structures in place to support students struggling with English (Tse, Shum, Ki, & Chan, 2007; Tsui, 2007). Tse et al. (2007) reported the impact of this HLE policy for mother tongue education: "Strict enforcement of this policy caused more than 300 secondary schools to switch from English to Chinese as the teaching medium. Out of the 430 secondary schools, only 113 were granted permission to teach lessons in English" (p. 138).

Two empirical studies have explored this policy dynamic in terms of teacher and student attitudes toward each language. The first study presented results from a survey of Hong Kong educators regarding HLE policy for Cantonese- and

English-medium instruction (Tse et al., 2007). Of Hong Kong's 430 government-supported schools, 334 participated, including 284 school administrators and 2,880 teachers. The response rate from Cantonese- and English-medium schools was the same, at 73%. Participants in both contexts reported that a school's medium of instruction should be determined by students' ability and "linguistic potential" (p. 153). In addition, participants from both contexts were in favor of a policy in which the medium depended on the subject of instruction, not a school-wide fixed policy. There was a discrepancy, however, in support for Cantonese-medium secondary programs. Participants in Cantonese-medium schools supported consistent Cantonese-medium schooling, while participants in English-medium schools supported a switch to English from the secondary level on. The researchers concluded that in order for HLE policies regarding medium of instruction to be effective, policymakers could not take a one-size-fits-all approach for all schools and contexts. The second study explored similar issues, but from a student perspective (Lai, 2005). Within the framework of instrumental versus integrative attitudes toward language study and use, Lai administered surveys to 1,048 secondary students (i.e., 15–17 years old). Respondents indicated in general positive instrumental attitudes to all three languages (i.e. Cantonese, Putonghua, and English). However, in terms of integrative attitudes, Lai stated that respondents "remain emotionally rather detached" from native speakers of Putonghua (p. 376). Based on the findings, Lai called into question the feasibility of official language policies aimed at trilingualism.

Other examples of recent research on HLE policy in Hong Kong consider the issue from ideological and critical-historical perspectives. Tsui (2007) situated Hong Kong HLE policy regarding medium of instruction in the general project of "resinicization" (p. 133), in which Chinese and Hong Kong officials have actively sought to recreate historical and cultural ties between China and Hong Kong, and to create a "Chinese cultural heritage and national identity [which] was perceived as lacking in Hong Kong. This identity was referred to as a *new* identity that Hong Kong people should take pride in" (p. 134, emphasis in original). Despite these overt efforts, HLE policy research has consistently found that the 1998 medium of instruction policy has not affected social stratification or the hegemony of English in Hong Kong prior to SAR status. For example, Tsui (2007) concluded that "the [Hong Kong] community's apprehension about losing the international flavor and competitive edge . . . because of reunification with China resulted in stronger than ever demands for more English and more English education" (p. 138). Lin (2005) reviewed a number of critical ethnographic studies of Hong Kong language policies from the late 1990s that have identified a continued stratification between working-class Cantonese speaking students, for whom "English remains something beyond their reach" (p. 50) and an English-speaking elite. She concluded that:

> The post-1997 years have so far not seen any significant changes in the English-dominant education system and society . . . and the dominance of English in post-1997 Hong Kong seems to be even more stead-fastly maintained by a neocolonial, complex modern capitalist regime of culture (p. 51).

INDIA

As with much of the literature on Africa, recent research on HLE policies in India has focused either on the mismatch between monolingual assumptions behind medium-of-instruction policy in a profoundly multilingual context, or on the divergent, contested attitudes toward the role of English in Indian schools. Many examples of Indian HLE policy analysis begin with historical overviews of language and education predating and during British colonization, as well as with discussion of the legal background to contemporary language policy (Agnihotri, 2007; Annamalai, 2005; Khubchandani, 2003; A. K. Mohanty, 2006; P. Mohanty, 2002). Currently, there are 22 constitutionally recognized languages in India. Moreover, the 1,652 languages (plus varieties of these languages) spoken in India have been classified into 300–400 languages belonging to five language families (A. K. Mohanty, 2006). Of these languages, 47 are used as media of instruction across India (Vaish, 2005), although A. K. Mohanty (2006) reported that this number has declined, especially the number of minority languages (i.e., languages other than Hindi or the regional language of the respective state). This linguistic landscape maps onto official HLE policy in India known as the "three languages formula," which calls for a regional mother tongue as medium of instruction for the first 5 years of school; Hindi (in non-Hindi states) or another Indian language (in Hindi states) to be taught as a school subject in lower secondary years; and English as a third language, introduced from the third year. In addition, where minority languages are spoken by 10% of the population, those languages may be used in lieu of the regional language as medium of instruction in the early primary years (Agnihotri, 2007; A. K. Mohanty, 2006).

A major focus of recent HLE policy research in India has been on the gap between official policies, such as the three languages formula, and actual practice in Indian schools. Descriptions of this gap have led to critical reexaminations of the usefulness of medium of instruction policies. For example, Khubchandani (2003) described a tripartite model of language practice in Indian schools based on the following distinctions: (a) "passive and active media" contexts, in which students receive instruction in one language while writing and responding in another; (b) "formal and informal media" contexts, in which formal teaching occurs in one language while informal explanations use another; and (c) "multitier media" contexts, in which different languages are taught in a succession from one grade or grade band to the next (p. 244). Khubchandani ascribed this gap between policy and practice in part to the imposition of standardized urban varieties of Indian languages that do not match the varieties or languages spoken in students' homes and communities. Agnihotri (2007) situated this gap between policy and practice in the historical context in which postcolonial Indian language policy was conceived. He argued that HLE policies regarding media of instruction in India have imposed monolingual categories onto a fluid multilingual context:

> What [the drafters of the constitution] could not anticipate however was that monolingual solutions to multilingual societies would not work. A multilingual society would need a multilingual perspective, and monolingual solutions that would eventually be formulated in terms, for example, of a three-language formula would not work. Any classroom in India is in general multilingual, and unless we conceptualize the school curriculum, syllabus, textbooks and classroom transaction in terms of multilingualism as a resource, strategy, and a goal ... we may not be able to arrive at a pedagogical breakthrough where an individual child's language and systems of knowledge are respected (p. 197).

An additional layer to Indian HLE policy consists of the role of English in education. As was the case in the literature on African HLE policies, recent research on India has taken various, indeed, competing perspectives on English and the extent to which it threatens Indian languages or constitutes a tool of postcolonial empowerment. These divergent perspectives are tied somewhat to differences in analytical framework adopted in each study. Annamalai (2005) considered HLE policy and English in India in terms of national development. He did not pit Indian languages against English, arguing that neither is necessarily useful for engendering social or political cohesion. Rather, he insisted that the metric for assessing medium-of-instruction policies should be the degree to which they allow for decolonization of Indian education that combines "inculcation of self-pride with self-criticism, of cultural rootedness with cosmopolitanism, of modernization with tradition" (p. 36). Such decolonized education is the key for Annamalai in national development and progress. Vaish (2005) is the most critical of applied linguistic research that conceives of English as an oppressing language. The author is the only among those reviewed here to ground the discussion on ethnographic work in schools investigating language practice. Vaish marshaled that research to argue that English is in fact used by the poorest and most disenfranchised students in Delhi as a means of upward mobility. A. K. Mohanty (2006) was also concerned with alleviating inequality but took a more critical position toward English. He stated that English is the most pervasive medium of instruction in the country, but that disparities in access and resources, both linguistic and material, have "provided the basis for a new social stratification of the literate groups" that places privileged students educated in expensive private English-medium schools at the top and subordinates the rest, including poorer students educated in "low cost English-medium" schools, below them (pp. 276–277). A. K. Mohanty argued for multilingual education in the mother tongue, not as an either-or proposition with respect to Hindi or English, but in conjunction with them, as the most effective means of realizing social justice.

NORTH AMERICA

Despite the fact that the term *heritage language* was coined in Canada, preparations for this article found almost no recent research on Canadian HLE policy. Duff (2008) indicated that most of the significant overviews of policies and programs in Canada were published in the 1980s and 1990s. She offered an explanation as to why so little research has been conducted since: "The dearth of scholarship on HL education in Canada since the early 1990s probably reflects the decline in federal funding for programs and research in the 1990s" (p. 72).

By contrast, a considerable amount of HLE policy research in the United States has appeared. Its emergence in the wake of the events of September 11, 2001, suggests that the focus for most analysis has been the relationship between HLE and national security. The U.S.-based policy research adopts almost universally a resource-based orientation (Ruiz, 1984); that is, in general, recent HLE policy research has identified heritage languages as resources for national security, for strengthening language teacher preparation programs, and for expanding multilingual competency generally. The following discussion takes each in turn.

Recent HLE policy research has focused overwhelmingly on the connections between heritage languages and national security. This connection is also invoked in more general analyses of whether the United States needs a formal language policy, and if so, what that policy should look like. Edwards (2004) acknowledged the increased attention paid to HLE post-9/11 and made the most explicit connection between increased language capacity and preventing terrorism. He referred specifically to Sen. Richard Shelby's (R-AL) comments in a 2002 interview with the *New York Times*, namely, that greater foreign language capacity might have prevented the events of September 11, and thus the intelligence community must recruit more heritage speakers of languages such as Arabic and Farsi. Brecht (2007) positioned HLE as a crucial component in a general language pipeline running from primary through higher education. He argued that HLE as part of such a system could meet three critical policy needs:

> a) an educated citizenry aware of the role of language and culture in the world and in human cognition, b) a broad base of school graduates with functional foreign language skills, and c) a cadre of advanced language specialists capabel of the highest level of linguistic and cultural performance (p. 264).

Additional research takes a language-specific approach to HLE policy. McGinnis (2005) reviewed the status of Chinese language instruction and found that the HL sector accounts for the largest enrollments, upwards of 150,000 HL learners across community, K–12, and university programs. Al-Batal (2007) and Sehlaoui (2008) presented similar overviews for Arabic language education, while Shinge (2008) considered the impact of the National Security Language Initiative of 2006 on Hindi programs.

A complementary set of HLE policy research interrogates the policy connections between national security and heritage languages. Scollon (2004) distinguished between state power, which privileges monolingual practice, and actual social power, which he argued is rooted in dynamic multilingual practice. Scollon maintained that HLE policies positioning multilingualism in the service of the state have pitted both power bases against one another, leading to an insurmountable paradox. Wiley (2007a, 2007b) reviewed contradictory historical policy responses that frame heritage languages at once as a threat and an expedient resource. He argued that policies tying HLE to security terms in fact represent a "crisis of monolingualist ideology" (2007a, p. 255). Allen (2007) raised his critique with respect to Arabic language education specifically and questioned the effectiveness of crisis-driven HLE policy. Lo Bianco (2008) conducted a close textual analysis of two policy documents positioning HLE in the service of national security. He finds that security-based policy "raises subtle and intangible matters of trust, loyalty and social categorization," which can ultimately undermine stated policy intentions (p. 159). Bale (2008) reported similar findings of self-defeating policy in an historical interpretive analysis of Title VI, a long-standing federal language policy tied to national defense and economic competitiveness, and its impact on Arabic as a heritage language.

Despite the overwhelming focus on HLE policy and national security, additional examples of recent scholarship position HLE as a resource for meeting other critical social and educational needs. With respect to preparing future language teachers, HL speakers are identified as a more effective source of language teacher candidates, and HL communities are described as an ideal venue for teacher candidate placements (Magnan, 2008; Zimmer-Loew, 2008). Met (2003) and Roca (2003) also framed their analysis of improving foreign language education in the United States by identifying the essential role that HL learners play in programs that lead to advanced proficiency. Wang (2007) connected her policy analysis of Chinese as a HL with a deeper discussion of developing biliteracy in the United States. She made several recommendations for improving Chinese HLE, with a focus on highly qualified teachers and expanded research, but also positioned Chinese HLE as a resource for expanding what she called "biliterate capital" that can be used in community, professional, and personal domains. Also at a broader ideological level, both García (2005) and Hornberger (2005) framed their analyses of HLE policy in terms of the opportunities HLE offers to break through the fossilized debate over bilingual education in the United States, to create more openness toward education in non-English languages, and to realize a more multilingual society.

The category of languages left out of HLE policy connections to national security and the existing foreign language education system are indigenous languages in the United States. This is not to say that HLE policy research has been silent on the issue. For example, McCarty (2008) presented an overview of indigenous languages as heritage languages in the United States and described three policy frameworks—tribal sovereignty, medium of instruction, and self-determination—that have been used to inform and implement indigenous language programs. Warhol (2009) presented the first comprehensive analysis of the Native American Languages Act of 1990 (NALA). She found two competing interpretations among policy actors involved with its formation and implementation. On the one hand, policy actors understood NALA as being too little, too late to have any significant impact on reversing native language shift; on the other hand, policy actors see NALA as integral to the realization of tribal sovereignty.

This review of HLE policy in the United States has generally excluded important recent research on bilingual education policy, which has focused largely on the silencing of bilingual education effected by the No Child Left Behind Act of 2001 (NCLB). This exclusion is based on the fact that most of this research frames language minority students as English language learners rather than heritage or bilingual students (see Menken, 2008b, and the recent special issue of *Language Policy* on NCLB [Menken, 2008a]).

The final world about HLE policy in the United States relates to intriguing theoretical and analytical developments in the field. Lomawaima and McCarty (2006) proposed safety zone theory in their reading of historical indigenous language education policy. Safety zone theory is an effort to explain, not merely describe, policy shifts over time. Its central premise concerns how dominant national interests and identities (ab)use notions of safety and threat to endorse or marginalize linguistic and cultural difference through policy. Johnson (2009) used his ethnographic study of bilingual education policy and practice in Philadelphia schools to propose a multilevel heuristic with which to analyze policy. The purpose of this analytic tool is to use ethnographic methods for understanding the policy appropriation process at micro and macro levels simultaneously.

OCEANIA

Although language revitalization efforts among the Maori in Aotearoa/New Zealand are both well documented and emulated, limited *recent* HLE policy analysis on these efforts were found. May (2004) and Benton (2007) provide comprehensive overviews of the history of language policy in Aotearoa/New Zealand.[4] May (2004) focused specifically on the development of language nests as a means of Maori language revitalization beginning in 1982. Language nests are immersion programs at the early childhood level that simulate the extended family in the schooling context to facilitate Maori language development. May's analysis highlighted three pressing issues not only for Maori efforts but also for indigenous language revitalization efforts generally. First, formal education programs cannot compensate for language attitudes and practice in society more broadly; thus revitalization efforts need to look beyond the classroom. May also addressed the issue of romanticizing past language use in revitalization efforts and stressed that Maori-medium instruction allows the Maori to pursue cultural and linguistic change on their own terms. Finally, May raised the paradox of state funding for indigenous language revitalization programs. On the one hand, state funding allows for expansion of such programs, but on the other, it may lead to state encroachment on community control.

Historical perspectives on Aboriginal and community languages in Australia form the background to several examples of recent research (Baldauf, 2005; Clyne & Kipp, 2006; de Courcy, 2005; Smolicz & Secombe, 2003). These overviews have traced the development of promotional HLE policy in Australia in support of heritage languages on three levels: as subjects in formal education, in Saturday community programs, and in after-hours programs auxiliary to the regular school day. In each case, the authors commented on the decline of state support for community languages. De Courcy (2005) argued, "we seem to have gone from a position in this country where we were the envy of other countries for our language policies to a position where the country now operates without a languages policy at all" (pp. 179–180). In addition, these overviews identified a connection between HLE policy and national interest concerns somewhat similar to those raised in the United States. Clyne and Kipp (2006), for example, analyzed HLE policy in Australia since the 1990s and found that official support for community, especially Asian, languages has often been framed in terms of their use for economic development and competition. They noted, however, that:

> The push for Asian languages and studies almost completely disregarded the local presence of communities of speakers of these languages, and other significant Asian languages in the Australian context, such as Vietnamese or Filipino, were not included at all (p. 10).

The authors questioned the effectiveness of tying support for community languages to instrumentalist aims.

Liu and Lo Bianco (2007) also pursued this theme of geopolitical rationales driving policy support for Asian languages in Australia. They described this support as connected to political discourses in Australia in the 1980s and 1990s that began to frame Asia as "our region" (p. 96) and raise the question of whether Australia were in fact an Asian nation. Concurrent to this discourse shift, education in Asian languages expanded greatly: "In a relatively short period of time key Asian languages came from the margins of education provision to be the most widely taught second languages at all levels of education, replacing the historical dominance of European languages" (p. 97). While the authors stated that Japanese has in fact been the main beneficiary of this expansion, their analysis comprised a case study of HLE policy toward Chinese. Their discussion focused largely on the mismatch between diverse types of Chinese language learners and the structure of Chinese language programs across the education system and in community schools.

Additional HLE policy in Australia research has focused on specific case studies of community languages or states. Smolicz and Secombe (2003) included in their extensive overview of HLE policy a discussion of Cambodians in South Australia. Their discussion was based on data regarding Cambodians, mostly of Chinese heritage, who were university students at the time the research was conducted. They found that these students successfully took advantage of community schools to develop literacy in Khmer while they acquired English language and literacy in public school. Smolicz and Secombe noted that a South Australian policy acknowledging Khmer as a subject for university entrance exams has benefited the students, but they also suggested that students have pursued literacy in Khmer for noninstrumentalist reasons. Mercurio and Scarino (2005) took a wider perspective on the South Australian policy of acknowledging community languages for secondary graduation and university entrance exam purposes. They framed policy as a process of legitimatization in which heritage languages are "grafted" (p. 145) onto socially accepted structures such as school administrations and curricula. The authors acknowledged the symbolic value of the South Australian policy, but they questioned its ultimate impact by analyzing data revealing low enrollments community languages in the state. Nicholls (2005) conducted an historical case study of Aboriginal HLE policy in the Northern Territory between 1972 and 1998. She recounted the rise and fall of bilingual Aboriginal-English programs and how state authorities' perceptions that English skills were in decline led to the dismantling of formal bilingual education policy. Beyond state-level analyses, research in Australia has considered HLE policy at the institutional level as well. For example, Hatoss (2006) conducted a micro-policy analysis of Hungarian language maintenance in Australia and found that nongovernmental community organizations have played a critical role in leveraging state financial support for community languages. The author concluded that micro-level HL planning, far from being merely local implementations of state or federal policy, is a "necessary complement" (p. 288) to macro-level efforts.

Baldauf (2005) and de Courcy (2005) conducted case studies in separate contexts but came to similar conclusions. The former study examined HLE policy vis-à-vis Aboriginal languages in New South Wales; the latter was a multiple case study of HLE policy in the Northern Territory toward Auslan, a deaf language, and Italian. In both articles, the authors identified a number of practical issues complicating the realization of HLE policy. Many factors related to teachers in HL programs. Baldauf (2005) acknowledged that, although teachers in community schools have brought extensive language and cultural skills, the spectrum of proficiency in the HL has varied significantly. Both authors stated that teachers in HL programs needed more extensive training in language teaching; de Courcy (2005) stressed that training for primary level education is also needed. Additional factors impacting the effectiveness of HL programs auxiliary to public schools included HLs not counting toward credit within formal school accreditation practices, waning state funding, and sociolinguistic factors such as prestige attached to the HL.

THE REPUBLIC OF IRELAND AND THE UNITED KINGDOM

Recent research on HLE policy in the Republic of Ireland and the United Kingdom has focused almost exclusively on policies related to Irish, Scottish Gaelic, and Welsh. Wei (2006) did review the history and contemporary status of complementary schools for immigrant and ethnic minority children in the United Kingdom, but policy was not a significant focus of the discussion. Jones and Martin-Jones (2004) and Smith (2003) both provided sociolinguistic overviews of Welsh and Scottish Gaelic, respectively, in their discussion of language revitalization efforts. Jones and Martin-Jones combined a critical-historical overview of national policy toward Welsh with a discussion of an ethnographic study of bilingual Welsh-English mathematics classrooms. They maintained that although policy support for Welsh-medium instruction has been strong, the language still faces formidable obstacles. First, despite a general increase in Welsh-medium programs, Welsh acquisition at home has continued to decline. Second, the shift among secondary students has continued to increase. And finally, there has been a greater diversity in Welsh proficiency among students entering school, straining the ability of Welsh-medium programs to cater to students' linguistic needs. They called for further ethnographic study to better understand classroom-level appropriation of Welsh HLE policy. While Smith's discussion was more focused on the legal framework behind Gaelic HLE policy, she cited similar challenges facing Gaelic. One specific factor she mentioned is the unwillingness of native speakers of Gaelic to become teachers in Gaelic-English bilingual programs. Nevertheless, she concluded that "the law is unequivocal in its support for mother tongue education" in Scotland (p. 143).

The policy status of Irish in Northern Ireland schools is examined in English- and Irish-medium contexts (McKendry, 2007; Ó Baoill, 2007). After presenting an overview of the Irish language and HLE policy toward it in Northern Ireland,

McKendry (2007) analyzed current education provisions for the language in English-medium schools. He raised doubts as to the future of the language in English-medium schools based on the fact that it has been most often offered in a "foreign language" structure, and that limited training has been provided through teacher preparation programs to teach the language. Ó Baoill (2007) also provided an historical overview of Irish in Northern Ireland with a specific focus on the central role played by Irish-medium HLE policy in revitalizing the language. He argued, however, that the limited amount of "pedagogical, educational, linguistic, and sociolinguistic research" (p. 423) on Irish immersion education has inhibited coordination across programs in Northern Ireland. In addition, he identified similar issues facing HLE policy for Irish-medium instruction, including lack of articulation across program levels and of well-trained teachers with sufficient competence in the language.

Laoire (2005) provided an extensive historical and sociolinguistic overview of Irish in the Republic of Ireland. His discussion emphasized that "since the inception of the Irish Free State in 1922, the education system has been seen as a cornerstone of the movement for the revitalization of Irish. In fact, the espoused planning policies for revitalization devolved almost entirely on the schools" (p. 261). The focus of much of this language planning has been in the Gaeltacht in western Ireland, a region the government considers to be Irish speaking. Immersion approaches to Irish education in the Gaeltacht date back to the 1930s, and the number of immersion programs began to rise again in the 1980s and 1990s. However, the majority of students across the Republic now study Irish as a school subject. Despite improvements in how Irish is studied—for example, the use of communicative syllabi focusing on "everyday" rather than "school" Irish (p. 276) and the fact that Irish has gained in prestige since becoming a working language of the European Union—Laoire (2005) argued that the language still faces important challenges. In addition to factors identified in other HLE policy research, Laoire added that immigration to Ireland, which has lead to an increase in students in school who speak neither English nor Irish, has further complicated the efforts to meet the needs of all its students while developing proficiency in Irish.

Two additional HLE policy studies in the Irish context shift their focus from national to institutional and interpersonal levels. Chríost (2006) analyzed census data from 2002 and found that there were more daily users of Irish in Greater

Dublin than in the Gaeltacht, despite decades of formal HLE policy focusing on Irish acquisition in the latter region. The data also reflected that school has been the primary site of Irish acquisition, not the home. Chríost argued that the discrepancy between formal policy and actual language practice suggests that micro-level language planning at the community level, modeled in fact on Welsh efforts, might provide better results in revitalizing the language. Ó hIfearnáin (2007) drew similar conclusions based on his fieldwork in specific communities in the Gaeltacht region of Ireland. He surveyed residents and their attitudes toward formal HLE policy, which calls for children to be raised exclusively in Irish and for Irish-medium instruction at school. Participants reported general support for Irish use at home, although responses describing their practice reflected divergence from their stated opinion. Participants also generally supported Irish-medium instruction, but claimed that their children were nevertheless English-dominant. Moreover, some 25% of respondents objected to Irish-medium schooling. Ó hIfearnáin identified a gap between official HLE policy that considers the Gaeltacht to be Irish speaking, when in fact it is a bilingual region, and argued:

> From the outset the paradox of the state wanting more Irish speakers, while the Gaeltacht Irish speakers themselves want to be bilingual, has led to what might be called a "discursive stand off" whereby the state seems to impose a monolingual model that is at variance with the wishes of those for whom it was planned (p. 526).

He concluded that what appears as lack of support for Irish-medium instruction is not a rejection of Irish per se but rather a preference for Irish-English bilingualism.

COMMON THREADS AND FUTURE RESEARCH

Before highlighting the common themes emerging from this broad review of HLE policy research, it is important to recall the caution referenced earlier about collapsing too many disparate linguistic, historical, cultural, and social contexts under one analytical term such as heritage language. Even while treading lightly with this caution in mind, the frequency with which similar logistical and programmatic concerns are cited in the research reviewed here is remarkable. In wealthy nations and developing ones alike, in rural contexts as in urban ones, and with respect to languages carrying the wide array of labels listed in the introduction to this article, researchers have consistently cited similar key factors impacting the success of HLE policies. These factors include linguistically and pedagogically competent teachers for HL programs, curricular materials in the target HL that are age and culturally appropriate, issues of language standardization and corpus planning, HL assessment, and finding ways to integrate multiple venues for HLE into existing administrative and accreditation systems.

While researchers consistently cite school-based factors impacting HLE, they also frequently conclude that formal schooling cannot be the lone site of HL revitalization or education programs. This conclusion holds not only in areas where schools have played a critical role in HLE and language revitalization, such as Aotearoa/New Zealand, Ireland, and the United Kingdom, but also where parental, educator, and community opinion is conflicted over where the HL should be taught (i.e., at home or in school).

The preceding discussion, however, uncovered two important tensions in the literature. The first relates to the historical and intellectual development of LPP overall. As LPP developed as a field of applied linguistic research, it often concerned itself with language "problems" faced by newly independent nations. Policy decisions regarding official languages, media of instruction, and language education generally were often tied closely to questions of national development. Those concerns still dominate much HLE policy research, as evidenced by the literature regarding HLE as a solution to "problems" of national security, economic competition, and socioeconomic development. This language-as-problem approach is deeply intertwined with assumptions about the role languages can, or better *should*, play in building, maintaining, and expanding nation-state power. The tension obtains inasmuch as HLE policy research increasingly adopts critical or postmodern theoretical frameworks that situate power and power conflicts at more localized levels in society that transcend the nation-state as a unit of analysis.

The second tension consistent across the research reviewed here is the contested relationship between HLs and English. Whether English is framed as a threat, as a nativized language, or a tool for empowerment and integration into a globalized world varied dramatically across the research reviewed here. Moreover, and particularly in postcolonial contexts, there is the additional issue where a regional language that is neither English nor the local HL was perceived by researcher and research participants as a linguistic threat. It is unlikely that consensus will be achieved with respect to whether English, or a national or regional language, is a threat or a tool of postcolonial identity construction and empowerment. Taken together, however, these common themes and tensions undergird another conclusion argued in much of the literature reviewed here, namely, that in order for HLE policy to be effective, there cannot be a one-size-fits-all approach.

In addition to these common themes, the literature reviewed here suggests multiple areas and questions in need of scholarly attention. The majority of the work cited here comprised single-nation case studies in which the bulk of the discussion was dedicated to an historical overview of language policy in pre-colonial, colonial, and postcolonial times. Another typical approach to analysis was to square HLE policies against sociolinguistic analysis of demographics and census data that included figures regarding language use and/or heritage. In some cases, the literature reviewed here was based on empirical research, and it seems that the most frequent approach included survey, questionnaire, and focus group data assessing attitudes and language ideologies of a given policy-relevant population. The two approaches to HLE policy analysis least frequently applied in the research reviewed here were historiography and ethnography. In each case, however, these approaches to HLE policy analysis stand to provide critical insights into how HLE policy works and has worked, especially when there seems to be such consensus that there can be no universal approach to HLE policy and practice.

NOTES

1 This list consciously excludes dialects and language varieties. This choice is merely pragmatic: To include research about dialects and language variation, (e.g. African American English, Scots, dialectal spectra in Africa or India, Singlish) would have broadened the scope of HLE policy research too far for one review.

2 The term *minoritized* recognizes that marginalized or otherwise disenfranchised languages may, in fact, be spoken by the majority of people.

3 However, the German literature regarding German language learners makes frequent use of the term *Herkunftsprache*, which translates to *heritage* or *ancestral*

language in English.
4 Aotearoa is the Maori name for New Zealand. Policy research on Maori often lists both names in this format.

REFERENCES

Adegbija, E. (2004). Language policy and planning in Nigeria. *Current Issues in Language Planning, 5*, 181–246.

Al-Batal, M. (2007). Arabic and national language education policy. *The Modern Language Journal, 91*, 268–271.

Allen, R. (2007). Arabic—flavor of the moment: Whence, why, and how? *The Modern Language Journal, 91*, 258–261.

Agnihotri, R. K. (2007). Identity and multilinguality: The case of India. In A. B. M. Tsui & J. W. Tollefson (Eds.), *Language policy, culture, and identity in Asian contexts* (pp. 185–204). Mahwah, NJ: Erlbaum.

Annamalai, E. (2005). Nation-building in a globalised world: Language choice and education in India. In A. M. Y. Lin & P. W. Martin (Eds.), *Decolonization, globalization: Language-in-education policy and practice* (pp. 20–37). Clevedon, UK: Multilingual Matters.

Baldauf, R. B., Jr. (2005). Coordinating government and community support for community language teaching in Australia: Overview with special attention to New South Wales. *International Journal of Bilingual Education and Bilingualism, 8*, 132–144.

Bale, J. (2008). *When Arabic is the "target" language: Title VI, national security, and Arabic language programs, 1958–1991*. Unpublished doctoral dissertation, Arizona State University. Tempe, AZ.

Bamgbose, A. (2004). *Language of instruction policy and practice in Africa*. Dakar, Senegal: Regional Office for Education in Africa, UNESCO. Retrieved June 5, 2009, from www.unesco.org/education/languages_2004/languageinstruction_africa.pdf.

Benton, R. A. (2007). Mauri or mirage? The status of the Maori language in Aotearoa New Zealand in the third millennium. In A. B. M. Tsui & J. W. Tollefson (Eds.), *Language policy, culture, and identity in Asian contexts* (pp. 163–181). Mahwah, NJ: Erlbaum.

Brecht, R. D. (2007). National language educational policy in the nation's interests: Why? How? Who is responsible? *The Modern Language Journal, 91*, 264–265.

Brutt-Griffler, J., & Makoni, S. (2005). The use of *heritage language:* An African perspective. *The Modern Language Journal, 89*, 609–612.

Chew, P. G.-L. (2007). Remaking Singapore: Language, culture, and identity in a globalized world. In A. B. M. Tsui & J. W. Tollefson (Eds.), *Language policy, culture, and identity in Asian contexts* (pp. 73–94). Mahwah, NJ: Erlbaum.

Chríost, D. M. G. (2006). Micro-level language planning in Ireland. *Current Issues in Language Planning, 7*, 230–250.

Clyne, M., & Kipp, S. (2006). Australia's community languages. *International Journal of the Sociology of Language, 180*, 7–21.

Cummins, J. (2005). A proposal for action: Strategies for recognizing heritage language competence as a learning resource within the mainstream classroom. *The Modern Language Journal, 89*, 585–592.

de Bot, K., & Gorter, D. (2005). A European perspective on heritage languages. *The Modern Language Journal, 89*, 612–616.

de Courcy, M. (2005). Policy challenges for bilingual and immersion education in Australia: Literacy and language choices for users of Aboriginal languages, Auslan, and Italian. *International Journal of Bilingual Education and Bilingualism, 8*, 178–187.

David, M. K., & Govindasamy, S. (2007). The construction of national identity and globalization in multilingual Malaysia. In A. B. M. Tsui & J. W. Tollefson (Eds.), *Language policy, culture, and identity in Asian contexts* (pp. 55–72). Mahwah, NJ: Erlbaum.

Djité, P. G. (2008). *The sociolinguistics of development in Africa*. Clevedon, UK: Multilingual Matters.

Dixon, L. (2009). Assumptions behind Singapore's language-in-education policy: Implications for language planning and second language acquisition. *Language Policy, 8*, 117–137.

Duff, P. A. (2008). Heritage language education in Canada. In D. M. Brinton, O. Kagan, & S. Bauckus (Eds.), *Heritage language education: A new field emerging* (pp. 71–90). New York & London: Routledge.

Edwards, J. D. (2004). The role of languages in a post-9/11 United States. *The Modern Language Journal, 88*, 268–271.

Fishman, J. A. (2001). 300-plus years of heritage language education in the United States. In J. K. Peyton, D. A. Ranard, & S. McGinnis (Eds.), *Heritage languages in America: Preserving a national resource* (pp. 81–98). Washington, DC, & McHenry, IL: Center for Applied Linguistics and Delta Systems.

Fishman, J. A. (2006). Three hundred-plus years of heritage language education in the United States. In G. Valdés, J. A. Fishman, R. Chávez, & W. Pérez (Eds.), *Developing minority language resources: The case of Spanish in California* (pp. 12–23). Clevedon, UK: Multilingual Matters.

García, O. (2005). Positioning heritage languages in the United States. *The Modern Language Journal, 89*, 601–605.

Gill, S. (2005). Language policy in Malaysia: Reversing direction. *Language Policy, 4*, 241–260.

Hatoss, A. (2006). Community-level approaches in language planning: The case of Hungarian

in Australia. *Current Issues in Language Planning, 7,* 287–306.
Hopkins, M. (2006). Policies without planning?: The medium of instruction issue in Hong Kong. *Language and Education: An International Journal, 20,* 270–286.
Hornberger, N. H. (2005). Opening and filling up ideological and implementational spaces in heritage language education. *The Modern Language Journal, 89,* 605–609.
Hornberger, N. H., & Wang, S. C. (2008). Who are our heritage language learners? Identity and biliteracy in heritage language education in the United States. In D. M. Brinton, O. Kagan, & S. Bauckus (Eds.), *Heritage language education: A new field emerging* (pp. 3–35). New York & London: Routledge.
Igboanusi, H., & Peter, L. (2004). Oppressing the oppressed: The threats of Hausa and English to Nigeria's minority languages. *International Journal of the Sociology of Language, 170,* 131–140.
Iyamu, E. O. S., & Aduwa Ogiegbaen, S. E. (2007). Parents and teachers' perceptions of mother-tongue medium of instruction policy in Nigerian primary schools. *Language, Culture, & Curriculum, 20,* 97–108.
Johnson, D. C. (2009). Ethnography of language policy. *Language Policy, 8,* 139–159.
Jones, D. V., & Martin-Jones, M. (2004). Bilingual education and language revitalization in Wales: Past achievements and current issues. In J. W. Tollefson & A. B. M. Tsui (Eds.), *Medium of instruction policies: Which agenda? Whose agenda?* (pp. 43–70). Mahwah, NJ: Erlbaum.
Kamwendo, G., & Mooko, T. (2006). Language planning in Botswana and Malawi: A comparative study. *International Journal of the Sociology of Language, 182,* 117–133.
Kamwendo, G. H. (2005). Language planning from below: An example from northern Malawi. *Language Policy, 4,* 143–165.
Khubchandani, L. M. (2003). Defining mother tongue education in plurilingual contexts. *Language Policy, 2,* 239–254.
Lai, M.-L. (2005). Language attitudes of the first postcolonial generation in Hong Kong secondary schools. *Language in Society, 34,* 363–388.
Laoire, M. Ó. (2005). The language planning situation in Ireland. *Current Issues in Language Planning, 6,* 251–314.
Levinson, B. A. U., & Sutton, M. (2001). Introduction: Policy as/in practice—a sociocultural approach to the study of educational policy. In M. Sutton & B. A. U. Levinson (Eds.), *Policy as practice: Toward a comparative sociocultural analysis of educational policy* (pp. 1–21). Westport, CT: Ablex.
Lin, A. M. Y. (2005). Critical, transdisciplinary perspectives on language-in-education policy and practice in postcolonial contexts: The case of Hong Kong. In A. M. Y. Lin & P. W. Martin (Eds.), *Decolonization, globalization: Language-in-education policy and practice*

(pp. 38–54). Clevedon, UK: Multilingual Matters.

Liu, G., & Lo Bianco, J. (2007). Teaching Chinese, teaching in Chinese, teaching the Chinese. *Language Policy*, *6*, 95–117.

Lo Bianco, J. (2008). Tense times and language planning. *Current Issues in Language Planning*, *9*, 155–178.

Lomawaima, K. T., & McCarty, T. L. (2006). *To remain an Indian: Lessons in democracy from a century of Native American education*. New York: Teachers College Press.

Magnan, S. S. (2008). What is needed for global literacy to become an education reality? Summary of a discussion group. *The Modern Language Journal*, *92*, 628–630.

Makoni, S. B., Dube, B., & Mashiri, P. (2006). Zimbabwe colonial and post-colonial language policy and planning practices. *Current Issues in Language Planning*, *7*, 377–414.

Makoni, S., Makoni, B., & Nyika, N. (2008). Language planning from below: The case of the Tonga in Zimbabwe. *Current Issues in Language Planning*, *9*, 413–439.

Martin, P. W. (2005). "Safe" language practices in two rural schools in Malaysia: Tensions between policy and practice. In A. M. Y. Lin & P. W. Martin (Eds.), *Decolonization, globalization: Language-in-education policy and practice* (pp. 74–97). Clevedon, UK: Multilingual Matters.

Matiki, A. J. (2006). Literacy, ethnolinguistic diversity, and transitional bilingual education in Malawi. *International Journal of Bilingual Education and Bilingualism*, *9*, 239–254.

May, S. (2004). Maori-medium education in Aotearoa/New Zealand. In J. W. Tollefson & A. B. M. Tsui (Eds.), *Medium of instruction policies: Which agenda? Whose agenda?* (pp. 21–41). Mahwah, NJ: Erlbaum.

McCarty, T. L. (2008). Native American languages as heritage mother tongues. *Language, Culture and Curriculum*, *21*, 201–225.

McKendry, E. (2007). Minority-language education in a situation of conflict: Irish in English-medium schools in Northern Ireland. *International Journal of Bilingual Education and Bilingualism*, *10*, 394–409.

McGinnis, S. (2005). More than a silver bullet: The role of Chinese as a heritage language in the United States. *The Modern Language Journal*, *89*, 592–594.

Menken, K. (2008a). Editorial 7.3: Introduction to thematic issue. *Language Policy*, *7*, 191–199.

Menken, K. (2008b). *English learners left behind: Standardized testing as language policy*. Clevedon, UK: Multilingual Matters.

Mercurio, A., & Scarino, A. (2005). Heritage languages at upper secondary level in South Australia: A struggle for legitimacy. *International Journal of Bilingual Education and Bilingualism*, *8*, 145–159.

Met, M. (2003). Developing language education policies for our schools. *The Modern*

Language Journal, 87, 589–592.

Mohanty, A. K. (2006). Multilingualism of the unequals and predicaments of education in India: Mother tongue or other tongue? In O. García, T. Skutnabb-Kangas, & M. E. Torres-Guzmán (Eds.), *Imagining multilingual schools: Languages in education and glocalization* (pp. 262–283). Clevedon, UK: Multilingual Matters.

Mohanty, P. (2002). British language policy in 19th century India and the Oriya language movement. *Language Policy, 1,* 53–73.

Musau, P. M. (2003). Linguistic human rights in Africa: Challenges and prospects for indigenous languages in Kenya. *Language, Culture & Curriculum, 16,* 155–164.

Nicholls, C. (2005). Death by a thousand cuts: Indigenous language bilingual education programmes in the Northern Territory of Australia, 1972–1998. *International Journal of Bilingual Education and Bilingualism, 8,* 160–177.

Ó Baoill, D. P. (2007). Origins of Irish-medium education: The dynamic core of language revitalisation in Northern Ireland. *International Journal of Bilingual Education and Bilingualism, 10,* 410–427.

Ó hIfearnáin, T. (2007). Raising children to be bilingual in the Gaeltacht: Language preference and practice. *International Journal of Bilingual Education and Bilingualism, 10,* 510–528.

Omoniyi, T. (2003). Local policies and global forces: Multiliteracy and Africa's indigenous languages. *Language Policy, 2,* 133–152.

Ricento, T. (Ed.). (2006). *An introduction to language policy: Theory and method.* Malden, MA: Blackwell.

Ricento, T., & Hornberger, N. (1996). Unpeeling the onion: Language planning and policy in the ELT profession. *TESOL Quarterly, 30,* 401–427.

Roca, A. (2003). Towards societal bilingualism: The complementary need for foreign and heritage language policies. *The Modern Language Journal, 87,* 588–589.

Rubdy, R. (2005). Remaking Singapore for the new age: Official ideology and the realities of practice in language-in-education. In A. M. Y. Lin & P. W. Martin (Eds.), *Decolonization, globalization: Language-in-education policy and practice* (pp. 55–73). Clevedon, UK: Multilingual Matters.

Ruiz, R. (1984). Orientations in language planning. *NABE Journal, 8,* 15–34.

Scollon, R. (2004). Teaching language and culture as hegemonic practice. *The Modern Language Journal, 88,* 271–274.

Sehlaoui, A. S. (2008). Language learning, heritage, and literacy in the USA: The case of Arabic. *Language, Culture and Curriculum, 21,* 280–291.

Shinge, M. (2008). The National security language initiative and the teaching of Hindi. *Language, Culture and Curriculum, 21,* 269–279.

Smith, R. K. (2003). Mother tongue education and the law: A legal review of bilingualism with reference to Scottish Gaelic. *International Journal of Bilingual Education and Bilingualism, 6*, 129–145.

Smolicz, J., & Secombe, M. (2003). Assimilation or pluralism? Changing policies for minority languages education in Australia. *Language Policy, 2*, 3–25.

Tembe, J., & Norton, B. (2008). Promoting local languages in Ugandan primary schools: The community as stakeholder. *The Canadian Modern Language Review / La Revue Canadienne des Langues Vivantes, 65*, 33–60.

Tse, S., Shum, M., Ki, W., & Chan, Y. (2007). The medium dilemma for Hong Kong secondary schools. *Language Policy, 6*, 135–162.

Tsui, A. B. M. (2007). Language policy and the social construction of identity: The case of Hong Kong. In A. B. M. Tsui & J. W. Tollefson (Eds.), *Language policy, culture, and identity in Asian contexts* (pp. 121–142). Mahwah, NJ: Erlbaum.

Vaish, V. (2005). A peripherist view of English as a language of decolonization in post-colonial India. *Language Policy, 4*, 187–206.

Valdés, G. (2001). Heritage language students: Profiles and possibilities. In J. K. Peyton, D. A. Ranard, & S. McGinnis (Eds.), *Heritage languages in America: Preserving a national resource* (pp. 37–80). Washington, DC, & McHenry, IL: Center for Applied Linguistics and Delta Systems.

Wang, S. C. (2007). Building societal capital: Chinese in the US. *Language Policy, 7*, 27–52.

Warhol, L. (2009). *Native American language education as policy-in-practice: An interpretive policy analysis of the Native American Languages Act of 1990/1992*. Unpublished doctoral dissertation, Arizona State University. Tempe, AZ.

Wei, Li. (2006). Complementary schools, past, present and future. *Language and Education: An International Journal, 20*, 76–83.

Wiley, T. G. (2005). The reemergence of heritage and community language policy in the U.S. national spotlight. *The Modern Language Journal, 89*, 594–601.

Wiley, T. G. (2007a). Heritage and community languages in the national language debate. *The Modern Language Journal, 91*, 252–255.

Wiley, T. G. (2007b). The foreign language "crisis" in the U.S.: Are heritage and community languages the remedy? *Critical Inquiry in Language Studies, 4*, 179–205.

Zimmer-Loew, H. (2008). An audacious goal: Recruiting, preparing, and retaining high-quality language teachers in the 21st century. *The Modern Language Journal, 92*, 625–628.

The Heart of Heritage: Sociocultural Dimensions of Heritage Language Learning

Agnes Weiyun He

The very notion of heritage language (HL) is a sociocultural one insofar as it is defined in terms of a group of people who speak it. Heritage languages also have a sociocultural function, both as a means of communication and as a way of identifying and transforming sociocultural groups. This article surveys two broad approaches to research on the sociocultural dimensions of HL learning. While both of these approaches acknowledge the close connection and mutual dependency between HL learning processes and sociocultural processes, they differ in that one of them takes a correlational perspective, and the other a social constructivist perspective. This article reviews a selective body of work conducted from each of the two perspectives and concludes with a discussion of the implications of the sociocultural complexity associated with HL learning for research and practice.

My home language is Chinese. My parents are from China. They praised me, scolded me, all in Chinese. ... My Chinese is really bad. I can't read and I can only write my name. But when I think of Chinese, I think of my mom, dad, and home. It is the language of my home, and my heart (Jason, a learner of Chinese as a heritage language).

INTRODUCTION

Researchers have not reached a consensus about a precise, scientific definition of a heritage language (HL) learner (Wiley & Valdés, 2000). In North America, the term *heritage language* has been used to refer to an immigrant, indigenous, or ancestral language that a speaker has a personal relevance and desire to (re)connect with (Cummins, 2005; Fishman, 2001; Wiley, 2001). The term has been used synonymously with *community language*, *native language*, and *mother tongue* to refer to a language other than English used by immigrants and their children. In addition, HL students have been referred to as *native speakers, quasi-native speakers, residual speakers, bilingual speakers*, and *home-background speakers* (Valdés, 1997). The range of terms reflects the range in proficiency among HL speakers and the diversity in the social status of the HLs.

While some have highlighted the learner's level of language proficiency, others, such as Fishman (2001), have emphasized whether the learner has a "particular family relevance" (p. 69) and an affiliation with and allegiance to an ethnolinguistic group. Valdés (2001) defined the HL learner broadly as "a language student who is raised in a home where a non-English target language is spoken and who speaks or at least understands the language and is to some degree bilingual in and in English" (p. 38). Van Deusen-Scholl (2003) characterized HL learners as "a heterogeneous group ranging from fluent native speakers to non-speakers who may be generations removed, but who may feel culturally connected to a language" (p. 221). She distinguished heritage learners from learners with a heritage motivation. The former are those who have achieved some degree of proficiency in the home language and/or have been raised with strong cultural connections, while the latter are "those that seek to reconnect with their family's heritage through language, even though the linguistic evidence of that connection may have been lost for generations" (Van Deusen-Scholl, p. 222). From an educational, pedagogical perspective, it is the students with some level of proficiency that present the most significant and practical challenges to the language teaching profession. Hence for the purposes of this article, I follow the definitions proposed by Valdés and Van Deusen-Scholl and consider HL learners as those who have an ethnolinguistic affiliation to the HL and who have some level of proficiency in oral and/or literacy skills but may need to make adjustments in their speech as they move from informal oral settings to formal settings or to written communication and to develop a wider range of registers and genres for settings, audiences, and purposes other than friends and family (Roca & Colombi, 2003). Furthermore, HL learners manifest a set of ambiguities and complications, which are perhaps less salient in the second or foreign language learner or mother tongue learner and which can be sources of both challenges and opportunities (He & Xiao, 2008).

To the HL learner, an HL may provide valuable personal, familial, and national resources, or it can become a linguistic and cultural liability. There have been substantive debates at social and political as well as cultural and linguistic levels on whether HLs should be maintained and whether the loss of HLs is part of the price to be paid for becoming acculturated into the mainstream society (Fishman, 1991; Wong Fillmore, 1991, 2000). The maintenance of HLs and cultures has been a major challenge for linguistic minorities, whether immigrant, refugee, or indigenous. Almost all societies around the world have witnessed overt or covert suppression of cultural and linguistic difference. As Hornberger (1997) put it, dominant languages such as English can become *predator* languages that endanger other languages. In response, some communities and individuals have taken active and proactive measures to ensure that their HL is passed down from one generation to the next, while other communities and individuals have let their HL disappear gradually or drastically.

What are the decisive factors for the success of HL development and maintenance? How do learner attitude, motivation, and social network enhance or hinder HL development? Why is it that we often witness a resistance to HL learning when learners are young but subsequently an embrace of HL after learners come of age? What is the impact of learner identity (projected as well as perceived, interactional as well as developmental) on the HL learning process? How do the political history, geography, demography, and social status of the HL impact its maintenance or attrition? What is the role of classroom cultural and interactional practices in shaping the HL development trajectory? What factors (e.g., amount of input, years of schooling, parental educational levels, and gender) determine whether HL learners are literate in the HL? Should the learners' home varieties of their HLs (e.g., various dialects in Chinese or varieties of Spanish) be revitalized or eradicated? How do language ideologies interact with particular pedagogical objectives?

The quintessential and intrinsic sociocultural nature is perhaps more salient in the case of HLs than other languages. The very notion of HL is a sociocultural one insofar as it is defined in terms of a group of people who speak it. Heritage languages also have a sociocultural function, both as a means of communication and as a way of identifying and transforming sociocultural groups. In this article, I will survey two broad approaches to research on the sociocultural dimensions of HL learning. While both of these approaches acknowledge the close connection and mutual dependency between HL learning processes and sociocultural processes, they differ in that one of them takes a correlational perspective, and the other a social constructivist perspective. I will review a selective body of work conducted from each of the two perspectives and conclude with a discussion of the implications of the sociocultural complexity associated with HL learning for research and practice.

CORRELATIONAL STUDIES OF SOCIOCULTURAL DIMENSIONS OF HERITAGE LANGUAGES

Rooted in essentialist paradigms and commonly adopted in developmental psycholinguistics and sociolinguistics, a correlational approach assumes sociocultural parameters as a priori givens and takes for granted these parameters as independent variables. It considers sociocultural parameters as having a sociohistorical reality that is independent of language behavior. It assumes that sociocultural traits are persistent and consistent across times and situations. It asks how an HL learner with specific, static traits behaves in the process of HL development. For example, do members of specific socioeconomic, ethnic, gender, generational or linguistic groups maintain their HLs, and if so, how? What is the relationship between phonological development and the learner's place of birth? What is the relationship between motivation and success in HL learning? In this framework, the researcher treats sociocultural variables as explanations for HL variation. Among the most common means of data collection are various measures of language proficiency (listening, speaking, reading, and writing), tests of academic performance, quantitative observations of language use, questionnaires, and attitude or motivation scales.

In one of the first few full-length books dedicated to one single HL population in a given setting, Gibbons and Ramirez (2004) examined the simultaneous development of English and Spanish as an HL in a given speech community in Sydney, Australia. The study investigated a set of variables that contribute to varying degrees of proficiency—societal factors, interpersonal contact, education, media and literacy practice, and attitudes and beliefs. It considered the impact of macro-level societal infrastructures and institutions on the development and maintenance of bilingualism and biliteracy. It listed societal variables including political history, geography, demography, status, institutions and media, and the many subcategories within each of these, and then examined each of them one by one for both English and Spanish. The authors correlated the sociodemographic information of the Hispanic teenager population under study with their levels of language proficiency, concluding that there was little correlation between social class and language achievement.

Gibbons and Ramirez (2004) also evaluated the impact of social practices and resources on spoken language development by correlating various categories of social network ties, the strength of the contact, and the mode of the contact (whether face to face or distant) with learners' oral proficiency, grammar, vocabulary, and overall confidence in using the language. By the same token, this study examined attitudes and beliefs that support or undermine the maintenance of minority languages. These attitudes and beliefs included aesthetic and social judgments of a particular language or variety, views concerning bilingualism and biculturalism, projections of the vitality of the minority language, and positioning of the learner vis-à-vis different cultures and languages, as well as beliefs about language proficiency. The researchers used a combination of open-ended and close-ended questions to provide a profile of the attitudes of their subjects and to identify attitude clusters and performed statistical correlations with the proficiency measures.

Similarly, Jia (2008) reported findings from a study on first-generation Chinese immigrants in New York City in terms of their speaking, reading, and writing skills for each 2-year interval of their residence in the United States. A grammaticality judgment task in Mandarin was also used to measure participants' sensitivity to Mandarin grammar. The findings showed that, in certain contexts, at the same time as the exposure to English and the English skills grew steadily, HL skills continuously declined over the years. Jia concluded that age of immigration, social economic status, and self-reported Chinese cultural identity are major variables that correlate with current proficiency in Chinese as a heritage language.

Treating learners' language status (HL learner versus foreign language learner) as an independent variable and adopting both proficiency tests and self-assessment measures, Kondo-Brown (2005) investigated (a) whether Japanese as a heritage language learners would demonstrate language behaviors distinctively different from those of traditional Japanese as a foreign language learners, and (b) which domains of language use and skills would specifically exhibit such differentiation. Kondo-Brown's findings suggested that there were striking similarities between the learner group and students with at least one Japanese-speaking grandparent, but without a Japanese-speaking parent, and students of Japanese descent without either a Japanese-speaking parent or grandparent. In contrast, students with at least one Japanese-speaking parent proved to be substantially different from other groups in (a) grammatical knowledge, (b) listening and reading skills, (c) self-assessed use or choice of Japanese, and (d) self-ratings of a number of can-do tasks that represented a wide range of abilities. Similarly, Kaufman (2005) took HL and native language as independent variables, investigated narratives produced by speakers of Hebrew as an HL and compared them to monolingual norms. The heritage narrative data showed considerable fragmentation in all aspects of the language. In comparison with monolingual native speakers, the heritage learners were lacking in communicative fluency, grammatical accuracy, and lexical specificity as evidenced in their use of developmental forms characterized by present-tense temporal anchoring, frequent pauses, false starts, repairs, lexical substitution, simplification, redundancy, and circumlocution.

Using place of birth as well as age as independent variables, Jia and Bayley (2008) investigated the (re)acquisition of the Mandarin Chinese perfective aspectual marker-*le* by 36 children and adolescents who either initially acquired Mandarin as a first language or were acquiring it as an HL. The results of several different measures indicate that, as expected, participants who were born in China outperformed their U.S. born counterparts, as did participants who reported using primarily Mandarin at home. Results for age show a more complicated picture, with younger speakers outperforming older speakers on a narrative retelling task, but older speakers outperforming younger speakers on cloze and sentence completion tasks.

Rothman (2007) compared Brazilian Portuguese heritage speakers' knowledge of inflected infinitives to advanced adult L2 learners and educated native controls. Unlike the latter groups, heritage speakers, who did not have formal education in the standard dialect, were shown to not have target knowledge of inflected infinitives. Rothman concluded that, whether it is the case of attrition or that of incomplete acquisition of the HL, literacy plays a significant role in the acquisition of this grammatical property in Brazilian Portuguese. Also conceptualizing literacy activities and print materials as crucial variables for HL growth, Koda, Zhang, and Yang (2008) addressed literacy development in Chinese as a heritage language among school-age students. These children typically use Chinese at home, receive primary literacy instruction in English at school, and pursue ancillary literacy in Chinese in a weekend school. As such, their primary literacy tends to build on underdeveloped oral proficiency, and secondary literacy reflects heavily restricted print input and experience. Hence, their literacy learning in both languages lacks sufficient linguistic resources. Despite these inadequacies, however, many children succeed in their primary literacy, and some even in HL literacy. Based on theories of cross-language transfer, reading universals, and metalinguistic awareness, their study explored what additional resources — metalinguistic and cognitive — are available to these children, and how such resources correlate with children's level of literacy.

Many researchers have correlated HL achievement with learner identity formation or transformation. Li (1994) posited that proficiency correlates positively with a well-developed sense of ethnic identity and network with their ethnic group, such that group members have a greater understanding and knowledge of their groups' cultural values, ethics, and manners. The same is echoed in Abdalla (2009), Bhatt (2009), Carreira (2009), Chinen and Tucker (2005), Cho (2000), Kaufman (2005), Kondo-Brown (2005), and Lee (2002), all of whom suggested that in addition to internal factors such as attitudes, motivation, and social identity, ethnic identity is also a key factor in HL development. Tse (2000) attempted to explain the relationships among ethnic identity, attitudes and motivation, and HL development. She examined published narratives of Americans of Asian descent to discover whether feelings of ethnic ambivalence or evasion extend to the HL, and if so, how they affect language beliefs and behaviors. The results suggested that for many, the HL is closely associated with the ethnic group so that attitudes toward the ethnic group and its language speakers also extend to the narrators' own language ability and their interest (or lack of interest) in maintaining and developing their HL. Tse concluded that language acquisition is facilitated when an individual has positive attitudes toward the language and feels positively about her ethnic group.

Bermel and Kagan (2000) examined correlations between variables such as the number of years the learners have spent in the United States, the number of years of schooling in Russia or the former Soviet Union, and learners' geographical background (whether originally from Armenia, Azerbaijan, Belarus, Georgia, Ukraine, Russia, etc.) with their self-reported Russian abilities in speaking, listening, reading, and writing as well as their received grades as a measure of command of written language. Although they were not able to identify a significant correlation, they speculated that émigré Russians' self-reported social status (whether their families belonged to the class of so-called intelligentsia and whether their parents held respectable professions in the former Soviet Union) may correlate with retention of greater speaking capacities in Russian.

Lu and Li (2008) correlated different motivational factors (integrative, instrumental, and situational) and heritage and nonheritage college students' Chinese learning in mixed classrooms. Their results indicate that both integrative and instrumental motivations are important to students' self-confidence in their language proficiency, but integrative motivation is more important to students' overall tests scores. Further, students are more influenced by instrumental motivation than nonheritage students but less influenced by situational factors (such as teacher effect and effect of mixed-classes).

Correlational research has long been one of the major approaches to second language research. It is no surprise that in researching the sociocultural factors in HL learning, this is a commonly adopted approach as well. Whether it is multivariate studies that examine relationships among a number of variables or bivariate studies that examine associations between two variables, collectively, these studies alert us to the paramount associations among the sociocultural variables that are important to HL learning and suggest general tendencies at certain given point in time. However, research from this perspective tends to rely on average frequencies or probabilities of usage and has yet to explain why a particular variable is associated with another. It tends to evaluate complex and evolving constructs such as motivation, attitude, ethnic identity, proficiency, and literacy in terms of numerical values and leads one to think that these sociocultural traits are essential, built-in, and unchanging qualities.

SOCIAL CONSTRUCTIVIST STUDIES OF SOCIOCULTURAL DIMENSIONS OF HERITAGE LANGUAGES

The constructivist approach to the relationship between (heritage) language learning and its sociocultural dimensions has its origin in the sociology of knowledge (Berger & Luckmann, 1966), phenomenology (Schutz, 1967), ethnomethodology (Garfinkel, 1967), practice theory (Bourdieu, 1977), and sociohistorical psychology (Vygotsky, 1978), among others. A social constructivist view sees sociocultural dimensions such as identities, attitudes, and motivation as accomplishments (outcomes) of linguistically encoded acts and stances. With respect to the notion of identity, for example, the cultural theorist Stuart Hall (1990) wrote:

> Identity is not as transparent or unproblematic as we think. Perhaps instead of thinking of identity as an already accomplished fact, which the new cultural practices then represent, we should think, instead, of identity as a "production," which is never complete, always in process, and always constituted within, not outside, representation. This view problematises the very authority and authenticity to which the term, "cultural identity," lays claim (p. 51).

Postcolonial theorist Homi Bhabha (1994) similarly asserted that individuals have not one, but multiple, identities and that the identification of those identities is "never the affirmation of a pre-given identity" (p. 64). In other words, identities are not determined by essence or nature, but are derived from and maintained through social interaction. One of the implications of this standpoint is an emphasis on the possibility of choice and transformation of identity.

In this view, then, sociocultural concepts and labels are constantly changing, constructed through human interactions and the conditions of our lives. The qualities and attributes that we attach to any specific type of human activities are products of social conventions that are open to revision and renewal. In applied linguistics, this view is most saliently expressed in the concern with the dynamic nature of language learning (de Bot, 2008; Larsen-Freeman & Cameron, 2008; Markee, 2008); the ecology of language learning (Kramsch, 2002; van Lier, 2004); the sociocultural foundation of language learning (Atkinson, 2002; Lantolf, 2000,

2006; Lantolf & Thorne, 2007); and the coconstructed nature of activities, affect, abilities, and identities (Ochs & Jacoby, 1995; Young & He, 1998).

Rather than treating HL as an independent variable, a constructivist approach considers HL as a dependent variable. It seeks to unravel the kinds of social cultural dimension a learner is attempting to construct by engaging in a specific kind of social interaction or expressing a particular kind of affect (Ochs, 1993). This approach emphasizes that in any given actual situation, at any given interactional moment, participants are actively (re)constructing themselves as members of a particular ethnicity, nationality, speech community, social rank, and profession and as learners of HLs at various proficiency levels (Ochs & Jacoby, 1995). Research from a social constructivist approach focuses on analyzing the organization of communicative practices through which HL learners and users acquire or maintain sociocultural knowledge and interactional competence and on the open-ended, negotiated, contested character of the interactional routine as a resource for language growth, maintenance, and change. In this line of work, the forms of language and the sociocultural contexts of language use become symbiotic with each other.

A social constructivist approach reconceptualizes (heritage) language development in the following ways. First, what does it mean to know an HL? A social constructivist approach considers language acquisition and socialization as an integrated process (Garrett & Baquedano-López, 2002; Kramsch, 2002; Ochs, 1990, 1996; Ochs & Schieffelin, 1995; Schieffelin & Ochs, 1986, 1996; Watson-Gegeo, 2004). Linguistic meanings and meaning makings are therefore necessarily embedded in cultural systems of understanding. An account of linguistic behavior must then draw on accounts of culture. The heritage culture is by definition a complex, developing, transnational, intercultural, cross-linguistic, and hybrid one. Accordingly, to know an HL means not merely to command the phonetic, lexical, and syntactic forms in both speech and writing, but also to understand or embrace a set of continually evolving norms, preferences and expectations relating linguistic structures to multifaceted, dynamic contexts (Polinsky & Kagan, 2007).

Second, how does heritage culture relate to HL? From a social constructivist perspective (Ochs & Schieffelin, 1995), HL learners' acquisition of linguistic forms requires a developmental process of delineating and organizing contextual dimensions in culturally sensible ways. Learners are tuned into certain indexical meanings of grammatical forms that link those forms to, for example, the social identities of interlocutors and the types of social events. This model relates learners' use and understanding of grammatical forms to complex yet orderly and recurrent, dispositions, preferences, beliefs, and bodies of knowledge that organize how information is linguistically packaged and how speech acts are performed within and across socially recognized situations.

Just as foreign or second language learners may have varying degrees of investment across space and time (Norton, 2000), HL learning is often motivated by neither strictly instrumental nor integrative goals; learner motivations are derived not merely from pragmatic or utilitarian concerns but also from the intrinsic cultural, affective, and aesthetic values of the language (Andrews, 1999; Bhatt, 2009; Campbell & Christian, 2003; Carreira, 2009; Cummins, 2005; He, 2006). Unlike mother tongue acquisition in a monolingual environment, an HL is in constant competition with the dominant language in the local community. How do HL learners position themselves vis-à-vis mainstream culture or language? A social constructivist approach enables us to examine the construction of multiple yet compatible or congruent identities, as well as blended or blurred identities in multilingual, multicultural, immigrant contexts.

Third, what constitutes evidence of learning? Social constructivist research has looked for culturally meaningful practices across settings and situations (Agha & Wortham, 2005; Bartlett, 2007; He, 2006, 2009b; Jeon, 2008; Markee, 2008). Heritage language learners can be viewed as acquiring repertoires of language forms and functions associated with complex and changing contextual dimensions (e.g., evolving and shifting role relationships, identities, acts, events) over developmental time and across space (He, 2006). It is not context-free frequency of occurrence of some linguistic forms but rather the understanding of the situational and interactional contingencies of the use of those forms that indexes the learner's competence.

The last but not the least important question to consider is the route by which HL is acquired and socialized. The transmission of HL takes place in not merely formal settings (e.g., classrooms) but also, and perhaps more importantly, informally (e.g., across generations at homes and in the communities). Both the propositional contents of message conveyed in the HL and the ways in which HL is used (e.g., how instructors or parents communicate with the learner) have a direct impact on how learners perceive the language and its associated culture (He, 2000, 2003).

There is a long tradition of conceptualizing language as an integral part of the development of the self, the mind, and the society that complements language learning. When language is seen not as a self-contained coherent system, but a context-specific tool for achieving our purposes, learner identity is then structured in the everyday flow of language and stabilized in the pragmatic narratives of our day-to-day, fluid social life. For HL learners, HL learning is thus constitutive of identity, which is accomplished in the everyday social conversations.

Rampton (1995), though not focusing on HL matters exclusively, provided a compelling example of such a social constructivist approach. Rampton examined the hybrid, emergent identities created as students navigate social relations through the use of home languages. He described language crossing in urban, multiethnic groups of adolescents in the United Kingdom, as White, south Asian, and Caribbean youth mixed features of Panjabi, Caribbean Creole, and stylized Asian English. Crossing involves inserting linguistic features from other languages into speech that takes place in a predominant language. It is a discursive strategy with which diverse youth contest and create relations around race, ethnicity, and youth culture. Instead of correlating the social status of minority home languages with the use of home languages by youth to resist stigmatization and discrimination, Rampton showed how these and other sociocultural effects are realized in situated practice. The uses of minority HLs involve contestation, teasing, resistance, irony, and other stances with respect to social issues surrounding minority identities in Britain. Home language, in this case, along with the dominant language, is shown to be used by minority youth as a resource to confront the specific challenges presented to them in a multiethnic society, rather than an abstract variable to be correlated with social injustice.

Researchers working from a socioconstructivist perspective attend to creativity and indeterminacy in HL use. In addition to learner identities, cultural values and speech roles have also been subjects of inquiry. Lo (2004) demonstrated how expressions of epistemic stance relate to moral evaluations by looking at cases in which teachers at a Korean HL school claim to read their students' mind with a high degree of certainty. Lo argued that Korean HL learners are socialized to portray their access to the thoughts and sensations of other individuals differently depending upon who these individuals are. If the individuals are perceived as morally worthy, then the access is portrayed as distant; if they are perceived as morally suspect, then the access is presented as self-evident.

He (2001, 2003, 2004, 2005, 2009a) examined the development of from a linguistic-anthropological and conversation-analytic perspective that aims to synthesize cognitive and sociocultural approaches by considering language development as largely originating in social interaction and shaped by cultural and social processes. She investigated, for example, speech roles and speech exchange systems in the classroom (He, 2003, 2005, 2009a), discourse markers (Chen & He, 2001), modal verbs and pronominal references (He, 2000, 2004, 2009b), and sequential and social bases of semantic ambiguity in learning (He, 2001) as rich resources for learner identity (trans)formation. He (2000), for example, detailed the discourse processes by which learners are socialized to values of respect for authority and group conformity through teachers' directives in weekend Chinese language schools, where teachers do not merely impart knowledge and facts but also function as moral guides to the students. She not only documented how teachers often use three-part moral directives to discipline students' disruptive behavior but also analyzed how teachers and students transform these directives as they construct particular stances in context.

Park (2008) investigated how parents and grandparents in three-generational Korean American households socialize young children through their use of a particular linguistic feature in Korean, the verb suffix -*ta*. Drawing on naturally occurring interaction in the household, Park showed that utterances ending in -*ta* are used mostly by Korean adults to socialize children into the distinction between culturally desirable and culturally dispreferred behavior, thereby reconstructing the hierarchical relationships among different generations. Park highlighted the importance of the three-generational Korean households which make it possible for children to observe and imitate the culturally appropriate verbal behavior of their parents as the latter are engaged in interactions with the children's grandparents. In Park's study, the language form of verb suffix -*ta* was not the end of socialization (i.e., children are not expected to use this form in their own speech), but rather the means to socialize children into cultural norms and values.

Drawing on Bourdieu's (1991) notion of habitus and symbolic capital, Dai and Zhang (2008) considered HL acquisition and maintenance as identity processes whereby the learner acquires and adjusts additional and alternative voices as resources for the positioning of self and of others. The authors situated the Chinese HL learners' habitus in the fields of language, culture, and social interaction and utilized *linguistic habitus, cultural habitus,* and *social habitus* to differentiate the ambivalent threshold of what the learners are inheriting. Linguistic habitus refers to a certain articulatory style (as reflected in the variations of pronunciations in various dialects, for instance) that learners have acquired at home. Sociocultural habitus refers to a set of durable dispositions regarding core values, customs, lifestyles, and demeanors that heritage learners have acquired through socialization by family, school, friendship groups, institutions, and the mass media. The sociocultural habitus disposes the learner to cope with different social agents in certain ways.

Jeon (2008) explored the role of language ideology in the maintenance of Korean. In a 3-year, multisite ethnographic study, she examined the range of language ideologies espoused by individuals in different phases of life. Drawing upon data from three separate venues—a university Korean language class of mostly heritage Korean speakers, a community-based English as second language program for Korean American senior citizens, and the home of a recent Korean immigrant family with teenage children—Jeon examined and compared the language attitudes of the mostly Korean-speaking elders in the community, those of the largely English-speaking second generation, and those of a recently emigrated father who insists that his children speak only English. Jeon concluded that language ideologies are continuously shaped by changing life circumstances and that promoting bilingualism at the societal level is a critical requirement in any language maintenance effort.

As we can see, the social constructivist approach is antithetical to correlational explanations of language development. It refrains from universalizing and allows social and language behavior to speak for itself, without imposing predetermined definitions of essential characteristics of HL learners. We fully expect future research along the social constructivist line to explore the challenges HL learners face across a spectrum of linguistic components and language skills and to reveal and specify the culturally situated ways in which these and other linguistic forms are learned and taught over interactional time, over historical time, and over developmental time (Lemke, 2002). We also expect to see research to be more sensitive and responsive to multiple sociocultural dimensions as heritage learners evolve in the course of social interaction, transforming in response to the acts and stances of other participants in order to provide a "rain forest" account of language learning with a "lush ecology" (Atkinson, 2002, p. 526).

In sum, from both correlational and social constructivist approaches, we have seen an increasingly large body of empirical studies documenting the various formal and functional aspects of HL learning that are concerned with different subgroups of HL learners ranging from developmental traits in learners who have minimal proficiency in the HL to maintenance issues in the case of highly proficient HL learners. These studies largely focus on one language proficiency level of the subjects at one life stage in one specific life circumstance. As Campbell and Christian (2003) pointed out, successful HL education is inseparable from the role of school systems, social institutions, and historical experiences of particular language communities, as well as language ideologies, suitable proficiency assessment instruments, and adequate literacy development. We have learned from previous research that a range of variables may influence language maintenance, including social prestige of the language, number of speakers, affinity to native country, vitality of HL schools, learners' social and ethnic positionings, degree of family bond, and discourse and interactional practices (Baker, 2006; Creeze & Martin, 2006; Feuerverger, 1991; Gibbons & Ramirez, 2004; He, 2006; He & Xiao, 2008; Jo, 2001; King, 2000; Shin, 2005; Stalikas & Gavaki, 1995; Tannenbaum & Howie, 2002; Zentella 1997). Given our definition of HL, neither the classroom nor the family is the only domain relevant to HL development or maintenance. Efforts to understand HL will be most fruitful if we take into account not only formal, institutional settings such as schools (e.g., Byon, 2003; He, 2000; Lo, 2004) but also patterns of HL use in informal settings such as home and communities (Bayley & Schecter, 2003, Brinton & Kagan, 2008; Kondo-Brown, 2006; Park, 2008; Xiao, 2008), not only the impact of face-to-face interaction but also the role of technology and popular culture (Lam, 2008; Lee, 2006). Temporally, like learning in other settings (e.g., Markee, 2008; Wortham, 2005), HL development is not limited to any specific given period of time; HL competencies, choices, and ideologies change over the learner's life span, reflecting changing motivations, social networks, opportunities, and other variables. In other words, we need to attend to the sociocultural complexity of HL development, a point to which I turn next.

THE SOCIOCULTURAL COMPLEXITY OF HERITAGE LANGUAGE DEVELOPMENT AND ITS IMPLICATIONS

In her analysis of efforts to protect cultural heritage, Kirshenblatt-Gimblett (2006) pointed out that people are not only passive cultural transmitters but also conscious, reflexive agents in the heritage enterprise itself. HL is not static but dynamic; it is constantly undergoing transformation by its learners and users, so that at the same time it serves as a resource for the transformation of learner identities, it is also transformed itself as a result of learners' and users' language ideologies and practices. It is important to realize that expert guidance in HL learning may be multiple, conflicting, and contested, as a result of different language ideologies held by different participants in the process. What constitutes an HL and what amounts to appropriate and adequate language learning can become debatable due to varying participant positions in terms of class, gender, generation, and so on. Beliefs about language articulated by learners, parents, and teachers to rationalize or justify the pedagogical decisions often play an important role in the outcome of school or community-based HL education. Ideological inconsistencies and tensions among those involved in HL education often affect the individuals' attitudes about their language maintenance and language learning.

Furthermore, the HL learner is engaged in multiple speech events in multiple settings for multiple purposes. The learning of HL, for example, takes place through the learner's interactions with multiple participants including language instructors, parents, grandparents, siblings, and peers, each of whom positions the learner in unique speech and social roles, and each of whose reactions and responses to the learner helps to shape the path of his or her language development. Research on sociocultural dimensions of development thus entails examination of the different stages as well as different domains of development and of the coconstructed, interactive nature of learning activities. He (2006), for example, delineated the complexity of HL socialization along temporal and spatial dimensions, with a focus on Chinese as an HL. Along the temporal dimension, she underscored the nonlinear, iterative, dynamic nature of development. Along the spatial dimension, she highlighted the multiagency and multidirectionality of development. In her study, learner identity is the centerpiece rather than the background of HL development. Identity is to be understood in association with its verb form, to *identify*, and thus as identification. In other words, identity is treated not as a collection of static attributes or as some mental construct existing prior to and independent of human actions, but rather as a process of continual emerging and becoming, a process that identifies what a person becomes and achieves through ongoing interactions with other persons (Bucholtz & Hall, 2004; Laroche, Kim, Hui, & Tomiuk, 1998; Ochs 1993). He (2006) asked whether development will place learners in interactional conditions of cultural and linguistic ambiguity that they are prepared to handle and whether the growing cultural complexity of communication as a result of development will lead to the withering away or the emergence of certain types of identity constructs.

In short, HL development is grounded in the learner's participation in social practice and continuous adaptation to the unfolding, multiple activities and identities that constitute the social and communicative worlds that he or she inhabits. Such a position compels us to take a more dialectical, dialogical, and ecological perspective on socialization, in the sense that the process will be viewed as reciprocal. It is important to keep in mind that learners are not merely passive, uniform recipients of socialization. As learners' allegiances and competencies evolve, the language choices and competencies of their parents, siblings, neighbors, and friends will also change, consequently and/or concurrently. In other words, learners contribute to the socialization process of the very people who socialize them to use the HL. Heritage language learning has the potential to transform all parties involved in the socialization process. It can also be expected that HL research will contribute to the very disciplines that have served as its theoretical or methodological guidance in terms of fundamental theoretical constructs, research methods, and units of analysis, among others. For example, HL learning provides fertile ground for us to reconsider dichotomous concepts such as native language versus target language, native speech community versus target speech community, instrumental versus integrative motivations, and basic interpersonal communication skills versus cognitive academic language proficiency. Last but not least, research will challenge us to reevaluate our unit of analysis from single snapshots of one-on-one, unidirectional interactional processes to trajectories of growth and change over space and time for all participants.

REFERENCES

Abdalla, M. (2009, June). *Negotiating the syllabus: The case of Arab heritage learners.* Paper presented at the Third Heritage Language Summer Institute, Urbana, IL.

Agha, A., & Wortham, S. (2005). Discourse across speech events: Intertextuality and interdiscursivity in social life [Special issue]. *Journal of Linguistic Anthropology, 15*(1).

Andrews, D. R. (1999). *Sociocultural perspectives on language change in diaspora.* Amsterdam: John Benjamins.

Atkinson, D. (2002). Toward a sociocognitive approach to SLA. *Modern Language Journal, 86*, 525–545.

Baker, C. (2006). *Foundations of bilingual education and bilingualism.* Clevedon, UK: Multilingual Matters.

Bartlett, L. (2007). Bilingual literacies, social identification, and educational trajectories. *Linguistics and Education, 18*, 215–231.

Bayley, R., & Schecter, S. (Eds.). (2003). *Language socialization in bilingual and multilingual societies.* Clevedon, UK: Multilingual Matters.

Berger, P. L., & Luckmann, T. (1966). *The social construction of reality: A treatise on the sociology of knowledge.* Garden City, NY: Anchor Books.

Bermel, N., & Kagan, O. (2000). The maintenance of written Russian in heritage speakers. In O. Kagan & B. Rifkin (Eds.), *The learning and teaching of Slavic languages and cultures* (pp. 405–436). Bloomington, IN: Slavica.

Bhabha, H. K. (1994). *The location of culture.* London: Routledge.

Bhatt, R. (2009, June). *Sociolinguistic inquiries into heritage language learning: The Indian diaspora.* Paper presented at the Third Heritage Language Summer Institute. Urbana, IL. Retrieved [October 2009] from http://www.international.ucla.edu/languages/nhlrc/2009summer/presentations/Bhatt.ppt.

Bourdieu, P. (1977). *Outline of a theory of practice.* Cambridge, UK: Cambridge University Press.

Bourdieu, P. (1991). *Language and symbolic power.* Cambridge, MA: Harvard University Press.

Brinton, D., & Kagan, O. (Eds.). (2008). *Heritage language acquisition: A new field emerging.* Hillsdale, NJ: Erlbaum.

Bucholtz, M., & Hall, K. (2004). Language and identity. In A. Duranti (Ed.), *A companion to linguistic anthropology* (pp. 369–394). Oxford, UK: Blackwell.

Byon, A. (2003). Language socialization and Korean as a heritage language: A study of Hawaiian classrooms. *Language, Culture and Curriculum, 16*, 269–283.

Campbell, R. N., & Christian, D. (Eds.). (2003). Directions in research: Intergenerational transmission of heritage languages. *Heritage Language Journal, 1*, 1–44. Retrieved [October

2009] from http://www.heritagelanguages.org.

Carreira, M. (2009, June). *Assessment and differentiation in mixed ability classes*. Paper presented at the Third Heritage Language Summer Institute, Urbana, IL.

Chen, Y., & He, A. W. (2001). Dui bu dui as a pragmatic marker: Evidence from Chinese classroom discourse. *Journal of Pragmatics, 33*, 1441–1465.

Chinen, K., & Tucker, G. R. (2005). Heritage language development: Understanding the role of ethnic identity and Saturday school participation. *Heritage Language Journal, 3*, 27–59. Retrieved [October 2009] from http://www.heritagelanguages.org.

Cho, G. (2000). The role of heritage language in social interactions and relationships: Reflections from a language minority group. *Bilingual Research Journal, 24*, 369–384.

Creeze, A., & Martin, P. (Eds.). (2006). Interaction in complementary school contexts [Special issue]. *Language and Education, 20* (1).

Cummins, J. (2005). A proposal for action: Strategies for recognizing HL competence as a learning resource within the mainstream classroom. *Modern Language Journal, 89*, 585–592.

Dai, J. E., & Zhang, L. (2008). What are the learners inheriting? Habitus of the learners. In A. W. He & Y. Xiao (Eds.), *Chinese as a heritage language* (pp. 3–51). Honolulu, HI: National Foreign Language Resource Center/University of Hawaii Press.

de Bot, K. (2008). Introduction: Second language development as a dynamic process. *Modern Language Journal, 92*, 166–178.

Fishman, J. A. (1991). *Reversing language shift*. Clevedon, UK: Multilingual Matters.

Fishman, J. A. (2001). 300-plus years of heritage language education in the United States. In J. K. Peyton, D. A. Ranard, & S. McGinnis (Eds.), *Heritage languages in America. Preserving a national resource* (pp. 81–89). McHenry, IL: Center for Applied Linguistics.

Feuerverger, G. (1991). University students' perceptions of heritage language learning and ethnic identity maintenance. *Canadian Modern Language Review, 47*, 660–677.

Garfinkel, H. (1967). *Studies in ethnomethodology*. Englewood Cliffs, NJ: Prentice Hall.

Garrett, P. B., & Baquedano-López, P. (2002). Language socialization: Reproduction and continuity, transformation and change. *Annual Review of Anthropology, 31*, 339–361.

Gibbons, J., & Ramirez, E. (2004). *Maintaining a minority language: A case study of Hispanic teenagers*. Clevedon, UK: Multilingual Matters.

Hall, S. (1990). Cultural identity and diaspora. In K. Woodward (Ed.), *Identity and difference* (pp. 51–59). London: Sage.

He, A. W. (2000). Grammatical and sequential organization of teachers' directives. *Linguistics and Education, 11*, 119–140.

He, A. W. (2001). The language of ambiguity: Practices in Chinese heritage language classes. *Discourse Studies, 3*, 75–96.

He, A. W. (2003). Novices and their speech roles in Chinese heritage language classes. In R. Bayley & S. Schecter (Eds.), *Language socialization in bilingual and multilingual societies* (pp. 128–146). Clevedon, UK: Multilingual Matters.

He, A. W. (2004). Identity construction in Chinese heritage language classes. *Pragmatics, 14*, 199–216.

He, A. W. (2005). Discipline, directives, and deletions: Grammar and interaction in Chinese heritage language classes. In C. Holten & J. Frodesen (Eds.), *The power of context in language teaching and learning: A festschrift for Marianne Celce-Murcia* (pp. 115–126). Boston, MA: Thomson Heinle.

He, A. W. (2006). Toward an identity theory of the development of Chinese as a heritage language. *Heritage Language Journal, 4*, 1–28. Retrieved [October 2009] from http://www.heritagelanguages.org.

He, A. W. (2009a). Sequences, scripts, and subject pronouns in the construction of Chinese heritage identity. In A. Reyes & A. Lo (Eds.), *Beyond yellow English: Toward a linguistic anthropology of Asian Pacific America* (pp. 366–384). New York: Oxford University Press.

He, A. W. (2009b, July). *Heritage language across the life span*. Lecture presented at the Third National Heritage Language Summer Research Institute. Urbana, Illinois.

He, A. W., & Xiao, Y. (Eds.). (2008). *Chinese as a heritage language: Fostering rooted world citizenry*. Honolulu, HI: University of Hawaii Press.

Hornberger, N. (1997). Literacy, language maintenance, and linguistic human rights: Three telling cases. *International Journal of the Sociology of Language, 127*, 87–103.

Jeon, M. (2008). Korean heritage language maintenance and language ideology. *Heritage Language Journal, 6*. Retrieved [October 2009] from http://www. heritagelanguages.org.

Jia, G. (2008). Heritage language development, maintenance, and attrition among recent Chinese immigrants in New York City. In A. W. He & Y. Xiao (Eds.), *Chinese as a heritage language* (pp. 189–203). Honolulu, HI: National Foreign Language Resource Center/ University of Hawaii Press.

Jia, L. & Bayley, R. (2008). Perfective aspect marking by learners. In A. W. He & Y. Xiao (Eds.), *Chinese as a heritage language* (pp. 205–222). Honolulu, HI: National Foreign Language Resource Center/University of Hawaii Press.

Jo, H. (2001). Heritage language learning and ethnic identity: Korean Americans' struggle with language authorities. *Language, Culture and Curriculum, 14*, 26–41.

Kaufman, D. (2005). Acquisition, attrition, and revitalization of Hebrew in immigrant children. In D. Ravid & H. Bat-Zeev Shyldkrot (Eds.), *Perspectives on Language and Language Development* (pp. 407–418). Dordrecht, Netherlands: Kluwer.

King, K. A. (2000). Language ideologies and heritage language education. *International Journal of Bilingual Education and Bilingualism, 3*, 167–184.

Kirshenblatt-Gimblett, B. (2006). World heritage and cultural economics. In G. Buntinx, C. Rassool, C. Kratz, L. Szwaja, T. Ybarra-Frausto, B. Kirshenblatt-Gimblett, & I. Karp (Eds.), *Museum frictions: Public cultures/global transformations* (pp. 161–202). Durham, NC: Duke University Press.

Koda, K., Zhang, Y., & Yang, C.-L. (2008). Literacy development in Chinese as a heritage language. In A. W. He & Y. Xiao (Eds.), *Chinese as a heritage language* (pp.137–149). Honolulu, HI: National Foreign Language Resource Center/University of Hawaii Press.

Kondo-Brown, K. (2005). Differences in language skills: Heritage language learner subgroups and foreign language learners? *The Modern Language Journal, 89*, 563–581.

Kondo-Brown, K. (Ed.). (2006). *Heritage language development: Focus on East Asian immigrants*. Amsterdam: John Benjamins.

Kramsch, C. (Ed.). (2002). *Language acquisition and language socialization*. New York: Continuum.

Lam, W. S. E. (2008). Language socialization in online communities. In P. Duff & N. H. Hornberger (Eds.), *Encyclopedia of language and education: Vol. 4. Language socialization* (pp. 301–312). New York: Springer.

Lantolf, J. P. (Ed.). (2000). *Sociocultural theory and second language learning*. Oxford, UK: Oxford University Press.

Lantolf, J. P. (2006). Sociocultural theory and L2: State of the art. *Studies in Second Language Acquisition, 28*, 67–109.

Lantolf, J. P., & Thorne, S. L. (2007). *Sociocultural theory and the genesis of second language development*. Oxford, UK: Oxford University Press.

Laroche, M., Kim, C., Hui, M., & Tomiuk, M. (1998). Test of a nonlinear relationship between linguistic acculturation and ethnic identification. *Journal of Cross-Cultural Psychology, 29*, 418–433.

Larsen-Freeman, D., & Cameron, L. (2008). *Complex systems and applied linguistics*. Oxford, UK: Oxford University Press.

Lee, J. S. (2002). The Korean language in America: The role of cultural identity and heritage language. *Language, Culture, and Curriculum, 15*, 117–133.

Lee, J. S. (2006). Exploring the relationship between electronic literacy and heritage language maintenance. *Language Learning and Technology, 10*, 93–113.

Lemke, J. (2002). Language development and identity: Multiple timescales in the social ecology of learning. In C. Kramsch (Ed.), *Language acquisition and language socialization* (pp. 68–87). New York: Continuum.

Li, W. (1994). *Three generations, two languages, one family.* Clevedon, UK: Multilingual Matters.

Lo, A. (2004). Evidentiality and morality in a Korean heritage language school. *Pragmatics, 14,*

235–256.
Lu, X., & Li, G. (2008). Motivation and achievement in Chinese language learning. In A. W. He & Y. Xiao (Eds.), *Chinese as a heritage language: Fostering rooted world citizenry* (pp. 89–108). Honolulu, HI: University of Hawaii Press.
Markee, N. (2008). Toward a learning behavior tracking methodology for CA-for-SLA. *Applied Linguistics, 29*(3), 404–427.
Norton, B. (2000). *Identity and language learning: Gender, ethnicity, and educational change.* Essex, England: Longman.
Ochs, E. (1990). Indexicality and socialization. In J. W. Stigler, R. Shweder, and G. Herdt (Eds.), *Cultural psychology: Essays on comparative human development* (pp. 287–308). Cambridge, UK: Cambridge University Press.
Ochs, E. (1993). Constructing social identity. *Research on Language and Social Interaction, 26*, 287–306.
Ochs, E. (1996). Linguistic resources for socializing humanity. In J. J. Gumperz & S. L. Levinson (Eds.), *Rethinking linguistic relativity* (pp. 407–437). Cambridge, UK: Cambridge University Press.
Ochs, E., & Jacoby, S. (Eds.). (1995). Co-construction [Special issue]. *Research on Language and Social Interaction, 28*(3).
Ochs, E., & Schieffelin, B. (1995). The impact of language socialization on grammatical development. In P. Fletcher & B. MacWhinney (Eds.), *The handbook of child language* (pp. 73–94). Cambridge, MA: Blackwell.
Park, E. (2008). Intergenerational transmission of cultural values in Korean American families: An analysis of the verb suffix *-ta*. *Heritage Language Journal, 6*. Retrieved [October 2009] from http://www.heritagelanguages.org.
Polinsky, M., & Kagan, O. (2007). Heritage languages: In the "wild" and in the classroom. *Languages and Linguistics Compass, 1*, 368–395.
Rampton, B. (1995). *Crossing language and ethnicity among adolescents.* New York: Longman.
Roca, A., & Colombi, M. C. (Eds.). (2003). *Mi lengua: Spanish as a heritage language in the United States.* Washington, DC: Georgetown University Press.
Rothman, J. (2007). Heritage speaker competence differences, language change and input type: Inflected infinitives in heritage Brazilian Portuguese. *International Journal of Bilingualism, 11*, 359–389.
Schieffelin, B., & Ochs, E. (Eds.). (1986). *Language socialization across cultures.* New York: Cambridge University Press.
Schieffelin, B. & Ochs, E. (1996). The microgenesis of competence. In D. Slobin, J. Gerhardt, A. Kyratzis, & J. Guo (Eds.), *Social interaction, social context, and language* (pp. 251–264).

Mahwah, NJ: Erlbaum.

Schutz, A. (1967). *Phenomenology of the social world.* Evanston, IL: Northwestern University Press.

Shin, S. J. (2005). *Developing in two languages: Korean children in America.* Clevedon, UK: Multilingual Matters.

Stalikas, A., & Gavaki, E. (1995).The importance of ethnic identity: Self-esteem and academic achievement of second-generation Greeks in secondary school. *The Canadian Journal of School Psychology, 11,* 1–9.

Tannenbaum, M., & Howie, P. (2002). The association between language maintenance and family relations: Chinese immigrant children in Australia. *Journal of Multilingual and Multicultural Development, 23,* 408–424.

Tse, L. (2000). The effects of ethnic identity formation on bilingual maintenance and development: An analysis of Asian American narratives. *International Journal of Bilingual Education and Bilingualism, 3,* 185–200.

Valdés, G. (1997). The teaching of Spanish to bilingual Spanish-speaking students: Outstanding issues and unanswered questions. In M. C. Colombi & F. X. Alarcón (Eds.), *La ensenanza del espannol a hispanohablantes: Praxis y teoria* [Teaching Spanish to Spanish speakers: practice and theory] (pp. 93–101). Boston: Houghton Mifflin.

Valdés, G. (2001). Heritage language students: Profiles and possibilities. In J. K. Peyton, D. A. Ranard, & S. McGinnis (Eds.), *Heritage languages in America. Preserving a national resource* (pp. 37–80). McHenry, IL: Center for Applied Linguistics.

Van Deusen-Scholl, N. (2003). Toward a definition of heritage language: sociopolitical and pedagogical considerations. *Journal of Language, Identity, and Education, 2,* 211–230.

van Lier, L. (2004). *The ecology and semiotics of language learning: A sociocultural perspective.* Boston: Kluwer.

Vygotsky, L. S. (1978). *Mind and society: The development of higher psychological processes.* Cambridge, MA: Harvard University Press.

Watson-Gegeo, K. A. (2004). Mind, language, and epistemology: Toward a language socialization paradigm for SLA. *The Modern Language Journal, 88*(3), 331–350.

Wiley, T. G. (2001). On defining heritage languages and their speakers. In J. K. Peyton, D. A. Ranard, & S. McGinnis (Eds.), *Heritage languages in America: Preserving a national resource* (pp. 29–36). McHenry, IL: Center for Applied Linguistics.

Wiley, T., & Valdés, G. (2000). Heritage language instruction in the United States: A time for renewal. *Bilingual Research Journal, 24,* i-v. Retrieved [October 2009] from http://brj.asu.edu/archive.html.

Wong Fillmore, L. (1991). When learning a second language means losing the first. *Early Childhood Research Quarterly, 6,* 323–346.

Wong Fillmore, L. (2000). Loss of family languages: Should educators be concerned? *Theory into Practice, 39*, 203–210.

Wortham, S. (2005). Socialization beyond the speech event. *Journal of Linguistic Anthropology, 15*, 95–112.

Xiao, Y. (2008). Home literacy environment in development. In A. W. He & Y. Xiao (Eds.), *Chinese as a heritage language: Fostering rooted world citizenry* (pp. 151–166). Honolulu, HI: University of Hawaii Press.

Young, R., & He, A. W. (Eds.). (1998). *Talking and testing: Discourse approaches to the assessment of oral language proficiency.* Philadelphia: Benjamins.

Zentella, A. (1997). *Growing up bilingual.* Oxford, UK: Blackwell.

SECTION B: RESEARCH METHODS AND TECHNIQUES

Meta-analysis in Second Language Research: Choices and Challenges

Frederick L. Oswald and Luke Plonsky

Applied linguists are increasingly conducting meta-analysis in their substantive domains, because as a quantitative approach for averaging effect sizes across studies, it is more systematic and replicable than traditional, qualitative literature reviews. Additional strengths, such as increased statistical power, moderator analyses, and model testing, have also contributed to its appeal. The current review describes typical stages of a meta-analysis in second language acquisition (SLA) research: (a) defining the research domain, (b) developing a reliable coding scheme, (c) analyzing data, and (d) interpreting results. Each stage has a host of equally reasonable decisions that can be made; each decision will influence the conduct of the meta-analysis, the nature of the results, and the substantive implications of findings for SLA. We highlight a number of benefits and challenges that inform these decisions. In general, when a meta-analysis in applied linguistics is well planned, employs sound statistical methods, and is based on a thorough understanding of relevant theory, it can provide critical information that informs theory as well as future research, practice, and policy.

INTRODUCTION

Meta-analysis is a statistical method that can appear complex and intimidating at first glance (Rosenthal & DiMatteo, 2001). But at its heart, a meta-analysis calculates the mean and variance of a set of numbers. The numbers are not individual scores, however, as researchers are accustomed to averaging, but instead are statistics reported across studies within a particular research domain, such as a set of study correlations, standardized mean differences between groups, or odds ratios. For at least 150 years, scientific researchers have engaged in the practice of averaging effects found across a set of studies or scientific observations; however, meta-analysis has developed relatively recently as a formalized statistical method for doing so (for information on the development of meta-analysis, see Borenstein, Hedges, Higgins, & Rothstein, 2009; Hunter & F. L. Schmidt, 2004; for early works on meta-analytic methods, see Cooper & Rosenthal, 1980; Glass, 1976; Hedges & Olkin, 1985; Rosenthal, 1978; F. L. Schmidt & Hunter, 1977).

Averaging quantitative effects across studies through meta-analysis overcomes three major problems of narrative or qualitative reviews in second language (L2) research. The first problem is having to wrestle with conflicting findings across studies: The magnitude of reported effect sizes across studies can vary wildly, ranging from large positive effects to large and possibly counterintuitive negative effects. Authors of narrative reviews may be correct in attributing such conflicting findings to the unique samples or theoretical orientations of each study, but an important competing explanation may be a simpler one involving sampling error variance. More specifically, small samples alone can contribute to large fluctuations in study outcomes, independent of the particular theories, samples, measures, or settings that were summarized. Researchers have a natural tendency to interpret significant statistics no matter what the sample size is (Tversky & Kahneman, 1971). This practice should generally be avoided because conceptually, small samples usually represent very little of the population of interest, and empirically, small-sample statistics (even significant ones) are highly unstable. However, small samples do have the potential to contribute meaningfully to the average meta-analytic effect across studies, given that the average is based on a cumulative sample size that is both conceptually representative of the population of interest as well as statistically significant.

The second problem of narrative reviews is an overreliance on the results from traditional null hypothesis significance testing (NHST). NHST has long since enjoyed a privileged status as the standard for empirical evidence (and, to some extent, publishability) in the field of second language acquisition (SLA), yet over five decades and thousands of pages of general debate on NHST have yielded many critics and few supporters (e.g., Balluerka, Gómez, & Hidalgo, 2005; Lykken,

1968; F. L. Schmidt, 1996). Applied linguists have also joined the fray, citing the weaknesses of NHST (Crookes, 1991; Ellis, 2006; Larson-Hall, 2010; Lazaraton, 1991; Norris & Ortega, 2006, 2007; Plonsky, 2009), and we similarly argue that progress in SLA will continue to be impaired by NHST until there is a widespread reform emphasizing effect sizes and practical significance, similar to what is already taking place in psychology, education, and other social sciences (e.g., see Wilkinson & the Task Force on Statistical Inference, 1999).

The root of the problem of NHST is that it reduces research findings into a dichotomy of statistical significance or nonsignificance based on the p value — and nothing more. This is problematic because statistical significance does not reflect the size or the importance of an effect. A p value for a t test, for instance, is a function of four numbers: the sample mean difference, the sample variances of the groups, the alpha level, and the sample size. Researchers can change any of these four numbers (incidentally, legitimately or deviously), to create a small p value and reject the null hypothesis, thereby achieving fame and fortune (or hopefully publication, at least). But the size or practical significance of an effect is what should matter, not only its statistical significance. As Tukey (1991) said in the context of finding a small p value, "the effects of A and B are always different — in some decimal place—for any A and B. Thus asking 'are the effects different?' is foolish" (p. 100). Once early research efforts provide empirical support for the presence of a relationship, it usually becomes important to understand magnitudes

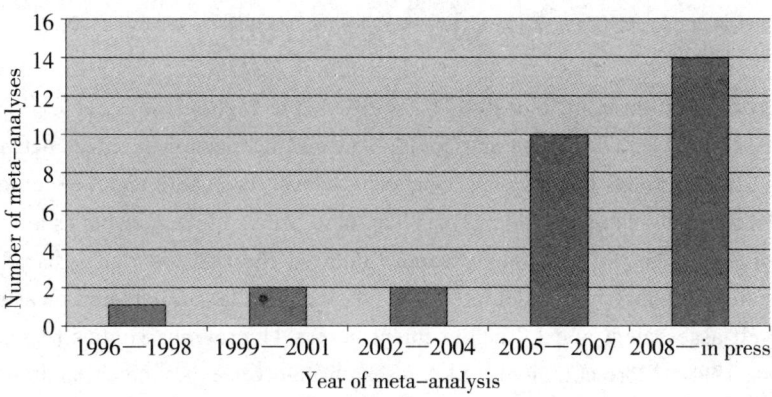

Fig. 1. Growth of meta-analysis in L2 research.

and patterns of relationships as well as the circumstances that affect them.

The third problem with narrative review concerns the limitations of the reviewers themselves, who even as experts are fallible human decision makers who can be inconsistent in the way they encode and interpret empirical findings across studies. They may also weigh quantitative findings more heavily for those studies whose authors make a verbally compelling case for their research or publish in prestigious journals, even though other empirical findings might be more informative, yet present a less interesting story line and/or reside in less-visible journals. To be clear, we are not implying that the expertise of a reviewer should ever be divorced from the process of a meta-analytic review; instead we are saying that experts reviewing L2 research should consider using meta-analysis as an important tool that may inject a more objective and systematic approach into the review process.

This article is fortunate to accompany the rise in prominence of meta-analysis in SLA (see Figure 1). We first highlight the many potential benefits of meta-analysis in the research enterprise, referring to meta-analyses conducted in SLA as cogent examples. We then outline the general process of conducting a meta-analysis, discussing critical steps and associated decision points that SLA researchers will inevitably encounter. We conclude with several take-home points regarding the promise and prospects of meta-analysis for the discipline.

USES AND POTENTIAL BENEFITS OF META-aNALYSIS

In its simplest form, meta-analysis quantifies and tests correlations between variables (such as L2 exposure and comprehension) or mean differences between identifiable groups (such as age, proficiency level, or experimental condition). Even relatively simple meta-analyses like these can be quite valuable as a quantitative summary of previous research findings. The first meta-analysis of L2 research, for instance, calculated the average correlation between measures of self-assessment and L2 achievement across 11 previous studies ($r = .63$; Ross, 1998). More commonly, SLA research involves experimental and quasi-experimental designs that measure the effect of a treatment on an outcome (Lazaraton, 2000; Teleni & Baldauf, 1989). For example, a recent meta-analysis provides an estimate of the overall effect of corrective feedback on L2 gains (d = .61; Li, 2010). In mature L2 research domains, meta-analysis can also be extended to test multiple hypotheses, thereby enabling researchers to test theoretical models broader than those contained in any of its constituent studies (Becker, 2009).

Meta-analysis clearly has much to offer by summarizing accumulated research and evaluating existing theoretical models; however, its influence should by no means be limited to retrospective accounts of the literature. On the contrary, a thorough meta-analysis catalogs the major substantive and methodological features of its primary studies; thus, one can learn from meta-analysis about the benefits and drawbacks of different designs and motivating theories across studies to determine what type of future research appears to be more productive. This has already happened in SLA meta-analyses in two ways.

First, based on their meta-analytic findings, some L2 researchers have called for additional studies to enhance the robustness, generalizability, and external validity of findings with different learner groups (e.g., preadolescents) and treatments (e.g., types of error correction; Poltavtchenko & Johnson, 2009; Russell & Spada, 2006). Second, Lee and Huang (2008) concluded from their meta-analysis that studies of input enhancement, and SLA research in general, needs to report their descriptive statistics, methods, and procedures more comprehensively if SLA meta-analyses are to reach their full informative potential (e.g., Norris & Ortega, 2000; Plonsky, in press).

Meta-analyses in SLA should also be useful for identifying specific variables, settings, and samples that have been underresearched yet can contribute to more integrated and well-developed theoretical models. Meta-analysis is a retrospective summary of research. A prospective meta-analysis is one that could be informed by a retrospective meta-analysis, where a series of planned empirical studies target specific research questions, with those findings to be accumulated in a future meta-analysis (see Berlin & Ghersi, 2005). The hope of a prospective meta-analysis is that the broad collaborative planning efforts of researchers would be of higher quality in terms of theory and research design. Because a prospective meta-analysis might yield greater empirical returns than an isolated set of primary studies, it may also receive greater interest and support by granting agencies.

CONSIDERATIONS AND CHOICES

Although meta-analysis is a data-driven procedure, the expert role of the SLA meta-analyst is a critical element, as we have mentioned (see Bangert-Drowns, 1995; Ortega, 2010). In fact, at the heart of this review lies the unavoidable interplay between researcher judgment and the meta-analysis procedures that require such judgment (Kavale, 1995; Norris & Ortega, 2007; Oswald & McCloy, 2003; Sutton & Higgins, 2008). Therefore, rather than prescribing one best practice for conducting a meta-analysis in SLA, we join other authors in emphasizing the fact that there are multiple options at each stage in carrying out a meta-analysis, each characterized by different strengths and weaknesses (see Hall & Rosenthal, 1995; Preiss & Allen, 1995; Wanous, Sullivan, & Malinak, 1989).

Defining the Research Domain

The first step in carrying out a meta-analysis is foundational: defining the conceptual umbrella of SLA research whose findings will be located and summarized. Just as primary researchers should carefully define the population of language learners and appropriately measure and/or manipulate relevant variables, meta-analysts must also delimit the research domain of interest to be investigated, which often requires balancing the prescriptive domain implied by a theory (or theories) with the descriptive domain defined post hoc by the set of studies on hand.

There are very different approaches one may take to this end. Consider the 11 L2 meta-analyses investigating the effectiveness of corrective feedback. Most meta-analyses in this area have been concerned with correction of spoken errors. One meta-analysis, however, focused on the effects of different types of both oral and written error correction, including recasts and metalinguistic feedback, but only with respect to gains in L2 grammar (d = 1.16; Russell & Spada, 2006). Of three recent meta-analyses, one took a broad approach by including dissertations and studies of computer-mediated feedback (d = .61; Li, 2010), while two others were much narrower, focusing only on recasts (Miller & Pan, 2009) and the effects of oral feedback in classroom settings (d = .74; Lyster & Saito, 2010). Seeking to settle perhaps one of the most highly polemic debates in SLA (see Chandler, 2004; Ferris, 1999, 2004; Truscott, 1996, 1999, 2004), two meta-analyses summarized the accumulated effects of corrective feedback on L2 writing (Poltavtchenko &

Johnson, 2009; Truscott, 2007). And finally, five meta-analyses have included studies of error correction within larger bodies of research on the effectiveness of instruction (Norris & Ortega, 2000, replicated by Goo, Granena, Novella, & Yilmaz, 2009; Spada & Tomita, 2010) and on the effects of L2 interaction (Keck, Iberri-Shea, Tracy-Ventura, & Wa-Mbaleka, 2006; Mackey & Goo, 2007). Our objective in pointing out this flurry of meta-analyses that include studies of corrective feedback is to illustrate two general points. First, many if not most theoretical and empirical questions in SLA can be addressed informatively at the meta-analytic level; second, even SLA meta-analyses in the same general domain can produce different results and interpretations, depending on how the L2 constructs of interest are defined.

Literature Searching

After deciding which constructs, group differences, theoretical relationships, experimental designs, and publication types to include in a meta-analysis, the search for studies that meet those criteria begins. In the same way that the method of recruiting participants affects the generalizability of a primary study's findings, the process of finding the primary studies that might be included in a meta-analysis requires principled and thorough literature-searching techniques. In this age of the Internet, a large variety of electronic databases and resources, both formal

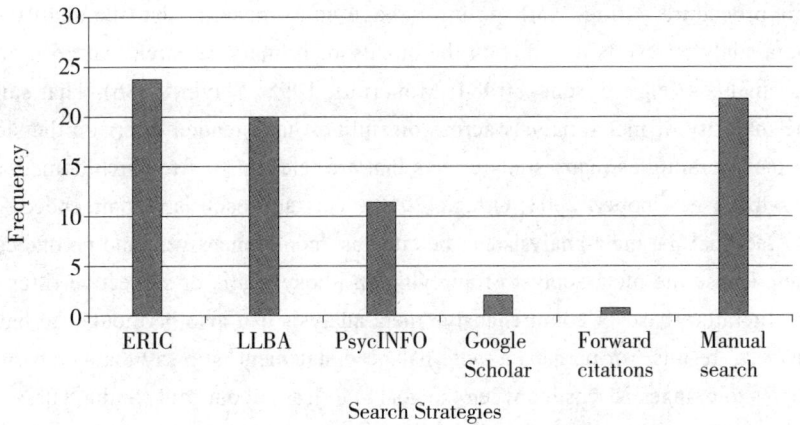

Fig. 2. Search strategies in meta-analyses of L2 research.

and informal in nature, are available to the meta-analyst. We would recommend searching in multiple ways, risking a high level of redundancy in order to ensure that any studies unique to a resource are retrieved.

As shown in Figure 2, the most popular database among SLA meta-analysts (24 out of 27) has been the Educational Resources Information Center (ERIC), followed by Linguistics and Language Behavior Abstracts (LLBA) and PsycINFO. Using resources such as Web of Science and Google Scholar that provide forward citations (i.e., the references to those who cited a particular study) is another common practice in present-day meta-analysis (White, 2009). Supplementing electronic database searches, older techniques are just as important, including manually scouring book chapters, journal archives, conference programs, and technical reports, requesting manuscripts from individual researchers, and asking prominent colleagues in the field if they know about any manuscripts in progress, in press, or on the scrap heap of statistical nonsignificance. The process of the entire literature search should be cataloged as it occurs, lest it be forgotten; then the process should be summarized and reported to inform readers' judgments about the nature and appropriateness of the meta-analysis.

Study Inclusion Criteria

An important choice in this early stage of a meta-analysis involves whether to filter out the low-quality studies before proceeding. Some scholars have recommended this procedure, citing "garbage in, garbage out," meaning that the quality of meta-analytic results depends on the quality of primary research that goes into the analysis (e.g., Eysenck, 1984; Moncrieff, 1998; Slavin, 1986). That said, the majority of meta-analysts across disciplines have tended to err on the side of incorporating as many study effects that are relevant to a research domain as possible (see Cooper, 2003; Ortega, 2010). This approach is recommended for the fact that the meta-analysis can be cited as "comprehensive," and no one can then accuse the meta-analyst of applying an idiosyncratic or subjective filter to the literature base. A comprehensive meta-analysis can also be thought to have "robust" results—or perhaps a more balanced statement is to say that comparing apples to oranges is sensible when the goal is to learn about fruit (Smith, Glass, & Miller, 1980). A notable exception in SLA to the principle of inclusiveness is a meta-analysis that applied strict methodological criteria when selecting studies of the effectiveness of written corrective feedback (Truscott, 2007). This decision affected both the size and even the direction of the results, when compared to Poltavtchenko and Johnson's (2009) inclusive meta-analysis of written corrective feedback ($d = -.16$ vs. $d = .33$, respectively). Specific exclusion criteria are always subject to debate, however, and any difference in effect sizes based on applying study exclusion criteria may be partially due to reducing the number of studies, independent of the level of study quality (e.g., $k = 5$ vs. $k = 13$ studies in the previous example).

An inclusive approach also enables the meta-analyst to examine study quality in a more empirical manner. Researchers can rate studies on one or more dimensions of quality, such as the quality of the measures, samples, and study designs. More commonly in meta-analysis, quality is quantified by the psychometric characteristics of the studies, such as sample sizes and alpha reliability coefficients (Hunter & F. L. Schmidt, 2004). No matter how quality is quantified, quality indices can be correlated with effect sizes to determine their relationship (Cooper, 1998). They can also be used to weight each study outcome, such that higher-quality studies contribute more to the meta-analytic average than do lower-quality studies (Rosenthal & DiMatteo, 2001; Valentine, 2009).

Two L2 meta-analyses serve as examples for examining quality empirically. One meta-analysis conducted meta-analyses on subgroups of studies based on a number of methodological criteria that reflect study quality, such as the level of control in experimental studies (studies with tight control: $d = .51$, weak control: $d = .38$, not controlled: $d = .59$; Adesope, Lavin, Thompson, & Ungerleider, 2009). Another meta-analysis found that studies that reported the reliability of their dependent measures tended to report higher effect sizes than studies that did not ($d = .65$ vs. $d = .42$; Plonsky, in press), suggesting that studies not reporting reliability coefficients may not have been as rigorous in nature.

Related to the issue in meta-analysis of the quality of primary studies in SLA is the decision of whether or not to exclude unpublished studies entirely (i.e., give them an implicit weight of zero). Some researchers may justifiably choose to include only peer-reviewed papers. Peer review helps ensure that published studies have met a standard of scientific quality as judged by experts in a given field (Burnham, 1990). Therefore, some SLA meta-analyses avoid sampling unpublished studies (e.g., Keck et al., 2006; Nekrasova & Becker, 2009), which also allows others to replicate the reported findings, if desired.

Other SLA meta-analysts instead decide to search for and include unpublished research. This is also a reasonable decision, and to date, approximately half of the 27 published and unpublished meta-analyses in SLA we review include unpublished studies, usually dissertations. One obvious statistical advantage of including unpublished studies is that the aggregated sample size increases, in turn increasing statistical power. Furthermore, meta-analyses containing unpublished research may be more robust, as mentioned, and also may be less vulnerable to distorted results due to publication bias, namely, the tendency of editors, reviewers, and individual researchers to favor only statistically significant or theoretically appealing findings (Moncrieff, 1998; Torgerson, 2006; Vevea & Woods, 2005; for a comprehensive review of this issue, see Rothstein, Sutton, & Borenstein, 2005).

Publication Bias

To assess publication bias, the fail-safe N is a statistic estimating how many nonsignificant studies (presumably unpublished and stashed in the file drawer) would need to be added to render a statistically significant meta-analytic effect nonsignificant (Orwin, 1983). When the fail-safe N is high, that is interpreted to mean that even a large number of nonsignificant studies may not influence the statistical significance of meta-analytic results too greatly. Although the fail-safe N has been calculated in SLA meta-analyses (Abraham, 2008; Adesope et al., 2009; Ross, 1998), it is not a very precise measure of publication bias (Becker, 2005).

To get better sense of publication bias in SLA, researchers have promoted the use of the funnel plot (see Li, 2010; Norris & Ortega, 2000; Plonsky, in press). In the funnel plot, effect sizes are plotted on the x-axis, and their corresponding sample sizes (or some function there of) on the y-axis. Assuming there is a single population effect underlying the set of effect sizes, the plot should take the form of an inverted funnel (see Figure 3a). In other words, smaller-sample studies will have less statistical power and will tend to produce a wider range of effect sizes that fan out at the bottom of the plot, while larger samples have more statistical power and will cluster toward the overall mean at the top center of the plot. Asymmetric plots indicate (but do not guarantee) some form of publication bias. For example, a funnel plot may be positively skewed (see Figure 3b) because small-sample studies that had small and nonsignificant effects were never published or reported.

Lumpy-looking funnel plots could indicate that moderator effects are present, where effects tend to be stronger for some subgroups of studies than for others (Sterne, Becker, & Egger, 2005). Out of the seven meta-analyses in SLA probing the issue of publication bias, three discovered a bias in favor of publishing statistically significant results. Future meta-analyses in SLA should continue the practice of plotting the distribution of study effect sizes as a visual aid for discovering possible publication bias, outliers, or other patterns of notable effects.

Coding

The coding stage of meta-analysis involves developing a scheme or template used to record important characteristics of each of the studies that may be included for meta-analysis. Coding requires identifying the most important char-acteristics of studies being meta-analyzed, and then deciding on the best coding format so that the coding data are representative and accurate. Typically, the study characteristics that are coded concern the nature of the sample (e.g., demographic composition, proficiency level) and the type of research design (e.g., classroom vs. laboratory, repeated-measures vs. between-subjects designs). These characteristics may be used simply to describe the pool of studies being meta-analyzed, just as a researcher would describe a sample of people being studied; they may be used to conduct meta-

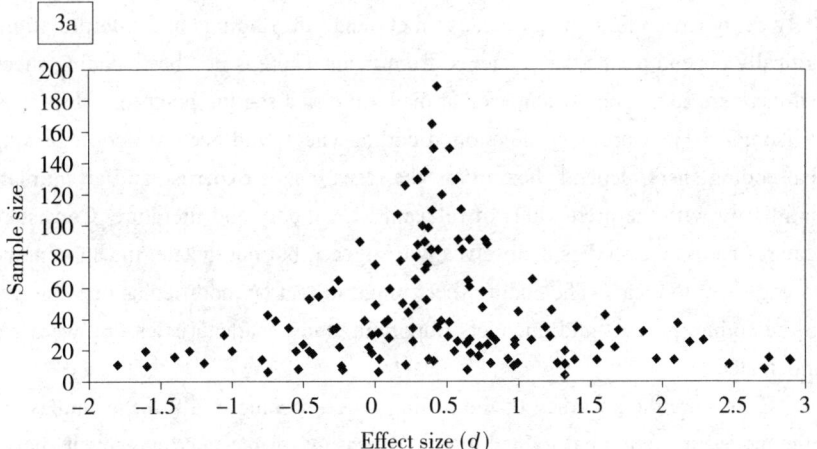

Fig. 3a. Example of a funnel plot without the presence of publication bias (modified from Plonsky, in press).

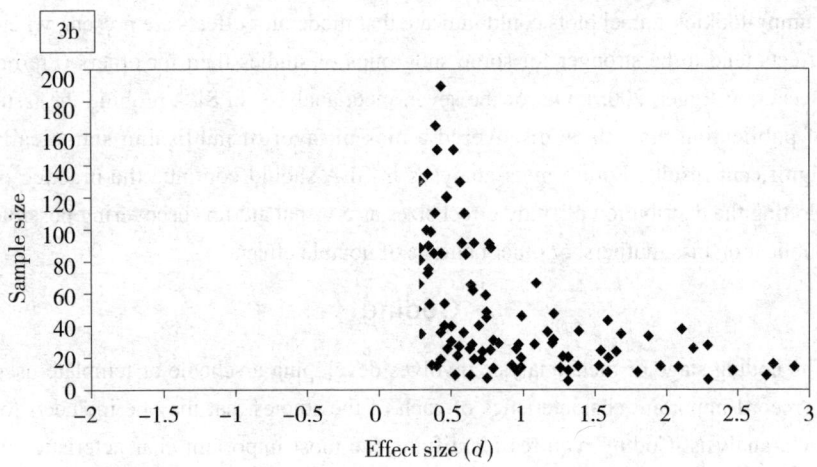

Fig. 3b. Example of a funnel plot with the presence of publication bias (modified from Plonsky, in press).

analyses within certain subgroups; or both. It is especially important to code the statistics reported in each study, such as descriptive statistics (e.g., sample sizes, means, standard deviations), and effect sizes (e.g., d values, correlations). In general, it may be useful to err on the side of coding more study information rather than less.

It is difficult to overemphasize the importance of a thorough and appropriately designed coding sheet, because meta-analytic findings and interpretations critically depend on the data obtained from them. There is no "best" coding sheet, but there are some good examples that may serve as a starting point (e.g., Lipsey & Wilson, 2001). A properly developed coding sheet, and accurate coding using that coding sheet, depends heavily on the researcher's expertise and an intimate familiarity with the predictions of relevant SLA theory and literature. Consistent features across the studies themselves will suggest, but not dictate, the appropriate coding sheet to create. The coding sheet might in fact be modified as one engages in the coding process and uncovers important study characteristics that were not anticipated.

To ensure the accuracy of the coding process, some or all of the studies are often coded by additional trained raters. A measure of interrater agreement should be calculated to determine accuracy of the ratings across raters (e.g., intraclass correlation, percent agreement, or number of rating discrepancies and how they were resolved). In SLA, 19 (70%) of the 27 meta-analyses we reviewed employed multiple raters, yet only 16 (59%) reported some form of interrater agreement. There is clearly a fundamental need for meta-analyses in this field to use multiple coders and report interrater agreement as a matter of habit (see Orwin & Vevea, 2009, for an excellent discussion of the need for multiple raters given the biases of coding).

We also urge future meta-analysts to publish their coding sheets (reported in 13 of 27 SLA meta-analyses) along with a clear description of the coding procedure. Ideally, the completed coding scheme for each study could be provided as online supplementary material. By making the entire meta-analytic process transparent, with the data on all study effects and study characteristics available for public inspection, consumers of meta-analyses can better understand and interpret the results. They also can replicate findings, combine additional study information of their own, or reanalyze the data in a different way that may provide additional insights.

The coding stage of a meta-analysis also requires the researcher to make decisions about unreported information, such as for those studies where the effect sizes, or the statistics required to calculate them (means, standard deviations, correlations), are not available. Three choices present themselves for dealing with this issue, and whatever choice is adopted should be reported by the meta-analyst. The most time-efficient alternative, and the option chosen for all but three meta-analyses in SLA, is to ignore or remove studies that contain missing data. Despite the appealing convenience of simply excluding these studies, it may not be the best choice for SLA meta-analysts who often must rely on a preciously small sample of primary studies. (The median number of studies across all published meta-analyses of L2 research is 16; the median number of samples is 23.) An alternative to removing missing data is to impute them. Although several procedures have been developed for estimating unreported values (see, e.g., Higgins, White, & Wood, 2008), only one SLA meta-analysis has done so. A meta-analyst must judiciously weigh the potential benefits of imputing data that are missing for a study, in order to salvage the other data available for that study, with the potential drawbacks of making too many imputations and abstractions from the original data. A third choice, reported by only two meta-analyses in SLA, is to request missing data directly from primary researchers themselves. We recommend this approach, but of course, researcher compliance will vary widely from such data requests, for a variety of reasons that are either stated or implied.

Analysis

As with the other stages previously described, many options also exist at the analysis stage, once the meta-analytic study data have been coded and organized into a database. Some meta-analytic approaches are relatively simple but as a result may carry overly simplistic assumptions of the data. Other meta-analytic methods lie at the other extreme, containing statistical nuances that strive to reach ultimate levels of precision that are not warranted by the data and often sacrifice some interpretability at the same time. It is the meta-analyst's responsibility to find a balance between these two extremes, conducting analyses that summarize the data in a faithful, reliable, and informative manner.

Meta-analysis would be a relatively simple endeavor if each primary study produced a single effect size based on a single outcome measure, particularly if measures, samples, and study designs were all the same. Studies in SLA are rarely, if ever, mere replications of one another, though; they are extensions or modifications of past work and may investigate multiple relationships, multiple groups, multiple instruments, and multiple time points. It is appropriate to average multiple effects within each study's sample when the effects reflect the same phenomenon. However, when a set of SLA studies each investigate a similar pattern of effects (e.g., relationships on multiple variables and measures within the same theoretical model), then the pattern of effects within each study is sample-dependent and should be analyzed that way (Cheung & Chan, 2004; Gleser & Olkin, 2009).

Another common analysis issue is when studies report effect sizes in different metrics (e.g., correlation coefficients and d values). These need to be converted to the same metric prior to meta-analysis. For example, repeated-measures and independent-groups designs require different formulas for calculating effect sizes and can only be combined when their estimates of sampling variance are suited to the designs (Morris & DeShon, 2002; see also Morris, 2008). Several resources provide appropriate formulas for converting effect sizes to a common metric prior to meta-analytic averaging (e.g., Lipsey & Wilson, 2001).

Weighted Averaging

When conducting the analysis, it is common to weight each study's effect size such that effects with higher weights will contribute more to the meta-analytic average. About half of the meta-analyses in SLA use weighted effect sizes, mostly weighting by sample size (nine studies) or similarly, weighting by the inverse of the sampling error variance (two studies). This form of weighting assumes that larger-sample effect sizes more accurately reflect true population effects and should therefore contribute more to the meta-analytic average than smaller-sample effects. Another common type of weighting is based on psychometric reliability, where studies with higher reliability contribute more to the meta-analytic average effect size. This weighting has been used in one SLA meta-analysis (Masgoret & Gardner, 2003). One can also create a weight that multiplies the individual weights for sample size, reliability, and other factors (see Hunter & F. L. Schmidt, 2004, and F. L. Schmidt, Le, & Oh, 2009, for detailed information on this approach). That said, SLA meta-analyses would greatly benefit even from a relatively simple sample-size weighting of effect sizes.

Fixed Versus Random Effects Models

In addition to the weighted average effect size in meta-analysis, there are estimates of the variance of study effect sizes. The observed variance can be mathematically decomposed in several ways, depending on the choice of meta-analysis model an SLA researcher decides to use. A *fixed effects* (FE) model assumes that study effects are homogeneous, or sample realizations of only one population effect size. Any variation in effects across studies, therefore, is assumed to be due to sampling error variance or other statistical artifacts (e.g., differences in measurement reliability). The Q test for homogeneity of effect sizes is a post hoc test of this assumption; a statistically significant Q statistic (chi-square with $k-1$ degrees of freedom) implies that the FE model does not hold, in other words, that study effects are heterogeneous even after artifacts are taken into account. A *random effects* (RE) model, by contrast, directly estimates this heterogeneity as a variance estimate (after accounting for sampling error variance). If the variance estimate has a confidence interval that does not include zero and is practically significant, then the conclusion is that study population effects are heterogeneous and do not have the same fixed value. A *mixed effects* model incorporates both fixed effects (variance in effects predicted by substantive variables) and random effects (unpredicted variance that remains).

If one had to select between the FE and RE model, the RE model is one that has a stronger conceptual motivation, because rather than assume homogeneity, the RE model tests for it (F. L. Schmidt, Oh, & Hayes, 2009). Only five meta-analyses in SLA appear to have mentioned the choice of model: In'nami and Koizumi (2009) used a mixed effects model; Taylor, Stevens, and Asher (2006), Li (2010), and Goo et al. (2009) calculated meta-analytic *d* values for both FE and RE models; and Norris and Ortega (2000) chose the RE model.

We wanted briefly to describe FE and RE models because these are now entrenched in the broader meta-analysis literature. Our perspective, however, is that SLA meta-analysis is much more productive and useful for its weighting and averaging procedures, and the choice of meta-analysis model generally does not change the average very much. Neither the FE nor RE model allows one to make strong substantive inferences about the homogeneity or heterogeneity of study effect sizes. First of all, statistical power for homogeneity tests are notoriously low, meaning that based on homogeneity tests, one may often mistakenly conclude that homogeneity exists when effects across studies are heterogeneous and vice versa (Hedges & Pigott, 2001; Oswald & Johnson, 1998), except perhaps in cases where the number of studies and their sample sizes are atypically large (Sutton & Higgins, 2008). Second, it is much better to use both theory and the available study data to suggest moderator analyses a priori, based on subgroups of studies, rather than conducting an overall test and conducting a subgroups analysis post hoc (e.g., a Q test or RE variance estimate).

In short, we urge SLA researchers to avoid homogeneity tests and rely more heavily on a combination of statistics, data visualization, and solid knowledge of the literature being analyzed to determine whether (a) all studies are similar (e.g., strict replications), (b) subgroups of studies differ (e.g., second vs. foreign language learners), or (c) most studies are relatively similar but some are unique (e.g., most are K–12 studies along with a single large-sample military study). Note that these efforts rely in part on the use and interpretation of confidence intervals (CIs). A 95% CI provides the expected range of 95% of the sampling variability for a given effect size, where smaller CIs indicate more precise effects (Kline, 2004). CIs can be built on a meta-analytic effect size or the effect size of an individual study. A CI for a meta-analytic effect size is based the number of effects in the meta-analysis, the variability in effects, and the sample size for each effect. The CI for the meta-analytic average effect across studies will usually be smaller than that for each constituent study effect—often much smaller when there are a large number of effects being meta-analyzed.

It is important to note that when examining the forest plot of effect sizes and CIs (shown in Figure 4 and Borenstein, 2005), nonoverlapping effect sizes indicate significant differences—but the converse is not true. When CIs overlap, the difference between effects may actually be statistically significant. For this latter situation, there are some rules of thumb for interpreting overlapping CIs appropriately (Cumming & Finch, 2005), or one may conduct a formal statistical test of the difference. Even with this caution in mind, the forest plot and funnel plot for publication bias are very useful visualization tools that can indicate meaningful patterns in the meta-analytic database.

Software

Space limitations prevent a critical review of current software programs available for meta-analysis, but we would be remiss if we did not indicate that a variety of commercial software, shareware, and freeware programs exist for coding

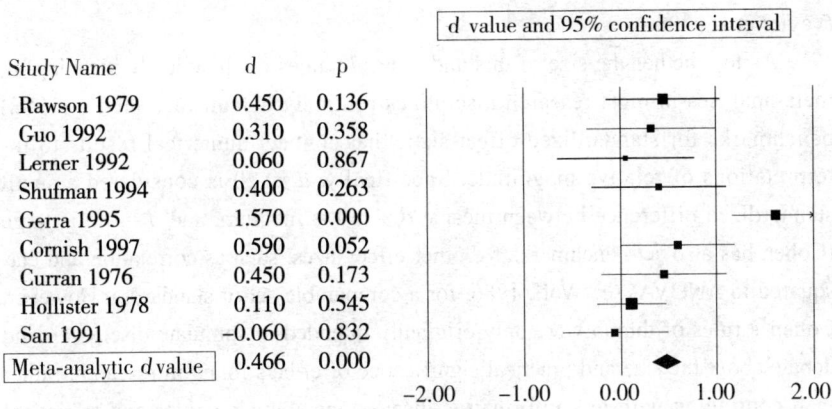

Fig. 4. Forest plot of *d* values and corresponding confidence intervals (from Borenstein, Hedges, Higgins, & Rothstein, 2005, used with permission).

and organizing data from the literature, computing and converting effect sizes, computing the meta-analytic effects, performing moderator analyses, determining publication bias, and creating publication-quality graphs of forest and funnel plots. Several sources provide recent reviews of a wide range of software and Internet resources useful for conducting a meta-analysis (e.g., Borenstein et al., 2009, chap. 44; Littell, Corcoran, & Pillai, 2008).

Interpreting Results from Meta-analysis

Having completed the more objective data collection and statistical procedures of the meta-analysis, the meta-analyst is faced with the critical task of asking and addressing key questions such as these: "How do I interpret the meta-analytic effect sizes averaged across studies?" "How big is a 'big' meta-analytic effect size and how small is 'small?'" "What are implications of the size and patterns of meta-analytic effect sizes for future research and practice?" (Kline, 2004). Answers to interpretational questions about effect sizes depend on the meta-analysis itself but also require the expert knowledge and experience of the meta-analyst (Kirk, 1996). Several SLA meta-analyses have interpreted meta-analytic d values using relative terms (e.g., small, medium, large effects). One SLA meta-analysis, for example, took a more literal approach, explaining that the overall d value of .54 means that the average L2 reader with access to first language (L1) glosses outperformed the average L2 reader without L1 glosses by approximately half a standard deviation (Taylor et al., 2006).

As to whether the size of this and other d values are practically meaningful, meta-analyses in most research disciplines routinely default to Cohen's (1988) benchmarks for standardized effect sizes that connect numerical results to interpretations of relative magnitude. Specifically, $d = .20$ is considered a small standardized difference between means, $d = .50$ is medium, and $d = .80$ is large (Cohen has also set benchmarks for other effect sizes, such as correlation and eta-squared in ANOVA; see Wolf, 1986, for a comparable set of standards). However, Cohen's rules of thumb were only originally intended to stimulate discussion and debate about the size and practical significance of effects found in research, rather than continuing with less informative discussions about p values and statistical significance.

Effect sizes are best understood when contextualized and interpreted with respect to other specific effects within a particular discipline (Valentine & Cooper, 2003). One would not expect Cohen's standards of small, medium, and large effect sizes to be identical for SLA and economics, for example, and they may even tend to be different for subtopics within SLA. Some applied linguists have responded to these suggestions by interpreting their research findings in relation to comparable meta-analyses of L1 (Plonsky, in press) and L2 research (e.g., Lee & Huang, 2008; Li, 2010), more often than not referring to Norris and Ortega (2000) as a point of reference. L2 research would surely benefit from a set of benchmarks reflecting the nature and size of effects across different sub-areas of SLA and meta-analyses could inform such benchmarks.

As a first step toward a more accurate understanding of the relative magnitude of effects in SLA, Table 1 presents 27 published and unpublished meta-analyses of L2 research and their effect sizes. These data indicate a fairly even dispersion of effects, ranging from a slightly negative difference to a large difference of approximately 1.5 standard deviations between control and experimental group means. As expected, differences in pre-post designs tend to be larger than for between-groups differences, because study participants serve as their own control in a pre-post design, increasing power to the extent that this effect offsets the smaller sample size typical of these designs (see Lipsey & Wilson, 1993; Morris, 2008). At this broad level of surveying effects across L2 meta-analyses in Table 1, Cohen's (1988) benchmarks appear to underestimate the experimental effects generally obtained in L2 research. Thus, we offer a preliminary and general set of SLA standards for effect sizes, with $d = .40$ representing a small effect, $d = .70$ medium, and $d = 1.00$ a large effect. We do not mean to offer these values as yet another gold standard; they do not apply with any precision to the entire population of research in SLA and should be refined further. Even with SLA-specific norms in place for small, medium, and large effect sizes, what appears to be a numerically large effect for a particular treatment, research design, or population of interest may reflect a theoretically or practically small effect, and conversely, small effects can have very important implications in other contexts (Kirk, 1996; Kline, 2004; Prentice & Miller, 1992; Volker, 2006).

When interpreting the magnitude of averaged effect sizes from meta-analysis, it may also be useful to reflect on the theoretical development of the research being synthesized. Early research is often characterized by experiments that induce strong manipulations to determine whether an effect even exists, let alone whether it is generalizable. Such experiments would tend to yield large effect sizes (Kline, 2004). Subsequently, after an effect is found and theory is advanced by an accumulating corpus of supportive empirical evidence, studies may shift toward examining the generalizability of an effect across samples and settings, leading to more variable effects.

Specifically, effects can be examined to determine whether correlations or group differences are a function of moderators or mediators (for a short and clear discussion of moderators and mediators, see Holmbeck, 1997). Moderator variables affect the strength of a relationship when they change. For example, classroom environment could by hypothesized as a moderator variable for the relationship between students' cognitive ability and L2 mastery. In this case, low-ability students

Table 1. Overall Findings from Meta-analyses of L2 Research

Study	Topic	d, CG-EG contrasts (k)	d, pre-post contrasts (k)
Goldschneider & DeKeyser (2001)	Causes of a natural order of acquisition	-	3.10[a] (12)
		-	2.67[a] (12)
Ross (1998)	Validity of self-assessment	-	1.62[a] (11)
Wa-Mbaleka (2006)	Effects of L2 reading on vocabulary	1.43 (48)	1.06 (13)
Nekrasova & Becker (2009)	L2 Practice	1.31 (69)	2.02 (10)
Dinsmore (2006)	Universal grammar and SLA	1.25 (22)	-
Russell & Spada (2006)	Corrective feedback	1.16 (15)	-
Zhao (2003)	Effects of technology	1.12 (9)	-
Taylor (2006)	Reading with CALL vs. traditional L1 glosses	1.09 (4)	-
		.39 (14)	-
Norris & Ortega (2000)	Effectiveness of instruction	.96 (49)	1.66 (19)
Keck et al. (2006)	Effects of interaction	.92 (24)	1.17 (16)

Study	Topic	d, CG-EG contrasts (k)	d, pre-post contrasts (k)
Spada & Tomita (2010)	Explicitness of instruction and complexity of linguistic features	.88 (24) .73 (20) .39 (29) .33 (9)	.84 (16) .88 (18) .29 (18) .66 (5)
Goo et al. (2009)	Effectiveness of instruction	.87 (36)	-
Abraham (2008)	Effect of computer-mediated glosses on vocabulary and reading comprehension	.73 (11) 1.40 (11)	- -
Mackey & Goo (2007)	Effects of interaction	.75 (22)	1.09 (41)
Lyster & Saito (2010)	Oral feedback	.74 (43)	-
Adesope et al. (2009)	Cognitive benefits of bilingualism	.73 (39)	-
Won (2008)	Vocabulary instruction	.69 (43)	-
In'nami & Koizumi (2009)	Format effects in test performance	.65 (22)	-
Li (2010)	Corrective feedback	.61 (28)	-
Jeon & Kaya (2006)	Pragmatics instruction	.59 (7)	1.57 (16)
Taylor et al. (2006)	Reading strategy instruction	.54 (23)	-
Masgoret & Gardner (2003)	Motivation and achievement	-	.49a (51)

Table 1. Continued

Study	Topic	d, CG-EG contrasts (k)	d, pre-post contrasts (k)
		-	.49[a] (55)
		-	.80[a] (55)
		-	.41[a] (49)
		-	.32[a] (49)
Plonsky (in press)	Strategy instruction	.49 (95)	-
Grgurović (2007)	CALL comparison studies	.39 (37)	-
Poltavtchenko & Johnson (2009)	Corrective feedback on writing	.33 (13)	.39 (18)
Lee & Huang (2008)	Input enhancement	.22 (17)	.55 (11)

		−.26 (7)	-
Truscott (2007)	Corrective feedback on writing	−.16 (5)	.15 (7)
Miller & Pan (2009)		-[b]	-[b]
Mean		.71	1.06
SD		.41	.80
95% CI	Lower	.56	.72
	Upper	.86	1.40

Note. Effect sizes listed in descending order. No distinctions have been made between models (i.e., random effects, fixed effects, or mixed effects) or weighting of effect sizes. CALL = computer-assisted language learning.
[a] Converted from Pearson's correlation coefficient; [b] Results could not be obtained from the authors.

might profit from a richer classroom environment, and therefore cognitive ability would have less of an effect in this setting compared with less stimulating classroom settings. In contrast with moderating variables that qualify the strength of a relationship, mediating variables either fully or partially explain a relationship between an independent and dependent variable. For instance, the relationship between cognitive ability and L2 mastery may be mediated by frequency of exposure to the target language, such that cognitive ability has a significantly reduced effect on mastery once exposure is taken into account.

SLA meta-analyses have carried out some of these more refined moderator analyses, including some of those we have mentioned: The meta-analysis relating self-assessment to achievement examined differences in correlations based on specific skills (e.g., listening, speaking; Ross, 1998); the meta-analysis examining the effect of corrective feedback on L2 gains went on to compare the effectiveness of immediate implicit versus explicit feedback (d = .54 vs. .69, respectively; Li, 2010); and a meta-analysis of the effectiveness of L2 strategy instruction examined whether longer interventions tended to yield greater improvements in L2 learning and use (Plonsky, in press). Note that the latter relationship is not addressed directly in any individual study, yet was able to be investigated meta-analytically.

The research setting is another very important moderator effect that can be discovered as a body of research accumulates over time. In particular, as theoretical models and research findings mature, research may migrate from experimental settings to educational settings that contain more uncontrolled and unmeasured factors. For example, one recent SLA meta-analysis found the effect of lab studies to be almost twice as large as those found in classroom studies ($d = .79$ vs. $d = .43$, respectively; Plonsky, in press).

In contrast with the scenario of discovering more subtle effects over time, there is an alternative scenario where advances in theory, design, and measurement enable researchers to overcome the historical shortcomings of past research, allowing them to design studies that generally result in larger effect sizes (Fern & Monroe, 1996). These two aforementioned trends are opposite in nature; they may be competitive explanations for a set of research findings, or they may run in parallel. Both trends should be considered when interpreting not only the set of effects available for analysis, but how the size of these effects may change over time as theory and research evolve.

To summarize, meta-analysts, just like primary researchers, have a responsibility for drawing appropriate conclusions based on the available body of research evidence — perhaps an even greater responsibility, to the extent that a meta-analysis has widespread visibility and impact. Although there have been two decades of ritual reliance on the same set of benchmarks for practical significance across most of the social sciences, and although we offered some SLA benchmarks ourselves, we want to argue that SLA research will benefit by considering the range of practically significant effect sizes within each of its subdisciplines, eventually moving away from donning small, medium, and large "t-shirt effect sizes" out of mere availability and convenience (Kline, 2009, p. 172).

For a meta-analysis to be interpreted in a balanced and scholarly manner, SLA researchers require a thorough understanding of the literature, with knowledge of (a) the development and progression of theories and paradigms underlying the substantive domain being meta-analyzed; (b) the nature of the independent variables and how they tend to be manipulated; (c) the psychometric reliability of outcome measures, because low reliability attenuates effect sizes; (d) the effectiveness (and problems) of the research methods used in primary research; and (e) whether size and patterns of the effects actually found in meta-analyses conform with theoretically expected predictions (Henson, 2006; Kirk, 1996; Kline, 2009).

CHALLENGES OF APPLYING META-ANALYSIS TO L2 RESEARCH

To this point, we have focused on the benefits and considerations when synthesizing research by means of meta-analysis; however, there are also several distinct challenges to meta-analysis that merit our attention, particularly as they pertain to L2 research. One concern is that seemingly conclusive findings from meta-analyses may either slow or shut down research activities in their respective areas prematurely (Bangert-Drowns, 1995). Especially at this early stage in the development of cumulative knowledge in SLA, we feel that meta-analysis most appropriately provides descriptive information of a literature base that suggests future research directions versus any sort of conclusive statistical summary that, by the sheer weight of the cumulative sample size, implies that any further research in an area is redundant. Narrative reviewing procedures should complement quantitative findings from meta-analysis by offering a conceptual model—often one that covers more ground than the models found within any individual study—that can then be used to identify specific areas in the literature that are important yet have been underresearched or ignored in the meta-analysis. In other words, meta-analysis is equally beneficial for both summarizing past empirical findings while stimulating future lines of research inquiry.

For future studies to meet the needs that are identified by SLA meta-analyses, we are in support of Norris and Ortega (2000, 2006, 2007; Ortega, 2010), who recommend shifting away from isolated research activities. There is a growing need for carefully designed collaborative research that seeks to replicate and thereby test the external validity of previous findings across contexts and learners that differ in theoretically important ways (*Language Teaching Review Panel*, 2008; Polio & Gass, 1997; Porte, 2009; Valdman, 1993). For instance, the conclusion of a meta-analysis of the effects of corrective feedback (CF) on grammar learning pointed out a need "for studies that investigate similar variables in a consistent manner," lamenting that the "wide range of variables examined in CF is spread rather thin" (Russell & Spada, 2006, p. 156). Unfortunately, this condition is not unique to CF, which has been the object of extensive research in SLA for decades. Ideally, broad agenda setting and collaboration would likely accelerate progress across most L2 research domains, if not all of them. We had mentioned this already in the context of a prospective meta-analysis.

SLA researchers could also collaborate when they disagree on construct definitions and operationalizations, as is common, because these conflicts tend to produce a set of studies that is challenging to meta-analyze. Consider, for example, the concept of "noticing" and the wide range of operationalizations and outcome measures that have been used to study its effects on L2 learning (e.g., R. Schmidt, 2001; Truscott, 1998). The prospect of meta-analyzing a set of studies as diverse and unsettled as the research on noticing is daunting. We do not mean to say that collaboration between those who disagree should lead to theoretical homogeneity. Instead we suggest that researchers who disagree might conduct an *adversarial collaboration* (Mitchell & Tetlock, 2009) to further the development of the research base, locating key constructs that can later be synthesized meaningfully and appropriately, whether it is in terms of a unified theory or in terms of a stronger bifurcation that of which each research camp ultimately achieves a better understanding. More generally, collaboration can serve to clarify and distinguish important theoretical definitions and models, perhaps leading to greater standardization of key measures and interventions that pave the way for more detailed meta-analyses and more reliable estimates of effects. Theoretical orientation, then, could serve as a moderator variable. This approach of adversarial collaboration might also reduce the high expectation of any single research effort or any single theory to provide conclusive answers within an L2 discipline (Norris & Ortega, 2007).

Even with theoretical disagreements in subdisciplines of SLA research, an agreed-upon set of appropriate definitions and measures would greatly facilitate meta-analysis as well as more fine-grained comparisons between studies. Although this is ideal, in reality, meta-analysis is constrained by what primary research ends up reporting—and not reporting. Unfortunately, and somewhat surprisingly, even the descriptive statistics needed to calculate effect sizes (usually the sample size, group means, and standard deviations) are all too often missing from published studies, forcing meta-analysts to exclude those studies from any analysis. To provide a concrete sense of this problem, the following numbers of studies were excluded from six SLA meta-analyses because of information that was not reported: 31 (194% of the studies that were meta-analyzed; Dinsmore, 2006), 19 (119%; Nekrasova & Becker, 2009), 32 (71%; Norris & Ortega, 2000),

36 (59%; Plonsky, in press), 16 (110%; Russell & Spada, 2006), and 20 (59%; Wa-Mbaleka, 2006). These studies could have provided valuable information to a meta-analysis, if the researchers had reported basic statistical information. SLA journals should require the reporting of appropriate descriptive statistics, correlations, and reliability coefficients where appropriate, if only for a greater understanding of the study itself, if not for future meta-analyses.

In addition to the issue of dealing with unreported descriptive statistics critical to meta-analysis, another issue is that the frequency of reporting the reliability of measures used in SLA research is extremely low (see Henning, 1986; Norris & Ortega, 2003). Nekrasova and Becker (2009) and Norris and Ortega (2000) both raised this problem, finding that 6% and 16% of the primary studies in their syntheses, respectively, reported the reliability of their dependent measures. It is important to consider the potential unreliability of measures that are implemented in those studies contributing to a meta-analysis, because just as completely unreliable measures lead to null effects, measures with low reliability will lead to reduced effect sizes—even when the actual effect being measured is large. As we have mentioned, coefficients for measurement reliability (e.g., Cronbach's alpha, test-retest reliability) can be used to weight each study's effect size in a meta-analysis, such that the effects from studies with more reliable measures contribute more to the average. Reporting reliability therefore allows a meta-analyst to weight studies in a more precise manner. More generally, by examining the distribution of reliability coefficients, SLA meta-analysts can summarize and interpret the psychometric quality of the substantive measures that are used in a given research area.

SUMMARY CONCLUSION

Meta-analysis generally improves traditional narrative reviews within a research domain by systematically identifying and coding the available quantitative effects, weighting and averaging them in a manner consistent with the statistical strength of the evidence. Meta-analysis is also informative for the results that are not provided, because this may indicate fruitful areas for future research (alternatively, these empirical lacunae may represent "danger zones" where no researcher dare tread!).

Given the growth of meta-analysis taking place in SLA, we close with three brief suggestions. First, we encourage searching for major substantive and statistical indicators of publication bias in a body of research. It is not unreasonable to think that journals tend to reject work that reports nonsignificant effects, and if this is true, then meta-analyses relying only on published effects in a research domain will likely overestimate the overall effect size across studies. At the very least, funnel plots can be provided in the journal space or as online supplementary material, and readers can visually examine effect sizes themselves for potential publication bias or other unique patterns that might not be revealed if one were to look at the summary results from meta-analysis alone. SLA meta-analysts might also more directly attempt to obtain studies in sources that are not readily accessible in hopes that bias is reduced.

Second, SLA researchers should be as transparent as possible about the process of meta-analysis that they undertook, so that readers can better understand and interpret the results, if not replicate them on their own. Transparency includes being open about decision points during the meta-analysis, and it also means making one's coding sheets available and publishing a clear table (or tables) listing the studies and all the data that were involved in the analysis (e.g., sample size, effect size, demographics, and reliability coefficients). Third, we recommend that meta-analysts emphasize practical significance but shift away from Cohen's benchmarks. These benchmarks should be revised within SLA subdisciplines in light of other issues such as manipulation of independent variables, practical significance, and theoretical maturity. We offer a different scale for general interpretations of effect size estimates based on findings from 27 meta-analyses in SLA.

Finally, we note that there is no substitute for well-conducted primary studies in SLA that attempt to satisfy the textbook ideals of representative sampling, careful experimental design, and psychometrically reliable measurement. Primary studies therefore have at least as much promise as meta-analysis, if not more, for answering challenging theoretical and practical research questions in SLA. Meta-analyses often inform primary research by pointing out which theoretical areas are more promising, which types of studies have yielded more compelling results, and how future research needs might increment existing research or blaze new territory previously undiscovered. We are excited about the potential for meta-analysis to summarize the history of research in applied linguistics and to guide its future.

REFERENCES

Abraham, L. B. (2008). Computer-mediated glosses in second language reading comprehension and vocabulary learning: A meta-analysis. *Computer Assisted Language Learning*, *21*, 199–226.

Adesope, O. O., Lavin, T., Thompson, T., & Ungerleider, C. (2009, April). S*ystematic review and meta-analysis on the cognitive benefits of bilingualism*. Paper presented at the annual meeting of the American Educational Research Association, San Diego, CA.

Balluerka, N., Gómez, J., & Hidalgo, D. (2005). The controversy over null hypothesis significance testing revisited. *Methodology*, *1*, 55–70.

Bangert-Drowns, R. L. (1995). Misunderstanding meta-analysis. *Evaluation & the Health Professions*, *18*, 304–314.

Becker, B. J. (2005). Failsafe *N* or file-drawer number. In H. R. Rothstein, A. J. Sutton, & M. Borenstein (Eds.), *Publication bias in meta-analysis: Prevention, assessment and adjustments* (pp. 111–126). Hoboken, NJ: Wiley.

Becker, B. J. (2009). Model-based meta-analysis. In H. Cooper, L. V. Hedges, & J. C. Valentine (Eds.), *The handbook of research synthesis and meta-analysis* (2nd ed., pp. 377–395). New York: Sage.

Berlin, J. A., & Ghersi, D. G. (2005). Preventing publication bias: Registries and prospective meta-analysis. In H. R. Rothstein, A. J. Sutton, & M. Borenstein (Eds.), *Publication bias in meta-analysis: Prevention, assessment and adjustments* (pp. 35–48). Hoboken, NJ: Wiley.

Borenstein, M. (2005). Software for publication bias. In H. R. Rothstein, A. J. Sutton, & M. Borenstein (Eds.), *Publication bias in meta-analysis: Prevention, assessment and adjustments* (pp. 193–220). Hoboken, NJ: Wiley.

Borenstein, M., Hedges, L. V., Higgins, J. P. T., & Rothstein, H. R. (2005). *Comprehensive meta-analysis* (*Version 2*). Englewood, NJ: Biostat.

Borenstein, M., Hedges, L. V., Higgins, J. P. T., & Rothstein, H. R. (2009). *Introduction to meta-analysis*. Hoboken, NJ: Wiley.

Burnham, J. C. (1990). The evolution of editorial peer review. *Journal of the American Medical Association*, *263*, 1323–1329.

Chandler, J. (2004). A response to Truscott. *Journal of Second Language Writing*, *13*, 345–348.

Cheung, S. F., & Chan, D. K.-S. (2004). Dependent effect sizes in meta-analysis: Incorporating the degree of interdependence. *Journal of Applied Psychology*, *89*, 780–791.

Cohen, J. (1988). *Statistical power analysis for the behavioral sciences* (2nd ed.). Hillsdale, NJ: Erlbaum.

Cooper, H. (1998). *Synthesizing research: A guide for literature reviews*. Thousand Oaks, CA: Sage.

Cooper, H. (2003). Editorial. *Psychological Bulletin*, *129*, 3–9.

Cooper, H. M., & Rosenthal, R. (1980). Statistical versus traditional procedures for summarizing research findings. *Psychological Bulletin, 87*, 442–449.

Crookes, G. (1991). Power, effect size, and second language research: Another researcher comments. *TESOL Quarterly, 25*, 762–765.

Cumming, G., & Finch, S. (2005). Inference by eye: Confidence intervals and how to read pictures of data. *American Psychologist, 60*, 170–180.

Dinsmore, T. H. (2006). Principles, parameters, and SLA: A retrospective meta-analytic investigation into adult L2 learners' access to Universal Grammar. In J. M. Norris & L. Ortega (Eds.), *Synthesizing research on language learning and teaching* (pp. 53–90). Philadelphia: John Benjamins.

Ellis, N. C. (2006). Meta-analysis, human cognition, and language learning. In J. M. Norris & L. Ortega (Eds.), *Synthesizing research on language learning and teaching* (pp. 301–322). Philadelphia: John Benjamins.

Eysenck, H. J. (1984). Meta-analysis: An abuse of research integration. *Journal of Special Education, 18*, 41–59.

Fern, E. F., & Monroe, K. B. (1996). Effect-size estimates: Issues and problems in interpretation. *Journal of Consumer Research, 23*, 89–105.

Ferris, D. (1999). The case for grammar correction in L2 writing classes: A response to Truscott (1996). *Journal of Second Language Writing, 8*, 1–11.

Ferris, D. (2004). The "grammar correction" debate in L2 writing: Where are we, and where do we go from here? (and what do we do in the meantime?). *Journal of Second Language Writing, 13*, 49–62.

Glass, G. V. (1976). Primary, secondary, and meta-analysis of research. *Educational Researcher, 5*, 3–8.

Gleser, L. J., & Olkin, I. (2009). Stochastically dependent effect sizes. In H. Cooper, L. V. Hedges, & J. C. Valentine (Eds.), *The handbook of research synthesis and meta-analysis* 2nd ed., (pp. 357–376). New York: Sage.

Goldschneider, J. M., & DeKeyser, R. M. (2001). Explaining the natural order of L2 morpheme acquisition: A meta-analysis of multiple determinants. *Language Learning, 51*, 1–50.

Goo, J., Granena, G., Novella, M., & Yilmaz, Y. (2009, October). *Implicit and explicit instruction in L2 learning: Norris and Ortega (2000) revisited and updated.* Paper presented at the Second Language Research Forum, East Lansing, MI.

Grgurović, M. (2007, October). *Research on CALL comparison studies: Can a meta-analysis inform instructed SLA?* Paper presented at the Second Language Research Forum, Urbana-Champaign, IL.

Hall, J. A., & Rosenthal, R. (1995). Interpreting and evaluating meta-analysis. *Evaluation & the Health Professions, 18*, 393–407.

Hedges, L. V., & Olkin, I. (1985). *Statistical methods for meta-analysis*. Orlando, FL: Academic Press.

Hedges, L. V., & Pigott, T. D. (2001). The power of statistical tests in meta-analysis. *Psychological Methods, 6*, 203–217.

Henning, G. (1986). Quantitative methods in language acquisition research. *TESOL Quarterly, 20*, 701–708.

Henson, R. K. (2006). Effect-size measures and meta-analytic thinking in counseling psychology research. *The Counseling Psychologist, 34*, 601–629.

Higgins, J. P. T., White, I. R., & Wood, A. M. (2008). Imputation methods for missing outcome data in meta-analysis of clinical trials. *Clinical Trials, 5*, 225–239.

Holmbeck, G. N. (1997). Toward terminological, conceptual, and statistical clarity in the study of mediators and moderators: Examples from the child-clinical and pediatric psychology literatures. *Journal of Counseling and Clinical Psychology, 65*, 599–610.

Hunter, J. E., & Schmidt, F. L. (2004). *Methods of meta-analysis: Correcting error and bias in research findings*. Thousand Oaks, CA: Sage.

In'nami, Y., & Koizumi, R. (2009). A meta-analysis of test format effects on reading and listening test performance: Focus on multiple-choice and open-ended formats. *Language Testing, 26*, 219–244.

Jeon, E. H., & Kaya, T. (2006). Effects of L2 instruction on interlanguage pragmatic development: A meta-analysis. In J. M. Norris & L. Ortega (Eds.), *Synthesizing research on language learning and teaching* (pp. 165–211). Philadelphia: John Benjamins.

Kavale, K. A. (1995). Meta-analysis at 20: Retrospect and prospect. *Evaluation & the Health Professions, 18*, 349–369.

Keck, C. M., Iberri-Shea, G., Tracy-Ventura, N., & Wa-Mbaleka, S. (2006). Investigating the empirical link between task-based interaction and acquisition: A meta-analysis. In J. M. Norris & L. Ortega (Eds.), *Synthesizing research on language learning and teaching* (pp. 91–131). Philadelphia: John Benjamins.

Kirk, R. E. (1996). Practical significance: A concept whose time has come. *Educational and Psychological Measurement, 56*, 746–759.

Kline, R. B. (2004). *Beyond significance testing: Reforming data analysis methods in behavioral research*. Washington, DC: American Psychological Association.

Kline, R. B. (2009). *Becoming a behavioral science researcher: A guide to producing research that matters*. New York: Guilford Press.

Language Teaching Review Panel (2008). Replication studies in language learning and teaching: Questions and answers. *Language Teaching, 41*, 1–14.

Larson-Hall, J. (2010). *A guide to doing statistics in second language research using SPSS*. New York: Routledge.

Lazaraton, A. (1991). Power, effect size, and second language research: A researcher comments. *TESOL Quarterly, 25*, 759–762.

Lazaraton, A. (2000). Current trends in research methodology and statistics in applied linguistics. *TESOL Quarterly, 34*, 175–181.

Lee, S.-K., & Huang, H.-T. (2008). Visual input enhancement and grammar learning: A meta-analytic review. *Studies in Second Language Acquisition, 30*, 307–331.

Li, S. (2010). The effectiveness of corrective feedback in SLA: A meta-analysis. *Language Learning, 60*, 309–365.

Lipsey, M. W., & Wilson, D. B. (1993). The efficacy of psychological, educational, and behavioral treatment: Confirmation from meta-analysis. *American Psychologist, 48*, 1181–1209.

Lipsey, M. W., & Wilson, D. B. (2001). *Practical meta-analysis.* Thousand Oaks, CA: Sage.

Littell, J. H., Corcoran, J. C., & Pillai, V. (2008). *Systematic reviews and meta-analysis.* New York: Oxford University Press.

Lykken, D. (1968). Statistical significance in psychological research. *Psychological Bulletin, 70*, 151–159.

Lyster, R., & Saito, K. (2010). Oral feedback in classroom SLA: A meta-analysis. *Studies in Second Language Acquisition, 32*, 265–302.

Mackey, A., & Goo, J. (2007). Interaction research in SLA: A meta-analysis and research synthesis. In A. Mackey (Ed.), *Conversational interaction in second language acquisition: A collection of empirical studies* (pp. 407–451). New York: Oxford University Press.

Masgoret, A.-M., & Gardner, R. C. (2003). Attitudes, motivation, and second language learning: A meta-analysis of studies conducted by Gardner and associates. *Language Learning, 53*, 123–163.

Miller, P. C., & Pan, W. (2009, March). *Recasts in the L2 classroom: A meta-analytic review.* Paper presented at the meeting of the American Association for Applied Linguistics, Denver, CO.

Mitchell, G. A., & Tetlock, P. E. (2009). A renewed appeal for adversarial collaboration. *Research in Organizational Behavior, 29*, 71–72.

Moncrieff, J. (1998). Research synthesis: Systematic reviews and meta-analysis. *International Review of Psychiatry, 10*, 304–311.

Morris, S. B. (2008). Estimating effect sizes from pretest-posttest-control group designs. *Organizational Research Methods, 11*, 364–386.

Morris, S. B., & DeShon, R. P. (2002). Combining effect size estimates in meta-analysis with repeated measures and independent-groups designs. *Psychological Methods, 7*, 105–125.

Nekrasova, T., & Becker, T. (2009). *Effectiveness of practice: A research synthesis and quantitative meta-analysis.* Manuscript in preparation.

Norris, J. M., & Ortega, L. (2000). Effectiveness of L2 instruction: A research synthesis and quantitative meta-analysis. *Language Learning, 50*, 417–528.

Norris, J. M., & Ortega, L. (2003). Defining and measuring SLA. In C. Doughty & M. Long (Eds.), *The handbook of second language acquisition* (pp. 717–761). Malden, MA: Blackwell.

Norris, J. M., & Ortega, L. (2006). The value and practice of research synthesis for language learning and teaching. In J. M. Norris & L. Ortega (Eds.), *Synthesizing research on language learning and teaching* (pp. 3–50). Philadelphia: John Benjamins.

Norris, J. M., & Ortega, L. (2007). The future of research synthesis in applied linguistics: Beyond art or science. *TESOL Quarterly, 41*, 805–815.

Ortega, L. (2010). Research syntheses. In B. Paltridge & A. Phakiti (Eds.), *Continuum companion to research methods in applied linguistics* (pp. 111–126). London: Continuum.

Orwin, R. G. (1983). A fail-safe N for effect size in meta-analysis. *Journal of Educational Statistics, 8*, 157–159.

Orwin, R. G., & Vevea, J. L. (2009). Evaluating coding decisions. In H. Cooper, L. V. Hedges, & J. C. Valentine (Eds.), *The handbook of research synthesis* (2nd ed., pp. 177–203). New York: Russell Sage Foundation.

Oswald, F. L., & Johnson, J. W. (1998). On the robustness, bias, and stability of results from meta-analysis of correlation coefficients: Some initial Monte Carlo findings. *Journal of Applied Psychology, 83*, 164–178.

Oswald, F. L., & McCloy, R. A. (2003). Meta-analysis and the art of the average. In K. R. Murphy (Ed.), *Validity generalization: A critical review* (pp. 311–338). Mahwah, NJ: Erlbaum.

Plonsky, L. (2009, October). *"Nix the null": Why statistical significance is overrated.* Paper presented at the Second Language Research Forum, East Lansing, MI.

Plonsky, L. (in press). *The effectiveness of second language strategy instruction: A meta-analysis.*

Polio, C., & Gass, S. (1997). Replication and reporting: A commentary. *Studies in Second Language Acquisition, 19*, 499–508.

Poltavtchenko, E., & Johnson, M. D. (2009, March). *Feedback and second language writing: A meta-analysis.* Poster session presented at the annual meeting of TESOL, Denver, CO.

Porte, G. (2009, March). *Encouraging replication research in the field of applied linguistics and second language acquisition.* Invited colloquium presented at the meeting of the American Association for Applied Linguistics, Denver, CO.

Preiss, R. W., & Allen, M. (1995). Understanding and using meta-analysis. *Evaluation & the Health Professions, 18*, 315–335.

Prentice, D. A., & Miller, D. T. (1992). When small effects are impressive. *Psychological*

Bulletin, 112, 160–164.
Rosenthal, R. (1978). Combining results of independent studies. *Psychological Bulletin, 85,* 185–193.
Rosenthal, R., & DiMatteo, M. R. (2001). Meta-analysis: Recent developments in quantitative methods for literature reviews. *Annual Review of Psychology, 51,* 59–82.
Ross, S. (1998). Self-assessment in second language testing: A meta-analysis and analysis of experiential factors. *Language Testing, 15,* 1–20.
Rothstein H. R., Sutton A. J., & Borenstein M. (Eds.). (2005). *Publication bias in meta-analysis: Prevention, assessment and adjustments.* Hoboken, NJ: Wiley.
Russell, J., & Spada, N. (2006). The effectiveness of corrective feedback for the acquisition of L2 grammar: A meta-analysis of the research. In J. M. Norris & L. Ortega (Eds.), *Synthesizing research on language learning and teaching* (pp. 133–164). Philadelphia: John Benjamins.
Schmidt, F. L. (1996). Statistical significance testing and cumulative knowledge in psychology: Implications for training of researchers. *Psychological Methods, 1,* 115–129.
Schmidt, F. L., & Hunter, J. E. (1977). Development of a general solution to the problem of validity generalization. *Journal of Applied Psychology, 62,* 529–540.
Schmidt, F. L., Le, H., & Oh, I.-S. (2009). Correcting for the distorting effects of study artifacts in meta-analysis. In H. Cooper, L. V. Hedges, & J. C. Valentine (Eds.), *The handbook of research synthesis and meta-analysis* (2nd ed., pp. 317–333). New York: Sage.
Schmidt, F. L., Oh, I.-S., & Hayes, T. (2009). Fixed versus random effects models in meta-analysis: Model properties and an empirical comparison of differences in results. *British Journal of Mathematical and Statistical Psychology, 62,* 97–128.
Schmidt, R. (2001). Attention. In P. Robinson (Ed.), *Cognition and second language instruction* (pp. 3–32). New York: Cambridge University Press.
Slavin, R. E. (1986). Best-evidence synthesis: An alternative to meta-analytic and traditional reviews. *Educational Researcher, 15,* 5–11.
Smith, M. L., Glass, G. V., & Miller, T. I. (1980). *The benefits of psychotherapy.* Baltimore, MD: Johns Hopkins.
Spada, N., & Tomita, Y. (2010). Interactions between type of instruction and type of language feature: A meta-analysis. *Language Learning, 60,* 263–308.
Sterne, J. A. C., Becker, B. K., & Egger, M. (2005). The funnel plot. In H. R. Rothstein, A. J. Sutton, & M. Borenstein (Eds.), *Publication bias in meta-analysis: Prevention, assessment and adjustments* (pp. 75–98). Hoboken, NJ: Wiley.
Sutton, A. J., & Higgins, J. P. T. (2008). Recent development in meta-analysis. *Statistics in Medicine, 27,* 625–650.
Taylor, A. (2006). The effects of CALL versus traditional L1 glosses on L2 reading com-

prehension. *CALICO Journal, 23*, 309–318.
Taylor, A., Stevens, J. R., & Asher, J. W. (2006). The effects of explicit reading strategy training on L2 reading comprehension: A meta-analysis. In J. M. Norris & L. Ortega (Eds.), *Synthesizing research on language learning and teaching* (pp. 213–244). Philadelphia: John Benjamins.
Teleni, V., & Baldauf, R. B. (1989). *Statistical techniques used in three applied linguistics journals*, Language Learning, Applied Linguistics *and* TESOL Quarterly *1980–1986: Implications for readers and researchers*. Unpublished research report. (ERIC Document Reproduction Service No. ED312905)
Torgerson, C. J. (2006). Publication bias: The Achilles' heel of systematic reviews? *British Journal of Educational Studies, 54*, 89–102.
Truscott, J. (1996). The case against grammar correction in L2 writing classes. *Language Learning, 46*, 327–369.
Truscott, J. (1998). Noticing in second language acquisition: A critical review. *Second Language Research, 24*, 103–135.
Truscott, J. (1999). The case for "The case against grammar correction in L2 writing classes": A response to Ferris. *Journal of Second Language Writing, 8*, 111–122.
Truscott, J. (2004). Evidence and conjecture on the effects of correction: A response to Chandler. *Journal of Second Language Writing, 13*, 337–343.
Truscott, J. (2007). The effect of error correction on learners' ability to write accurately. *Journal of Second Language Writing*, 16, 255–272.
Tukey, J. W. (1991). The philosophy of multiple comparisons. *Statistical Science*, 6, 100–116.
Tversky, A., & Kahneman, D. (1971). Belief in the law of small numbers. *Psychological Bulletin, 76*, 105–110.
Valdman, A. (1993). Replication study. *Studies in Second Language Acquisition, 15*, 505.
Valentine, J. C. (2009). Judging the quality of primary research. In H. Cooper, L. V. Hedges, & J. C. Valentine (Eds.), *The handbook of research synthesis* (2nd ed., pp. 129–146). New York: Russell Sage Foundation.
Valentine, J. C., & Cooper, H. (2003). *Effect Size Substantive Interpretation Guidelines: Issues in the Interpretation of Effect Sizes*. Washington, DC: What Works Clearinghouse.
Vevea, J. L., & Woods, C. M. (2005). Publication bias in research synthesis: Sensitivity analysis using a priori weight functions. *Psychological Methods, 10*, 428–443.
Volker, M. A. (2006). Reporting effect size estimates in school psychology research. *Psychology in the Schools, 43*, 653–672.
Wa-Mbaleka, S. (2006). *A meta-analysis investigating the effects of reading on second language vocabulary learning*. Unpublished doctoral dissertation, Northern Arizona University, Flagstaff, AZ.

Wanous, J. P., Sullivan, S. E., & Malinak, J. (1989). The role of judgment calls in meta-analysis. *Journal of Applied Psychology, 74*, 259–264.

White, H. D. (2009). Scientific communication and literature retrieval. In H. Cooper, L. V. Hedges, & J. C. Valentine (Eds.), *The handbook of research synthesis* (2nd ed., pp. 51–71). New York: Russell Sage Foundation.

Wilkinson, L., & Task Force on Statistical Inference. (1999). Statistical methods in psychology journals: Guidelines and explanations. *American Psychologist, 54*, 594–604.

Wolf, F. M. (1986). *Meta-analysis: Quantitative methods for research synthesis.* Beverly Hills, CA: Sage.

Won, M. (2008). *The effects of vocabulary instruction on English language learners: A meta-analysis.* Unpublished doctoral dissertation, Texas Tech University, Lubbock, TX.

Zhao, Y. (2003). Recent developments in technology and language learning: A literature review and meta-analysis. *CALICO Journal, 21*, 7–27.

Concurrent Verbal Reports in Second Language Acquisition Research

Melissa A. Bowles

This article provides an overview of the ways in which concurrent verbal reports, sometimes referred to as think-alouds, have been used in cognitivist second language acquisition (SLA) research. It addresses two issues related to the validity of verbal reports—reactivity and veridicality—and reviews studies that have examined the validity of verbal reports in SLA. On the basis of the results of a meta-analysis of studies comparing the performance of silent and think-aloud groups (Bowles, 2010), this article concludes with suggestions for further research into the issue of validity and recommendations for the careful use of think-alouds in research.

INTRODUCTION

Language acquisition research consists (at least in part) of measuring and describing learners' knowledge about a language. But it is well known that the evidence stemming from learners' language production is incomplete; some other method is needed to elicit a more complete data set. Verbal reports have been used in first (L1) and second (L2) language research to provide insight on a variety of issues that production data alone cannot address, such as language learners' thought processes and strategies. Simply put, verbal reports are verbalizations learners make either while they complete a task or sometime thereafter. Verbal reports completed during a task are referred to as concurrent reports (or think-alouds), and those completed after the task are referred to as retrospective reports (or stimulated recalls).

This article provides an overview of how think-alouds have been used in language research and seeks to provide some answers to questions about the validity and use of think-alouds. Readers interested in the use of stimulated recalls are referred to Gass and Mackey (2000), which is indispensable on the topic.

USE OF AND ASSUMPTIONS ABOUT VERBAL REPORTS

Decades before they were first applied in language research, verbal reports were used extensively in cognitive psychology, where they were traditionally used to investigate problem-solving strategies on nonverbal tasks and puzzles (J. H. Davis, Carey, Foxman, & Tarr, 1968; Gagné & Smith, 1962). Since the 1980s, "both concurrent and retrospective verbal reports [have become] generally recognized as major sources of data on subjects' cognitive processes in specific tasks" (Ericsson & Simon, 1993, p. xi). The collection of verbal reports has become standard in many fields, such as accounting (Anderson, 1985); care planning (Fowler, 1997); counseling (Bozarth, 1970); drug and alcohol addiction treatment (Midanik & Hines, 1991); ergonomics (Brinkman, 1993); marketing (Biehal & Chakravarti, 1989); nursing (Greenwood & King, 1995); software engineering (Hughes & Parkes, 2003); medicine, where verbal reports are routinely used in the treatment of autism and developmental disorders (Berg, 2002; Friedman & Mulhern, 1976); speech pathology (Karsenty, 2001); neurology (Chan, Hoosain, & Lee, 2002); and cardiology (Bernardi et al., 2000). In each of these fields, verbal reports provide insight into the cognitive processes of clients and patients.

Think-alouds have also been used to investigate many aspects of first and second language acquisition and use. In the L1 literature, there have been numerous studies on reading, which have tended to focus on reading strategies used by older and younger, more and less successful readers (Cohen, 1986, 1987; Earthman, 1992; Folger, 2001; Gordon, 1990). Think-alouds have also been used to study the L1 writing process (Breetvelt, 1994; Zellermayer & Cohen, 1996). In some cases, think-alouds have been used as one component of programs designed to improve students' reading (Baumann, Jones, & Seifert Kessell, 1993; Robertson, 1995; Walczyk, Marsiglia, Bryan, & Naquin, 2001; Wilhelm, 2001) and writing ability (Box, 2002; Cushman, 2002; Fresch, Wheaton, & Zutell, 1998; Scardamalia, 1984).

In second language acquisition (SLA) research, think-alouds have also been used to study reading (Carrell, 1989; Cohen, 1986, 1987; Cohen & Cavalcanti, 1987; Hosenfeld, 1976, 1977, 1979, 1984; Pressley & Afflerbach, 1995; Pritchard, 1990) and writing (Qi & Lapkin, 2001; Sachs & Polio, 2007). However, they have also been used to investigate a wide array of other phenomena, including L1 and L2 strategy use (Chamot & El Dinary, 1999; J. Davis & Bistodeau, 1993; Yamashita, 2002), lexical organization (Herwig, 2003), the use of translation in L2 learning (Kern, 1994), interlanguage pragmatics (Woodfield, 2008), the role of different levels of awareness in L2 learning (Leow, 1997, 1998a, 1998b, 1999, 2000, 2001a, 2001b; Rosa & Leow, 2004a, 2004b; Rosa & O'Neill, 1999), and the relationship between explicit and implicit L2 knowledge (Ellis, 2004; Hu, 2002).

As this brief review shows, verbal reports have been used to answer a wide array of research questions in SLA. Verbal reports have been used in cognitivist approaches to SLA, where they are viewed as a window into the minds of learners, that is, as a means of gathering information about their internal thought processes. Crucially, an underlying assumption is that verbalizations can accurately reflect thought processes without altering them and can therefore be a data collection tool.

CONTROVERSY OVER THE USE OF VERBAL REPORTS

Indeed, despite the frequency with which verbal reports are gathered, their use is not uncontroversial. More than three decades ago cognitive psychologists raised questions about whether verbal reports actually capture thought processes accurately, or whether they alter those processes (Nisbett & Wilson, 1977; Payne, Braunstein, & Carroll, 1978). Similar concern has since been voiced in SLA. For instance, Jourdenais (2001) specifically cautioned that "the think-aloud data collection method itself acts as an additional task which must be considered carefully when examining learner performance" (p. 373).

Specifically, the two main validity issues surrounding the use of verbal reports are reactivity and veridicality. Verbalization is said to be reactive if it alters task performance, and it is said to be *veridical* if it accurately *reflects* the participant's cognitive processes. Ericsson and Simon's (1993) classic model of verbalization speaks to the validity of think-alouds. The model does not treat all verbal reports alike; rather it distinguishes them along two dimensions: time of reporting (concurrent vs. retrospective) and level of detail. It predicts that concurrent reports will be more complete and accurate (veridical) than retrospective reports, since participants who think aloud during a task are not subject to memory decay, unlike those who are asked to report their thoughts some time after completing a task. The model furthermore makes different predictions based on how detailed the verbalizations are required to be. Verbalizations that are generated as a normal part of the solution process (what Ericsson & Simon refer to as Type 1 verbalizations, or nonmetacognitive verbalizations) will be largely nonreactive; that is, they will reflect the nature of cognitive processes fairly accurately, while slowing processing slightly. Conversely, their model predicts that verbalizations that include additional reasoning or justifications that would not normally figure into the normal solution process (what Ericsson & Simon refer to as Type 2 and 3 verbalizations, or metacognitive verbalizations) are more likely to be reactive, or to affect task performance.

Experimental studies examining the effects of think-alouds on problem-solving and decision-making tasks have been conducted in the field of cognitive psychology since the 1950s. To assess the extent to which verbalization affected participants' task performance, one group would complete a task silently, while another would complete the same task while verbalizing. Overall, a synthesis of the studies reviewed in Ericsson and Simon (1993) reveals a clear pattern of results. When participants were asked to think aloud nonmetacognitively, their task performance (usually measured as accuracy) was generally not significantly different from that of the participants in the silent groups. On the other hand, when participants were asked to think aloud metacognitively, their task performance was, in most studies, significantly different from that of participants in silent groups. In some cases, participants in verbalization groups outperformed silent participants, and in others, the verbal ones underperformed the silent, suggesting that sometimes verbalization is facilitative and sometimes it is detrimental. Furthermore, participants who verbalized (either nonmetacognitively or metacognitively) tended to take significantly more time to complete the task than silent participants, because the additional time needed for verbalization increases the overall solution time. These findings support the predictions of Ericsson and Simon's model. However, most of the studies used nonverbal and/or problem-solving tasks, limiting their relevance to SLA.

REVIEW OF SLA STUDIES ON REACTIVITY

Leow and Morgan-Short (2004) was the first SLA study to empirically investigate the reactivity of think-alouds. Their study investigated the effects of nonmetacognitive think-alouds on 77 beginning Spanish learners' text comprehension and intake and written production of formal imperative morphology in Spanish. Learners in the control condition read and completed the tasks silently, while learners in the experimental condition read and completed the tasks while thinking aloud. Results showed nonreactivity, since the two groups did not differ significantly on either text comprehension or posttask assessments of the targeted inflectional morphology. Time on task was not a dependent variable measured in the study, so it was not possible to determine whether thinking aloud affected solution time.

Expanding on Leow and Morgan-Short (2004), Bowles and Leow (2005) sought to investigate the reactivity of both metacognitive and nonmetacognitive think-alouds on text comprehension and item and system learning of the pluperfect subjunctive. Participants were 45 fifth-semester Spanish learners who were randomly assigned to either a control or to one of two verbalization groups (nonmetacognitive or metacognitive). All participants read a text that included tokens of the targeted structure and then completed the same comprehension and written production tasks. The only difference between the groups were verbalization instructions: Participants in the control group were silent; those in the nonmetacognitive group were instructed to "say whatever passed through [their] minds"; and those in the metacognitive group were instructed to comment specifically about their processes. Similar to Leow and Morgan-Short (2004), the results indicated that, compared with a control group, nonmetacognitive verbalization did not significantly affect either comprehension or written production of the targeted form. However, metacognitive verbalization caused a significant decrement in text comprehension but no significant difference for production when compared with either the control or to the nonmetacognitive group. Results also indicated that both verbalization groups took significantly more time to read the text and complete the postassessment tasks than the control group, but that there was no significant difference between the two think-aloud groups in terms of time on task.

Sachs and Polio (2007) examined the reactivity of think-alouds on an L2 writing task. The study was carried out in two experiments. In Experiment 1, 15 adult English as a second language (ESL) learners participated in a three-stage, composition-comparison-revision task. Each learner participated in the three-stage process three times, once receiving written corrections on their compositions, once receiving reformulations of their errors, and once receiving reformulations of their errors and verbalizing while they compared their original composition to the reformulated version. Results of a Wilcoxon signed rank test indicated that when learners were silent during the comparison stage (reformulation), they subsequently revised more errors in their composition than when they verbalized during the comparison stage (reformulation + think aloud), although the effect size ($\eta^2 = 0.28$) was weak, suggesting that the difference in performance between the two groups, though statistically significant, was small. Experiment 2 was then conducted as a nonrepeated-measures study, this time with 54 ESL learners, randomly assigned to one of four conditions: (1) error correction, (2) reformulation, (3) reformulation + think aloud, or (4) control, in which learners received no feedback on their writing. A Mann-Whitney test comparing the reformulation and reformulation + think-aloud conditions revealed no significant differences ($p = .77$), indicating that in Experiment 2, learners who verbalized during the comparison stage and those who did not corrected a similar number of errors during the revision stage. In summary, verbalization was found to be reactive in Experiment 1, since it appeared to hinder learners' ability to make revisions to their compositions. In Experiment 2, however, verbalization was found to be nonreactive. In both Experiment 1 and Experiment 2, learners were instructed to verbalize in English (their L2), unlike in the previous SLA studies (Bowles & Leow, 2005; Leow & Morgan-Short, 2004), which gave learners the option to speak in either their L1 or L2. This difference between Sachs and Polio (2007) and previous studies, combined with the repeated-measures nature of Experiment 1, is cause for the results to be interpreted with caution.

Sachs and Suh (2007) investigated the issue of reactivity of think-alouds in the context of synchronous computer-mediated communication (CMC). Thirty ESL learners participated in the study, which targeted sequence of tense in English. All learners interacted individually with the researcher via CMC, first taking a written text completion and interactive story-retelling pretest, followed by a story-retelling task either with or without textually enhanced recasts, and with or without thinking aloud. Each learner then completed an interactive story-retelling posttest and a text completion posttest. Learners were allowed to speak in either their L1 (Korean) or in their L2 (English) while thinking aloud, as they preferred. Results indicated that the + and − think-aloud groups did not differ significantly in the amount of time spent on task (t (28) = − 0.113, p = .91), indicating that verbalization was nonreactive for time on task, in contrast to the findings of Bowles and Leow (2005), the one previous SLA study that examined time as a dependent variable. Repeated-measures ANOVAs were then run with ± think-aloud as the between-subjects factor, time as the within-subjects factor, and text completion and production (story retelling) as the dependent variables. There was a significant between-group main effect on text completion ($F(1,26)$ = 6.478, p = .02), which indicates that the group that verbalized performed differently on the text completion test than the group that did not verbalize, regardless of time. No significant interaction effect between time and group was found for either the story retelling or the text completion test, leading the authors to conclude that strong generalizations regarding reactivity should not be drawn from the data.

In a study investigating the role of lexical temporal indicators, such as temporal adverbs, in the incidental acquisition of the Spanish future tense, Rossomondo (2007) compared groups of first-semester Spanish students who read a passage silently and those who read the same passage while thinking aloud nonmetacognitively. Following recommendations from Ericsson and Simon (1993) and from previous SLA studies, Rossomondo gave participants a sample think-aloud as well as a short warm-up text during which they were instructed to think aloud. After reading the experimental passage, all participants completed a 13-item multiple-choice comprehension test in English, followed by either a 13-item form-recognition task, or a 13-item form-production task. The form-recognition task consisted of 13 target sentences taken from the passage (presented without lexical temporal markers) with a blank where the inflected verb should have been. Participants had to choose the correct inflected form (the future) from among four options. The form-production task consisted of the same 13 target sentences taken from the text, but in this case each blank was followed by the infinitive form of a verb in parenthesis, and participants were instructed to conjugate the verb in the same form as in the passage. No reaction time or time on task data were collected. Results indicated that participants who thought aloud while reading scored statistically similarly on comprehension measures to participants who read the passage silently ($F(1,159) = 0.078, p = .781$). For recognition and production of the target form, results were quite different, with participants who thought aloud scoring significantly higher on both the form-recognition ($F(1,77) = 12.194, p < .001$) and form-production (F(1,80) = 7.352, p < .008) tests.

Bowles (2008) investigated the effects of completing nonmetacognitive and metacognitive think-alouds while performing an L2 problem-solving task on subsequent written production of previously encountered and new exemplars of a target form. A total of 194 first-semester learners of Spanish were randomly assigned to one of six experimental conditions, which differed in terms of the type of verbalization (metacognitive, nonmetacognitive, or silent) and the type of feedback (implicit or explicit). Learners were instructed to speak in either L1 (English) or L2 (Spanish), as they felt most comfortable. Results showed that metacognitive verbalization significantly increased time on task ($F(2,193) = 15.763, p < .0001$), with the metacognitive think-aloud group taking significantly more time to complete the task than either the nonmetacognitive or silent group. Metacognitive verbalization also hindered participants' ability to produce exemplars of the target structure that they had seen during the experimental task ($F(2,193) = 3.778, p < .05$). However, neither type of verbalization significantly affected participants' ability to produce novel exemplars of the target structure ($F(2,193) = 1.713, p = .183$), and there was no interaction between verbalization and feedback. These results as a whole indicate that nonmetacognitive verbalization was nonreactive for both item and system learning, in accordance with Ericsson and Simon's model. However, the results indicate that metacognitive verbalization was reactive on item learning but nonreactive on system learning.

Yoshida (2008) investigated the role that verbalization plays in an L2 reading task, thereby building on the work of Leow and Morgan-Short (2004) and Bowles and Leow (2005). In her study, 64 Japanese ESL students were randomly assigned to a verbalization condition (think-aloud or non-think-aloud) and to one of three reading conditions (a control passage, the same passage with questions embedded throughout, or the passage with guidance to help students produce an outline). Students were allowed to think aloud in their L1 (Japanese) or L2 (English), so that their verbalizations would not be constrained by their language ability. The instructions required students to produce metacognitive think-alouds, since they were asked to explain how they made each decision provided in their responses to written while-reading tasks. After reading the passage and completing a corresponding while-reading task, each learner completed a written recall of the propositions in the passage. The recall scores were taken as an indication of reading comprehension, and results of a two-way ANOVA found no significant main effect for reading condition ($F(1,58) = 0.795, p = .376$) or for task type ($F(2,58) = 0.392, p = .677$), and no significant interaction was found between reading condition and task type ($F(2,58) = 0.182, p = .834$). These results indicate that learners who verbalized performed similarly to learners who did not verbalize, regardless of the task they engaged in while reading. A two-way ANOVA revealed that the think-aloud group took considerably more time on task than the non-think-aloud group ($F(1,58) = 12.76, p = .001$).

Sanz, Lin, Lado, Bowden, and Stafford (2009) reported on two studies investigating the reactivity of concurrent verbal reports in an L2 instructional lesson. In Experiment 1, 24 L1 English-speaking students, 11 in the think-aloud group and 13 in a silent group, completed a computerized lesson on the Latin case system. After the lesson, participants took an aural interpretation test, a written grammaticality judgment test, and a sentence production test that required them to drag and drop appropriate morphemes to create a sentence describing an on-screen photograph. On all tests, there was a main effect only for time, indicating that students in both the silent and think-aloud groups learned as a result of the lesson, and that verbalizing during the lesson had neither a facilitative nor a detrimental effect on performance. Furthermore, Sanz et al. (2009) used a more precise measurement than that used in previous studies to measure time. They measured mean reaction times on correct responses from the three pre- and posttests and calculated a grand mean on which to base their overall time measure for each participant. The think-aloud group had longer reaction times than the silent group on just one of the posttests, the grammaticality judgment, indicating mixed results for latency in this experiment.

In Experiment 2, 24 college-age students, 11 in the think-aloud group and 13 in the silent group, completed a less explicit version of the treatment used in

Experiment 1. The only difference between the two instructional treatments was that the treatment in Experiment 1 included an explicit grammar lesson on the case system, whereas the second treatment did not. Instead, students had to rely on knowledge they gained from task-essential practice and explicit feedback. All pre- and posttest measures were the same as in Experiment 1. As in the first experiment, there were main effects for time for all tests, indicating that the treatment caused students to improve in their ability to interpret and produce sentences in Latin. But, in contrast to Experiment 1, there were also reactivity effects because students in the think-aloud group performed significantly better than those in the silent group on both the grammaticality judgment and production tests. In this case, verbalization had a facilitative effect on subsequent performance. As for latency, there were no significant differences in reaction times for the two groups across the three tests, indicating that in this experiment, although verbalization enhanced performance, it did not cause any change in the speed with which participants responded to stimuli in the L2.

Finally, in a study similar to Leow and Morgan-Short (2004), Polio and Wang (2005) examined the reactivity of think-alouds with advanced-proficiency learners completing a reading task. The authors hypothesized that the reading strategies of advanced learners might be different enough from those of the beginning learners in the original study to cause a change in reactivity. In Polio and Wang (2005), 30 Chinese L1 learners of English were randomly assigned to a think-aloud or to a silent reading group and were instructed to read a passage in English, seeded with both frequent and infrequent phrasal verbs. Upon completing the reading task, participants took a comprehension test (in the L2, English) as well as written production and recognition tests targeting the phrasal verbs found in the passage. Since there were 15 participants per group, less powerful nonparametric statistical tests (Mann-Whitney U tests) were used to compare the performance of the think-aloud and silent groups on the three measures. The only significant difference occurred in comprehension, where participants in the think-aloud group comprehended the text significantly worse than participants in the silent group ($p = .01$). Polio and Wang then examined the contents of the think-alouds to investigate the nature of the reading process for this group of learners. They determined that whereas in Leow and Morgan-Short, translation was the predominant reading strategy, for these advanced learners who used English for academic purposes, translation was relatively uncommon. The researchers hypothesized that this difference in strategy use may have been largely responsible for the differing findings between the original and the replication. Since learners in Leow and Morgan-Short relied heavily on translation, they were easily able to verbalize the contents of their short-term memory without any effect on comprehension. On the other hand, the learners in the replication were engaging in other, more complex strategies, so it may have been more cognitively demanding for them to verbalize, contributing to the finding of reactivity in comprehension.

META-ANALYSIS OF STUDIES ON REACTIVITY

As the review in the preceding section shows, there is a mounting body of primary research investigating the reactivity of think-alouds on verbal tasks. However, no one study on reactivity, regardless of its size, complexity, or number of participants, can provide reliable answers, since individual study findings are susceptible to chance variability and any number of idiosyncrasies in design and sampling. This section therefore presents the results of a quantitative research synthesis, or meta-analysis, which was carried out on reactivity studies that used verbal tasks. A complete description of the meta-analysis is provided in Bowles (2010).

Besides providing a summary of existing research in different fields, a meta-analysis compares the outcomes of a range of studies with an array of independent variables, in an attempt to identify patterns. In SLA, meta-analyses have increased in frequency in the past decade, as researchers in the field have started to adopt the method to provide more comprehensive answers to long-standing questions, such as the role of instruction in SLA (Norris & Ortega, 2000), the efficacy of different types of corrective feedback (Russell & Spada, 2006), the effects of conversational interaction (Keck, Iberri-Shea, Tracy-Ventura, & Wa-Mbaleka, 2006; Mackey & Goo, 2007), the impact of attitude and motivation (Masgoret & Gardner, 2003), and visual/textual input enhancement (Lee & Huang, 2008) on language learning.

Identification of Studies

Since reactivity studies involving verbal tasks have been conducted both in psychology and in linguistics, Bowles searched the *PsycInfo* database, in addition to *Linguistics and Language Behavior Abstracts* (LLBA) and the *Education Resources Information Center* (ERIC) database, using the following subject, abstract, and keywords, and combinations thereof: *concurrent verbal report(s)*, *concurrent verbal protocol(s)*, *reactivity*, *think aloud(s)*, *verbal task*, and *language task*. Then, the search was replicated in major SLA journals to ensure that published studies had not been missed. Specifically, separate searches were conducted in each of the following journals: *Applied Linguistics, Applied Psycholinguistics, Canadian Modern Language Review, Computer Assisted Language Learning, Foreign Language Annals, International Journal of Educational Research, Language Learning, Language Learning & Technology, Language Teaching Research, The Modern Language Journal, ReCALL, Second Language Research, Studies in Second Language Acquisition, System,* and *TESOL Quarterly*.

Following recommendations in the SLA literature (Norris & Ortega, 2006), unpublished papers, sometimes referred to as the *fugitive literature* (Rosenthal, 1994), were included in the meta-analysis to the extent possible.

Selection Criteria

The studies identified through the subject, abstract, and keyword searches were narrowed down by using the following selection criteria.

Inclusion Criteria

(1) The study was published, in press, or accepted for publication prior to November 2009.

(2) The study compared one or more verbalization groups to a silent (control) group, or it compared one or more verbalization groups to each other, in the absence of a silent (control) group.

(3) At least one of the verbalization groups required participants to verbalize concurrently, while performing some type of verbal task (involving either language comprehension or production).

(4) Participants in the studies could be either adults or children. It is important to note that children in all of the studies were verbalizing (and completing verbal tasks) in their L1. To disentangle the variety of variables, language of verbalization and language of the task were coded separately for each study.

(5) The study included sufficient descriptive statistics to enable the calcu-

lation of effect sizes. (Three studies—Rhenius & Deffner, 1990; Russo, Johnson, & Stephens, 1989; Stratman & Hamp-Lyons, 1994—were excluded from the meta-analysis on this basis.)

(6) The study included sufficient information to be coded according to the coding scheme adopted.

(7) Studies written in English, French, and German all appeared as results in the database searches and were evaluated for inclusion. That is, no study was excluded simply on the basis of language of publication.

Exclusion Criteria

Studies were excluded from the analysis if concurrent verbalization, although a part of the study design, was not an independent variable (Piolat & Olive, 2000; Witte & Cherry, 1994).

Based on the foregoing criteria, a total of 14 unique sample studies, described in 12 research reports, were identified for inclusion in the meta-analysis. Those studies are identified in the references with a single asterisk.

Combining Effect Sizes

One advantage of a meta-analysis is that it enables the combination of many studies to produce one effect size. Effect sizes of studies cannot be combined at random, however. Even when the meta-analyst has good reason to believe that studies are similar in terms of their substantive and/or methodological characteristics, it is necessary to quantitatively analyze the studies using a homogeneity test to determine whether the variability across effect sizes is greater than or less than what would be expected from sampling error alone. If the group of studies is found to be homogeneous, "the mean effect size is clearly a representative and meaningful summary of the distribution of effect size values" (Lipsey & Wilson, 2001, p. 162).

Sometimes even when studies have been grouped by substantive and methodological variables and are considered to be similar enough to warrant averaging their effect sizes, the homogeneity test determines that they are heterogenous (i.e., that the variability observed is larger than what would be due to different samples across the different studies). In these cases, it is not advisable to combine effect sizes but rather to determine whether some other variable explains a significant portion of the between-study variance. "When studies that presumably examine the same thing disagree, it is neither wise nor especially meaningful to resolve their differences simply by averaging them all together. The average over contrary results is not likely to converge on the truth, just muddle it" (Lipsey & Wilson, 2001, p. 162).

Main Findings

It was not possible to average the effect sizes of all studies to produce grand weighted mean effect sizes for accuracy or for latency because those effect size distributions violated the assumption of homogeneity. This result indicates that the answer to the question of reactivity and think-alouds is not unidimensional but rather is dependent on a host of variables.

Nonetheless, the fact that almost all of the effect size means overlapped the zero value indicates that think-aloud groups do not consistently perform significantly differently than silent control groups. Furthermore, the small effect sizes of $d \leq 0.5$ for 18 of the 22 (81%) calculations done as part of the meta-analysis indicate that any posttest differences between silent and think-aloud groups tend to be small. In other words, compared to participants completing the same tasks silently, participants who think aloud tend to perform only slightly better or slightly worse on posttests.

The results for time on task were more decisive, indicating across the board that thinking aloud increases time on task. Nevertheless, effect sizes for latency ranged from small ($d = 0.16$) to very large ($d = 1.16$), with the largest effects demonstrated when participants were required to think aloud while performing reading tasks.

FUTURE RESEARCH DIRECTIONS

The systematic coding and analysis of reactivity studies that was conducted as part of the meta-analysis (Bowles, 2010) revealed several areas that, despite their theoretical importance, have been underinvestigated. At the same time, the meta-analysis highlighted the role that several previously untested variables unique to the context of language research may have on whether thinking aloud is or is not reactive.

Needed are studies such as Polio and Chiu (2007) that examine the effect of using just one language (either L1 or L2) in thinking aloud. This is because most of the studies conducted so far have examined the reactive effects of think-alouds when participants were allowed to select either the L1 or the L2, or to use a combination of the two languages, in their reports. Certainly, this is a gap in the research that should be filled.

Similarly, some task types have been investigated more heavily than others with regard to reactivity. Topping the list are studies that have examined the reactivity of think-alouds on reading ($n = 6$) and grammar learning tasks ($n = 7$). But the effect of think-alouds on the writing process has only been investigated in two unique sample studies, making it untenable to draw firm conclusions about reactivity with this task type.

More research is clearly needed overall in examining reactivity in conjunction with verbal tasks, given the paucity of reactivity research with language tasks as compared to nonverbal and problem-solving tasks. Empirical studies are needed to test the sources of between-study variance identified in this meta-analysis to determine to what extent they affect reactivity. Analyses to identify the sources of between-study variance revealed that a portion of the variance could be attributed to expected sources, such as type of report (metacognitive vs. nonmetacognitive), which has been discussed at length in the psychology literature (Ericsson & Simon, 1993). The other sources of between-study variance that were identified, L2 proficiency and explicitness of instruction, are unique to the language research context. Future research is clearly needed to determine how verbalizing affects learners (a) at different proficiency levels and (b) in conjunction with more and less explicit instruction.

Although reactivity has been the focus of the majority of research on think-alouds, both in psychology and in SLA, the issue of veridicality should not be forgotten. In research studies that use think-alouds as a data elicitation tool, once the think-aloud group has been shown to perform statistically similarly to a silent control group, it is also important to examine the issue of veridicality. The small number of studies in psychology that have investigated veridicality have demonstrated that concurrent verbal reports tend to be more accurate (Robinson, 2001) and to include more information (Kuusela & Paul, 2000) than retrospective reports. In SLA, only Polio and Chiu (2007) have addressed veridicality directly, using a within-subjects design to examine concurrent and retrospective reports of the

L2 writing process. In the study, advanced ESL learners completed concurrent verbal reports while writing and were then asked to provide a retrospective report (stimulated recall). Results showed that learners were indeed able to provide additional information in the retrospective reports, indicating that although concurrent verbalization seemed to accurately reflect thought processes, they were somewhat incomplete. So in cases where think-alouds are shown not to have been reactive, researchers should next examine the question of veridicality to determine how accurate and complete the reporting was.

CONCLUSIONS

On the basis of the body of research on reactivity in SLA, it is possible to draw some conclusions. The findings of the meta-analysis detailed in Bowles (2010) have important implications for researchers from a variety of different theoretical perspectives. Crucially, a variety of factors seem to play a role in determining whether or not verbalization is reactive on a given task.

Based on the evidence available to date, it appears that in some cases verbal reports can indeed be a source of learning, as sociocultural theory would suggest. For instance, Bowles (2010) reported that participants who thought aloud nonmetacognitively scored moderately higher ($d = 0.67$) on receptive tests of form learning than did participants who completed the same task silently. This result suggests that verbalizing facilitated form learning, at least as measured by receptive tests. On tests of productive form learning, however, thinking aloud had a small, detrimental effect ($d = -0.12$).

By the same token, the small effect sizes of $d \leq 0.5$ in 81% of the effect size calculations indicate that any posttest differences between silent and think-aloud groups tend to be small. In 86% of the effect size calculations, the 95% confidence interval overlaps zero, indicating that the d value is not significantly different from zero. This finding suggests that verbal reports can be used as a data collection tool. The results of the meta-analysis in Bowles (2010) stress the importance of including a (silent) control group in the design of any study using verbal reports as a data collection tool.

Since the first reactivity study in SLA (Leow & Morgan-Short, 2004) was conducted less than a decade ago, there are undoubtedly more questions than answers about verbal reports and reactivity. This safeguard allows the researcher to determine whether verbalizing caused significantly different task performance compared to silent participants. The findings also highlight the need for more fine-grained research to determine under what circumstances verbalizations are likely to accurately reflect processing and in what circumstances they are not.

REFERENCES

Anderson, M. (1985). Some evidence on the effect of verbalization on process: A methodological note. *Journal of Accounting Research, 23*, 843–852.

Baumann, J. F., Jones, L. A., & Seifert Kessell, N. (1993). Using think alouds to enhance children's comprehension monitoring abilities. *Reading Teacher, 47*, 184–193.

Berg, H. P. (2002). *Remediating cognitive perspective-taking in children with autism.* Unpublished doctoral dissertation, Columbia University Teachers College, New York.

Bernardi, L., Wdowczyk-Szulc, J., Valenti, C., Castoldi, S., Passino, C., Spadacini, G., et al. (2000). Effects of controlled breathing, mental activity, and mental stress with or without verbalization on heart rate variability. *Journal of the American College of Cardiology, 35*, 1462–1469.

Biehal, G., & Chakravarti, D. (1989). The effects of concurrent verbalization on choice processing. *Journal of Marketing Research, 26*, 84–96.

*Bowles, M. (2008). Task type and reactivity of verbal reports in SLA: A first look at a task other than reading. *Studies in Second Language Acquisition, 30*, 359–387.

Bowles, M. (2010). *The think-aloud controversy in language acquisition research.* New York: Routledge.

*Bowles, M., & Leow, R. P. (2005). Reactivity and type of verbal report in SLA research methodology: Expanding the scope of investigation. *Studies in Second Language Acquisition, 27*, 415–440.

Box, J. A. (2002). Guided writing in the early childhood classroom. *Reading Improvement, 39*, 111–113.

Bozarth, J. (1970). Verbal protocol patterns of college dormitory counselors. *Counselor Education and Supervision, 10*, 23–29.

Breetvelt, I. (1994). Relations between writing processes and text quality: When and how? *Cognition and Instruction, 12*, 103–123.

Brinkman, J. A. (1993). Verbal protocol accuracy in fault diagnosis. *Ergonomics, 36*, 1381–1397.

Carrell, P. L. (1989). Metacognitive awareness and second language reading. *Modern Language Journal, 73*, 121–134.

Chamot, A. U., & El Dinary, P. B. (1999). Children's learning strategies in language immersion classrooms. *Modern Language Journal, 83*, 319–338.

Chan, R. C., Hoosain, R., & Lee, T. M. (2002). Talking while performing a task: A better attentional performance in patients with closed head injury? *Journal of Clinical Experimental Neuropsychology, 24*, 695–704.

Cohen, A. D. (1986). Mentalistic measures in reading strategy research: Some recent findings. *English for Specific Purposes, 5*, 131–145.

Cohen, A. D. (1987). Recent uses of mentalistic data in reading strategy research. *Revista de Documentação de Estudos em Lingüística Teorica e Aplicada, 3*, 57–84.

Cohen, A. D., & Cavalcanti, M. C. (1987). Viewing feedback on compositions from the teacher's and the student's perspective. *ESPecialist, 16*, 13–28.

Cushman, D. (2002). From scribbles to stories. *Instructor, 111*, 32–33.

Davis, J., & Bistodeau, L. (1993). How do L1 and L2 reading differ? Evidence from think aloud protocols. *Modern Language Journal, 77*, 459–472.

Davis, J. H., Carey, M. H., Foxman, P. N., & Tarr, D. B. (1968). Verbalization, experimenter presence, and problem solving. *Journal of Personality and Social Psychology, 8*, 299–302.

Earthman, E. A. (1992). Creating the virtual work: Readers' processes in understanding literary texts. *Research in the Teaching of English, 26*, 351–384.

Ellis, R. (2004). The definition and measurement of L2 explicit knowledge. *Language Learning, 54*, 227–275.

Ericsson, K. A., & Simon, H. A. (1993). *Protocol analysis: Verbal reports as data* (Rev. ed.). Cambridge, MA: MIT Press.

Folger, T. L. (2001). Readers' parallel text construction while talking and thinking about the reading process. *Dissertation Abstracts International, 62* (4), 1329A. (UMI No. 3012966)

Fowler, L. P. (1997). Clinical reasoning strategies used during care planning. *Clinical Nursing Research, 6*, 349–361.

Fresch, M. J., Wheaton, A., & Zutell, J. B. (1998). Thinking aloud during spelling word sorts. *National Reading Conference Yearbook, 47*, 285–294.

Friedman, P., & Mulhern, S. T. (1976). Relationship of clinician feedback to child-initiated verbalization during language training. *Journal of Communication Disorders, 9*, 289–299.

Gagné, R. H., & Smith, E. C. (1962). A study of the effects of verbalization on problem solving. *Journal of Experimental Psychology, 63*, 12–18.

Gass, S., & Mackey, A. (2000). *Stimulated recall methodology in second language research.* Mahwah, NJ: Erlbaum.

Gordon, C. J. (1990). Modeling an expository text structure strategy in think alouds. *Reading Horizons, 31*, 149–167.

Greenwood, J., & King, M. (1995). Some surprising similarities in the clinical reasoning of expert and novice orthopaedic nurses: Report of a study using verbal protocols and protocol analysis. *Journal of Advanced Nursing, 22*, 907–913.

Herwig, A. (2003). Plurilingual lexical organisation: Evidence from lexical processing in L1-L2-L3-L4 translation. In J. Cenoz, B. Hufeisen, & U. Jessner (Eds.), *Cross linguistic influence in third language acquisition: Psychological perspectives* (pp. 115–137). Clevedon, UK: Multilingual Matters.

Hosenfeld, C. (1976). Learning about learning: Discovering our students' strategies. *Foreign Language Annals, 9*, 117–129.

Hosenfeld, C. (1977). A preliminary investigation of the reading strategies of successful and nonsuccessful second language learners. *System, 5*, 110–123.

Hosenfeld, C. (1979). Cindy: A learner in today's foreign language classroom. In W. Borne (Ed.), *The foreign language learner in today's classroom environment* (pp. 53–75). Montpelier, VT: Northwest Conference on the Teaching of Foreign Languages.

Hosenfeld, C. (1984). Case studies of ninth grade readers. In J. C. Alderson & A. H. Urquhart (Eds.), *Reading in a foreign language* (pp. 231–249). London, UK: Longman.

Hu, G. (2002). Psychological constraints on the utility of metalinguistic knowledge in second language production. *Studies in Second Language Acquisition, 24*, 347–386.

Hughes, J., & Parkes, S. (2003). Trends in the use of verbal protocol analysis in software engineering research. *Behaviour & Information Technology, 22*, 127–141.

Jourdenais, R. (2001). Cognition, instruction, and protocol analysis. In P. Robinson (Ed.), *Cognition and second language instruction* (pp. 354–375). Cambridge, UK: Cambridge University Press.

Karsenty, L. (2001). Adapting verbal protocol methods to investigate speech systems use. *Applied Ergonomics, 32*, 15–22.

Keck, C. M., Iberri-Shea, G., Tracy-Ventura, N., & Wa-Mbaleka, S. (2006). Investigating the empirical link between task-based interaction and acquisition: A quantitative meta-analysis. In J. M. Norris & L. Ortega (Eds.), *Synthesizing research on language learning and teaching* (pp. 91–131). Amsterdam: John Benjamins.

Kern, R. G. (1994). The role of mental translation in second language reading. *Studies in Second Language Acquisition, 16*, 441–461.

Kuusela, H., & Paul, P. (2000). A comparison of concurrent and retrospective verbal protocol analysis. *The American Journal of Psychology, 113*, 387–404.

*Lass, U., Klettke, W., Lüer, G., & Ruhlender, P. (1991). Does thinking aloud influence the structure of cognitive processes? In R. Schmid & D. Zambarbieri (Eds.), *Oculomotor control and cognitive processes* (pp. 385–396). New York: North-Holland.

Lee, S.-K., & Huang, H.-T. (2008). Visual input enhancement and grammar learning: A meta-analytic review. *Studies in Second Language Acquisition, 30*, 307–331.

Leow, R. P. (1997). Attention, awareness, and foreign language behavior. *Language Learning*, *47*, 467–505.

Leow, R. P. (1998a). The effects of amount and type of exposure on adult learners' L2 development in SLA. *Modern Language Journal*, *82*, 49–68.

Leow, R. P. (1998b). Toward operationalizing the process of attention in SLA: Evidence for Tomlin and Villa's (1994) fine-grained analysis of attention. *Applied Psycholinguistics*, *19*, 133–159.

Leow, R. P. (1999). The role of attention in second/foreign language classroom research: Methodological issues. In F. M.-G. J. Gutiérrez-Rexach (Ed.), *Advances in Hispanic Linguistics: Papers from the 2nd Hispanic Linguistics Symposium* (pp. 60–71). Somerville, MA: Cascadilla Proceedings Project.

Leow, R. P. (2000). A study of the role of awareness in foreign language behavior: Aware versus unaware learners. *Studies in Second Language Acquisition*, *22*, 557–584.

Leow, R. P. (2001a). Attention, awareness, and foreign language behavior. *Language Learning*, *51*(Suppl. 1), 113–155.

Leow, R. P. (2001b). Do learners notice enhanced forms while interacting with the L2? An online and offline study of the role of written input enhancement in L2 reading. *Hispania*, *84*, 496–509.

*Leow, R. P., & Morgan-Short, K. (2004). To think aloud or not to think aloud: The issue of reactivity in SLA research methodology. *Studies in Second Language Acquisition*, *26*, 35–57.

Lipsey, M. W., & Wilson, D. B. (2001). *Practical meta-analysis*. Thousand Oaks, CA: Sage.

Mackey, A., & Goo, J. (2007). Interaction research in SLA: A meta-analysis and research synthesis. In A. Mackey (Ed.), *Conversational interaction in second language acquisition* (pp. 407–452). Oxford, UK: Oxford University Press.

Masgoret, A. M., & Gardner, R. C. (2003). Attitude, motivation, and second language learning: A meta-analysis of studies conducted by Gardner and associates. *Language Learning*, *53*, 123–163.

*Mathews, R. C., Buss, R. R., Stanley, W. B., Blanchard-Fields, F., Cho, J. R., & Druhan, B. (1989). Role of implicit and explicit processes in learning from examples: A synergistic effect. *Journal of Experimental Psychology: Learning, Memory, and Cognition*, *15*, 1083–1100.

Midanik, L. T., & Hines, A. M. (1991). "Unstandard" ways of answering standard questions: Protocol analysis in alcohol survey research. *Drug and Alcohol Dependence*, *27*, 245–252.

Nisbett, R. E., & Wilson, T. D. (1977). Telling more than we can know: Verbal reports on mental processes. *Psychological Review*, *84*, 231–259.

Norris, J. M., & Ortega, L. (2000). Effectiveness of L2 instruction: A research synthesis and quantitative meta-analysis. *Language Learning*, *50*, 417–528.

Norris, J. M., & Ortega, L. (Eds.). (2006). *Synthesizing research on language learning and teaching. Amsterdam:* John Benjamins.

Payne, J. W., Braunstein, M. L., & Carroll, J. S. (1978). Exploring predecisional behavior: An alternative approach to decision research. *Organizational Behavior and Human Performance, 22*, 17–44.

Piolat, A., & Olive, T. (2000). Comment étudier le coût e le déroulement de la rédaction de textes? La méthode de la triple tăche: Un bilan méthodologique [How can the process and cost of writing texts be studied? The triple task methodology]. *L'Annee Psychologique, 100*, 465–502.

Polio, C., & Chiu, S. C.-H. (2007, April). *Reactivity, veridicality, and language choice in L2 writing concurrent verbal protocols.* Paper presented at the American Association of Applied Linguistics Conference, Costa Mesa, CA.

*Polio, C., & Wang, J. (2005, October). *Another look at the reactivity of concurrent verbal protocols in second language reading research.* Paper presented at the Second Language Research Forum, New York.

Pressley, M., & Afflerbach, P. (1995). *Verbal protocols of reading: The nature of constructively responsive reading.* Hillsdale, NJ: Erlbaum.

Pritchard, R. (1990). The effects of cultural schemata on reading processing strategies. *Reading Research Quarterly, 25*, 273–295.

Qi, D., & Lapkin, S. (2001). Exploring the role of noticing in a three-stage second language writing task. *Journal of Second Language Writing, 10*, 277–303.

Rhenius, D., & Deffner, G. (1990). Evaluation of concurrent thinking aloud using eye-tracking data. In M. E. Wiklund (Ed.), *Proceedings of the Human Factors Society 34th Annual Meeting* (pp. 1265–1269). Santa Monica, CA: Human Factors Society.

Robertson, B. (1995). Why think along? Using "think alouds" in the classroom. *State of Reading, 2*, 19–22.

Robinson, K. M. (2001). The validity of verbal reports in children's subtraction. *Journal of Educational Psychology, 93*, 211–222.

Rosa, E., & Leow, R. P. (2004a). Awareness, different learning conditions, and L2 development. *Applied Psycholinguistics, 25*, 269–292.

Rosa, E., & Leow, R. P. (2004b). Computerized task-based exposure, explicitness, type of feedback, and Spanish L2 development. *Modern Language Journal, 88*, 192–216.

Rosa, E., & O'Neill, M. (1999). Explicitness, intake, and the issue of awareness. *Studies in Second Language Acquisition, 21*, 511–556.

Rosenthal, M. C. (1994). "The fugitive literature." In H. Cooper & L. Hedges (Eds.), *Handbook of research synthesis.* New York: Russell Sage Foundation.

*Rossomondo, A. E. (2007). The role of lexical temporal indicators and text interaction format in the incidental acquisition of the Spanish future tense. *Studies in Second Language Acquisition, 29*, 39–66.

Russell, J., & Spada, N. (2006). The effectiveness of corrective feedback for the acquisition of L2 grammar: A meta-analysis of the research. In J. M. Norris & L. Ortega (Eds.), *Synthesizing research on language learning and teaching* (pp. 133–164). Amsterdam: John Benjamins.

*Russo, J. E., Johnson, E. J., & Stephens, D. L. (1989). The validity of verbal protocols. *Memory and Cognition, 17*, 759–769.

*Sachs, R., & Polio, C. (2007). Learners' uses of two types of written feedback on an L2 writing revision task. *Studies in Second Language Acquisition, 29*, 67–100.

*Sachs, R., & Suh, B. R. (2007). Textually enhanced recasts, learner awareness, and L2 outcomes in synchronous computer-mediated interaction. In A. Mackey (Ed.), *Conversational interaction in second language acquisition: A collection of empirical studies* (pp. 197–227). Oxford, UK: Oxford University Press.

*Sanz, C., Lin, H.-J., Lado, B., Bowden, H. W., & Stafford, C. A. (2009). Concurrent verbalizations, pedagogical conditions, and reactivity: Two CALL studies. *Language Learning, 59*, 33–71.

Scardamalia, M. (1984). Teachability of reflective processes in written composition. *Cognitive Science: A multidisciplinary journal of artificial intelligence, 8*, 173–190.

Stratman, J. F., & Hamp-Lyons, L. (1994). Reactivity in concurrent think-aloud protocols. In P. Smagorinsky (Ed.), *Speaking about writing: Reflections on research methodology* (pp. 89–112). London: Sage.

Walczyk, J., Marsiglia, C. S., Bryan, K. S., & Naquin, P. J. (2001). Overcoming inefficient reading skills. *Journal of Educational Psychology, 93*, 750–757.

Wilhelm, J. (2001). Getting kids into the reading game: You gotta know the rules. *Voices from the Middle, 8*, 25–36.

Witte, S. P., & Cherry, R. D. (1994). Think-aloud protocols, protocol analysis, and research design: An exploration of the influence of writing tasks on writing processes. In P. Smagorinsky (Ed.), *Speaking about writing: Reflections on research methodology* (pp. 20–54). London: Sage.

Woodfield, H. (2008). Problematising discourse completion tasks: Voices from verbal report. *Evaluation and Research in Education, 21*, 43–69.

Yamashita, J. (2002). Reading strategies in L1 and L2: Comparison of four groups of readers with different reading ability in L1 and L2. *ITL, Review of Applied Linguistics, 135–136*, 1–35.

*Yoshida, M. (2008). Think-aloud protocols and type of reading task: The issue of reactivity in L2 reading research. In M. Bowles, R. Foote, S. Perpiñán, & R. Bhatt (Eds.), *Selected* *proceedings of the 2007 Second Language Research Forum* (pp. 199–209). Somerville, MA: Cascadilla Proceedings Project.

Zellermayer, M., & Cohen, J. (1996). Varying paths for learning to revise. *Instructional Science, 24,* 177–195.

Qualitative Interviews in Applied Linguistics: From Research Instrument to Social Practice

Steven Talmy

Interviews have been used for decades in empirical inquiry across the social sciences as one or the primary means of generating data. In applied linguistics, interview research has increased dramatically in recent years, particularly in qualitative studies that aim to investigate participants' identities, experiences, beliefs, and orientations toward a range of phenomena. However, despite the proliferation of interview research in qualitative applied linguistics, it has become equally apparent that there is a profound inconsistency in how the interview has been and continues to be theorized in the field. This article critically reviews a selection of applied linguistics research from the past 5 years that uses interviews in case study, ethnographic, narrative, (auto)biographical, and related qualitative frameworks, focusing in particular on the ideologies of language, communication, and the interview, or the communicable cartographies of interviewing, that are evident in them. By contrasting what is referred to as an *interview as research instrument* perspective with a *research interview as social practice* orientation, the article argues for greater reflexivity about the interview methods that qualitative applied linguists use in their studies, the status ascribed to interview data, and how those data are analyzed and represented.

INTRODUCTION

Interviews have been used for decades in empirical inquiry across the social sciences as one or the primary means of generating data. In applied linguistics, interview studies have increased dramatically in recent years, particularly research that adopts case study, ethnographic, narrative, (auto)biographical, and related qualitative frameworks. This developing literature continues to address a rich array of topics and to yield notable insights concerning research participants' identities, experiences, beliefs, attitudes, and orientations toward a range of phenomena. However, despite the proliferation of interview research in qualitative applied linguistics, it has become equally apparent in recent years that there is a profound inconsistency in how the interview has been and continues to be theorized. As Block (2000, p. 757) described it, there is a "tendency" in qualitative applied linguistics research that uses interview methods "to take research participants 'at their word,'" that is, to offer "presentation of data plus content analysis, but no problematization of the data themselves or the respective roles of interviewers and interviewees" (also see Johnston, 1997; Pavlenko, 2007). Writing nearly 10 years later, in a major review of qualitative research in language teaching, Richards (2009) was more resolute:

> There is still work to be done to encourage yet deeper engagement with methodological issues, especially where interviews are concerned. We need to have more details of methodological and especially analytical matters in published papers, and it would be satisfying to see the demise of summaries [of interview data] amounting to no more than a couple of sentences or a short paragraph (p. 168).

As such comments suggest, it seems that qualitative applied linguistics researchers have engaged only partially and variably with debates concerning their ideologies of interviewing (Briggs, 2007b), debates that have taken place for some time in neighboring disciplines, particularly sociology, anthropology, and (discursive) psychology (e.g., Briggs, 1986; Cicourel, 1964; Drew & Heritage, 1992; Gubrium & Holstein, 2002a; Holstein & Gubrium, 1995, 2003, 2004; Mishler, 1986; van den Berg, Wetherell, & Houtkoop-Steenstra, 2003). As a result, a usually implicit and intuitive, or commonsensical, perspective on the interview remains evident in many qualitative studies in applied linguistics that employ interview methods (Block, 2000; Pavlenko, 2007; Richards, 2003, 2009).

In this article, I refer to this commonsensical conceptualization of the interview as an *interview as research instrument* perspective. It is contrasted with an orientation that I call *research interviews as social practice*, in which the research interview is explicitly conceptualized and analyzed as social action. I employ this basic classificatory scheme as a heuristic to organize my discussion of a selection of qualitative applied linguistics interview research published in refereed journals over the past 5 years or so. I restrict the range of studies I consider to qualitative studies that primarily use face-to-face semistructured and unstructured interviews as one or the sole means of data generation in the qualitative frameworks mentioned earlier.[1] I note at the outset that my discussion does not concern the *practicalities* of conducting interviews: for example, how to develop interview guides or protocols, what types of questions to ask and when, effective techniques for developing rapport, interview ethics, computer-mediated communication interviewing, and so forth. There are many excellent resources concerning these matters both in applied linguistics (e.g., Richards, 2003) and qualitative research more generally (e.g., Fontana & Prokos, 2007; Gubrium & Holstein, 2002b; Kvale, 2007; Kvale & Brinkman, 2009; Spradley, 1979; Warren, 2002; Warren & Karner, 2010). Instead, my focus in this review is on the ideologies of *interviewing* evident in these studies, as they are realized by the relative status that is ascribed to interview data (i.e., as direct reports or accounts of phenomena), as well as how those data are described, analyzed, and represented.

CARTOGRAPHIES OF COMMUNICABILITY IN "THE INTERVIEW SOCIETY"

Although interviews have become a method of choice in a great deal of qualitative applied linguistics research, the scarcity of material that addresses how they might be theorized is "quite curious" (Wooffitt & Widdicombe, 2006, p. 32), especially since there is no shortage of methodologically oriented texts concerning how interviews should be conducted. The comparative lack of consideration of the ontological, epistemological, and ideological assumptions underpinning interviews in applied linguistics and elsewhere has been traced to their "ubiquity" in contemporary social life: as Briggs (1986) argued, "because the interview is an accepted speech event in our own ... speech communities, we take for granted that we know what it is and what it produces" (p. 2; also see Mishler, 1986, p. 23).

Atkinson and Silverman (1997, pp. 304–305) similarly located "the stubbornly persistent ... special faith" that many researchers place in the interview to what they call the contemporary "interview society," where interviews are a pervasive feature of the discursive landscape: indeed are "everywhere" (Sarangi, 2003, p. 69). The "contemporary uses of the interview" have, Atkinson and Silverman (1997, pp. 309–310) maintained, "give[n] researchers, amid a diversity of methodological and epistemological positions, a spurious sense of stability, authenticity, and security." This has led to

> the widespread, sometimes uncritical, adoption of the interview, and an unreflective endorsement of the core assumptions of the interview society...[whereby] unexamined models of the social actor and of the research process [are implicitly introduced] into the particular styles of interviewing that [researchers] recommend" (Atkinson & Silverman, 1997, p. 310).

The core assumptions of the interview society can be explicated in terms of what Briggs (2007a, 2007b) called the *cartographies of communicability* that constitute particular conceptualizations of interviewing. A communicable cartography of interviewing is essentially a conceptual map consisting of certain ideologies of language, communication, and the institution of the interview, which are temporally and spatially located, and which produce certain (contestable) social roles, subject positions, agency, and social relations that allow individuals in the interview society to *make sense* of interviews and interview data, to *understand what they are*, and to *interpret* them as particular kinds of social phenomena. Communicable cartographies of interviewing can also work to *naturalize* and *project* themselves, to ensure their continued circulation.

Briggs (2007a) argued that three particular ideologies of language and communication have converged in a communicable cartography of interviewing that has been naturalized in contemporary times: language as a transparent medium, separation of the private from the public spheres, and a "nostalgia for the supposedly primordial face-to-face basis of communication and social life." Interviews from this perspective "magically appear to embody all three ideologies, producing discourse that seems to transform inner voices into public discourse by constructing particular types of subjectivity and inducing subjects to reveal their inner voices (attitudes, beliefs, experiences, etc.)" (pp. 553–554).

I use the label *interviews as research instrument* to refer to a similar communicable cartography of interviewing, as it is manifested in qualitative applied linguistics. As a research instrument, interviews are theorized (often tacitly) as a resource for investigating truths, facts, experience, beliefs, attitudes, and/or feelings of respondents. Language tends to be conceptualized in referential terms, as a neutral medium that reflects or corresponds to objective or subjective reality (Alvesson, 2003; Baker, 2002; Briggs, 1986; Holstein & Gubrium, 1995; Richards, 2003; Roulston, 2010; Sarangi, 2003; Silverman, 2001). Interview data are ontologically ascribed the status of "reports" of respondents' biographical, experiential, and psychological worlds, with the interview thus conceptualized as the epistemological conduit to those worlds: the interviewer reveals what "really" happened, or what participants "actually" felt through the technology of the interview, with closer approximations of reality depending on the interviewer's skill at developing rapport, for example, or not asking leading questions. (Neo)positivist approaches such as survey or structured interviewing take the interview as research instrument perspective (see Alvesson, 2003; Roulston, 2010), as do "naturalistic" (Lincoln & Guba, 1985), "romantic" (Alvesson, 2001), or "emotionalist" (Silverman, 2001) approaches, such as those utilizing so-called open-ended or in-depth interview methods, which "suggest that it is possible...to unravel a deeper or more essential reality" (van den Berg et al., 2003, p. 3) than allowed by structured interviewing.

Clearly, *interviews as social practice* share with the *interview as research instrument* perspective an interest in generating research data for the purpose of analysis, answering research questions, a concern with interview techniques, and so forth. However, the former position departs from the latter by problematizing the assumptions that constitute the research instrument perspective, and treating interviews *themselves* as topics for investigation (also see Sarangi, 2003; see Table 1). In this respect, the research interview as social practice orientation aligns with Holstein and Gubrium's (1995, *inter alia*) well-known active interview. In terms similar to Silverman (2001), Holstein and Gubrium (2003) contrasted the active interview with conventional approaches by arguing that the latter privilege the *whats* of the interview, that is, the interview content, whereas active interviews are interested in both the *whats* and *hows*, that is, the content *and* the "interactional

[and] narrative procedures of knowledge production" (p. 68). Holstein and Gubrium argued that conceiving of the interview as a fundamentally social encounter rather than a conduit for accessing information means that the interview becomes "a site of, and occasion for, producing reportable knowledge" (p. 68). Further, by "activating" the subject "behind" the respondent, the interviewee is transformed from a "passive vessel of answers" to someone who "not only holds facts and details of experience, but, in the very process of offering them up for response, constructively adds to, takes away from, and transforms the facts and details" (p. 70). In this respect, bias and distortion, validity and reliability, topics of great concern in (neo)positivist and naturalistic theories of interview are transformed since the "respondent can hardly 'spoil' what he or she is, in effect subjectively creating" (p. 70; also see Briggs, 1986, pp. 21–23).[2]

Table 1. Contrasting conceptualizations of the research interview

	Interview as research instrument	Research interview as social practice
Status of interview	• A tool or resource for "collecting" or "gathering" information.	• A site or topic for investigation itself.
Status of interview data	• Data are "reports," which reveal truths and facts, and/or the attitudes, beliefs, and interior, mental states of self-disclosing respondents.	• Data are "accounts" of truths, facts, attitudes, beliefs, interior, mental states, etc., coconstructed between interviewer and interviewee.
Voice	• Interviews "give voice" to interviewees.	• "Voice" is situationally contingent and discursively coconstructed between interviewer and interviewee.
Bias	• Interviewers must strive to obviate data contamination.	• Reflexive recognition that data are collaboratively produced (and analysis of how they are); data cannot therefore be contaminated.
Analytic approaches	• Content or thematic analysis, summaries of data, and/or straightforward quotation, either abridged or verbatim, i.e., the data "speak for themselves."	• Data do not speak for themselves; analysis centers on how meaning is negotiated, knowledge is coconstructed, and interview is locally accomplished.
Analytic focus	• Product-oriented. • "What".	• Process-oriented. • "What" and "how".

Analyzing not only the whats, or the *product* of the interview, but also the hows, or the *process* involved in the coconstruction of meaning, has significant implications for data analysis. In conventional approaches, analysis of interview data often takes form in content or thematic analysis, "systematically grouping and summarizing the descriptions" of experience produced by respondents by common themes or content categories, such that their "interpretive activity is subordinated to the substance of what they report." In an active interview analysis, by contrast, "[t] he focus is as much on the assembly process as on what is assembled" (Holstein & Gubrium, 2003, p. 78; cf. Braun & Clarke, 2006). A range of analytic approaches can be adopted for this undertaking but all in some way account for the fundamental sociality of the interview.

INTERVIEWS AS RESEARCH INSTRUMENT IN APPLIED LINGUISTICS

There is an impressive diversity of topics addressed by qualitative applied linguistics studies that conceptualize interviews as a research instrument. For this reason, the discussion in this section is organized by the qualitative approach that authors indicated they adopted, using the following subheadings: ethnographic and case study research; narrative/life-history research; and a more generic class of interview studies that were identified as qualitative, or were not identified at all.

Ethnographic and Case Study Research

Interviews are frequently used in ethnography and case studies, employed in tandem with methods such as participant observation and document analysis as a means of developing in-depth understandings of phenomena through triangulation (by method and source) (Denzin & Lincoln, 2000; Lincoln & Guba, 1985). In this respect, it might come as a surprise that only a minority of the studies that were reviewed here presented findings based on an evident synthesis of the research methods employed. Among them was Vickers's (2007) ethnography of the second language (L2) language socialization of an Indonesian electrical engineering student into the practices of a community of student engineers. Featuring a sophisticated design that included participant observation, interviews, document analysis, playback sessions of videorecorded team meetings, and micro-analysis of face-to-face interaction, the study traced the development of the focal student's participation in project team meetings, using interview data to provide important contextual information about the participants' perspectives on the project and each other. In Rankin and Becker's (2006) action research case study, observational data were similarly integrated with written student and teacher reflections, stimulated recall sessions of videorecorded classes, and interviews in a small-scale investigation of a German as a foreign language teacher's oral corrective feedback practices. Interviews in this study were used "to trace the long-term development of [the teacher's] thinking" about his provision of the practice in question. In Creese's (2006) ethnographic study of an English as a second language (ESL) teacher and a subject teacher who were partnered in a secondary geography class, interviews were used to document these teachers' contrasting views of their pedagogical roles and responsibilities. Having thus "set the scene" (p. 444), the two teachers' views were then compared in an analysis of their actions in the actual classroom.

More typical of the ethnographic and case study research that was reviewed was the relative foregrounding of interviews from a larger ethnographic project, with these data composing the majority of the data presented (in some cases, the only data). As in the studies reviewed earlier, interviews were used most often as a means of accessing and presenting participants' beliefs, attitudes, perceptions, and experiences. For example, in Motha's (2006) critical feminist ethnography about the links between ESL and (neo)colonialism, data from interviews, conversations, and afternoon teas served as the primary record, used "to listen to voices that have traditionally been delegitimized within educational research" (p. 80), as four practicing teachers and the researcher discussed monolingualism, assimilationism, and linguicism in public schools. Canagarajah's (2008) ethnography concerning the role of the family in processes of language shift in three Sri Lankan diasporic communities, used interviews to gain an emic or "insider perspective on how the community explains its language choice and attitudes" (p. 148). Interviews also predominated in Golombek and Jordan's (2005) case study (data from reaction papers were provided, too, although it is not always clear which data came from which source). These data were used to present the thoughts and beliefs of two Taiwanese preservice L2 English teachers during and following a poststructuralist pronunciation pedagogy course, as they confronted such (language) ideologies as the native speaker myth and worked to "assert their right" (p. 514) to teach English pronunciation. Similarly, interview data were supplemented by language autobiographies in Haddix's (2008) insightful study of two White, monolingual-English teacher candidates in a sociolinguistics course. L. Taylor's (2006) short-term study of the experiences of a group of racially and ethnically diverse high school ESL students in a "Freirean-styled, antidiscrimination leadership camp" (p. 520) also relied heavily on interview data, as did K. King and Ganuza's (2005) ethnographic investigation into the national, ethnic, and linguistic identifications of Chilean-Swedish transmigrant youth, as manifested in interview talk.

Narrative/Life-History Research

It is no surprise that interviews were the central method of data generation in the studies that were reviewed, which focused on participant life histories and narratives (see, e.g., Andrews, Squire, & Tamboukou, 2008; Benwell & Stokoe, 2006; Clandinin & Connelly, 2000; Gubrium & Holstein, 2008). Nor is it a surprise that these studies investigated "subject realities" and "life realities" (Pavlenko, 2007), nor, for that matter, that the kinds of analyses undertaken were as varied (and variable) as they were. Nevertheless, there was considerable methodological and analytic overlap between studies in this section and the previous one, particularly those ethnographic and case studies that foregrounded interviews. On the one hand, these overlaps are an artifact of the categories I have used to organize this section, and the leakage (Trinh, 1989) between them. On the other, they may serve as evidence of some slippage in terms of how ethnography, case study, and narrative research have been conceptualized in applied linguistics: in fact, at times, the only way to discover whether a given study was an ethnography, a case study, a narrative inquiry, life-history research, or a phenomenological study, was by the terminology used to identify it. Even then, these terms were at times used as if they were interchangeable (cf. Creswell, 1998; Hatch, 2002; Polkinghorne, 1995; Silverman, 2001).

An exception is Menard-Warwick's (2005) life-history study of two Central American women and their contrasting educational experiences following their immigration to the United States. Menard-Warwick used data from interviews and classroom observations to represent the sociohistorically situated "life trajectories" (p. 171) of Brenda and Serafina as they attempted to balance English-language learning with family, work, scheduling difficulties, and U.S. immigration policy. Tsui's (2007) narrative inquiry concerning a Chinese EFL (English as foreign language) learner and teacher's negotiation of multiple conflicting identities utilized a design more common to other narrative/life-history studies reviewed, drawing on face-to-face interviews and diaries for Min-Fang's stories about struggling to identify with the professional identity of "communicative language teacher." Gao (2008) included some welcome methodological detail concerning her (thematic) data analysis, although her decision to employ life-history interviews to investigate 14 Chinese students' language-learning strategies is curious, given the topical focus, and the number (two) and length (45 minutes) of the interviews. Nonetheless, the study generally succeeded in its goal of "capturing learners' voices" (p. 173), at least as those voices were represented in the study. Participant voices were also well-represented in Carroll, Motha, and Price (2008), which analyzed narratives (written and spoken) from two separate studies to examine how "social structures and contexts can behave simultaneously as powerfully tyrannizing regimes of truth and powerfully liberating imagined communities" (p. 189). However, there is less detail than might be expected about the procedures of the content and thematic analyses that were undertaken, and little consideration of implications that the modalities of the narrative data might have had for the analysis. A point of contrast here can be found in Cheung's (2005) study of teachers' narratives about their career development, which provided a remarkable amount of information about the interviews and data analytic procedures that were undertaken.

"Qualitative" Interview Research

The studies considered in this section were identified by their authors simply as qualitative or were not identified at all; despite substantive differences between them, all used interviews as the primary method for generating empirical data. Palfreyman (2005), for example, relied almost exclusively on interviews in his important study about processes of Othering (cf. Said, 1978) among Turkish teachers and expatriate administrators at a Turkish university's English-language center. B. King (2008) provided a comparatively robust analytic framework based on Sacks (1972) to consider the pervasive but little-investigated problem of heteronormativity in L2 English education, using what appeared to be a single group interview with three gay male Korean L2 learners for his dataset.

In Baek and Damarin (2008), interviews were used to describe "the complex inner stories" (p. 195) of seven female L2-English-speaking university students from Korea and their experiences with computer-mediated communication in the L2. Atay and Ece (2009) "explore[d] the ideas" (p. 21) and "identity clash" (p. 31) of Turkish preservice teachers of English through a rich display of quotes from their 34 participants, although it was unclear whose voices belonged to whom since quotes were not attributed to particular participants. In Sarkar and Allen's (2007) qualitative study of identity and language use in a community of multilingual, multiethnic hip-hop artists in Montreal, interviews "focused on rappers' use of mixed language and the links they perceive to their identities as Quebec hip-hoppers" (p. 122). In a related study, Pennycook (2007) used interview data in his analysis of hip-hop in such countries as Malaysia, Korea, and Tanzania, and studied the challenges these localized varieties posed to the African American hip-hop ideology of "keepin' it real." Varghese and Johnston (2007) indicated that the participants in their qualitative study of evangelical Christian L2 English teachers were "very articulate" and "very pleased" to be interviewed, and as a result, that the researchers "had the impression that ... the interviewees' words could at one level ... be taken as a reasonably accurate record of what they actually thought" (p. 13). Interviews were also used in K. King and Fogle's (2006) study of ways that parents discursively positioned themselves to justify their bilingual parenting practices and policies, with parents' quotes about these matters organized around common themes that "emerged" from the data.

SUMMARY

As the review here suggests, qualitative research in applied linguistics that conceives of interviews as research instrument is remarkably diverse, in terms of the topics addressed, the theoretical frameworks adopted, the research methods employed, and the ways that data and analyses are represented. Certainly, these studies illustrate how common the interview as a methodological option in qualitative applied linguistics has become. As well, they underscore the utility, flexibility, and convenience of qualitative interviews for investigating an impressive array of matters of relevance to applied linguistics. At the same time, each of these studies illustrates in different ways one or more of the features of the communicable cartography of interview as research instrument described earlier. I alluded earlier to several of these features; here I elaborate briefly on four of them: the status of interview data as "reports," the obfuscation of power, the interview as giving "voice" to participants, and matters concerning data analysis.

Status of Data as "Reports"

There is an evident propensity in the research discussed earlier to conceptualize interview data as participant "reports" of objective or subjective reality, with a generally exclusive focus on "content," or the "what" of the interview. Perhaps the clearest indication of the status ascribed to these data is in how they are displayed: frequently as decontextualized, stand-alone quotes of respondents' answers, as if they were "discrete speech events isolated from the stream of social interaction in which—and for which—they were produced" (Wooffitt & Widdicombe, 2006, p. 39). Even when interviewers are included in representations of data, there tends to be little analysis concerning their role in the production of data. Both points are significant analytically, for, as a long line of research in conversation analysis has demonstrated, "answers" are normatively oriented to and designed for the questions that occasion them (Sacks, 1992; Sacks, Schegloff, & Jefferson, 1974; Schegloff, 2007). In other words, interviewees' answers are "shaped by, and oriented to, the interactional context. This [insight] … invites [researchers] to give serious consideration to the ways in which *the interviewer's participation is significantly implicated in what the respondents end up saying, and how they say it*" (Wooffitt & Widdicombe, 2006, p. 56, my emphasis). This valuable analytic resource disappears, however, when data are represented as direct reports—as if the interviewer were invisible—and consequently, a wide range of potentially important insights concerning the data, analysis, and interpretations of a given study can be lost. For example, although Canagarajah (2008) provided important contextual information by mentioning differences in religion, caste, and class between his participants and him, there was no analysis of the impact this may have had on his interviews. L. Taylor (2006), too, mentioned her own race (White), but did not consider implications of this for her interviews or her findings, a curious omission given the study's focus on race, and that many interviewees were youth of Color. Although Menard-Warwick (2005) indicated that she made "every effort to take into account [her] own presence as an Anglo, Spanish-speaking, former teacher" (p. 170), she, too, was largely absent in her analysis of interview data. Similarly, in my (Talmy, 2006) ethnographic study concerning the struggles of a group of Micronesian students at a Hawai'i high school, I failed to consider my raced and "placed" (Blommaert, 2005) status as an adult White male researcher whose first language is English, interviewing ESL youth of Color. The same can be said of Palfreyman (2005), who inexplicably did not consider his own identity as a British expatriate in a study of Othering between expatriates and Turks at a Turkish university; and Varghese and Johnston (2007), who, although clear that as "atheists" their "interpretations, findings, and conclusions will be colored by and filtered through our subject positions" (p. 13), were less informative concerning the actual implications of this for their interviews with evangelical Christians. In Golombek and Jordan (2005), one of the researchers was the teacher of the two focal students, and apparently, was one of the interviewers, too; yet nothing was discussed about this relationship or its potential effect on the interviews. The same is true of Motha (2006), who was her focal participants' course advisor, university teacher, and practicum coordinator; and Chavez (2007), who was her participants' course supervisor, though she did briefly acknowledge (p. 185) that this relationship may have had some relevance for her findings. This is not to single out these studies as being unusual in any way; indeed, the neglect of the role of the researcher/interviewer in coconstructing interview data—*whatever* their relationship to the interviewee—is common across studies that conceive of interviews as a research instrument.

Power

Relatedly, the interview is constituted by complex relations of power, which can be differentially realized in many ways: who chooses what—and what not—to discuss; who asks what questions, when, and how; who is ratified to answer them (and who is not); who determines when to terminate a line of questioning; and so on. There are also other potentially important asymmetries that may be less directly observable but equally relevant, if not more so, ranging from differences in institutional status, age, language expertise, social class, and more. Analyses that conceive of interviews as providing access to what participants think or believe, ascribe interview data the status of reports, or do not account for the "complex pragmatics of interview practices" (Briggs, 2007a, p. 555) obscure such power imbalances by simply not attending to them. Additionally, important power asymmetries can be enacted *beyond* the immediate interactional context of the interview, in terms of data representation, specifically in what Bauman and Briggs (1990) have called *entextualization*, "the process of rendering discourse extractable, of making a stretch of linguistic production [e.g., talk from an interview] into a unit—*a text*—that can be lifted out of its interactional setting" (p. 73) so that it can be *recontextualized*, that is, placed into another context. Thus, as Briggs (2007a) noted: "power lies not just in controlling how discourse unfolds in the context of its production but [in] gaining control over its *recontextualization*—shaping how it draws on other discourses and contexts and when, where, how, and by whom it will be subsequently used" (p. 562). Just as interviews as research instrument do not address power within the interview itself, neither do they attend to power in terms of how those data are entextualized, decontextualized, and subsequently recontextualized, for example, as stand-alone quotes of "what participants think."

Voice

A frequently cited rationale for adopting qualitative interview methods is that they allow participants' own "voices" to be "heard" rather than obscured, for example, in summaries, tables, or statistics; indeed, participant voices were communicated in resounding fashion in the studies reviewed earlier. However, such a conception of voice carries with it a range of assumptions that may go unexamined: for example, that a person speaks with a single voice; that voice does, or at least can, given the right circumstance, express one's true self; and that the researcher or interviewer plays a central role in creating the liberatory conditions for this voice to be heard, by establishing trust, asking the right questions, and not interrupting. All caveats concerning "multiple," "conflicting," and "contradictory" identities notwithstanding, such an unproblematized notion of voice suggests the existence of a *unitary, coherent,* and *essential* self that the participant "gives voice to." As Mazzei and Jackson (2009) sum up:

> Qualitative researchers have recognized the dangerous assumptions in trying to represent a single truth (seemingly articulated by a single voice) and have therefore pluralized voice, intending to highlight the polyvocal and multiple

nature of voice.... This practice of "more is better" has indeed highlighted the ways in which voices are not singular, yet the obsession for more full voices side-steps ... the problem: these practices remain attached to notions of voice inherited from metaphysics—voice as present, stable, authentic, and self-reflective. Voice is still "there" to search for, retrieve, and liberate (pp. 1–2).

Data Analysis

All of the studies reviewed earlier analyzed their interview data using some combination of content and thematic analysis, an approach to analysis that is well-aligned with a conceptualization of the interview as a research instrument (cf. Braun & Clarke, 2006).[3] As one might expect for a collection of studies so diverse, the type and quality of analyses were variable, ranging from sophisticated thematic analyses, to general summaries of the content of what participants said, to little or no provision of analytic comment at all. In her important review of autobiographic narrative research in applied linguistics, and with clear relevance to the present discussion, Pavlenko (2007) noted that the key advantage of content and thematic analyses is their "sensitivity to recurrent motifs salient in participants' stories and thus to themes that are important to L2 learners but [that] may not have been reflected in previous scholarship" (p. 166). This is indeed the case with each of the studies discussed here, from B. King's (2008) welcome discussion of heteronormativity in applied linguistics, to Canagarajah's (2008) problematization of the pivotal role of family in language maintenance, to the insights yielded by Menard-Warwick's (2005) memorable life histories of Brenda and Serafina, to Sarkar and Allen's (2007) significant contribution to the growing literature on hybridity, globalization, and hip-hop. However, in addition to the benefits that attend content and thematic analyses, Pavlenko (2007) enumerates five of what she calls their major weaknesses:

> The first is the lack of a theoretical premise, which makes it unclear where conceptual categories come from and how they relate to each other. The second is the lack of established procedure for matching of instances to categories. The third is the overreliance on repeated instances, which may lead analysts to overlook important events or themes that do not occur repeatedly or do not fit into pre-established schemes. The fourth is an exclusive focus on

what is in the text, whereas what is excluded may potentially be as or even more informative. The fifth and perhaps the most problematic for applied linguistics is the lack of attention to ways in which storytellers use language to interpret experiences and position themselves as particular kinds of people.... In other words, content analysis may result in a laundry list of observations, factors, or categories, illustrated by quotes from participants, that misses the links between the categories, essentializes particular descriptions, and fails to describe the larger picture where they may fit (pp. 166–167).

Perhaps a sixth *potential* weakness concerns issues of theoretical (in)compatibility, that is, when studies that are explicitly formulated with post-structuralist, social constructionist, and/or social practice theoretical frameworks adopt for their theory of interview a research instrument perspective. There is, of course, always the possibility that a deliberate decision has been made to do this; if that is the case, however, some meta-methodological discussion about that choice would be anticipated (see Roulston, 2010; Silverman, 2001).

RESEARCH INTERVIEWS AS SOCIAL PRACTICE IN APPLIED LINGUISTICS

As mentioned earlier, studies that conceive of research interviews as social practice treat the interview not as a resource for extracting data held within a univocal respondent, but as a site for investigation itself. Rather than direct reports, data are conceptualized as accounts of phenomena, jointly produced by interviewer and interviewee. Rather than a concern with researcher bias, there is a fundamentally reflexive orientation to the collaborative character of knowledge production and data generation. Rather than an exclusive focus on interview content, or the "what" of the data, attention is directed both to the "what" and "how," that is, the content *and* the linguistic and/or interactional resources used in coconstructing content and locally achieving the interview as speech event. Taken together, these features constitute a communicable cartography of the interview as participation in social practice(s)—the "(partially) routine activities through which people carry out (partially) shared goals based on (partially) shared (conscious or unconscious) knowledge of the various roles or positions people can fill [or do] in these activities" (Gee, 2004, p. 33; also see Giddens, 1984). A wide range of analytic approaches can be adopted for the analysis of research interviews as social practice; among the most common are various types of (critical) discourse analysis (see, e.g., Blommaert, 2005; Eggins, 2005; Fairclough, 2003; Gee, 2005; Johnstone, 2008; Schiffrin, Tannen, & Hamilton, 2001; cf. Wooffitt, 2005), narrative analysis (e.g., Andrews et al., 2008; Gubrium & Holstein, 2008), conversation analysis (Sacks, 1992) especially work in "institutional" (Heritage, 2005) or "applied" (ten Have, 2007) conversation analysis (see especially Drew & Heritage, 1992), membership categorization analysis (Sacks, 1972, 1992; for work on interviews, see Baker, 2002, 2004), positioning analysis (e.g., Bamberg, 2000; Harré & van Langenhove, 1992), and interactional sociolinguistics (e.g., Gumperz, 1982), to name but a few. Depending on the design of a study and its scope, research questions, and theoretical framework, analytic focus can range from the comparatively "micro" (e.g., sequential organization, recipient design, discourse markers, contextualization cues, evidentiality, category-bound activities), to the "macro" (e.g., narrative structure, membership categorization devices, negotiation of identities, power relations, intertextuality, interdiscursivity), to more general orientations that engage less with the "how" than the "what," but still challenge the conception of interviews as a conduit into what people really think, know, or believe. In other words, to presume that analysis of interviews as social practice *necessarily* involves some form of micro-analysis, for example, would be as much a mistake as presuming that it does not. Instead, the primary issue for a social practice analysis entails an ontological and epistemological *shift*, by problematizing the ideologies that constitute the cartography of communicability that is referred to earlier as interviews as research instrument.[4]

To demonstrate implications of this discussion, I consider in the remainder of this section several qualitative applied linguistics studies that conceive of the research interview as social practice. Each study uses interviews for a different purpose, and each analyzes the data generated from them using a different approach, ranging from micro-analysis to more general orientations that problematize the status of the interview, the data, and the role of the interviewer. My aim in discussing these studies is not to hold them up as exemplars of any kind, but to provide some illustrative examples of this particular conception of the research interview.

Liebscher and Dailey-O'Cain's (2009) qualitative study of language attitudes provides a useful entry point for this discussion. In terms that parallel the different conceptualizations of the interview referred to above, Liebscher and Dailey-O'Cain identified three different approaches taken in the analysis of qualitative data on language attitudes, which are typically drawn from interviews: a "content-based approach" (pp. 197–198), which aligns with the interview as research instrument perspective; and two alternatives, "turn-internal semantic and pragmatic approaches" (pp. 198–199) and "interactional approaches" (pp. 199–201), which can be situated under the rubric of research interview as social practice. The authors make a strong case for integrating these three "levels" of analysis, drawing on interviews they conducted with western Germans who had moved to Saxony and German émigrés in Canada, concerning attitudes about the Saxon dialect. Using an analytic framework that combined interactional sociolinguistics, positioning analysis, and critical discourse analysis, they showed not only that there was, for western Germans, a "stigma" associated with the Saxon dialect, but also how it was interactionally worked up among focus group participants. The authors also demonstrated the comparative nonsalience of the stigma among German émigrés in Canada, suggesting that it was more important for these participants to index a "common ground in the German language" than to mark differences based on regional variation. As a result, the interviews themselves became central analytic sites, where participants not only *talked about* language attitudes but also *produced* them with one another and the researcher(s) in the interactions that constituted the interviews.

Johnson's (2006) study of the construction and negotiation of teacher identity in a research interview uniquely foregrounds the interview as site for knowledge production. The study posed the following research question: "Can a poststructural approach to critical reflection encourage teachers to become more critical?" (p. 215). Rather than providing a thematic analysis based on the teacher's reports about her reflections on teaching, whether they were critical or not, and if, as a result, she became more or less critical, Johnson investigated how the identities of a "good teacher" and a "good research participant" became salient in her interviews. Drawing on conversation analysis and membership categorization analysis, she described in substantive detail the ways that the teacher "portrayed herself as *doing* reflective practice from a 'critical perspective'" (p. 217, my emphasis), as well as how she oriented to being an "excellent interviewee, in the terms laid out by the researcher/interviewer" (p. 219). Consequently, the answer to her research question is based on a notably reflexive analysis: that "the interviewer primarily position[ed] the interviewee through the assignation of a teacher as excellent reflective practitioner category [with that] option ... taken up by the teacher ... in the ensuing [interview]" (p. 232).

Prior (in press) utilizes discursive psychology (e.g., Edwards & Potter, 1992, 2005) and narrative analysis to examine two versions of the "same" emotionally charged narrative told on two separate occasions by Trang, a multilingual, multiethnic adult immigrant for whom English was an L2. From an interview as research instrument perspective, such a study might be concerned with issues related to reliability, for example, the degree of consonance between Trang's two tellings of a frustrating experience at a bank in Canada, whether they diverged and if so, in what ways, and so forth, with the similarities and differences pointing to how truthful Trang was, how dependable his memory was, and whether his story was to be believed as a report of what really happened. However, Prior located important differences between the two narrative versions, characterizing them not as an indication of inconsistency but as evidence that the tellings served substantially different rhetorical purposes in the different contextual circumstances of the two interviews (also see Pavlenko, 2007). The analysis is, once again, fundamentally reflexive, as it accounts not only for the "content" of the two versions of the bank narrative but also the interactional and interpersonal circumstances of their local production.

Campbell and Roberts (2007) continue a long line of work by Gumperz and associates (e.g., Roberts, Davies, & Jupp, 1992) concerning interethnic communication in workplace encounters. The article examined the variable performance of White and of Color "British born" applicants versus "born abroad" applicants in job interviews, accounting for the comparatively unsuccessful performance of the latter group in terms of their failure to "synthesize" what the authors called *personal* and *institutional* discourses in the job interview. The interview data were subjected to a methodologically eclectic discourse analysis, as the authors displayed differences in how both groups of applicants negotiated the interview, although it is not always clear what role the interviewer played in coconstructing successful and unsuccessful interview performances. However, one concern that stood out in the study, given the analysis of the job interview data, is what emerges as a central analytic inconsistency: the conceptualization of the status of a secondary stream of data used from stimulated recall interviews. In contrast to the job interview data, the stimulated recall data were taken at face value, as accurate representations of what participants were really thinking in the job interviews; that is, the stimulated recall interviews were treated as research instruments, in contrast to the job interviews. Unfortunately, the authors did not comment upon this apparent tension, leaving one to wonder whether it was a deliberate analytic move or not.

Finally, Hawkins (2005) provides a good example of a study that engages less with the "how" than the "what" of her interviews, but still problematizes the ideologies that constitute the communicable cartography of interview as research instrument (also see Block, 2000). This is likely due, at least in part, to the fact that her interview participants were young children. Stating at one point that what was missing in her previous research on young children's school-based language and literacy development was "their voices and opinions" (p. 67), Hawkins and her research collaborator devised several ways of including them, one of which involved interviewing. The analysis of these data connects the contrasting patterns of communication and school engagement of two kindergarten boys: interactional patterns that were observed in classrooms are shown to be recontextualized and repeated in the interviews themselves. The analytic focus on how these boys participated in the interviews thus served as an important secondary source of data for Hawkins' larger argument about their differing ways of participating in school.

CONCLUSION

It may appear from the preceding discussion that I am advancing the position that qualitative applied linguists using interview methods should theorize them as social practice. That is not the case. Studies that adopt (neo)positivist or naturalistic/romantic theoretical frameworks, for example, need not conceptualize research interviews as social practice, though I believe there are clear advantages if they do. Rather, my goal is to call for greater attention to the theories of interview that *all* qualitative applied linguistics studies adopt, to highlight the communicable cartography of interviewing that has been naturalized in "the interview society," and to raise questions about it so that the ideologies of language, communication, and the interview that constitute it are not imported into qualitative applied linguistics studies, at least *without due consideration*. As Briggs (2007a) argued, when interviews are not adequately theorized, and ideologies of interviewing go unexamined, interviews "largely remain black boxes ... technologies so widely accepted that [researchers] can just feed in questions and get quotations for [their] publications without worrying about the complex pragmatics that make them work. Our own assimilation of these ideologies [can] thus limit ... the ways we interview and reflect on our own and other people's interviews" (p. 555). In this respect, I would suggest that there is considerable need for heightened reflexivity about the interview methods that applied linguistics researchers use in their studies, on the role of the interviewer in occasioning interview answers, on the subject "behind" the interviewee, on the status ascribed to interview data, and on how those data are analyzed and represented, regardless of whether one opts to conceive of interviews as research instrument, or research interviews as participation in social practices.

NOTES

1 Due to space constraints, I do not consider in this article experimental studies that incorporate qualitative interviews. There is a great deal that could (and should) be said about this important stream of "mixed methods" research. However, although I must side-step the discussion, I will state that these studies tend to adopt a theory of interview—as research instrument—that aligns well with the (e.g., [neo]positivist) theoretical frameworks of the larger studies in which the interviews are used. At the same time, I do believe that quantitative researchers, like their qualitative colleagues, would do well to work toward greater reflexivity concerning the ontological, epistemological, and ideological assumptions guiding their decisions to use interviews, the status they ascribe to interview data, and the claims they make based on this particular research method.

2 Holstein & Gubrium (2003) elaborate:

When the interview is viewed as a dynamic, meaning making occasion ...

different criteria [regarding reliability and validity] apply. The focus is on how meaning is constructed, the circumstances of construction, and the meaningful linkages that are assembled.... While interest in the content of answers persists, it is primarily in how and what the subject/respondent, in collaboration with an equally active interviewer, produces and conveys about the subject/respondent's experience under the interpretive circumstances at hand. One cannot expect answers on one occasion to replicate those on another because they emerge from difference circumstances of production. Similarly, the validity of answers derives not from their correspondence to meanings held within the respondent, but from their ability to convey situated experiential realities in terms that are locally comprehensible (p. 71).

3 However, it was indicated in several studies that some form of discourse analysis had in fact been undertaken. For example, Haddix (2008, p. 261) and Miller (2007, p. 152) stated that they used Gee's approach for analysis; Golombek & Jordan (2005, p. 519) mentioned Fairclough; while L. Taylor (2006, p. 526) referred generically to "discourse analysis." K. King & Ganuza (2005) mentioned Preston's (1994) "content-oriented discourse analysis," but it is not clear what this involved, how it was done, or what analytic benefit it provided. Hayes (2005) provided a sophisticated theoretical discussion about the role of the researcher in coconstructing interview data, but did not, unfortunately, apply these insights to his analysis. B. King (2008) attempted to use Sacks' (1972) membership categorization analysis, but was ultimately unsuccessful in his attempt at following through. Only Varghese & Johnston (2007) actually delivered on a Bakhtinian analysis, although it is minimal enough that it is ultimately subordinated to the content analysis featured in the study. See Antaki, Billig, Edwards, & Potter (2003); Burman (2004); and S. Taylor (2001) for more on criteria that can be used to determine what constitutes a discourse analysis.

4 An excellent discussion and useful set of guidelines for undertaking an analysis of qualitative applied linguistics interviews as social practice can be found in Richards (2003, pp. 79–103).

REFERENCES

Alvesson, M. (2003). Beyond neopositivists, romantics, and localists: A reflexive approach to interviews in organizational research. *Academy of Management Review, 28*, 13–33.

Andrews, M., Squire, C., & Tamboukou, M. (Eds.). (2008). *Doing narrative research*. Los Angeles: Sage.

Antaki, C., Billig, M., Edwards, D., & Potter, J. (2003). Discourse analysis means doing analysis: A critique of six analytic shortcomings. *Discourse Analysis Online, 1*. Retrieved January 1, 2004, from http://extra.shu.ac.uk/daol/articles/open/2002/002/antaki2002002-paper.html.

Atay, D., & Ece, A. (2009). Multiple identities as reflected in English-language education: The Turkish perspective. *Journal of Language, Identity, & Education, 8*, 21–34.

Atkinson, P., & Silverman, D. (1997). Kundera's Immortality: The interview society and the invention of the self. *Qualitative Inquiry, 3*, 304–325.

Baek, M., & Damarin, S. K. (2008). Computer-mediated communication as experienced by Korean women students in U.S. higher education. *Language and Intercultural Communication, 8*, 192–208.

Baker, C. (2002). Ethnomethodological analyses of interviews. In J. F. Gubrium & J. A. Holstein (Eds.), *Handbook of interviewing: Context and method* (pp. 777–795). Thousand Oaks, CA: Sage.

Baker, C. (2004). Membership categorization and interview accounts. In D. Silverman (Ed.), *Qualitative research: Theory, method, and practice* (2nd ed., pp. 162–176). London: Sage.

Bamberg, M. (2000). Critical personalism, language and development. *Theory & Psychology, 10*, 749–767.

Bauman, R., & Briggs, C. (1990). Poetics and performance as critical perspectives on language and social life. *Annual Review of Anthropology, 19*, 59–88.

Benwell, B., & Stokoe, E. H. (2006). *Discourse and identity*. Edinburgh, UK: Edinburgh University Press.

Block, D. (2000). Problematizing interview data: Voices in the mind's machine? *TESOL Quarterly, 34*, 757–763.

Blommaert, J. (2005). *Discourse: A critical introduction*. Cambridge, UK: Cambridge University Press.

Braun, V., & Clarke, V. (2006). Using thematic analysis in psychology. *Qualitative Research in Psychology 3*(2), 77–101.

Briggs, C. (1986). *Learning how to ask: A sociolinguistic appraisal of the role of the interview in social science research*. Cambridge, UK: Cambridge University Press.

Briggs, C. (2007a). Anthropology, interviewing, and communicability in contemporary society. *Current Anthropology, 48*, 551–567.

Briggs, C. (2007b). The Gallup poll, democracy, and vox populi: Ideologies of interviewing and the communicability of modern life. *Text & Talk, 27*(5/6), 681–704.

Burman, E. (2004). Discourse analysis means analysing discourse: Some comments on Antaki, Billig, Edwards and Potter: "Discourse analysis means doing analysis: A critique of six analytic shortcomings." *Discourse Analysis Online, 2*. Retrieved January 1, 2004, from http://extra.shu.ac.uk/daol/articles/open/2003/003/burman2003003-paper.html.

Campbell, S., & Roberts, C. R. (2007). Migration, ethnicity and competing discourses in the job interview: Synthesizing the institutional and personal. *Discourse & Society, 18*, 243–271.

Canagarajah, A. S. (2008). Language shift and the family: Questions from the Sri Lankan Tamil diaspora. *Journal of Sociolinguistics, 12*, 143–176.

Carroll, S., Motha, S., & Price, J. N. (2008). Accessing imagined communities and reinscribing regimes of truth. *Critical Inquiry in Language Studies, 5*, 165–191.

Chavez, M. M. (2007). The orientation of learner language use in peer work: Teacher role, learner role and individual identity. *Language Teaching Research, 11*, 161–188.

Cheung, E. (2005). Hong Kong secondary schoolteachers' understanding of their careers. *Teachers and Teaching: Theory and Practice, 11*, 127–149.

Cicourel, A. V. (1964). *Method and measurement in sociology.* New York: Free Press.

Clandinin, D. J., & Connelly, F. M. (2000). *Narrative inquiry: Experience and story in qualitative research.* San Francisco, CA: Jossey-Bass.

Creese, A. (2006). Supporting talk? Partnership teachers in classroom interaction. *International Journal of Bilingual Education and Bilingualism, 9*, 434–453.

Creswell, J. W. (1998). *Qualitative inquiry and research design: Choosing among five traditions.* Thousand Oaks, CA: Sage.

Denzin, N. K., & Lincoln, Y. S. (2000). The discipline and practice of qualitative research. In N. K. Denzin & Y. S. Lincoln (Eds.), *Handbook of qualitative research* (2nd ed., pp. 1–28). Thousand Oaks, CA: Sage.

Drew, P., & Heritage, J. (1992). *Talk at work: Interaction in institutional settings.* Cambridge, UK: Cambridge University Press.

Edwards, D., & Potter, J. (1992). *Discursive psychology.* Thousand Oaks, CA: Sage.

Edwards, D., & Potter, J. (2005). Discursive psychology, mental states, and description. In H. te Molder & J. Potter (Eds.), *Conversation and cognition* (pp. 241–259). Cambridge, UK: Cambridge University Press.

Eggins, S. (2005). *Introduction to systemic function linguistics* (2nd ed.). London: Continuum.

Fairclough, N. (2003). *Analysing discourse: Textual analysis for social research.* London: Routledge.

Fontana, A., & Prokos, A. H. (2007). *The interview: From formal to postmodern.* Walnut Creek, CA: Left Coast Press.

Gao, X. (2008). You had to work hard 'cause you didn't know whether you were going to wear shoes or straw sandals! *Journal of Language, Identity, & Education, 7*, 169–187.

Gee, J. P. (2004). Discourse analysis: What makes it critical? In R. Rogers (Ed.), *Critical discourse analysis in education* (pp. 19–50). Mahwah, NJ: Erlbaum.

Gee, J. P. (2005). *An introduction to discourse analysis: Theory and method* (2nd ed.). New York: Routledge.

Giddens, A. (1984). *The constitution of society: Outline of a theory of structuration.* Berkeley, CA: University of California Press.

Golombek, P., & Jordan, S. R. (2005). Becoming "black lambs" not "parrots" : A poststructuralist orientation to intelligibility and identity. *TESOL Quarterly, 39,* 513–533.

Gubrium, J. F., & Holstein, J. A. (2002a). From the individual interview to the interview society. In J. F. Gubrium & J. A. Holstein (Eds.), *Handbook of interview research: Context and method* (pp. 3–32). Thousand Oaks, CA: Sage.

Gubrium, J. F., & Holstein, J. A. (Eds.). (2002b). *Handbook of interview research: Context and method.* Thousand Oaks, CA: Sage.

Gubrium, J. F., & Holstein, J. A. (2008). *Analyzing narrative reality.* Thousand Oaks, CA: Sage.

Gumperz, J. J. (1982). *Discourse strategies.* New York: Cambridge University Press.

Haddix, M. (2008). Beyond sociolinguistics: Towards a critical approach to cultural and linguistic diversity in teacher education. *Language and Education, 22,* 254–270.

Harré, R., & van Langenhove, L. (1992). Varieties of positioning. *Journal for the Theory of Social Behaviour, 20,* 393–407.

Hatch, J. A. (2002). *Doing qualitative research in education settings.* Albany, NY: SUNY Press.

Hawkins, M. (2005). Becoming a student: Identity work and academic literacies in early schooling. *TESOL Quarterly, 39,* 59–82.

Hayes, D. (2005). Exploring the lives of non-native speaking English educators in Sri Lanka. *Teachers and Teaching: Theory and Practice, 11,* 169–194.

Heritage, J. (2005). Conversation analysis and institutional talk. In K. L. Fitch & R. E. Sanders (Eds.), *Handbook of language and social interaction* (pp. 103–147). Mahwah, NJ: Erlbaum.

Holstein, J. A., & Gubrium, J. F. (1995). *The active interview.* Thousand Oaks, CA: Sage.

Holstein, J. A., & Gubrium, J. F. (2003). Active interviewing. In J. F. Gubrium & J. A. Holstein (Eds.), *Postmodern interviewing* (pp. 67–80). Thousand Oaks, CA: Sage.

Holstein, J. A., & Gubrium, J. F. (2004). The active interview. In D. Silverman (Ed.), *Qualitative research: Theory, method, and practice* (pp. 140–161). London: Sage.

Johnson, G. C. (2006). The discursive construction of teacher identities in a research interview. In A. de Fina, D. Schiffrin, & M. Bamberg (Eds.), *Discourse and identity* (pp. 213–232). Cambridge, UK: Cambridge University Press.

Johnston, B. (1997). Do ESL teachers have careers? *TESOL Quarterly, 31,* 681–712.

Johnstone, B. (2008). *Discourse analysis* (2nd ed.). Malden, MA: Blackwell.

King, B. W. (2008). "Being gay guy, that is the advantage" : Queer Korean language learning and identity construction. *Journal of Language, Identity, & Education, 7,* 1–33.

King, K., & Fogle, L. (2006). Bilingual parenting as good parenting: Parents' perspectives on family language policy for additive bilingualism. *International Journal of Bilingual Education and Bilingualism, 9,* 695–712.

King, K., & Ganuza, N. (2005). Language, identity, education, and transmigration: Chilean adolescents in Sweden. *Journal of Language, Identity, & Education, 4,* 179–199.

Kvale, S. (2007). *Doing interviews.* London: Sage.

Kvale, S., & Brinkman, S. (2009). *InterViews: Learning the craft of qualitative research interviewing* (2nd ed.). Thousand Oaks, CA: Sage.

Liebscher, G., & Dailey-O'Cain, J. (2009). Language attitudes in interaction. *Journal of Sociolinguistics, 13,* 195–222.

Lincoln, Y. S., & Guba, E. G. (1985). *Naturalistic inquiry.* Newbury Park, CA: Sage.

Mazzei, L. A., & Jackson, A. Y. (2009). The limit of voice. In A. Y. Jackson & L. A. Mazzei (Eds.), *Voice in qualitative inquiry: Challenging conventional, interpretive, and critical conceptions in qualitative research.* London: Routledge.

Menard-Warwick, J. (2005). Intergenerational trajectories and sociopolitical context: Latina immigrants in adult ESL. *TESOL Quarterly, 39,* 165–185.

Miller, J. (2007). Identity construction in teacher education. In Z. Hua, P. Seedhouse, L. Wei, & V. Cook (Eds.), *Language learning and teaching as social interaction* (pp. 148–162). London: Palgrave Macmillan.

Mishler, E. G. (1986). *Research interviewing: Context and narrative.* Cambridge, MA: Harvard University Press.

Motha, S. (2006). Decolonizing ESOL: Negotiating linguistic power in U.S. public school classrooms. *Critical Inquiry in Language Studies, 3,* 75–100.

Palfreyman, D. (2005). Othering in an English language program. *TESOL Quarterly, 39,* 211–233.

Pavlenko, A. (2007). Autobiographic narratives as data in applied linguistics. *Applied Linguistics, 28,* 163–188.

Pennycook, A. (2007). Language, localization, and the real: Hip-hop and the global spread of authenticity. *Journal of Language, Identity, & Education, 6,* 101–115.

Polkinghorne, D. E. (1995). Narrative configuration in qualitative analysis. In J. A. Hatch & R. Wisniewski (Eds.), *Life history and narrative* (pp. 5–23). London: Falmer Press.

Preston, D. (1994). Content-oriented discourse analysis and folk linguistics. *Language Sciences, 16,* 285–331.

Prior, M. (in press). Self-presentation in L2 interview talk: Narrative versions, accountability, and emotionality. *Applied Linguistics.*

Rankin, J., & Becker, F. (2006). Does reading the research make a difference? A case study of teacher growth in FL German. *Modern Language Journal, 90,* 353–372.

Richards, K. (2003). *Qualitative inquiry in TESOL.* Basingstoke, UK: Palgrave Macmillan.

Richards, K. (2009). Trends in qualitative research in language teaching since 2000. *Language Teaching, 42,* 147–180.

Roberts, C. R., Davies, E., & Jupp, T. (1992). *Language and discrimination: A study of communication in multi-ethnic workplaces.* London: Longman.

Roulston, K. (2010). *The reflective researcher: Learning to interview in the social sciences.* Thousand Oaks, CA: Sage.

Sacks, H. (1972). On the analyzability of stories by children. In J. J. Gumperz & D. Hymes (Eds.), *Directions in sociolinguistics: The ethnography of communication* (pp. 325–345). New York: Holt, Rinehart, and Winston.

Sacks, H. (1992). *Lectures on conversation* (Vols. 1– 2). Oxford, UK: Blackwell.

Sacks, H., Schegloff, E. A., & Jefferson, G. (1974). A simplest systematics for the organization of turn-taking for conversation. *Language, 50,* 696–735.

Said, E. W. (1978). *Orientalism.* New York: Random House.

Sarangi, S. (2003). Institutional, professional, and lifeworld frames in interview talk. In H. van den Berg, M. Wetherell, & H. Houtkoop-Steenstra (Eds.), *Analyzing race talk: Multidisciplinary perspectives on the research interview* (pp. 64–84). Cambridge, UK: Cambridge University Press.

Sarkar, M., & Allen, D. (2007). Hybrid identities in Quebec hip-hop: Language, territory, and ethnicity in the mix. *Journal of Language, Identity, & Education, 6,* 117–130.

Schegloff, E. A. (2007). *Sequence organization in interaction: Vol. 1. A primer in conversation analysis.* Cambridge, UK: Cambridge University Press.

Schiffrin, D., Tannen, D., & Hamilton, H. E. (Eds.). (2001). *The handbook of discourse analysis.* Oxford, UK: Blackwell.

Silverman, D. (2001). *Interpreting qualitative data* (2nd ed.). Thousand Oaks, CA: Sage.

Spradley, J. P. (1979). *The ethnographic interview.* New York: Holt, Rinehart, & Winston.

Talmy, S. (2006). The other Other: Micronesians in a Hawai'i high school. In C. C. Park, R. Endo, & A. L. Goodwin (Eds.), *Asian and Pacific American education: Learning, socialization, and identity* (pp. 19–49). Greenwich, CT: Information Age.

Taylor, L. (2006). Wrestling with race: The implications of integrative antiracism education for immigrant ESL youth. *TESOL Quarterly, 40,* 519–544.

Taylor, S. (2001). Evaluating and applying discourse analytic research. In M. Wetherell, S. Taylor, & S. J. Yates (Eds.), *Discourse as data: A guide for analysis* (pp. 311–330). London: Sage/Open University.

ten Have, P. (2007). *Doing conversation analysis: A practical guide* (2nd ed.). London: Sage.

Trinh, T. M. (1989). *Woman, native, other.* Bloomington, IN: Indiana University Press.

Tsui, A. B. M. (2007). Complexities of identity formation: A narrative inquiry of an EFL teacher. *TESOL Quarterly, 41*, 657–680.

van den Berg, H., Wetherell, M., & Houtkoop-Steenstra, H. (2003). *Analyzing race talk: Multidisciplinary perspectives on the research interview.* Cambridge, UK: Cambridge University Press.

Varghese, M. M., & Johnston, B. (2007). Evangelical Christians and English language teaching. *TESOL Quarterly, 41*, 5–31.

Vickers, C. H. (2007). Second language socialization through team interaction among electrical and computer engineering students. *Modern Language Journal, 91*, 621–640.

Warren, C. A. B. (2002). Qualitative interviewing. In J. F. Gubrium & J. A. Holstein (Eds.), *Handbook of interview research: Context and method* (pp. 83–101). Thousand Oaks, CA: Sage.

Warren, C. A. B., & Karner, T. X. (2010). *Discovering qualitative methods: Field research, interviews, and analysis* (2nd ed.). New York: Oxford University Press.

Wooffitt, R. (2005). *Conversation analysis and discourse analysis: A comparative and critical introduction.* London: Sage.

Wooffitt, R., & Widdicombe, S. (2006). Interaction in interviews. In P. Drew, G. Raymond, & D. Weinberg (Eds.), *Talk and interaction in social research methods* (pp. 28–49). London: Sage.

AUTHOR NOTE

My thanks to Keith Richards, Charlene Polio, and the anonymous reviewers for comments on earlier drafts of this article, and to Gabi Kasper, who several years ago introduced me to many of these ideas. All errors in the article are my responsibility.

Uses of Eye-Tracking Data in Second Language Sentence Processing Research

Paola E. Dussias

When hearing or reading words and sentences in a second language (L2), we face many uncertainties about how the people and objects referred to are connected to one another. So what do we do under these conditions of uncertainty? Because relatively proficient L2 speakers have access to the grammar and lexicon of each language when comprehending words and sentences or when planning spoken utterances, and because the recent research suggests that these linguistic systems are not entirely independent, there is a critical question about how the knowledge of two languages affects basic aspects of language processing. In this article, I review how eye-tracking methodology has been used as a tool to address this question. I begin by discussing why eye movements are a useful methodology in language processing research, and I provide a description of one experimental paradigm developed to explore eye movements during reading. Second, I present recent developments in the use of eye tracking to study L2 spoken-language comprehension. I also highlight the importance of using multiple measures of online sentence processing by discussing results obtained using a moving window task and eye-tracking records while L2 speakers read syntactically ambiguous relative clauses. Next, I discuss research investigating syntactic processing when L2 speakers process mixed language. I end with suggestions for future research directions.

INTRODUCTION

Second language (L2) acquisition has been studied using a variety of techniques. Syntacticians have relied on introspective intuitions—from binary to gradient grammaticality judgments—as the main source of evidence for their theorizing (e.g., Montrul & Bruhn de Garavito, 1999; Schwartz & Sprouse, 1996; Sorace, 1993; White, 2003). Sociolinguists have employed survey data, sociolinguistic interviews, questionnaires, and other methods typically used in field work as data collection techniques to study the impact of social context on learner language and L2 acquisition (e.g., Bayley & Preston, 2008; Tarone, 2007). Phonologists perform acoustic comparisons of recorded speech samples to study the variables involved in the perception and production of nonnative sounds (e.g., Elliott, 2003; Flege & Eefting, 1987; Flege, Schirru, & MacKay, 2003; Smiljanic & Bradlow, 2005). Psycholinguists have used a variety of behavioral measures to study how L2 speakers engage linguistic knowledge online during comprehension and production (e.g., Dussias, 2003; Dussias & Sagarra, 2007; Felser & Roberts, 2007; Fernández, 2003; Frenck-Mestre, 2002, 2005; Jackson & Dussias, 2009; Juffs, 1998; Juffs & Harrington, 1996; Kroll & de Groot, 2005; Kroll & Stewart, 1994; Love, Maas, & Swinney, 2003; Marian & Spivey, 2003a, 2003b; Papadopoulou & Clahsen, 2003; Roberts, Gullberg, & Indefrey, 2008). Neuroscientists have employed measures of brain activity such as event-related potentials (ERPs) and functional magnetic resonance imaging (fMRI) to study what brain structures are involved in computing different kinds of information during the processing of a nonnative language and to investigate the cognitive and neural consequences of housing two or more languages in a single mind (e.g., Abutalebi, Cappa, & Perani, 2005; Hahne & Friederici, 2001; Stowe & Sabourin, 2005; Tokowicz & MacWhinney, 2005; van Hell & Tokowicz, 2009; Weber-Fox & Neville, 1996). What is significant from this list is that scholars have made use of the wide range of methodological tools available to them to study how L2s are acquired and processed. Among this family of techniques, the recording of eye movements is becoming increasingly popular among researchers interested in uncovering how structural processing proceeds when adult L2 speakers comprehend sentences in their L2.

What is it about eye-movement records that are especially informative and attractive? Theories of sentence processing have generally been interested in the online or incremental nature of comprehension processes. As soon as each word is encountered, readers are assumed to make structural decisions about how to integrate each word within the ongoing syntactic structure. Over three decades of eye-movement research shows that when eye movements are recorded during reading, there are systematic relations between fixation durations and the characteristics of the fixated words (Ehrlich & Rayner, 1981; Just & Carpenter, 1980; Rayner, 1978, 1983). Readers spend more time fixating on harder words and on more important words than on easier words. Longer words are also more likely to be fixated on than shorter words, and words that are likely to be skipped are short, function words.

We also know that eye movements are influenced by textual and typographical variables. Print quality, length of the line of text, and amount of space between letters all influence processing. Eye movements are likewise heavily influenced by variations in the content of the text. For example, when the text becomes more complex or contains uncommon or contextually implausible words, eye fixation duration increases, and saccade length (i.e., small jumps made by the eye to move through text) decreases (Duchowski, 2002). What is crucial for researchers is that this variation in fixations can be captured in the gaze duration of readers (i.e., the initial amount of time a reader spends in a region from first entering it until the eyes move to another word). Word frequency has the most influential effect on gaze duration: a high-frequency word like *rain* in *The heavy rain damaged the crops* decreases gaze duration (O'Regan & Lévy-Schoen, 1987; Rayner & Pollatsek, 1987) compared to a lower-frequency word like *hail*, which is matched for length, number of syllables, meaning, and sentence frame. Unpredictable words also have immediate effects on fixation duration. Readers tend to look at unpredictable words for 60–90 milliseconds longer than predictable words and they skip over predictable words more frequently than unpredictable words (Ehrlich & Rayner, 1981). Moreover, when disambiguating information in a structurally ambiguous sentence is inconsistent with the syntactic interpretation assigned by a reader, there is considerable disruption in eye movement. Thus, participants reading the syntactically ambiguous sentence *The photographer accepted the money might not be legally obtained*[1] (from Wilson & Garnsey, 2009) show long fixation durations at the disambiguating region *might not*, launch regressive saccades from the disambiguating point to the syntactically ambiguous noun phrase *the money*, or reread the sentence for a second time. The fact that inconsistencies associated with the structural analysis of a particular word (or collection of words) are noticed by readers as soon as they arise provides support for the *immediacy assumption*—the assumption that readers do not wait to interpret text until a number of words have been encountered, but rather interpret each word of a text as soon as it is encountered (Carpenter & Just, 1983). These facts suggest that recordings of eye movements can be very informative when studying the structural decisions that people make during reading.

In the remainder of this article, I review some facts about eye movements during skilled reading and provide a description of an experimental paradigm developed to arrive at these facts. Next, I present recent developments in the use of eye tracking to study L2 spoken-word processing. Then, I discuss the work that has investigated ambiguity resolution processes in L2 speakers for which eye-tracking and self-paced reading data are available to highlight differences in the results that may be attributed to the differences in the two methods. Finally, I discuss research investigating syntactic processing when L2 speakers process mixed language. I end with suggestions for future directions.

SOME FACTS ABOUT EYE MOVEMENTS DURING READING

When we read, our eyes do not move smoothly across the text, as our expe-rience as readers might suggest. Instead, we make very small, high velocity jumps called *saccades*. Four types of saccadic movements have been identified in reading: forward or rightward movements, regressions, return sweeps, and corrective movements (McConkie, 1983). Approximately 10–15% of the time, readers perform regressive saccadic movements to go back to material that has already been read. The average length of a saccade is approximately eight letter spaces. Readers normally make about three to four saccadic movements per second, each lasting between 20 and 40 milliseconds. Saccades are separated by moments during which our eyes remain still. These are called *fixations* and allow readers to extract important and useful information about the text.

McConkie, Kerr, Reddix, and Zola (1988; see also Rayner, 1998; Reichle, Pollatsek, Fisher, & Rayner, 1998) reported a landing position effect for fixations such that readers tend to fixate about halfway between the beginning and the middle of a word. An average fixation lasts approximately 200–250 milliseconds, although there is considerable within- and between-reader variability.

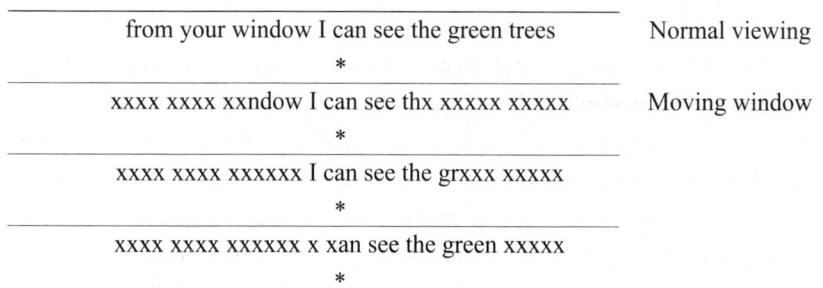

Fig. 1. Example of the moving window paradigm. The first line shows a normal line of text; the fixation point is marked with an asterisk.

Thus, a fixation can range from a little under 100 milliseconds to more than 500 milliseconds. Variation is also found in saccadic length, which can range from 1 to 15 letter spaces—although such long saccades typically occur following a regression. The variability in fixation duration and saccadic length is thought to be associated to the cognitive processes related with the ease or difficulty of comprehending text (Rayner, 1998).

An important question in reading research concerns the amount of information that readers acquire at each fixation. Experiments using three types of paradigms, *the moving window, boundary*, and *foveal mask*, have been instrumental in providing some answers. Given space limitations, I will explain only the first technique. In the moving window technique developed by McConkie and Rayner (1975), a window is sized to include a number of letter spaces to the left and the right of a fixated word, so that only a portion of the text to each side of the fixation is visible to the reader. Outside that window, the text is replaced by Xs, and spaces between words are preserved. When the reader advances the eyes, the window advances, too (see Figure 1). The idea behind this technique is that when the window is as large as the region from which the reader can obtain information, there should be no difference between reading in this condition and reading during normal viewing (i.e., when there is no window).

Using this technique, a large number of experiments have confirmed that the *perceptual span*, or the region from which readers are able to acquire useful information, is quite small. For readers of left-to-right languages like Dutch, French or English, the span is asymmetric: it extends from not more than three or four letter spaces to the left of the fixation to approximately 14–15 letter spaces to the right of the fixation. For readers of languages printed from right-to-left (such as Hebrew), the span is also asymmetric but in the opposite direction; it is larger to the left of the fixation than to the right of it (Pollatsek, Bolozky, Well, & Rayner, 1981). Pollatsek et al. (1981) have also found that orthography modulates the size of the span. The span of English readers is larger than that of Hebrew readers, presumably because English is less "densely packed" than Hebrew—that is, it takes more characters to write the same sentence in English than in Hebrew (Rayner, 1994). Studies with Japanese readers (e.g., Osaka, 1987, 1990) indicate that their span is even smaller.

To the right of a fixation, different types of information are acquired. Information needed for identifying a word is obtained within the region providing the highest degree of visual resolution, called the foveal region, and at the beginning of the parafoveal region—the area immediately surrounding the foveal region. Word length information, which guides eye movements to the next location, is acquired at about 15 letter spaces to the right of the fixation.

Experiments have also reported that word identification span (the area from which words can be identified on a given fixation) is smaller than perceptual span—it generally does not exceed seven or eight letter spaces to the right of the fixation (Rayner, 1998; Rayner, Well, Pollatsek, & Bertera, 1982; McConkie & Rayner, 1975). However, this value is influenced by word length and the ease or difficulty that readers experience in processing the word. When two or three short words occur in succession, readers are typically able to identify all of them, but if the fixated word is difficult to process, readers obtain less information from the upcoming word (Henderson & Ferreira, 1990).

What dependent variables are available to the investigator when collecting eye-movement records? For any critical region or regions of interest, a number of measurements can be distinguished. The earliest measure is *first fixation*, defined as the first time the eyes land on a region (whether a single word or a string of words). This measure appears to be sensitive to lexical information such as word frequency. The next measure is *first pass* time, which refers to the sum of all fixations in a region, from first entering it until the eyes first exit to the left or right of the region. On regions with only one word, first pass time equals *gaze duration* (e.g., Rayner & Duffy, 1986). First pass time has been found to be most informative in revealing detections of syntactic anomalies. *Regression path time* (the sum of all temporally contiguous fixations from the time the reader first enters the region of interest until advancing to the right beyond that region) has also been interpreted as a sensitive measure of immediate anomaly detection, given that readers often respond to processing difficulties by regressing to earlier portions of the sentence (e.g., Liversedge, Paterson, & Pickering, 1998; Wilson & Garnsey, 2009). Another commonly used measure is *second pass time*, which refers to the time spent reading a region after leaving the region (in other words, excluding first pass time). Finally, *total time* is the sum of all fixations in a region (effectively, the sum of first pass time and second pass time). In addition to the measurement of time, another useful dependent measure is the *probability of a regression*, defined as the percentage of regressive eye movements (leftward movements in a language like English) out of a region. This index is usually restricted to first pass regressions.

The major advantage of the eye-movement recording technique is that it allows researchers to obtain evidence about what is happening during the comprehension of a sentence moment by moment, as processing unfolds, without significantly altering the normal characteristics of either the task or the presentation of the stimuli. Eye movements are a normal characteristic of reading, and while eye-movement records are collected, participants are free to move their eyes along the printed line of text. Recent advancements in eye-movement technology also make available eye-tracking equipment that is extremely versatile, and replaces traditional, fixed eye-tracking systems with more flexible head-mounted systems, or remote systems that do not require the use of a headband or head (i.e., chin or forehead) support. In addition, to obtain the dependent measure, participants are not required to perform a secondary task (such as a button or pedal press) that might disrupt the normal comprehension process. Furthermore, thanks to several decades of eye-movement research during reading, we have a very good understanding of the amount of visual information processed while our eyes fixate on text.

EYE-TRACKING APPLICATIONS IN SECOND LANGUAGE RESEARCH

Eye-movement records have been employed in L2 research primarily to ask how proficient L2 speakers manage the presence of two languages in a single mind. If it were the case that L2 speakers could be characterized as two monolinguals in one head, then this question would not be very interesting. However, the available evidence from the word-recognition and sentence-processing literature suggests that when two linguistic systems are housed in a single brain, they interact closely with one another, and these interactions influence the way in which L2 speakers read and understand spoken words in each of their language (e.g., Dussias & Sagarra, 2007). In this section, I review two major areas of research activity that illustrate how eye-tracking methodology has been used in L2 processing research. The first examines the way in which L2 speakers recognize words when they are spoken in each language. The second concerns the comprehension of sentences and asks whether the specific syntactic subprocesses engaged during L2 language comprehension are different when monolingual and L2 speakers process input in the target language. Although the review will necessarily be brief, its scope is to illustrate the benefits of using eye-tracking techniques in L2 acquisition research.

Monitoring Eye Movements to Investigate Processing at the Word Level

Building on work by Cooper (1974), researchers studying language processing have employed an eye-tracking method known as the *visual world paradigm* to test the seriality of lexical selection mechanisms (Allopenna, Magnuson, & Tanenhaus, 1998; Altmann & Kamide, 1999; Tanenhaus & Spivey-Knowlton, 1996; Tanenhaus, Spivey-Knowlton, Eberhard, & Sedivy, 1995; Trueswell, Sekerina, Hill, & Logrip, 1999). In the version of the paradigm used in Allopenna et al. (1998), auditory material is concurrently presented with a related visual scene containing pictured objects that are displayed on a computer screen. The auditory material plays spoken instructions related to the objects (e.g., *click on the bell*), which participants are asked to follow. During the experiment, participants' eye movements to the objects are monitored as the name of the target object (i.e., the object mentioned in the instruction) unfolds over time. On some crucial trials, a distractor object that is phonologically similar to the name of the target is included in the visual scene. For instance, the target object *bell* in Figure 2 may be presented together with the picture of a competitor object such as *bed*, which overlaps at the onset. The general finding from these

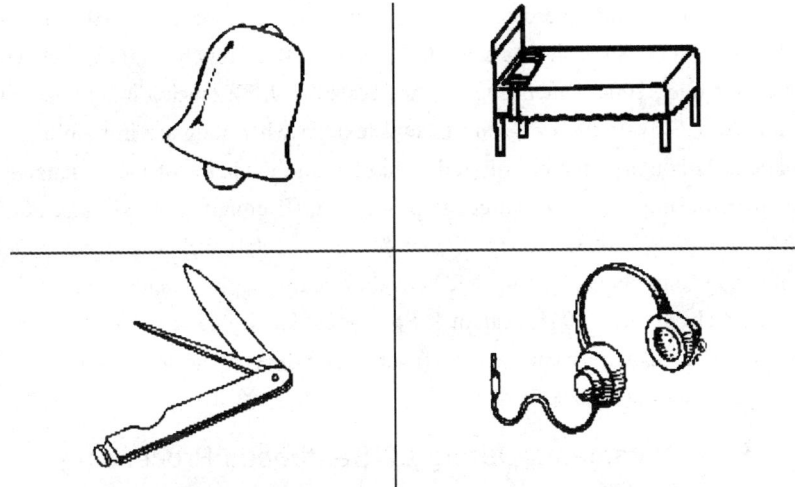

Fig. 2. Example of a display in the visual world eye-tracking paradigm.

studies is that participants are equally likely to fixate on the target word and the competitor word early during the processing of the auditory input stimulus (e.g., in Figure 2, before participants hear the phoneme that allows selection of *bell* over *bed*). This indicates that eye movements to the visual scene are closely time-locked with the auditory input.

In recent years, the visual world paradigm has been extended to the L2 domain to investigate whether proficient L2 speakers activate words from their two languages in parallel when they hear words in one language alone (e.g., Ju & Luce, 2004; Marian & Spivey, 2003a; Spivey & Marian, 1999). The critical manipulation in these studies is the presence of objects whose spoken name in one language is phonologically similar to the name of an unrelated object in the other language. To illustrate, in Spivey and Marian (1999), first language (L1) Russian speakers proficient in English heard the instruction "Put the marker below the cross" in the presence of a visual display that contained four objects: a marker, a stamp (whose translation in Russian, *marka*, shares initial phonetic features with the English *marker*), and two other objects whose English and Russian names had no phonetic similarity to the target word. Findings showed that when Russian-English speakers heard the word *marker* in English, they were likely to also look at the Russian between-language competitor *marka*. This result, replicated with L2 speakers of other language backgrounds (e.g., Canseco-Gonzalez, Brick, Fischer, & Wagner, 2005, Spanish-English; Ju & Luce, 2004, French-English speakers; Weber & Cutler, 2004, Dutch-English), suggests that L2 listeners do not appear to be able to deactivate the irrelevant mental lexicon when they are in a unilingual situation. Although a number of studies have found evidence of native language activation during nonnative language processing (Blumenfeld & Marian, 2005; Marian & Spivey, 2003a, 2003b; Weber & Cutler, 2004; Weber & Paris, 2004), results indicating nonnative language activation during native language processing are mixed (Ju & Luce, 2004; Marian & Spivey, 2003b; Weber & Cutler, 2004) and seem to be modulated by language proficiency and the cognate status of the words (Blumenfeld & Marian, 2007).

Eye Movements During L2 Sentences Processing

What are the semantic, morphological, and syntactic variables that constrain sentence comprehension in a L2? When L2 speakers read in their L2, they face many uncertainties about how the people or objects referred to in the text are connected to one another. This is so because as they move their eyes along a line of printed text, the information needed to establish correct dependencies among each of the words being encountered may not be immediately available. Because learners who are relatively proficient in two or more languages have access to the grammar and lexicon of each language when they comprehend written sentences, one critical question concerns whether the specific semantic and syntactic subprocesses engaged during L2 language comprehension are different when monolingual speakers and L2 learners process input in the target language.

  Recent online behavioral investigations of L2 structural processing have employed the recording of eye movements in large part because of its high temporal resolution and the ability to divide reading time into distinct components that may provide detailed information about the cognitive processes engaged during online L2 sentence comprehension (e.g., Dallas, Cowles, & Kaan, 2009; Dussias, 2003; Dussias & Sagarra, 2007; Felser, Cunnings, Batterham, & Clahsen, 2009; Felser, Sato, & Bertenshaw, 2009; Frenck-Mestre, 2002; Keating, 2009; Roberts et al., 2008; Witzel, Witzel, & Nicol, 2009). It is common in native sentence processing research to seek for converging evidence using the eye-movement technique and other laboratory methods (e.g., moving window paradigm or phrase-by-phrase self-paced reading) because such convergence enhances the confidence in the phenomenon being observed and makes for a coherent set of results (Carreiras & Clifton, 2004). However, there is only one syntactic structure in the L2 sentence processing literature that has been investigated using different online behavioral techniques. The resolution of relative clause ambiguities has received a disproportionate amount of attention relative to other syntactic constructions, because the existence of cross-linguistic differences in relative clause attachment provides a fertile ground to test whether sentence parsing in the L2 is influenced by the reader's native language. In the next section the focus is on the research that has examined resolution of syntactically ambiguous relative clauses because it provides the clearest illustration that we can learn more about the set of variables that constrain L2 sentence processing by studying experiments in which the results diverge.

Ambiguity Resolution in L2 Reading

One of the recurring questions in the L2 processing literature concerns whether the same structure-based principles that have been identified during monolingual syntactic processing are also found in nonnative language processing. Structure-based principles have been postulated to explain the preference by the parser (i.e., the mechanism responsible for constructing a syntactic tree for a given string of words) to initially compute a certain syntactic analysis over other analyses. A classic example of this is given in (a):

(a) Molly said that she will go to New Jersey yesterday.

In this case, the ambiguous constituent (yesterday) can be linked either to the higher clause or to the lower clause. If linked to the higher clause, the sentence means roughly, "It was yesterday that Molly said that she would go to New Jersey." Linking it to the lower clause will result in the implausible interpretation that "Molly will go to New Jersey yesterday." For the vast majority of readers, the tendency is to link the ambiguous constituent to the lower clause. The realization that the outcome yields an incorrect interpretation forces reanalysis of the ambiguous site.

Two structure-based principles that are assumed to be operative during monolingual sentences processing are *recency*, which refers to a tendency by the parser to reduce the distance between a potential host site and a modifier within the sentence, and *predicate proximity*, the preference to attach a modifier as close as possible to the head of a predicate phrase (Gibson, Pearlmutter, Canseco-Gonzalez, & Hickock, 1996). The principles have been proposed to explain cross-linguistic differences in attachment preferences involving potential attachment sites for a modifier. Specifically, preferences reflecting the application of recency have been found in languages like English, Brazilian Portuguese, and Arabic, but the application of predicate proximity has been reported in other languages like Spanish, Dutch, German, and French (e.g., Abdelghany & Fodor, 1999; Brysbaert & Mitchell, 1996; Carreiras & Clifton, 1999; Zagar, Pynte & Rativeau, 1997). To illustrate, consider the temporarily ambiguous sentence *The man called the daughter of the psychologist who lives in California*, in which the relative clause *who lives in California* can be interpreted as referring to one of the two potential attachment sites in the complex noun phrase the *daughter of the psychologist* (hence the temporary ambiguity). Empirical evidence suggests that in English recency dominates over predicate proximity, so the preferred resolution of the ambiguity is to "attach" the relative clause to the noun closest to it (*NP2* attachment or *low attachment*). This results in an interpretation in which *the psychologist lives in California*. Contrary to this, in Spanish, predicate proximity is strong enough to dominate over recency. In this case, the ambiguity is resolved in favor of *NP1* attachment or *high attachment*, resulting in an interpretation in which *the daughter lives in California*.

Whether L2 speakers use structure-driven or structure-based parsing principles during L2 sentence parsing in a matter of debate. Clahsen and Felser (2006) have recently argued that the structure-building processes during online L2 sentence comprehension are fundamentally different from the representations built by native speakers of the target language. According to their *shallow structure hypothesis*, the syntactic representations that L2 learners construct while processing input in their L2 are "shallower" and less detailed than those computed by adult L1 speakers. In their view, whereas L1 speakers prioritize on structure-driven strategies and syntactic information during sentence processing, L2 speakers privilege lexical-semantic and pragmatic information.

One of the pieces of evidence that Clahsen and Felser (2006) present in favor of shallow processing by L2 speakers is their finding that proficient L2 speakers do not show a particular preference for high or low attachment when processing constructions in their L2 that contain temporarily ambiguous relative clauses. They present data from several self-paced reading studies that examine the behavior of L1 and L2 speakers while processing syntactically ambiguous relative clauses (*The dean liked the secretary of the professor who was reading a letter.*). To investigate the processing of these constructions in L2 learners, Papadopoulou and Clahsen (2003) asked native readers of high-attaching languages to read ambiguous constructions in their L2 Greek, a language where high attachment is also the preferred strategy. The online behavioral method used for data collection was a noncumulative self-paced reading task. In this task, a sentence was divided into segments, and participants pressed a button to read each segment. Participants began the trial by pressing a key that displayed the first segment. Once they finished reading it, the next key press removed the first segment from the computer screen and displayed the second segment. Participants continued until they reached the end of the text. In this task, the dependent measure was the time participants spent reading each segment.

Using this technique, Papadopoulou and Clahsen (2003) found that proficient L2 speakers showed no preference for high or low attachment when processing a L2 that, like their L1, also favored high attachment (similar results are reported in Felser, Roberts, Gross & Marinis, 2003). This finding, coupled with the fact that clear attachment preferences were observed when lexical cues guided attachment decisions, was interpreted as evidence that L2 speakers do not use structure-based information but rather are mainly guided by lexical cues.

There is some indication coming from the L2 eye-tracking literature, however, that suggests that the choices that L2 speakers make while parsing temporarily ambiguous structures could be explained via the application of structure-based principles of parsing. For example, Dussias and Sagarra (2007) collected eye-movement records with Spanish-English bilinguals and monolingual Spanish speakers to investigate the effect that intense contact with English had on attachment preferences in Spanish, their L1. L1 Spanish speakers proficient in English, who had lived in an L2 environment for an extended period of time, and functionally monolingual Spanish speakers participated in the study. The structure under investigation contained a complex noun phrase followed by a relative clause (e.g., *El policía arrestó a la hermana del criado que estaba enferma desde hacía tiempo* / The police arrested the sister of the (male) servant who had been ill (fem) for a while). Analyses of total time fixations at disambiguating region (i.e., the adjective within the relative clause) revealed that the Spanish monolingual participants showed the conventional bias for high attachment reported in the literature. Conversely, the Spanish-English speakers showed a consistent preference for low attachment when reading sentences in their L1, suggesting that the parsing routines used to process the L2 had an impact on the processing of the L1 as well. This finding was taken to indicate that parsing routines in bilinguals are permeable, but importantly for the present purposes, the Spanish-English speakers showed a robust preference that emerged in eye-tracking records of the participants.

In a more recent study, Witzel et al. (2009) examined the eye movements of highly proficient Chinese learners of English on sentences involving temporarily ambiguous structures that have been used to reveal biases based on structure-based parsing principles. Three kinds of syntactically ambiguous structures were investigated (syntactically ambiguous material is underlined): (a) Relative clause attachment ambiguity (The son of the actress who shot himself on the set was under investigation); (b) adverb attachment ambiguity (Jack will meet the friend he phoned yesterday, but he doesn't want to) and (c) noun phrase versus sentence coordination ambiguity (The nurse examined the mother and the child played quietly in the corner). Regression path duration—a measure usually taken to reflect initial processing—and total times showed that like the monolingual English controls, the Chinese-English speakers show clear attachment biases on all three structures, suggesting, contra Clahsen and Felser (2006), that the L1 and L2 parsers behave similarly with respect to establishing abstract structural relations between phrases.

In addition, another eye-tracking study by Frenck-Mestre and Pynte (1997) shows that under some circumstances, the L2 parser initially favors structure-based parsing principles such as low attachment. These authors used eye-movement records to investigate the way in which advanced English-speaking learners of French and French native speakers resolved attachment ambiguities involving prepositional phrases. The pattern of first pass reading times as well as regression time revealed that the L2 speakers momentarily experienced greater difficulty than native speakers with verb phrase attachment (i.e., high attachment) of the prepositional phrase in sentences such as *He rejected the manuscript on purpose because he hated its author.* No such difficulty was observed when the L2 speakers read structures in which the correct analysis required attachment of the prepositional phrase to the noun phrase immediately preceding it (i.e., low attachment or late closure), as would be the case in *He rejected the manuscript on horses because he hated its author*. In other words, L2 speakers temporarily adopted a strategy of attaching the ambiguous prepositional phrases low, to the most recently processed constituent. This analysis resulted in an incorrect interpretation in the first example but not in the second example. To account for this finding, Frenck-Mestre and Pynte proposed that nonnative readers may have a general preference for a low attachment (late closure) strategy, which, in this case, amounts to attaching the prepositional phrase to the noun phrase immediately preceding it.

The collection of studies already presented suggests that differences in the methods used for data collection may be responsible for some of the divergent findings reported in the literature. Reading studies that have used self-paced reading or phrase-by-phrase reading tasks as the method of data collection have generally concluded that during L2 sentence processing, L2 speakers are not guided by phrase-structure-based parsing principles of the kind that have been attested in L1 processing. Studies using methods of data collection that are more sensitive to the time course of processing, such as eye tracking, suggest that the pattern of results produced when nonnatives read syntactically ambiguous structures in their L2 show evidence of the application of phrase-structure-based parsing principles.

SPOKEN-LANGUAGE COMPREHENSION IN AN L2

Although reading processes have provided important insights into the mechanisms involved during L2 sentence processing, one question that has not been adequately addressed is whether the processing characteristics uncovered to date are specific to L2 reading or can be generalized to L2 spoken-language comprehension. One experimental methodology that has had great success in research on auditory language processing with monolingual participants is the *visual world paradigm*. In addition to the competitor effect discussed earlier, previous research has shown that participants are able to anticipate forthcoming linguistic reference to objects in the visual scene before these objects are actually mentioned in the auditory input (e.g., Altmann & Kamide, 1999). For example, Lew-Williams and Fernald (2007) showed that when Spanish-speaking children are shown different-gender objects, they orient their eyes to the object whose gender is congruent with the article they hear, even before they hear the name of the object. In the experiment, children were presented with visual scenes showing same-gender objects (e.g., *galleta[fem]*/cookie and *pelota[fem]*/ball) as well as different-gender objects (*galleta[fem]* and *zapato[masc]*/shoe), while they listened to instructions about the objects (*encuentra la pelota* / find the ball), which they were asked to follow. The main finding was that shortly after the article accompanying the noun was available in the auditory input, children had already launched reliably more and longer looks to the appropriate noun in the picture (i.e., the noun that matched the gender of the article) than to the inappropriate noun. This suggests that the most likely forthcoming referent was anticipated on the basis of the linguistic and visual information available.

Only one study to date has used the visual world paradigm to ask whether grammatical information known to affect native language processing also influences processing when speakers are hearing mixed-language input. Valdés Kroff, Guzzardo, Dussias, Gerfen, and Gullifer (2008) investigated whether gender-marked articles are an informative cue when L1 Spanish speakers of English process spoken code-switched utterances. The question is theoretically relevant because corpus data containing spoken and written mixed-language switches suggest that the masculine article *el* can precede an English noun whose Spanish translation equivalent is masculine (*el candy*) or feminine (*el candle*), possibly due to the default status of masculine grammatical gender in Spanish. However, in mixed-language speech *la* only appears with feminine translation equivalents (*la candle* but not *la candy*). Given this asymmetry, it is possible that the gender-marking of articles facilitates to a lesser extent the processing of code-switched speech.

Pairs of objects were displayed on a computer screen as the eye movements of 24 Spanish-English speakers were recorded. Participants listened to sentences naming one of the objects and were instructed to click on the named object. Pictures were presented in three blocks: a block of English-only sentences, in which participants heard sentences such as *There is a boy looking at the candle on the window sill*, while the picture of two objects that were phonological competitors in English (e.g., candy and candle) was displayed on a computer screen, and a Spanish block in which participants heard sentences like *La chica está comprando la vela para su amiga* ("the girl is buying the candle for her friend") in two conditions: a condition in which the two objects matched in grammatical gender (e.g., *vela* and *galleta*) and a condition in which they did not match (*vela-caramelo*). Materials in the code-switching block were phonological competitors in English (e.g., candy/ candle) for which the Spanish translation equivalents contrasted in grammatical gender (e.g., *el caramelo* [the candy] vs. *la vela* [the candle]). Finally, target English words were spoken with a Spanish article that matched the gender of the Spanish translation equivalents (e.g., *El high school student que está mirando la candle lleva new sunglasses* / The high school student who is looking at the[*fem*] candle is wearing new sunglasses) or did not match (*El high school student que está mirando el candle lleva new sunglasses* / The high school student who is looking at the[*masc*] candle is wearing new sunglasses).

Data were analyzed by comparing the proportion of looks to the objects in each condition. In the Spanish-only trials, the L2 speakers oriented their eye movements to the referent more rapidly on different-gender trials (i.e., when the article was potentially informative) than on same-gender trials, replicating the results reported in Lew-Williams and Fernald (2007). In the English-only trials, when the scene included two objects that were phonological competitors, participants temporarily considered both objects until the disambiguating information in the word became available. This finding replicates the competitor effect reported in previous literature with native English speakers (e.g., Allopenna et al., 1998). However, the bilinguals exhibited differential processing of masculine and feminine articles in the code-switching block. For example, in the mixed-language block, when the article was masculine, participants waited until the disambiguating information was spoken before committing to one of the two pictures. Taken together, the findings suggest that L2 speakers instantiate different linguistic behavior when processing mixed language that is not evident from either unilingual mode.

FUTURE DIRECTIONS

The field of L2 sentence comprehension has reached an exciting point. The number of findings involving different types of syntactic structures is rapidly growing, and explanations are beginning to emerge that attempt to characterize the type of processing that L2 learners engage while constructing a syntactic parse. The framing question underlying much of the L2 processing research is to what extent L2 processing is qualitatively similar or different from L1 processing. Current research shows that a number of linguistic variables affect reading processing among L2 learners and that learners' characteristics, such as proficiency and type of linguistic experience, often interact with linguistic aspects of the input in producing a parsing outcome. As the nature of the research questions have become more refined, the need for more sophisticated online behavioral measures has become central. The use of these methods has raised the prospect of addressing increasingly subtle issues.

Further research needs to explore the use of different online measures that are closely time-locked to the input so that short-lived input-driven processes are not missed (see also White, Bruhn-Garavito, Kawasaki, Pater, & Prévost, 1997, for a related argument). The visual world paradigm brings with it a new set of exciting possibilities to study real-time spoken-language comprehension. In addition, because participants interact with the world, other lesser studied types of information, such as referential and pragmatic information, can be brought into the study of L2 language comprehension. Increasingly, researchers will also need to invest some effort in replicating the findings produced by one particular method with other techniques. Relying on multiple response measures for our theorizing has the advantage that the weaknesses of one method can be compensated by the strength of another method. Some obvious pairings include the use of ERPs and eye tracking with the same materials (see Rayner & Clifton, 2009, for a recent discussion of the two methodologies to investigate language processing during reading and listening) and the monitoring of eye movements during reading and spoken-language processing to ensure that the findings from reading studies are generalizable to spoken-language processing as well. Finally, one very important direction in the use of eye-tracking methodology is to investigate language processing at various stages of L2 development to understand the developmental trajectory of reading processes as learners gradually become more proficiency in the L2. Taken together, the advantage of the approaches is that they will produce a stable body of results that will widen the range of theoretical issues in our field.

NOTE

1 The syntactic ambiguity in this sentence arises because the noun phrase *the money* can function either as the direct object of *accept* or as the subject of the

ensuing clause. It is only after participants read the disambiguating region *might not* that the correct interpretation of the noun phrase is confirmed.

REFERENCES

Abdelghany, H., & Fodor, J. D. (1999, September). *Low attachment of relative clauses in Arabic*. Poster presented at the annual meeting of Architecture and Mechanisms for Language Processing (AMLaP), Edinburgh, UK.

Abutalebi, J., Cappa, S. F., & Perani, D. (2005). What can functional neuroimaging tell us about the bilingual brain? In J. Kroll & A. M. B. de Groot (Eds.), *Handbook of bilingualism: Psycholinguistic perspectives* (pp. 497–515). Oxford, UK: Oxford University Press.

Allopenna, P. D., Magnuson, J. S., & Tanenhaus, M. K. (1998). Tracking the time course of spoken word recognition using eye movements: Evidence for continuous mapping models. *Journal of Memory and Language, 38*, 419–439.

Altmann, G. T. M., & Kamide, Y. (1999). Incremental interpretation at verbs: Restricting the domain of subsequent reference. *Cognition, 73*, 247–264.

Bayley, R., & Preston, D. R. (2008). Variation and second language grammars. *Studies in Hispanic and Lusophone Linguistics, 1*, 385–397.

Blumenfeld, H. K., & Marian, V. (2005). Covert bilingual language activation through cognate word processing: An eye-tracking study. *Proceedings of the 27th Annual Meeting of the Cognitive Science Society* (pp. 286–291). Mahwah, NJ: Erlbaum.

Blumenfeld, H. K., & Marian, V. (2007). Constraints on parallel activation in bilingual spoken language processing: Examining proficiency and lexical status using eye-tracking. *Language and Cognitive Processes, 22*, 233–260.

Brysbaert, M., & Mitchell, D. C. (1996). Modifier attachment in sentence processing: Evidence from Dutch. *Quarterly Journal of Experimental Psychology, 49A*, 664–695.

Canseco-Gonzalez, E., Brick, C., Fischer, K., & Wagner, K. (2005). "Carpet or Carcel" effects of speaker type, fluency, and language mode on bilingual lexical access. *Proceedings of the International Symposium on Bilingualism, Spain, 5*, 156–157.

Carpenter, P. A., & Just, M. A. (1983). What your eyes do while your mind is reading. In K. Rayner (Ed.), *Eye movements in reading* (pp. 275–307). New York: Academic Press.

Carreiras, M., & Clifton, C. (1999). Another word on parsing relative clauses: Eyetracking evidence from Spanish and English. *Memory and Cognition, 27*, 826–833.

Carreiras, M., & Clifton, C. (2004). On the on-line study of language comprehension. In C. Carreiras & C. Clifton, (Eds.), *The on-line study of sentence comprehension: Eyetracking, ERPs, and beyond* (pp. 1–14). New York: Psychology Press.

Clahsen, H., & Felser, C. (2006). Grammatical processing in language learners. *Applied*

Psycholinguistics, 27, 3–42.

Cooper, R. M. (1974). The control of eye fixation by the meaning of spoken language. A new methodology for the real-time investigation of speech perception, memory, and language processing. *Cognitive Psychology, 6*, 84–107.

Dallas, A., Cowles, H., W., & Kaan, E. (2009, May). *The use of verbal properties during the processing of complex sentences.* Paper presented at the Workshop on Second Language Processing and Parsing: State of the Science, Lubbock, TX.

Duchowski, A. T. (2002). A breadth-first survey of eye tracking applications. *Behavior Methods, Research, Instruments, and Computers, 1*, 1–15.

Dussias, P. E. (2003). Syntactic ambiguity resolution in L2 learners: Some effects of bilinguality on L1 and L2 processing strategies. S*tudies in Second Language Acquisition, 25*, 529–557.

Dussias, P. E., & Sagarra, N. (2007). The effect of exposure on syntactic parsing in Spanish-English bilinguals. *Bilingualism: Language and Cognition, 10*, 101–116.

Ehrlich, S. F., & Rayner, K. (1981). Contextual effects on work perception and eye movements during reading. *Reading Research Quarterly, 16*, 227–235.

Elliott, A. R. (2003). Staking out the territory at the turn of the century: Integrating phonological theories, research and the effect of formal instruction on pronunciation in the acquisition of Spanish as a second language. In B. Lafford & R. Salaberry (Eds.), *Spanish second language acquisition: State of the science*, pp. 19–46. Washington, DC: Georgetown University Press.

Felser, C., Cunnings, I., Batterham, C., & Clahsen, H. (2009, May). *Constraints on L2 learners' processing of wh-dependencies: Evidence from eye movements.* Paper presented at the Workshop on Second Language Processing and Parsing: State of the Science, Lubbock, TX.

Felser, C., & Roberts, L. (2007). Processing wh-dependencies in a second language: A cross-modal priming study. *Second Language Research, 23*, 9–36.

Felser, C., Roberts, L., Gross, R., & Marinis, T. (2003). The processing of ambiguous sentences by first and second language learners of English. *Applied Psycholinguistics, 24*, 453–489.

Felser, C., Sato, M., & Bertenshaw, N. (2009). The on-line application of Binding Principle A in English as a second language. *Bilingualism: Language and Cognition, 12*, 485–502.

Fernández, E. M. (2003). *Bilingual sentence processing: Relative clause attachment in English and Spanish.* Amsterdam: John Benjamins.

Flege, J. E., & Eefting, W. (1987). The production and perception of English stops by Spanish speakers of English. *Journal of Phonetics, 15*, 67–83.

Flege, J. E., Schirru, C., & MacKay, I. R. A. (2003). Interaction between the native and second language phonetic subsystems. *Speech Communication, 40*, 467–491.

Frenck-Mestre, C. (2002). An on-line look at sentence processing in the second language. In R.

R. Heredia & J. Altarriba (Eds.), *Bilingual sentence processing* (pp. 218–236). Amsterdam: Elsevier.

Frenck-Mestre, C. (2005). Ambiguities and anomalies: What can eye movements and event-related potentials reveal about second language sentence processing? In J. Kroll & A. M. B. de Groot (Eds.), *Handbook of bilingualism: Psycholinguistic perspectives* (pp. 268–281). Oxford, UK: Oxford University Press.

Frenck-Mestre, C., & Pynte, J. (1997). Syntactic ambiguity resolution while reading in second and native languages. *Quarterly Journal of Experimental Psychology, 50*, 119–148.

Gibson, E., Pearlmutter, N., Canseco-Gonzalez, E., & Hickock, G. (1996). Recency preferences in the human sentence processing mechanism. *Cognition, 59*, 23–59.

Hahne, A., & Friederici, A. D. (2001). Processing a second language: Late learners' comprehension mechanisms as revealed by event-related brain potentials. *Bilingualism: Language and Cognition, 4*, 123–142.

Henderson, J. M., & Ferreira, F. (1990). Effects of foveal processing difficulty on the perceptual span in reading: Implications for attention and eye movement control. *Journal of Experimental Psychology: Learning, Memory, and Cognition, 16*, 417–429.

Jackson, C., & Dussias, P. E. (2009). Cross-linguistic differences and their impact on L2 sentence processing. *Bilingualism: Language and Cognition, 12*, 65–82.

Ju, M., & Luce, P. A. (2004). Falling on sensitive ears. *Psychological Science, 15*, 314–318.

Juffs, A. (1998). Main verb vs. reduced relative clause ambiguity resolution in L2 sentence processing. *Language Learning, 48*, 107–147.

Juffs, A., & Harrington, M. (1996). Garden path sentences and error data in second language sentence processing research. *Language Learning, 46*, 286–324.

Just, M., & Carpenter, P. (1980). A theory of reading: From eye fixations to comprehension. *Psychological Review, 87*, 329–354.

Keating, G. (2009). Sensitivity to violations of gender agreement in native and nonnative Spanish: An eye-movement investigation. *Language Learning, 59*, 503–535.

Kroll J. F., & de Groot A. M. B. (Eds.). (2005). *Handbook of bilingualism: Psycholinguistic perspectives*. Oxford, UK: Oxford University Press.

Kroll, J. F., & Stewart, E. (1994). Category interference in translation and picture naming: Evidence for asymmetric connections between bilingual memory representations. *Journal of Memory and Language, 33*, 149–174.

Lew-Williams, C., & Fernald, A. (2007). Young children learning Spanish make rapid use of grammatical gender in spoken word recognition. *Psychological Science. 18*, 193–198.

Liversedge, S. P., Paterson, K. B., & Pickering, M. J. (1998). Eye movements and measures of reading time. In G. Underwood (Ed.), *Eye guidance in reading and scene perception* (pp. 55–75). New York: Elsevier.

Love, T., Maas, E., & Swinney, D. (2003). The influence of language exposure on lexical and syntactic language processing. *Experimental Psychology*, *50*, 204–216.

Marian, V., & Spivey, M. (2003a). Bilingual and monolingual processing of competing lexical items. *Applied Psycholinguistics*, *24*, 173–193.

Marian, V., & Spivey, M. (2003b). Competing activation in bilingual language processing: Within and between-language competition. *Bilingualism: Language and Cognition*, *6*, 97–115.

McConkie, G. W. (1983). Eye movements and perception during reading. In K. Rayner (Ed.), *Eye movement in reading: Perceptual and language processes*, (pp. 65–96). New York: Academic Press.

McConkie, G. W., Kerr, P. W., Reddix, M. D., & Zola, D. (1988). Eye movement control during reading: The location of initial fixations on words. *Vision Research*, *28*, 1107–1118.

McConkie, G. W., & Rayner, K. (1975). The span of the effective stimulus during a fixation in reading. *Perception & Psychophysics*, *17*, 578–586.

Montrul, S., & Bruhn de Garavito, J. (1999). Generative approaches to the second language acquisition of Spanish [Special issue]. *Second Language Research*, *15*, 111–114.

O'Regan, J. K., & Lévy-Schoen, A. (1987). Eye-movement strategy and tactics in word recognition and reading. In M. Coltheart (Ed.), *Attention and performance: XII. The psychology of reading* (pp. 363–383). London: Erlbaum.

Osaka, N. (1987). Effect of peripheral visual field size upon eye movements during Japanese text processing. In J. K. O'Regan & A. Levy-Schoen (Eds.), *Eye movements: From physiology to cognition* (pp. 421–429). Amsterdam: North-Holland.

Osaka, N. (1990). Spread of visual attention during fixation while reading Japanese text. In R. Groner, G. d'Ydewalle, & R. Parham (Eds.), *From eye to mind: Information acquisition in perception, search and reading* (pp. 167–178). Amsterdam: North-Holland.

Papadopoulou, D., & Clahsen, H. (2003). Parsing strategies in L1 and L2 sentence processing: A study of relative clause attachment in Greek. *Studies in Second Language Acquisition*, *25*, 501–528.

Pollatsek, A., Bolozky, S., Well, A. D., & Rayner, K. (1981). Asymmetries in the perceptual span for Israeli readers. *Brain and Language*, *14*, 174–180.

Rayner, K. (1978). Eye movements in reading and information processing. *Psychological Bulletin*, *85*, 618–660.

Rayner, K. (1983). The perceptual span and eye movement control during reading. In K. Rayner (Ed.), *Eye movement in reading: Perceptual and language processes* (pp. 97–139). New York: Academic Press.

Rayner, K. (1994). Eye movements during skilled reading. In J. Ygge & G. Lennerstrand (Eds.), *Eye movements in reading* (pp. 205–218). Oxford, UK: Pergamon Press.

Rayner, K. (1998). Eye movements in reading and information processing: 20 years of research. *Psychological Bulletin, 124*, 372–422.

Rayner, K., & Clifton, C. (2009). Language processing in reading and speech perception is fast and incremental: Implications for event-related potential research. *Biological Psychology, 80*, 4–9.

Rayner, K., & Duffy, S. A. (1986). Lexical complexity and fixation times in reading: Effects of word frequency, verb complexity, and lexical ambiguity. *Memory and Cognition, 14*, 191–201.

Rayner, K., & Pollatsek, A. (1987). Eye movements in reading: A tutorial review. In M. Coltheart (Ed.), Attention and performance: XII. *The psychology of reading* (pp. 327–362). London: Erlbaum.

Rayner, K., Well, A. D., Pollatsek, A., & Bertera, J. H. (1982). The availability of useful information to the right of fixation in reading. *Perception & Psychophysics, 31*, 537–550.

Reichle, E. D., Pollatsek, A., Fisher, D. L., & Rayner, K. (1998). Toward a model of eye movement control in reading. *Psychological Review, 105*, 125–157.

Roberts, L., Gullberg, M., & Indefrey, P. (2008). Online pronoun resolution in L2 discourse: L1 influence and general learner effects. *Studies in Second Language Acquisition, 30*, 333–357.

Schwartz, B. D., & Sprouse, R. (1996). L2 cognitive states and the full transfer/full access model. *Second Language Research, 12*, 40–72.

Smiljanic, R., & Bradlow, A. R. (2005). Production and perception of clear speech on Croatian and English. *Journal of the Acoustical Society of America, 118*, 1677–1688.

Sorace, A. (1993). Incomplete vs. divergent representations of unaccusativity in non-native grammars of Italian. *Second Language Research, 9*, 24–47.

Spivey, M., & Marian, V. (1999). Cross talk between native and second languages: Partial activation of an irrelevant lexicon. *Psychological Science, 10*, 281–284.

Stowe, L., & Sabourin, L. (2005). Imaging the processing of a second language: Effects of maturation and proficiency on the neural processes involved. The entity from which ERIC acquires the content, including journal, organization, and conference names, or by means of online submission from the author. *International Review of Applied Linguistics in Language Teaching, 43*, 329–353.

Tanenhaus, M. K., & Spivey-Knowlton, M. J. (1996). Eye-tracking. *Language and Cognitive Processes, 11*, 583–588.

Tanenhaus, M. K., Spivey-Knowlton, M. J., Eberhard, K. M., & Sedivy, J. C. (1995). Integration of visual and linguistic information in spoken language comprehension. *Science, 268*, 1632–1634.

Tarone, E. (2007). Sociolinguistic approaches to second language acquisition research, 1997–2007. *Modern Language Journal, 91*, 837–848.

Tokowicz, N., & MacWhinney, B. (2005). Implicit and explicit measures of sensitivity to violations in second language grammar. *Studies in Second Language Acquisition, 27*, 173–204.

Trueswell, J. C., Sekerina, I., Hill, N. M., & Logrip, M. L. (1999). The kindergarten-path effect: Studying on-line sentence processing in young children. *Cognition, 73*, 89–134.

Valdés Kroff, J., Guzzardo, R., Dussias, P. E., Gerfen, C., & Gullifer, J. (2008, March). *Grammatical gender in processing Spanish-English code-switches: A visual world study.* Paper presented at the CUNY Conference on Human Sentence Processing, University of North Carolina, Chapel Hill, NC.

van Hell, J. G., & Tokowicz, N. (2009). Event-related brain potentials and second language learning: Syntactic processing in late L2 learners at different L2 proficiency levels. *Second Language Research, 25*, 465–496.

Weber, A., & Cutler, A. (2004). Lexical competition in non-native spoken-word recognition. *Journal of Memory and Language, 50*, 1–25.

Weber, A., & Paris, G. (2004). The origin of the linguistic gender effect in spoken-word recognition: Evidence from non-native listening. *Proceedings of the 26th Annual Meeting of the Cognitive Science Society, 26*, 1446–1451.

Weber-Fox, C., & Neville, H. J. (1996). Maturational constraints on functional specializations for language processing: ERP and behavioral evidence in bilingual speakers. *Journal of Cognitive Neuroscience, 8*, 231–256.

White, L. (2003). *Second language acquisition and Universal Grammar.* Cambridge, UK: Cambridge University Press.

White, L., Bruhn-Garavito, J., Kawasaki, T., Pater, J., & Prévost, P. (1997). The researcher gave the subject a test about himself: Problems of ambiguity and preference in the investigation of reflexive binding. *Language Learning, 47* , 145–172.

Wilson, M. P., & Garnsey, S. (2009). Making simple sentences hard: Verb bias effects in simple direct object sentences. *Journal of Memory and Language, 60*, 368–392.

Witzel, J., Witzel, N., & Nicol, J. (2009, May). *The reading of structurally ambiguous sentences by English language learners.* Paper presented at the Workshop on Second Language Processing and Parsing: State of the Science, Lubbock, TX.

Zagar, D., Pynte, J., & Rativeau, S. (1997). Evidence for early closure attachment on first-pass reading times in French. *Quarterly Journal of Experimental Psychology, 50A*, 421–438.

AUTHOR NOTE

The writing of this article was supported in part by National Science Foundation grant BCS-0821924 to Paola E. Dussias and Chip Gerfen. I would like to thank Charlene Polio and an anonymous reviewer for insightful comments and for their close reading of the manuscript. All errors are my own.

SECTION C: LANGUAGE SOCIALIZATION

Language Socialization into Academic Discourse Communities

Patricia A. Duff

Although much has been written about academic discourse from diverse theoretical perspectives over the past two decades, and especially about English academic discourse, research on socialization into academic discourse or literacies in one's first or subsequently learned languages or into new discourse communities has received far less attention. Academic discourse socialization is a dynamic, socially situated process that in contemporary contexts is often multimodal, multilingual, and highly intertextual as well. The process is characterized by variable amounts of modeling, feedback, and uptake; different levels of investment and agency on the part of learners; by the negotiation of power and identities; and, often, important personal transformations for at least some participants. However, the consequences and outcomes of academic discourse socialization are also quite unpredictable, both in the shorter term and longer term. In this review I provide a brief historical overview of research on language socialization into academic communities and describe, in turn, developments in research on socialization into oral, written, and online discourse and the social practices associated with each mode. I highlight issues of conformity or reproduction to local norms and practices versus resistance and contestation of these. Next, studies of socialization into academic publication and into particular textual identities are reviewed. I conclude with a short discussion of race, culture, gender, and academic discourse socialization, pointing out how social positioning by oneself and others can affect participants' engagement and performance in their various learning communities.

INTRODUCTION

Academic discourse, and especially English academic discourse, has been examined from a number of theoretical perspectives over the past two decades in applied linguistics, particularly at the postsecondary level (e.g., Hyland, 2006), socialization being one of the more recent. Basic questions this latter work addresses are the following: How do newcomers to an academic culture learn how to participate successfully in the oral and written discourse and related practices of that discourse community? How are they socialized, explicitly or implicitly, into these local discursive practices? How does interaction with their peers, instructors, tutors, and others facilitate the process of gaining expertise, confidence, and a sense of authority over those practices over time?

A perusal of the *Journal of English for Academic Purposes*, the *Journal of Second Language Writing*, *English for Specific Purposes*, and other publications reveals that research on *academic discourse* has generally been associated with two sets of topics: (a) the linguistic and discursive structure and conventions of different kinds of written texts or genres, as determined by corpus-based studies (e.g., Biber, 2006; Connor & Upton, 2004) or other types of analysis; and (b) challenges involved in first language (L1) and second language (L2) writing at the postsecondary level, both undergraduate and graduate, in composition courses, mainstream content courses, and students' thesis or dissertation writing (e.g., Johns, 2005; Starfield & Ravelli, 2006).

Important research, to be sure, has been conducted on aspects of academic discourse not centrally considered here, such as the cognitive and rhetorical processes of composing and assessing writing; the effects of feedback on the quality of writing (e.g., Hyland & Hyland, 2006); textual borrowing, citation, and plagiarism (e.g., Flowerdew & Li, 2007; Pecorari, 2008; Shi, 2004, 2010); metadiscourse (Hyland, 2004); and various other topics in L2 writing (e.g., Casanave, 2004). (For a synthesis of research on L2 writing in the North American context, see Leki, Cumming, & Silva, 2008). However, insufficient research has examined, in an ethnographic or otherwise in-depth, longitudinal, and qualitative manner, the nature and effects of scaffolding and enculturation on students' acquisition and production of target genres and of the tacit cultural knowledge represented by such genres. The 2002 issue of the *Annual Review of Applied Linguistics*, on discourse and applied linguistics, for instance, which was otherwise quite comprehensive, had no article on discourse socialization. Yet a central concern of educators, learners, and applied linguists is how best to help novices participate effectively in new academic discourse communities and their practices. The development of novices' own voices and identities as budding scholars in academic and professional disciplines, whether in speech or writing, over time, has not been examined fully enough either, especially from sociocultural and anthropological perspectives.

Academic discourse is not just an entity but a social, cognitive, and rhetorical process and an accomplishment, a form of enculturation, social practice, positioning, representation, and stance-taking. Identity work and the negotiation of institutional and disciplinary ideologies and epistemologies are core aspects of the production and interpretation of academic discourse. Academic discourse is therefore a site of internal and interpersonal struggle for many people, especially for newcomers or novices. Considerable emotional investment and power dynamics may therefore be involved. In short, it is dialogic, not monologic (Molle & Prior, 2008). Affective issues and tensions, commonplace in writing but just as pervasive in oral discourse, may be especially acute in intercultural contexts—in which local and global (or remote) language codes, cultures, and ideologies of literacy may differ; furthermore, the expectations of students producing academic language and those assessing it (instructors, journal editors, or reviewers) may be at odds (Reder & Davila, 2007).

Problems of academic discourse and the processes of being socialized into it are not new though. Bourdieu, Passeron, and de Saint Martin (1994), in a piece that first appeared in French in the mid-1960s, described some of the challenges for French university students and also suggested that the inaccessibility of academic discourse to novices is perhaps deliberate: It serves to perpetuate the distance between experts and novices to some extent, to the experts' advantage.

ACADEMIC LITERACIES, ACADEMIC (DISCOURSE) SOCIALIZATION, OR ACADEMIC ENCULTURATION?

Several literacy theorists in the United Kingdom distinguish between *academic literacies* and *academic (discourse) socialization* on the grounds, they claim, that the former takes into account issues of power relations, identity, institutional practices, and contestation in a way that the term *socialization* does not (e.g., Ivanič, 2004; Lea & Street, 1998; Lillis, 2003). In this view, academic literacies represent a higher-order, value-added perspective. However, language and literacy socialization experiences and accounts will almost inevitably involve the negotiation of power and identity, and especially when examined within a larger sociopolitical and sociocultural context. Macro-social dimensions, by definition, are constituted in the very micro-social practices that novices are being inducted or socialized into (Duff, 1995, 1996, 2002), and vice versa. As a noun phrase, *discourse socialization* places more emphasis on social processes, negotiation, and interaction than the (arguably) more static noun *literacies* suggests. One seems to be about process, and the other about what is learned and the wider contexts of learning (e.g., literacy events, multiple forms of literacy), although that is an overly simplistic distinction, especially given current conceptualizations of literacy(ies). Both, in effect, are concerned with learning processes, with macro and micro contexts for language development, forms of knowledge and practice valued, material products or tools involved in literacy, and outcomes. *Socialization*, as currently used by applied linguists and linguistic anthropologists, does not denote a mindless, passive conditioning that leads invariably, with exposure or feedback or practice, to desired homogeneous responses, competencies, behaviors, and stances on the part of novices engaged in them (Duff, 2003, 2007a). On the contrary, the socializers may also be socialized by their junior associates or peers; that is, socialization is a bi- or multidirectional, contingent process (e.g., Duff, 1995; Talmy, 2008). Those being socialized have agency and powers of resistance, innovation, and self-determination and are not likely to simply reproduce or internalize the complete repertoire of linguistic and ideological resources in their midst (Kulick & Schieffelin, 2004); even if they wanted to, it would likely not be possible, at least not right away (Garrett & Baquedano-López, 2002). Full mastery of target genres may not be their goal or expectation in any event.

Finally, in terms of terminology, other scholars, describing very similar processes, frame their work in terms of *academic* (*disciplinary*) *enculturation* (e.g., Berkenkotter & Huckin, 1995; Casanave, 2002; Casanave & Li, 2008; Prior, 1998), using *enculturation* and *socialization* as synonyms (cf. Casanave,1990). Others may use the nouns induction or *initiation* (Berkenkotter, Huckin, & Ackerman, 1991), or alternatively, the verb *inculcate*, to refer to the same process as socialization (e.g., Barnard & Torres-Guzman, 2009; Mertz, 2007). In what follows, I use *academic* (*discourse*) *socialization*, *academic literacies*, and *academic enculturation* more or less synonymously, but I prefer the first term. I focus mainly on work done in the past 5 years but must also lay the foundation for current developments in this area by citing some important earlier work.

EXAMINING SOCIALIZATION INTO ORAL AND WRITTEN DISCOURSE ACROSS EDUCATIONAL CONTEXTS

Although researchers have examined issues in postsecondary written academic discourse to a great extent, and especially at the undergraduate and doctoral levels, fewer have examined the academic discourse demands of L2 or multilingual school-aged writers (see Johns & Snow, 2006; Schleppegrell, 2004, for some current directions). Similarly, too little attention has been paid to oral academic discourse; the intermodal and intertextual relationships between oral and written discourse; multilingual, multivocal (heteroglossic) academic discourse; or the sometimes blended modes of communication found in online academic discourse, such as in course-related discussion forums. In this article, I therefore examine work that directly examines social processes in the apprenticeship of oral, written, and online or networked language for academic purposes. However, rather than review or repeat the substantial work on academic discourse itself, I examine the intersection of language socialization and academic discourse research. I begin by providing a brief description of language socialization and academic discourse.

Language Socialization

Language socialization, as an area of study, represents an orientation to language and literacy development in particular communities and settings that is informed by anthropology, sociology, (socio)linguistics, and education (Duff, 2010, in press; Duff & Hornberger, 2008). It also draws on cultural psychology and especially neo-Vygotskyan sociocultural theory (Duff, 2007a). A language socialization perspective, of which discourse socialization is but one (sub-) focus, sees development as culturally situated, as mediated, and as replete with social, cultural, and political meanings in addition to propositional or ideational meanings carried or *indexed* by various linguistic, textual, and paralinguistic forms. The core theoretical premise of language socialization is that language is learned through interactions with others who are more proficient in the language and its cultural practices and who provide novices explicit and (or) implicit mentoring or evidence about normative, appropriate uses of the language, and of the worldviews, ideologies, values, and identities of community members. Major early intellectual forces in the development of this theoretical focus from anthropology, sociology, and linguistics were Dell Hymes (see review of his work in Ervin-Tripp, 2009), Schieffelin and Ochs (1986), and Bernstein (1972). Halliday (e.g., 1980/2003) examined language development (socialization) in terms of (a) learning language, (b) *learning through* language, and (c) learning *about* language. Finally, Heath's (1983) seminal book *Ways with Words* demonstrated the relationship between language and literacy socialization practices in the home, at school, and in work contexts and was therefore another important precursor to contemporary work on language socialization into academic discourse.

According to language socialization theory, as learners gain knowledge of language and an ability to participate in new discourse communities by using language appropriately, they gain various other kinds of information or cultural knowledge about ideologies, identities or subjectivities, affective orientations, linguistic and nonlinguistic content (history, mathematics) and practices valued by the local community (Ochs, 1986). For example, students in classrooms are often socialized into and through discourses of (showing) respect (and self-control, decorum) to teachers, to one another, and to the subject matter itself (e.g., Howard & Lo, 2009; Talmy, 2009); that is, they are not just socialized into the pragmatics or sociolinguistics of showing respect but also into ideologies of respect, including aspects of social stratification, ranks, roles, and values — which they, in turn, may either internalize or, rather, challenge or resist. In elementary school classrooms, classroom discourse can provide clear evidence of other types of ideologies, too, such as the need for autonomous and independent academic work versus collaboration and shared knowledge production and ownership (e.g., Toohey, 1998). In bilingual, diglossic, or multilingual contexts, the language or code used in classrooms, and the norms related to whether, when, and with whom other linguistic codes are allowed are themselves important aspects of socialization.

Textbooks and other publications (e.g., journals) often have a clear socializing or enculturating role as well, regarding the objectivity or objectification of science (Viechnicki & Kuipers, 2008), for example, or ideologies of "perseverance, seniority, the importance of education and modesty," in the case of

Chinese heritage-language textbooks (Curdt-Christiansen, 2008, p. 100). In U.S. law schools, students are socialized to the authority of legal texts. Mertz (2007) demonstrated how the ability to use past legal cases (legal precedents) for current purposes is a crucial component of legal education. Socratic classroom questioning often centers on the legal cases and related notes and reports in textbooks, with a focus on facts, technical legal vocabulary, and prior legal decisions or opinions (i.e., hierarchically layered legal authority from different levels of courts or legislatures). Such classroom discourse also serves to socialize students into adversarial, doctrinal courtroom discourse and also into how to "build analogies between the case before them and earlier cases" (p. 61).

Numerous overviews of language socialization exist. Duff and Hornberger's (2008) edited volume includes a 30-year historical review of language socialization as a subfield of linguistic anthropology (Ochs & Schieffelin, 2008), a chapter on academic discourse socialization in university mainstream content areas (Morita & Kobayashi, 2008), another on language socialization and schooling (Baquedano-López & Kattan, 2008), and a chapter looking at the intersections between language socialization for higher education and for professional work (Duff, 2008). Bronson and Watson-Gegeo (2008), in the same volume, emphasized the need for studies of language socialization that incorporate critical theoretical perspectives; using the example of one writer, a Japanese doctoral student in California, they also argued that the student, Keiko, deliberately resisted certain grammatical forms in English (definite articles) as a way to preserve her identity and voice as a Japanese person (see also Bronson, 2004, and the discussion that follows here). Garrett and Baquedano-López (2002) provided a very comprehensive earlier review of language socialization and issues of cross-generation reproduction versus transformation in norms of language use and code choice across transcultural contexts and Bayley and Schecter's (2003) edited volume includes studies of school-based or postsecondary language socialization as well. Finally, Zuengler and Cole (2005) reviewed 17 studies taking a language socialization perspective, a number of them dealing with school language and literacy.

Elsewhere, I have considered various dimensions of language/discourse socialization into academic communities, based on research in both L1 and L2 settings. I have also problematized certain aspects of academic discourse socialization by examining some of the misconceptions often held about it, such as that so-called experts are necessarily good, competent socializers (e.g., good presenters, writers, mentors) or that the biggest challenge for students in academia is formal technical or academic written discourse rather than other more interpersonal forms of discourse and communication found in class discussions or other informal academic interactions (Duff, 2004, 2007b; see also Bunch, 2009).

Socialization into academic discourse, especially in middle-class Anglo-European families, typically begins in the home during early childhood as children are prepared for the kind of school-related literacies and language practices (e.g., show and tell, picture book reading interactions, reader response, discussions about current events, problem solving, and hypothesizing in North American schooling). This preparation affects one's ability to engage in more sophisticated literacy activities later, which in turn affects subsequent workplace, professional, or vocational socialization and performance (Duff, 2008; Heath, 1983; Ochs & Taylor, 1992). Language socialization research now focuses more than before on both older learners in a variety of activity settings (rather than young children) and on socialization into academic literacy practices and not only, or primarily, oral ones (e.g., Séror, 2008; Zappa-Hollman, 2007b). The newer research on postsecondary academic literacy socialization extends scholarship on genre and written composition produced nearly two decades earlier (e.g., Berkenkotter, Huckin, & Ackerman, 1988; Casanave, 1990).

Regardless of the age of learners or the context involved in (academic) language socialization research, much of it has also incorporated the notion of apprenticeship (Rogoff, 1990) into the ways of thinking and acting in a particular community of practice (CoP; Lave & Wenger, 1991), while also (increasingly) noting the limitations of the CoP construct in classroom discourse studies (Duff, 2007b; Haneda, 2006; Zuengler & Miller, 2008). Zappa-Hollman (2007b) suggested that a social network approach (what she called *individual networks of practice*) may account for students' simultaneous engagements with richly distributed human, material, and symbolic resources and relationships (their individual networks) better than the typically narrower, more immediate, apolitical, and tightly circumscribed sense of discourse socialization associated with CoP.

Academic Discourse

Academic discourse (or academic language, academic literacies) refers to forms of oral and written language and communication — genres, registers, graphics, linguistic structures, interactional patterns — that are privileged, expected, cultivated, conventionalized, or ritualized, and, therefore, usually evaluated by instructors, institutions, editors, and others in educational and professional contexts. (Professional discourse is subsumed here under the cover term of academic discourse because generally professional socialization has a strong academic component prior to or concurrent with internships and other field experience in the professions and because academia itself is a professional site.) Martin and Rose (2007) described discourse as "meaning beyond the clause.... the social as it is constructed through texts, ... the constitutive role of meanings in social life" (p. 1). Academic discourse is usually connected with specific disciplines or professional areas and is embodied both in texts and in other modes of interaction and representation. It is normally inculcated within academic communities such as school or university programs and classrooms. Some students, in postcolonial or lingua franca settings, for example (Duff, 1996; Moore, 2008), may have opportunities to be socialized bilingually or multilingually into academic discourse(s). However, in English-dominant immigrant-receiving settings or other multilingual contexts, students may be expected to develop proficiency in English academic discourse but not in their home languages and literacies, or not to the same extent. Regardless, academic discourse is a complex representation of knowledge and authority and identity that comprises language(s), ideologies, and other semiotic or symbolic resources, often displayed in texts, but one that has strong social, cultural, institutional, and historical foundations and functions (Leki, 2007). As Fairclough (1989) put it, discourse is text, interaction, and context.

Academic discourse is continually evolving, and many new, sometimes experimental and highly personal, creative genres exist (e.g., Kouritzen, Piquemal, & Norman, 2009), some of which complement—even transgress—traditional norms of standard academic discourse(s), such as those requiring that research articles follow the structure of introduction, methods, results and discussion, commonly referred to as IMRAD. Nevertheless, applied linguists usually associate academic discourse with particular genres, genre sets, and registers, and often a relatively formal register, with subject-specific (or disciplinary) linguistic, discursive, and multimodal conventions (see, e.g., Biber, 2006). Studies of academic discourse and the socialization of students to engage with it and to participate in new discourse communities have tended to be associated primarily with written or visual texts and their production although that more limited notion is changing (Molle & Prior, 2008). Despite sometimes being described as such, academic discourse or even individual genres are not homogeneous, singular, pure, or static forms of discourse; they often contain hybrid and multimodal features and change over time and across contexts and are enacted within the constraints and contingencies of each local setting (Prior, 1998).

Students entering academic institutions have different amounts and kinds of prior experience with academic discourse, even when their home language is the same as that of the educational institution. Mature English-speaking students entering English-medium higher education after some years of absence may experience "change, difficulty, crises of confidence, conflicts of identity, feelings of strangeness, the need to discover the rules of an unfamiliar world" (Ivanič, 1998, p. 7). For students coming from disadvantaged or minority languages and backgrounds, the challenges become particularly salient. Leibowitz (2005) described black isiXhosa-speaking students' socialization into academic discourse in an English-medium South African university. Students' discomfort often stems from an acute awareness of differences across the worlds of their homes, communities, or prior school experiences and those in the current educational setting. Starfield's (2002) ethnographic case studies in a South African first-year university sociology program illustrated similar disjunctions.

However, students' discomfort is often not simply a perception on their part, an internally generated form of anxiety or a lack of immediate identification or familiarity with the new target discourses and community practices. It is also coconstructed through interactions and other social practices, by dominant power structures and prevailing discourses of exclusion, including gendered discourses (Morita, 2004, 2009; Tracy, 1997). Thus, also affecting students' experiences of socialization is the way newcomers and their histories and aspirations are viewed and by how they are positioned—by themselves, by others, and by their institutions—as capable (or incapable), as worthy, legitimate, showing potential for fuller participation or membership (or not), as insiders (or outsiders), and so on. Unfortunately, as many language socialization researchers have found, some programs, activities, and instructors are more effective socializing agents or mediators than others (Casanave & Li, 2008; Morita, 2004, 2009; Séror, 2008;

Zappa-Hollman, 2007a, 2007b). Those who are most successful not only display, but also make explicit, the values and practices implicit in the culture and provide novices with the language, skills, support, and opportunities they need to participate with growing competence in the new culture and its core activities (Duff, 2007b, 2010). With students coming from a range of linguistic and cultural backgrounds and variable levels of out-of-school support for their academic literacies, the challenges are typically magnified (Morita, 2000). As Heath (1983) and others (e.g., Hawkins, 2005) have demonstrated, young children from minority cultures must learn academic or "school" discourse very early on in order to succeed, particularly if they do not come to school with the vaunted cultural, symbolic, and discursive capital and social practices of mainstream educational culture. Older newcomers have less time to catch up and have a very steep linguistic, discursive, and cultural learning curve once mainstreamed in content or professional areas.

LANGUAGE SOCIALIZATION AND ACADEMIC DISCOURSE ACROSS MODALITIES

Oral Academic Discourse Socialization

As much research has demonstrated (e.g., Biber, 2006), oral and written academic discourse are quite distinct and so too are the ways in which students are socialized into target practices, genres, registers, and speech events. Oral academic discourse is normally much more spontaneous and public than written discourse, the latter often produced in relative isolation by a writer (student, professor)—although with a great deal of social academic experience leading up to the writing—and then submitted to someone else for private assessment or comment. Yet the two modalities, oral and written, are not completely distinct, because oral presentations or lectures typically draw on a variety of written texts and may also incorporate visual texts by means of PowerPoint, handouts, or other media, to facilitate communication (e.g., Kobayashi, 2003, 2004). Similarly, any given text, oral or written, is not a stand-alone construction because, especially in academic discourse, it normally draws on and interweaves many other texts. Nevertheless, in this section I consider issues in oral academic discourse socialization first, since it has been the most neglected in studies of academic discourse.

There is more to academic socialization than just learning to read and write standard academic discourse, which is nevertheless a crucial form of knowledge construction, representation, and assessment. For example, learning to participate effectively in initiation-response-evaluation (IRE) exchanges, which are a staple in many teacher-fronted classes around the world, may pose challenges for many learners but must be mastered (Mehan, 1979). IRE has therefore been researched a great deal from many theoretical and methodological approaches, including language socialization. Contributors to Barnard and Torres-Guzman's (2009) volume illustrated how students in elementary and secondary schools in different parts of the world are inducted or socialized through oral classroom discourse, including IRE, into locally sanctioned knowledge and practice.

Oral communication skills displayed in presentations, mini-lectures, group project work, and class discussions are now being stressed and assessed by instructors and peers more than before and are therefore being researched more by language socialization scholars as well (e.g., Duff, 1995, 2009; Duff & Kobayashi, 2010; Kobayashi, 2006; Morita, 2000; Tracy, 1997; Zappa-Hollman, 2007b). This emphasis on orality reflects, in part, the amount and quality of collaboration and communication (and not just textbook knowledge or theory) that are now required in real-world knowledge building and knowledge sharing in a variety of professional and academic fields—from medicine to engineering, pharmacy, education, social work, and clinical psychology (Duff, 2010). The students themselves in these new discourse communities may be asked to evaluate their own and others' participation in these highly oral, collaborative activity settings, normally on the basis of participants' social interaction skills as well as their knowledge of academic discourse. Although oral academic discourse has not received as much attention in the relevant research in applied linguistics as written discourse has to date, new research demonstrates just how socially, cognitively, and discursively complex and variable a standard oral activity such as oral presentation can be, whether in the context of a classroom or boardroom, a thesis or dissertation defense theatre, or a conference.

Tracy (1997), a professor of communication, was a participant observer in a 2-year study of a weekly academic colloquium series in communication departments at two U.S. universities. She documented the academic discourse socialization and related identity work taking place for members of the department:

graduate students, visitors, and professors of different rank and gender, for whom every week a colleague was scheduled to make a formal presentation on their work. The socialization practices were associated (potentially) with conflict, tensions, the loss of face, and dilemmas, as her book's subtitle, *Dilemmas of Academic Discourse*, reveals. Furthermore, the colloquium involved a complex merging of oral and literate practices and of less contextualized, impersonal language as well as more contextualized, interpersonal language and interaction.

Unlike most written discourse, oral presentations are often commented upon publicly immediately after the speaker has finished, which makes them potentially face-threatening to both presenters and audience members who are expected to provide commentary, critique, and stimulating questions and points for follow up discussion (e.g., Duff, 2009). In a study of doctoral students and postdoctoral fellows in physics, Jacoby (1998) examined the functions served by the conference talk rehearsal, as part of the discursive and professional socialization of physicists in physics labs with fellow graduate students, postdoctoral fellows, supervisors, and others. One significant part of Jacoby's analysis was the problem-solving comment sequences and complaints (based on what she called *indigenous assessment*) following the practice sessions. She described these as being specifically "designed and heard as not only concerned with particular problems in particular presentations, but also as communicating general lessons about the alleged conventional and moral expectations of a conference talk presentation, as a genre and as an event, in the communication of science" (p. 364).

Kobayashi (2003, 2004, 2006) examined how undergraduate Japanese exchange students at a Canadian university were socialized into required practices in support of their final group project presentations (see also Beckett, 2005, for research on socialization through project work at the secondary school level). He traced the in-class and out-of-class development of the project, a kind of living, organic process, as students became coagents of socialization, coaching one another through a variety of meetings and rehearsals and strategies, using both Japanese and English, in order to ultimately deliver an effective English presentation. They also worked together to produce grammatical PowerPoint slides and concoct pragmatic strategies to engage their audience and teacher in appropriate, sometimes humorous, ways.

Zappa-Hollman (2007a) and Morita (2000) examined the very different specifications and characteristics of oral presentations across disciplines (e.g., applied linguistics, neuroscience, history, and engineering). In addition, each presentation they observed was not viewed as independent of the others but was contingent upon prior experience and moment-by-moment developments. Students often chose strategies for their own implementation of the activity based on what they perceived to be successful, unsuccessful, original, or unoriginal in previous presentations by themselves and by peers in the same courses. Elements of reproduction were reported but so too were innovation and experimentation by students, precisely to showcase their originality, considered to be a valuable trait by some students and a way of distinguishing themselves from other graduate students.

Vickers (2007) conducted ethnographic research on L2 socialization in electrical and computer engineering team meetings at an American university, during which engineering projects were designed by student teams. A sample project was a device to render sound-producing devices mute. The instructors socialized students into the "industry" culture of teamwork in the engineering profession beyond university as well as within their program. "Efficiency, clarity, and engagement" (p. 628) in the design process were valued attributes of engineering students—and competent engineers—in the local academic and professional communities. Explicit advice to that effect was therefore pervasive. Vickers analyzed participation and relative expertise in managing the conversational floor in the design meetings, demonstrating how, linguistically, the more technically expert students initially assumed the role of information providers or explainers (socializers) to the novices, whose role it was to ask questions seeking technical information. With time and observation, experience, scaffolding, confidence building, and control over the content, the novices had learned enough technical content to themselves become information providers and to "think, design, and talk like a competent engineer" (p. 637). One new student had to "position himself as a competent, expert, core member of the team before he could take on the language behaviors typical of such team members" (p. 637).

Turning now to socialization within public school content classroom discourse, my research in grade 10 high school content-area classrooms in Hungary and Canada revealed how students were socialized into multimodal, intertextual, heteroglossic literacies and ways of knowing and speaking about history and social studies, respectively (Duff, 1995, 1996, 2002, 2004, 2009; cf. Maybin, 2003).

I examined teacher-fronted discussions and also student recitations and presentations in the form of mini-lectures. In the dual-track Hungarian-English bilingual schools in Hungary, the discourse in Hungarian-medium classes socialized students into a highly ritualized form of oral recitation similar in some ways to the sometimes nerve-wracking Socratic discourse practiced in law classes described in Mertz's (2007) book. In the English-medium programs in Hungary, however, new, ostensibly more democratic discourse practices were being introduced, involving not only a different code choice (English) but also new genres (e.g., voluntary student mini-lectures, small-group discussions on historical topics such as the Russian Revolution, and only some years later, written essays) by means of which students could present their knowledge and teachers could assess it.

The most valued components of oral academic discourse became very clear in each setting, often in the form of feedback from the teacher. However, for many of the English language learners in the mainstream social studies classes who were analyzed, the vernacular discourse and pervasive extracurricular references (to *The Simpsons* and other iconic pop culture TV programs) were especially perplexing, and students were seemingly being socialized into the appropriation of two (diglossic) registers and not just one. Furthermore, students needed to learn how to make logical connections between topics from the news and other content and their academic material and also contribute to these discussions meaningfully, a very challenging prospect for newcomers to Canada without a strong command of English.

Socialization into Written Academic Discourse and (Inter)Textuality

Much of the early work on written academic discourse socialization, particularly at the postsecondary level, is not based on language socialization theory and research practice as developed by Ochs, Schieffelin, and others (e.g., Ochs, 1986; Schieffelin & Ochs, 1986) but on compatible work in sociology, rhetoric, the history and sociology of science, and other traditions.

In-depth case studies and ethnographies have been conducted of individual learners and their interlocutors negotiating the textual requirements, and especially their own writing processes and struggles, across courses, or throughout the dissertation writing or publishing experience, in some cases longitudinally over one or more years (e.g., Berkenkotter & Huckin, 1995; Berkenkotter et al., 1988, 1991; Casanave, 1992, 2002; Casanave & Vandrick, 2003; Spack, 1997). Leki (1995) examined the challenges faced by international students from Europe and Asia in their first semester at a U.S. university and their coping mechanisms including, in some cases, their resistance to professors' demands or requirements rather than their accommodation.

Casanave (2002) focused on academic and professional writing socialization at the postsecondary and professoriate levels. Dozens of key case studies in the field of L2 writing were reviewed, both those conducted by her (e.g., Casanave, 1992, 1998) and by others (e.g., Ivanič, 1998; Prior, 1998; Spack, 1997). The studies dealt with such topics as plagiarism, agency, authority, authorship, authenticity in writing, doctoral student mentoring, article revising strategies, silence, power and (textual) identities, voice, disciplinary enculturation, experiences of multilingual writers, and resistance. The changing cultures and practices within and across disciplines such as sociology were also examined.

Academic enculturation or discourse socialization is viewed by Casanave (2002) as a set of "writing games" (the title of her book) for which students and new professionals must learn the rules—or learn how to bend the rules—in order to participate and succeed. Several of the students profiled were in the field of sociology. Most of the studies look at the processes involved in writing papers as single-authors (acknowledging, however, that even single-authored papers blend many different voices and texts and may be coconstructed through interactions between supervisor and student or larger research team and students). A few studies (see Prior, 1998) also deal with the processes involved in coauthored academic discourse, by groups of students and/or professors. Prior underscored the importance of textual practices and activities to disciplinary enculturation: "providing opportunity spaces for (re)socialization of discursive practices, for foregrounding representations of disciplinarity, and for negotiating trajectories of participation in communities of practice" (p. 32).

Too often it is taken for granted that language learners (and other newcomers) will be fully accommodated and apprenticed within their new communities and will also have ample access to the target discourse practices they are expected to emulate (Duff, 2002, 2003, 2007b; Haneda, 2006). Such assumptions of facile apprenticeship, accommodation and access are problematic in the light of evidence to the contrary (e.g., Belcher, 1994). Research has found, not surprisingly perhaps, that many instructors do not provide explicit and appropriate scaffolding, modeling, or feedback to support students' performance of oral assignments (e.g., presentations, critiques, projects; e.g., Zappa-Hollman, 2007a, 2007b). It is simply expected that most students are already familiar with the genres required for academic essays or presentations and the criteria for evaluating them, even though these attributes and criteria may vary greatly from one context to the next.

Two dissertations demonstrate this point. Both examined academic literacy socialization from, or in, the margins—that is, the kinds of messages, intended or not, provided by instructors to nonnative English-speaking students, typically in the margins or at the end of their assignments or written drafts and their impact on the students (already at risk of being marginalized linguistically) who read the comments. Séror (2008) reported that the Japanese undergraduate students in his yearlong study in Canada were often deeply disappointed, confused, or simply not helped by the comments on their assignments, which were illegible and incomprehensible to many students; but beyond that, comments were often negative, terse, global, and uninstructive. He also observed how students were sometimes positioned disadvantageously by the instructors' comments (e.g., as nonnative speakers and writers), denying the students any sense of legitimacy in their courses—or any possibilities for other identities, such as successful writer or insightful scholar or someone with a strong background in the content area.

Bronson's (2004) multiple case study, also using ethnographic methods and language socialization theory, reached a similar conclusion, but by focusing on graduate students' academic literacy socialization at a university in California. Both studies reported that the feedback provided was contingent on many other sociopolitical and socioeducational factors, such as the value and reward structures in place for teaching (as opposed to research) at the university, the instructors' status and rank at the university, the number of students per course, the availability of teaching assistants, and other considerations, such as whether instructors felt qualified or obligated (able or willing) to assist students in their courses to become better writers (in both form and content) and whether students could locate good (peer) proofreaders or tutors. In some cases, it was reported, students received only a grade, but their articles were never returned. Opportunities for meaningful enculturation into written academic discourse were thus lost, to students' great disappointment and detriment.

Zappa-Hollman (2007b), referred to earlier, examined the importance and density of Mexican undergraduate exchange students' individual social networks and the other institutional resources they availed themselves of in both Mexico and Canada for their socialization into literate practices valued in the Canadian university context she studied. She also contrasted the academic cultures and modes of academic discourse socialization surrounding literacy and higher education in universities in the two countries as a way of explaining some of glaring differences and difficulties that students encountered. She then followed the students back to Mexico to determine what effect their English (Canadian) experiences had on their subsequent academic discourse socialization and performance in Mexico (e.g., they now felt the instruction in Mexico was unchallenging, required too many weekly assignments, and did not acknowledge them as mature and independent thinkers; they also reported transferring some process writing practices from Canada to their assignments in Mexico).

In a study summarized briefly in Duff (2007a), I found that, for many of the Korean undergraduate exchange students in a similar study, accessing suitable English-speaking or English-supporting networks was not at all straightforward for a variety of reasons (social, cultural, pragmatic). Most ended up seeking the assistance of bilingual and bicultural Generation 1.5 Korean Canadians or other Asian students as their socializing agents or cultural and linguistic brokers rather than local, native English speakers. The latter were often unable to provide the support needed. Their Asian-background peers, on the other hand, socialized them not into a local Anglo-Canadian university CoP so much as a Pan-Asian, transnational, multilingual one, a kind of hybrid/third space. Korean-Canadian Generation 1.5 university students, for their part, may also experience complicated, nonlinear trajectories as they are socialized into English academic discourse and communities; and as their investments in maintaining their bilingualism and biculturalism, and their identities, dominant languages, primary linguistic networks, and academic goals change over time. Kim's (2008) dissertation demonstrates this point very well with longitudinal data from seven Korean-Canadian case study participants.

In her discussion of the socialization of first-year law students into American legal discourse and into the law profession, Mertz (2007) argued that the process entails not simply learning to write or read or speak like a lawyer, essential though these skills and discourses are for lawyers. Rather, the novice law students or initiates, as she called them, must learn, first and foremost, to *Think Like a Lawyer* — the subtitle of her book. The epistemologies, worldviews, and language ideologies underlying the behaviors she observed (e.g., the Socratic method of teaching) in her study of language use and interaction in contracts classes at eight different law schools strongly favored distancing oneself morally and emotionally from cases, tragedies, or conflicts. Instead, students were socialized into dispassionately interpreting and applying the letter of the law in what was presumed and claimed to be a neutral and technical manner. Philips's (1982) earlier study examined the discursive socialization of U.S. law students into the legal cant, that is, the specialized, complex, and often publicly inaccessible or impenetrable legal terminology and discourse patterns, both oral and written, associated with appellate (case) law and practice.

Similar processes occur in other advanced degree and professional programs such as medicine. Using a discourse socialization perspective, Hobbs (2004) analyzed medical residents' and doctors' handwritten progress reports (treatment notes) as well as physicians' implicit socialization into these practices and genres by means of their supervisors' reviews and their concurrence on cases. The physicians' progress reports she examined used a mixture of Latin, English abbreviations, and other symbols. To produce and interpret such reports accurately, and to develop their clinical judgment and expertise, physicians had to have considerable theoretical and clinical experience and enculturation.

The criteria for genres of writing in graduate school courses and for later writing may sometimes differ from actual practice requiring that people continue to be socialized or apprenticed into new target discourse practices in the professional workplace. Studies by Parks (2001) and Parks and Maguire (1999) analyzed the important and pervasive genres of nursing reports and care plans taught in nursing programs for use by nurses during or at the end of their hospital shifts. However, the texts Francophone student nurses (in Quebec) had been socialized to produce in their study actually differed from those expected in either Francophone or Anglophone Montreal hospitals, requiring further socialization into workplace literacy practices.

In general, substantial discussion has focused on postsecondary language and literacy socialization, particularly in work coming out of academic writing. An edited volume by Australian scholars, *Learning Discourses and the Discourses of Learning* (Marriott, Moore, & Spence-Brown, 2007), highlighted many of the challenges associated with academic discourse socialization in a variety of program contexts in that country.

To date, less research has examined written academic discourse socialization at the elementary or secondary levels than at the postsecondary level. Poole (2008) illustrated the competing discourses of (so-called) decontextualized and contextualized language use in the literacy socialization of grade 5 students in reading groups in which nonfictional, illustrated essayist (expository) texts about dinosaurs, for example, were being discussed. Other work has looked at socialization into scientific discourse (e.g., Huang, 2004) and religious as opposed to secular schooling contexts for school-aged learners. A special issue on the "spirit of reading ... sacred texts" (Sterponi, 2008) features work on Talmudic, Koranic, and Catholic (*doctrina*) text recitation and related code choice issues, particularly in multilingual contexts, as well as gender norms, the socialization of morality, and related issues (see Baquedano-López & Kattan, 2008; Fader, 2001, 2006; Garrett & Baquedano-López, 2002; Moore, 2008).

In summary, a substantial body of new research exists on language socialization into oral and written discourse across an increasingly wide range of academic and educational discourse contexts. In the next section I consider emergent, blended, digital modes of communication.

Blurred, Blended or Hybrid Modes of Academic Discourse Socialization

Much academic discourse that takes place in the written mode is now mediated by electronic networks, and some genres represent a blend of oral and written discourse that permits the inclusion of graphics and hyperlinks as well. With an increasing number of mixed-mode courses offered at universities, involving both face-to-face and online discussion components, students and teachers have opportunities to participate in new kinds of discourse communities and new genres mediated by these new technologies. In her research in Canada on computer-mediated communication (CMC) in mixed-mode graduate courses in education, Yim (2005) found that students, both native and nonnative speakers of English, needed to learn appropriate roles, registers, and technological skills to participate in asynchronous, threaded, bulletin-board discussions related to course content. In one course, the instructor insisted on highly academic discourse and carefully formulated responses to course content, which all students struggled with to some extent. In another course, however, the instructor provided a more informal, interactional forum for discussion, and in that discourse community, students were socialized into different kinds of language use, pragmatics, and role-taking. The CMC speech functions there involved conveying knowledge and expressing opinions (initiating and reacting to postings), making requests for additional information and commands, and then using a range of social formulas or speech acts, such as greeting, thanking, acknowledging, and apologizing. Although the instructor set up the online component and offered suggestions for how the students would engage with it, the students really learned how to participate through observation of their peers' interaction styles and registers. In the course that required less formal academic discourse, students produced more postings on average and reported feeling more ownership over their writing and also others' writing. In the more formal environment, on the other hand, there was tension between the instructor's preferred style of communicating online and that of students, and an attendant lack of social formulas and positive appraisal of one another's messages. There was also resistance to this mode and register of socialization.

Potts (2005) also examined CMC discourse in mixed-mode graduate courses in language and literacy education and, similarly, reported on the bidirectional or multilateral socialization taking place as everyone in the discourse community over time, in response to others' forms of participation, learned together how they wanted to communicate with one another. They negotiated, typically online, how to participate most meaningfully and also how to project their (desired) identities as intelligent, informed graduate students. One nonnative English speaker in the course reflected on her academic discourse socialization as follows: "I try to learn how ... other participants post their message, and then I try to cite their postings into my posting, not exactly the expression, I try to imitate their style, their writing style and then I try to imply [apply] the way of writing into my posting" (p. 151). Deliberately analyzing, borrowing, and imitating certain others' postings was commonly reported, reflecting their jointly achieved enculturation into a new educational mode for which the norms and conventions were still under negotiation (cf. Lu & Nelson, 2008).

Finally, Warschauer (2002) and Lam (2008) have looked at the role of online discussion and participation in other forms of electronic networking on students' well-being and especially as it affects their academic literacies and identities. Clearly, research in this area will be of increasing importance in the future as greater collaboration in project work, report writing, presentations within and across communities and disparate mediating networks, and electronically mediated education becomes the norm rather than the exception.

SOCIALIZATION INTO ACADEMIC PUBLICATION AND TEXTUAL IDENTITIES

In a series of articles based on her dissertation, Li (2005, 2006a, 2006b, 2007) conducted a multiple case study of the experiences of Chinese doctoral students at a university in Nanjing, China, learning to publish in international journals in English, typically as a PhD requirement. She noted the complex and arduous processes of enculturation experienced by the participants, science students who might not have a strong background in academic English writing. Li also described the multiple community memberships the doctoral students were simultaneously negotiating, in their departments, their disciplinary fields in China, and the international scientific community mediated by English. She carefully documented their enculturation (socialization) into the world of English scholarly publication, which required, among other things, grappling with editors' and reviewers' comments on manuscript submissions and the revising process.

Turning now to academic literacy socialization at more advanced levels, many articles and chapters provide authors' personal perspectives on how they, as new professors (or from even earlier stages), were socialized into valued academic writing practices leading to scholarly publication, tenure, and esteem or acknowledged authority. Well-known applied linguists have published their personal reflections on their own multilingual literacy development or socialization along their academic journeys as graduate students and now professors (e.g., Belcher & Connor, 2001; Casanave, 2002; Casanave & Vandrick, 2003; Pavlenko, 2003) or have described the tensions when scholars trained in one linguistic and/ or discourse community (e.g., the United States) later return to their home country (e.g. China), where other academic discourse traditions prevail (Shi, 2002, 2003).

Belcher and Connor (2001) edited narratives by 18 other established applied linguists, many of whom are known for their research on L2 literacy and writing and contributed chapters about their own formative bilingual or L2 literacy experiences and their current "multiliterate lives," as professors in North America, Asia, Israel, or Scandinavia, and elsewhere. They described their experiences of discourse socialization across languages, text types, and contexts, illuminating the many factors affecting emerging professionals.

RACE, CULTURE AND GENDER IN ACADEMIC DISCOURSE SOCIALIZATION

Although much research has examined gender in relation to first and second language socialization in everyday, mostly oral, language contexts (e.g., Gordon, 2008; Howard, 2008; Kyratzis & Cook-Gumperz, 2008; Pavlenko & Piller, 2008), particularly from a poststructural perspective, relatively few studies have examined it explicitly in relation to academic discourse socialization. Morita's (2009) research on gender, language and culture is a longitudinal case study of a Japanese international student at a Canadian university. The stances her participant, Kota, took in interactions with his female professor indexed certain gendered expectations, both on his part and hers (cf. Schleef, 2008, on gender and academic discourse; Casanave, 2002; Mertz, 2007). Morita determined that "[w]hereas feminism, critical theories, and issues of minority education were popular in the department, Kota was interested in exploring university–industry collaboration from a perspective of economics—a viewpoint that he felt might be considered as 'a male perspective' " (p. 453). His professor, a feminist scholar, resented some of the behaviors and attitudes of the male international students in her class, which she attributed to a lack of respect for the teaching/learning situation and for her as a female instructor. Morita interpreted the gendering practices, identities, and (perceived) membership in the new academic community as highly coconstructed, situational, and based on several interrelated contextual factors.

Morita (2002, 2004) also conducted a larger, longitudinal, multiple case study that examined six Japanese women's academic discourse socialization into graduate and senior-level undergraduate courses at a Canadian university, focusing on the women's variable levels and forms of participation (including silence) in class discussions. Many factors influenced the way they performed their multiple identities in different course contexts: their status as English teachers, nonnative English speakers, non-Canadians, older versus younger Japanese nationals, women, and so on, and their positioning by teachers and classmates in particular ways (as "outsiders," MA not PhD students). They each negotiated these positionings and their sense of agency (e.g., to receive assistance) within each class over time leading to variable outcomes. These two studies illustrate the value of taking a nuanced, nonessentialist perspective on issues connected with race, culture, and gender to see how students and instructors, through various kinds of socialization, experiences, and contestation, negotiate their legitimacy and identities in academic discourse communities. More research of this sort is needed.

CONCLUSION

Language socialization is a dynamic, socially and culturally situated, multimodal, and often multilingual process with unpredictable uptake, intentions, behind-the-scenes power plays, investment on the part of learners, and outcomes. Such dynamics are particularly visible in academic communities. Some implications of this overview are that applied linguists need to better understand the actual discursive practices and requirements of various fields and the ways in which students, instructors, and scholars are positioned by academic discourse, by institutions, and by interactions within them. Greater attention must be paid to the process of developing intersubjectivity in academic activity settings among participants and developing new knowledge, competencies, and textual identities in these learning communities through appropriate mediation and scaffolding. Instructors, students, and colleagues also have a joint responsibility to serve as better agents of one another's socialization and development as writers, speakers, and scholarly thinkers. The successful socialization of both nonnative and native writers worldwide has, it seems, become a higher-stakes enterprise as assessments for scholarships, grants, degrees, and jobs require more strategic and visible output with greater perceived impact than ever before. Therefore, schools, universities, and other sites for socialization into academic discourse and into academic discourse communities need to increase the metadiscursive support made available to students and instructors to enhance the quality of language and literacy socialization in their midst and to accommodate and support newcomers—from all language backgrounds—within these discourse communities more satisfactorily and seamlessly as well.

ACKNOWLEDGMENTS

I acknowledge, with thanks, the very helpful and detailed editorial suggestions of an anonymous reviewer. Unfortunately, due to space constraints, I could not elaborate on some of the points raised.

REFERENCES

Baquedano-López, P., & Kattan, S. (2008). Language socialization and schooling. In P. A. Duff & N. H. Hornberger (Eds.), *Encyclopedia of language and education: Vol. 8. Language socialization* (pp. 161–173). New York: Springer.

Barnard, R., & Torres-Guzman, M. (Eds.). (2009). *Creating communities of learning in schools.* Clevedon, UK: Multilingual Matters.

Bayley, R., & Schecter, S. (Eds.). (2003). *Language socialization in bilingual and multilingual societies.* Clevedon, UK: Multilingual Matters.

Beckett, G. H. (2005). Academic language and literacy socialization through project-based instruction: ESL student perspectives and issues. *Journal of Asian Pacific Communication, 15*, 191–206.

Belcher, D. (1994). The apprenticeship approach to advanced academic literacy: Graduate students and their mentors. *English for Specific Purposes, 13*, 23–34.

Belcher, D., & Connor, U. (Eds.). (2001). *Reflections on multiliterate lives.* Clevedon, UK: Multilingual Matters.

Berkenkotter, C., & Huckin, T. N. (1995). *Genre knowledge in disciplinary communication.* Hillsdale, NJ: Erlbaum.

Berkenkotter, C., Huckin, T. N., & Ackerman, J. (1988). Conventions, conversations, and the writer: Case study of a student in a rhetoric Ph.D. program. *Research in the Teaching of English, 22*, 9–45.

Berkenkotter, C., Huckin, T. N., & Ackerman, J. (1991). Social contexts and socially constructed texts: The initiation of a graduate student into a writing research community. In C. Bazerman & J. Paradis (Eds.), *Textual dynamics of the professions: Historical and contemporary studies of writing in academic and other professional communities* (pp. 191–215). Madison: University of Wisconsin Press.

Bernstein, D. (1972). Social class, language and socialization. In P. P. Giglioli (Ed.), *Language and social context* (pp. 157–178). New York: Penguin Books.

Biber, D. (2006). *University language: A corpus-based study of spoken and written registers.* Amsterdam: John Benjamins.

Bourdieu, P., Passeron, J.-C., & de Saint Martin, M. (1994). Students and the language of teaching. In P. Bourdieu, J.-C. Passeron, & M. de Saint Martin (Eds.), *Academic discourse: Linguistic misunderstanding and professorial power* (pp. 35–79). Palo Alto, CA: Stanford University Press.

Bronson, M. D. (2004). *Writing passage: Academic literacy socialization among ESL graduate students, A multiple case study.* Unpublished doctoral dissertation, University of California, Davis.

Bronson, M. C., & Watson-Gegeo, K. A. (2008). The critical moment: Language socialization and the (re)visioning of first and second language learning. In P. A. Duff & N. H. Hornberger (Eds.), *Encyclopedia of language and education: Vol. 8. Language socialization* (pp. 43–55). New York: Springer.

Bunch, G. C. (2009). "Going up there": Challenges and opportunities for language minority students during a mainstream classroom speech event. *Linguistics and Education, 20*, 81–108.

Casanave, C. P. (1990). *The role of writing in socializing graduate students into an academic discipline in the social sciences.* Unpublished doctoral dissertation, Stanford University, Palo Alto, CA.

Casanave, C. P. (1992). Cultural diversity and socialization: A case study of a Hispanic woman in a doctoral program in sociology. In D. E. Murray (Ed.), *Diversity as resource: Redefining cultural literacy* (pp. 148–182). Alexandria, VA: TESOL.

Casanave, C. P. (1998). Transitions: The balancing act of bilingual academics. *Journal of Second Language Writing, 7*, 175–203.

Casanave, C. P. (2002). *Writing games: Multicultural case studies of academic literacy practices in higher education.* Mahwah, NJ: Erlbaum.

Casanave, C. P. (2004). *Controversies in second language writing.* Ann Arbor: University of Michigan Press.

Casanave, C. P., & Li, X. (Eds.). (2008). *Learning the literacy practices of graduate school: Insiders' reflections on academic enculturation.* Ann Arbor: University of Michigan Press.

Casanave, C. P., & Vandrick, S. (Eds.). (2003). *Writing for scholarly publication: Behind the scenes in language education.* Mahwah, NJ: Erlbaum.

Connor, U., & Upton, T. (Eds.). (2004). *Discourse in the professions: Perspectives from corpus linguistics.* Amsterdam: John Benjamins.

Curdt-Christiansen, X. (2008). Reading the world through words: Cultural themes in heritage Chinese language textbooks. *Language and Education, 22,* 95–113.

Duff, P. A. (1995). An ethnography of communication in immersion classrooms in Hungary. *TESOL Quarterly, 29,* 505–537.

Duff, P. A. (1996). Different languages, different practices: Socialization of discourse competence in dual-language school classrooms in Hungary. In K. Bailey & D. Nunan (Eds.), *Voices from the language classroom: Qualitative research in second language acquisition* (pp. 407–433). New York: Cambridge University Press.

Duff, P. A. (2002). The discursive construction of knowledge, identity, and difference: An ethnography of communication in the high school mainstream. *Applied Linguistics, 23,* 289–322.

Duff, P. A. (2003). New directions in second language socialization research. *Korean Journal of English Language and Linguistics, 3,* 309–339.

Duff, P. A. (2004). Intertextuality and hybrid discourses: The infusion of pop culture in educational discourse. *Linguistics and Education, 14,* 231–176.

Duff, P. A. (2007a). Second language socialization as sociocultural theory: Insights and issues. *Language Teaching, 40,* 309–319.

Duff, P. A. (2007b). Problematising academic discourse socialisation. In H. Marriott, T. Moore, & R. Spence-Brown (Eds.), *Learning discourses and the discourses of learning* (pp. 1–18). Melbourne, Australia: Monash University e-Press/University of Sydney Press.

Duff, P. A. (2008). Language socialization, higher education, and work. In P. A. Duff & N. H. Hornberger (Eds.), *Encyclopedia of language and education: Vol. 8. Language socialization* (pp. 257–270). New York: Springer.

Duff, P. A. (2009). Language socialization in a Canadian secondary school: Talking about current events. In R. Barnard & M. Torres-Guzman (Eds.), *Creating communities of learning in schools* (pp. 165–185). Clevedon, UK: Multilingual Matters.

Duff, P. A. (2010). Language socialization. In N. H. Hornberger & S. McKay (Eds.), *Sociolinguistics and language education* (pp. 427–452). Bristol, UK: Multilingual Matters.

Duff, P. A. (in press). Second language socialization. In A. Duranti, E. Ochs, & B. B. Schieffelin (Eds.), *Handbook of language socialization.* Malden, MA: Wiley-Blackwell.

Duff, P. A., & Hornberger, N. H. (Eds.). (2008). *Encyclopedia of language and education: Vol. 8. Language socialization.* New York: Springer.

Duff, P. A. & Kobayashi, M. (2010). The intersection of social, cognitive, and cultural processes in language learning. In R. Batstone (Ed.), *Sociocognitive perspectives on language use and language learning* (pp. 75–93). Oxford, UK: Oxford University Press.

Ervin-Tripp, S. (2009). Hymes on speech socialization. *Text and Talk, 29,* 245–256.

Fader, A. (2001). Literacy, bilingualism, and gender in a Hasidic community. *Linguistics and Education*, *12*, 261–283.

Fader, A. (2006). Learning faith: Language socialization in a community of Hasidic Jews. *Language in Society*, *35*, 205–229.

Fairclough, N. (1989). *Language and power.* London: Longman.

Flowerdew, J., & Li, Y. (2007). Language re-use among Chinese apprentice scientists writing for publication. *Applied Linguistics*, *28*, 440–465.

Garrett, P. B., & Baquedano-López, P. (2002). Language socialization: Reproduction and continuity, transformation and change. *Annual Review of Anthropology*, *31*, 339–361.

Gordon, D. (2008). Gendered second language socialization. In P. Duff & N. H. Hornberger (Eds.), *Encyclopedia of language and education: Vol. 8. Language socialization* (pp. 231–242). New York: Springer.

Halliday, M. (2003). Three aspects of children's language development: Learning language, learning through language, learning about language. In J. Webster (Ed.), *The language of early childhood* (pp. 308–326). London: Continuum. (Reprinted from *Oral and written language development: Impact on schools— Proceedings from the 1979 and 1980 IMPACT Conferences*, pp. 7–19, by Y. Goodman, M. Haussler, & D. Strickland, Eds., 1980, Newark, DE: International Reading Association)

Haneda, M. (2006). Classrooms as communities of practice: A reevaluation. *TESOL Quarterly*, *40*, 807–817.

Hawkins, M. (2005). Becoming a student: Identity work and academic literacies in early schooling. *TESOL Quarterly*, *39*, 59–82.

Heath, S. B. (1983). *Ways with words: Language, life, and work in communities and classrooms.* Cambridge, UK: Cambridge University Press.

Hobbs, P. (2004). The role of progress notes in the professional socialization of medical residents. *Journal of Pragmatics*, *36*, 1579–1607.

Howard, K. M., & Lo, A. (Eds.). (2009). Mobilizing respect and politeness in classrooms [Special issue]. *Linguistics and Education*, *20*(3).

Howard, K. M. (2008). Language socialization and language shift among school-aged children. In P. A. Duff & N. H. Hornberger (Eds.), *Encyclopedia of language and education: Vol. 8. Language socialization* (pp. 187–199). New York: Springer.

Huang, J. (2004). Socialising ESL students into the discourse of school science through academic writing. *Language and Education*, *18*, 97–123.

Hyland, K. (2004). *Metadiscourse.* London: Continuum.

Hyland, K. (2006). *English for academic purposes.* New York: Routledge.

Hyland, K., & Hyland, F. (Eds.). (2006). *Feedback in second language writing: Contexts and issues.* Cambridge, UK: Cambridge University Press.

Ivanič, R. (1998). *Writing and identity: The discoursal construction of identity in academic writing.* Philadelphia: John Benjamins.

Ivanič, R. (2004). Discourses of writing and learning to write. *Language and Education, 18,* 220–245.

Jacoby, S. (1998). *Science as performance: Socializing scientific discourse through the conference talk rehearsal.* Unpublished doctoral dissertation, University of California, Los Angeles.

Johns, A. (2005). English for academic purposes: Issues in undergraduate reading and writing. In P. Bruthiaux, D. Atkinson, W. Eggington, W. Grabe, & V. Ramanathan (Eds.), *Directions in applied linguistics* (pp. 101–116). Clevedon, UK: Multilingual Matters.

Johns, A., & Snow, M. A. (Eds.). (2006). Academic English in secondary schools [Special issue]. *Journal of English for Academic Purposes, 5*(4).

Kim, J. (2008). *Negotiating multiple investments in languages and identities: The language socialization of Generation 1.5 Korean-Canadian university students.* Unpublished doctoral dissertation, University of British Columbia, Vancouver, British Columbia, Canada.

Kobayashi, M. (2003). The role of peer support in students' accomplishment of oral academic tasks. *Canadian Modern Language Review, 59,* 337–368.

Kobayashi, M. (2004). *A sociocultural study of second language tasks: Activity, agency, and language socialization.* Unpublished doctoral dissertation, University of British Columbia, Vancouver, Canada.

Kobayashi, M. (2006). Second language socialization through an oral project presentation: Japanese university students' experience. In G. H. Beckett & P. C. Miller (Eds.), *Project-based second and foreign language education* (pp. 71–93). Charlotte, NC: Information Age.

Kouritzen, S., Piquemal, N., & Norman, R. (Eds.). (2009). *Qualitative research challenging the orthodoxies in standard academic discourse(s).* New York: Routledge.

Kulick, D., & Schieffelin, B. (2004). Language socialization. In A. Duranti (Ed.), *A companion to linguistic anthropology* (pp. 349–368). Malden, MA: Blackwell.

Kyratzis, A., & Cook-Gumperz, J. (2008). Language socialization and gendered practices in childhood. In P. A. Duff & N. H. Hornberger (Eds.), *Encyclopedia of language and education: Vol. 8. Language socialization* (pp. 145–157). New York: Springer.

Lam, W. S. E. (2008). Language socialization in online communities. In P. A. Duff & N. H. Hornberger (Eds.), *Encyclopedia of language and education: Vol. 8. Language socialization* (pp. 301–311). New York: Springer.

Lave, J., & Wenger, E. (1991). *Situated learning: Legitimate peripheral participation.* New York: Cambridge University Press.

Lea, M., & Street, B. (1998). Student writing in higher education: An academic literacies approach. *Studies in Higher Education, 23,* 157–172.

Leibowitz, B. (2005). Learning in an additional language in a multilingual society: A South African case study on university-level writing. *TESOL Quarterly, 39*, 661–681.

Leki, I. (1995). Coping strategies of ESL students in writing tasks across the curriculum. *TESOL Quarterly, 29*, 235–260.

Leki, I. (2007). *Undergraduates in a second language: Challenges and complexities of academic literacy development.* Mahwah, NJ: Erlbaum.

Leki, I., Cumming, A., & Silva, T. (2008). *A synthesis of research on second language writing in English.* London: Routledge.

Li, Y. (2005). Multidimensional enculturation: The case study of an EFL Chinese doctoral student. *Journal of Asian Pacific Communication, 15*, 153–170.

Li, Y. (2006a). Negotiating knowledge contribution to multiple discourse communities: A doctoral student of computer science writing for publication. *Journal of Second Language Writing, 15*, 159–178.

Li, Y. (2006b). *Writing for international publication: The case of Chinese doctoral science students.* Unpublished doctoral dissertation, City University of Hong Kong.

Li, Y. (2007). Apprentice scholarly writing in a community of practice: An intraview of an NNES graduate student writing a research article. *TESOL Quarterly, 41*, 55–79.

Lillis, T. (2003). Student writing as "academic literacies": Drawing on Bakhtin to move from critique to design. *Language and Education, 17*, 192–207.

Lu, Y., & Nelson, G. (2008). Negotiating on-line postings and publication: Identity construction through writing. In C. Casanave & Y. Li (Eds.), *Learning the literacy practices of graduate school: Insiders reflections on academic enculturation* (pp.150–165). Ann Arbor: University of Michigan Press.

Marriott, H., Moore, T., & Spence-Brown, R. (Eds.). (2007). *Learning discourses and the discourses of learning.* Melbourne, Australia: Monash University e-Press/University of Sydney Press.

Martin, J., & Rose, D. (2007). *Working with discourse: Meaning beyond the clause.* London: Continuum.

Maybin, J. (2003). Voices, intertextuality and induction to schooling. In S. Goodman, T. Lillis, J. Maybin, & N. Mercer (Eds.), *Language, literacy and education: A reader* (pp. 159–170). Stoke on Trent, UK: Trentham Books, Stoke on Trent.

Mehan, H. (1979). *Learning lessons.* Cambridge, MA: Harvard University Press.

Mertz, E. (2007). *The language of law: Learning to think like a lawyer.* Oxford, UK: Oxford University Press.

Molle, D., & Prior, P. (2008). Multimodal genre systems in EAP writing pedagogy: Reflecting on a needs analysis. *TESOL Quarterly, 42*, 541–566.

Moore, L. C. (2008). Language socialization and second/foreign language and multilingual education in non-Western settings. In P. A. Duff & N. H. Hornberger (Eds.), *Encyclopedia of language and education: Vol. 8. Language socialization* (pp. 175–185). New York: Springer.

Morita, N. (2000). Discourse socialization through oral classroom activities in a TESL graduate program. *TESOL Quarterly, 34*, 279–310.

Morita, N. (2002). Negotiating participation in second language academic communities: *A study of identity, agency, and transformation.* Unpublished doctoral dissertation, University of British Columbia, Vancouver, Canada.

Morita, N. (2004). Negotiating participation and identity in second language academic communities. *TESOL Quarterly, 38*, 573–603.

Morita, N. (2009). Language, culture, gender, and academic socialization. *Language and Education, 23*, 443–460.

Morita, N., & Kobayashi, M. (2008). Academic discourse socialization in a second language. In P. A. Duff & N. H. Hornberger (Eds.), *Encyclopedia of language and education: Vol. 8. Language socialization* (pp. 243–256). New York: Springer.

Ochs, E. (1986). Introduction. In B. B. Schieffelin & E. Ochs (Eds.), *Language socialization across cultures* (pp. 1–13). New York: Cambridge University Press.

Ochs, E., & Schieffelin, B. B. (2008). Language socialization: An historical overview. In P. A. Duff & N. H. Hornberger (Eds.), *Encyclopedia of language and education: Vol. 8. Language socialization* (pp. 3–15). New York: Springer.

Ochs, E., & Taylor, C. (1992). Science at dinner. In C. Kramsch & S. McConnell-Ginet (Eds.), *Text and context: Cross-disciplinary perspectives on language study* (pp. 29–45). Lexington, MA: D.C. Heath.

Parks, S. (2001). Moving from school to the workplace: Disciplinary innovation, border crossings, and the reshaping of a written genre. *Applied Linguistics, 22*, 405–438.

Parks, S., & Maguire, M. (1999). Coping with on-the-job writing skills in ESL: A constructivist-semiotic perspectives. *Language Learning, 49*, 143–175.

Pavlenko, A. (2003). The privilege of being an immigrant woman. In C. Casanave & S. Vandrick (Eds.), *Writing for scholarly publication: Behind the scenes in language and multicultural education* (pp. 177–193). Mahwah, NJ: Erlbaum.

Pavlenko, A., & Piller, I. (2008). Language education and gender. In S. May & N. H. Hornberger (Eds.), *Encyclopedia of language and education: Vol. 1. Language policy and political issues in education* (pp. 57–69). New York: Springer.

Pecorari, D. (2008). *Academic writing and plagiarism: A linguistic analysis.* London: Continuum.

Philips, S. U. (1982). The language socialization of lawyers: Acquiring the "cant." In G. Spindler (Ed.), *Doing the ethnography of schooling* (pp. 176–209). New York: Holt, Rinehart, and Winston.

Poole, D. (2008). The messiness of language socialization in reading groups: Participation in and resistance to the values of essayist literacy. *Linguistics and Education, 19*, 378–403.

Potts, D. (2005). Pedagogy, purpose, and the second language learner in on-line communities. *Canadian Modern Language Review, 62*, 137–160.

Prior, P. A. (1998). *Writing/disciplinarity: A sociohistoric account of literate activity in the academy.* Mahwah, NJ: Erlbaum.

Reder, S. & Davila, E. (2007). Context and literacy practices. *Annual Review of Applied Linguistics, 25*, 170–187.

Rogoff, B. (1990). *Apprenticeship in thinking: Cognitive development in social context.* New York: Oxford University Press.

Schieffelin, B. B., & Ochs, E. (Eds.). (1986). *Language socialization across cultures.* Cambridge, UK: Cambridge University Press.

Schleef, E. (2008). Gender and academic discourse: Global restrictions and local possibilities. *Language in Society, 37*, 515–538.

Schleppegrell, M. J. (2004). *The language of schooling: A functional linguistics approach.* Mahwah, NJ: Erlbaum.

Séror, J. (2008). *Socialization in the margins: Second language writers and feedback practices in university content courses.* Unpublished doctoral dissertation, University of British Columbia, Vancouver, Canada.

Shi, L. (2002). How Western-trained Chinese TESOL professionals publish in their home environment. *TESOL Quarterly, 36*, 625–634.

Shi, L. (2003). Writing in two cultures: Chinese professors return from the West. *Canadian Modern Language Review, 59*, 369–391.

Shi, L. (2004). Textual borrowing in second language writing. *Written Communication, 21*, 171–200.

Shi, L. (2010). Textual appropriation and citing behaviors of university undergraduates. *Applied Linguistics, 31*, 1–24.

Spack, R. (1997). The acquisition of academic literacy in a second language: A longitudinal case study. *Written Communication, 14*, 3–62.

Sterponi, L. (Ed.). (2008). The spirit of reading. Practices of reading sacred texts [Special issue]. *Text and Talk, 28*(5).

Starfield, S. (2002). "I'm a second-language English speaker": Negotiating writer identity and authority in Sociology One. *Journal of Language, Identity, and Education, 1*, 121–140.

Starfield, S., & Ravelli, L. J. (2006). "The writing of this thesis was a process that I could not explore with the positivistic detachment of the classical sociologist": Self and structure in the *New Humanities* research theses. *Journal of English for Academic Purposes, 5*, 222–243.

Talmy, S. (2008). The cultural productions of ESL student at Tradewinds High: Contingency, multidirectionality, and identity in L2 socialization. *Applied Linguistics, 29*, 619–644.

Talmy, S. (2009). A very important lesson: Respect and the socialization of order(s) in high school ESL. *Linguistics and Education, 20*, 235–253.

Toohey, K. (1998). "Breaking them up, taking them away" : Constructing ESL students in grade one. *TESOL Quarterly, 32*, 61–84.

Tracy, K. (1997). *Colloquium: Dilemmas of academic discourse.* Norwood, NJ: Ablex.

Vickers, C. (2007). Second language socialization through team interaction among electrical and computer engineering students. *Modern Language Journal, 91*, 621–640.

Viechnicki, G. B., & Kuipers, J. (Eds.). (2008). Objectification and the inscription of knowledge in science classrooms. *Linguistics and Education, 19*, 203–318.

Warschauer, M. (2002). Networking into academic discourse. *Journal of English for Academic Purposes 1*, 45–58.

Yim, Y. K. (2005). *Second language speakers' participation in computer-mediated discussions in graduate seminars.* Unpublished doctoral dissertation, University of British Columbia, Vancouver, Canada.

Zappa-Hollman, S. (2007a). Becoming socialized into diverse academic communities through oral presentations. *Canadian Modern Language Review, 63*, 455–485.

Zappa-Hollman, S. (2007b). *The academic literacy socialization of Mexican exchange students at a Canadian university.* Unpublished doctoral dissertation, University of British Columbia, Vancouver, Canada.

Zuengler, J., & Cole, K. M. (2005). Language socialization and L2 learning. In E. Hinkel (Ed.), *Handbook of research in second language teaching and learning* (pp. 301–316). Mahwah, N.J.: Erlbaum.

Zuengler, J., & Miller, E. (2008). Apprenticing into a community: Challenges of the Asthma Project. In K. M. Cole & J. Zuengler (Eds.), *The research process in classroom discourse: Current perspectives* (pp. 129–148). New York: Erlbaum/Taylor & Francis.

Becoming National: Classroom Language Socialization and Political Identities in the Age of Globalization

Debra A. Friedman

Although schools have long been recognized as primary sites for creating citizens of the modern nation-state, in recent years traditional assimilationist and exclusionist notions of national identity have been challenged by competing values of multiculturalism, hybridity, and transnationalism. This article surveys recent language socialization research that has examined classrooms as sites for socializing novices into political identities associated with membership in a national or transnational community. It explores five broad themes: (a) socialization into the national language, (b) socialization of immigrants, (c) socialization into new forms of national identity, (d) socialization of minority political identities within nation-states, and (e) socialization and transnational identities. The survey concludes with a review of the contributions of a language socialization approach to the study of these issues as well as suggested directions for future research.

Scholars of nationalism have long considered universal education and the spread of literacy as primary mechanisms for cultural and linguistic homogenization, thus creating the social conditions that make it possible for individuals to identify themselves as members of the *imagined community* (Anderson, 1991, p. 6) of the nation (e.g., Gellner, 1983; Weber, 1976). Public education has also been identified as a crucial site for acculturating new immigrants (e.g. Olneck, 2004) and instilling democratic values (e.g., Dewey, 1916/1966; Levinson, 2005), and popular recognition of the role of education in legitimating cultural identity and developing national consciousness has sometimes turned schools into sites of struggle among competing ethnolinguistic and national groups (e.g., Langman, 2002).

However, in recent years traditional assimilationist models of civic education have been challenged by the competing values of multiculturalism, while social forces such as transborder labor migration, globalization, and mass communication have blurred the boundaries between nations and national cultures, thus highlighting the limitations of the exclusionary or essentialist conceptualizations of national identity often promoted by schooling (e.g., Mitchell, 2001). Drawing from a corpus of studies appearing over the last 10 years, this survey will review the contributions of a language socialization approach to understandings of the role of schooling in the formation and transformation of national political identities in the age of globalization. It will explore five broad and sometimes overlapping themes: (a) socialization into the national language, (b) socialization of immigrants, (c) socialization into new forms of national identity, (d) socialization of minority political identities within nation-states, and (e) socialization and transnational identities. The survey will conclude with a review of the strengths of a language socialization approach to the study of these issues as well as suggested directions for future research.

METHODOLOGICAL ISSUES

Language Socialization and Political Identities

Language socialization research is concerned with the process through which individuals become "culturally intelligible subjects" (Kulick & Schieffelin, 2004, p. 351); that is, how they acquire the ways of speaking, acting, and being in the world that are recognized as legitimate within a community (or communities) of practice. Part of this process involves developing an awareness of the range of subject positions (i.e., identities) that one is expected or allowed to take up and how these are performed in the course of everyday interaction. As novices interact with other community members in various activities, they are socialized into the social acts (i.e., socially recognized goal-directed verbal behavior) and stances (i.e., a verbal display of a socially recognized perspective or attitude) that are conventionally associated with particular social identities within the community and into the language ideologies that imbue these acts and stances with social meaning (Ochs,

1992, 1993, 1996, 2002). They in turn may use these acts, stances, and ideologies as resources for enacting their own roles, relationships, and group memberships and for interpreting and categorizing the actions of others.

The studies to be reviewed here examine schools as sites for socialization into the language behaviors and language ideologies associated with membership in the imagined community called *the nation* or its political manifestation, the *nation-state*. For social scientists, the term *nation* refers to a form of social organization whose precise definition remains elusive, but which is generally understood to be a community based on a (supposedly) shared language and culture (e.g., Anderson, 1991, Gellner, 1983). While sometimes overlapping with ethnic affiliation, *national identity* is generally distinguished from *ethnic* or *cultural identity* in that it is associated with claims for political autonomy or independence.[1] A variety of terms have been used to refer to this form of identification, reflecting the various ways in which the relationship between individuals and national communities may be constructed. For example, *national identity* carries with it assumptions of a deeply felt, internalized identification with the nation, while the more legalistic *citizenship* signifies a set of rights and obligations conferred through community membership. For purposes of this review, the term *political identity* will be employed to encompass a range of such relationships as well as alternative forms of political identification, such as *transnationalism*, which reference membership in multiple national communities.

Setting the Parameters

A primary characteristic of language socialization research is its focus on everyday language use as the central locus for cultural production, reproduction, and transformation. Its aim is not simply to describe the practices of a particular community (as is the case with ethnography more generally), but to trace the processes through which novices become competent in these practices and are accepted as members (or, conversely, how they fail to become competent and are not accepted as members). This emphasis on developmental processes does not limit language socialization research to its traditional focus on young children; the approach has always emphasized that socialization occurs across the life span (e.g., Schieffelin & Ochs, 1986) and has been productively applied to examine the experiences of adolescents and adults who are entering new or evolving communities of practice (see Garrett & Baquedano-López, 2002). Nor does it presume an unproblematic transmission of cultural knowledge from expert to novice, but it considers socialization as something achieved (or resisted) through negotiation in the context of everyday interaction (Kulick & Schieffelin, 2004; Ochs, 1988; Schieffelin, 1990).

The question of what constitutes a language socialization study has engendered considerable discussion in recent years as the approach has expanded beyond its origins and been taken up by researchers in a variety of disciplines (e.g., Baquedano-López & Kattan, 2007; Bayley & Schecter, 2003; Garrett, 2006; Kulick & Schieffelin, 2004). According to Kulick and Schieffelin, a language socialization study must be ethnographic and longitudinal, and it must "demonstrate the acquisition (or not) of particular linguistic and cultural practices over time and across contexts" (p. 350). Garrett proposed that language socialization research (a) be longitudinal and ethnographic, (b) incorporate analysis of audio or video recorded interaction, and (c) attend to both macro- and micro-levels of analysis. He further argued that it is not possible to ignore one or more of these areas and still be counted as language socialization research. However, as Baquedano-López and Kattan have noted, the term *language socialization* may be used to refer not only to a theoretical and methodological approach but also to a research focus; that is, a study that examines the role of language in the process of socialization may be called a language socialization study even though it may not necessarily adhere to the methodology just delineated.

For purposes of this survey, a language socialization study will be understood to be one that (a) focuses on the process of becoming national as opposed to the practices of being national, (b) incorporates analysis of the language use and language ideologies of everyday classroom practices as they relate to this process, and (c) situates classroom practices within a larger sociopolitical context. While the majority of studies to be reviewed here explicitly evoke language socialization as the operating theoretical framework, the survey will also take selective note of other relevant ethnographic research that is broadly consistent with the aims of the approach.

LANGUAGE AND NATION: SOCIALIZATION INTO THE NATIONAL LANGUAGE

Among the behaviors deemed to constitute identities as members of a national community, speaking the national language (or languages)[2] is arguably the most powerful, such that failure to do so may call into question an individual's political loyalties or rights to community membership (e.g., Woolard & Schieffelin, 1994, p. 61). The past decade has seen an increasing number of language socialization studies conducted in multilingual settings in which the national language differs from what is spoken in the local community, a number of which have examined how children are socialized into speaking the national language in school (Augsburger, 2004; Fellin, 2001; Howard, 2003, 2004, 2009; Moore, 2004, 2006; Paugh, 2001, 2005). While formation of political identities has not been the primary focus of this research, it has nevertheless revealed the complex and often subtle ways that school language practices contribute to the construction of associations linking different languages and language varieties to various social identities, values, and group memberships, with consequences for patterns of civic or cultural identification.

Howard's (2003, 2004, 2009) research in a village in northern Thailand examined how children were being socialized into showing respect across the contexts of home, Buddhist temple, and school. In the school setting, Howard found that showing respect was represented as an essential feature of being Thai, a form of national identification encompassing the range of diverse cultural, ethnic, and linguistic groups that constitute modern Thailand. She further showed how kindergartners were being socialized into displaying respect in the classroom through the medium of the national language, Standard Thai, which since the late 19th century has served as an emblem of a unified Thai national identity, rather than in the local vernacular Kam Muang. For example, although children were free to speak Kam Muang in class (on the assumption that they were "not yet ready to receive" [Howard, 2003, p. 327] Standard Thai), teachers insisted on use of Standard Thai politeness particles to show respect to teachers during certain classroom activities. Howard concluded that through such practices children were not only being socialized into appropriate forms of showing respect but also into language ideologies positioning Standard Thai as the language through which identities as Thai citizens were to be performed.

In her study of language socialization in Q'uranic and public schools in Cameroon, Moore (2004, 2006) compared how rote learning practices, or *guided repetition*, served different socialization goals in these two settings. In Cameroon, public education has been charged with the goal of fostering a Cameroonian identity and a modern understanding of the world in opposition to so-called traditional or tribal forms of identification. Part of this process involves socializing children into speaking the national language, French, and the primary focus of education in the primary grades is to develop basic competence in the language by having the children listen to, memorize, and perform scripted role plays. However, Moore noted that the guided repetition routines that she observed in French language classrooms served other social goals as well by, for example, providing models of appropriate language behavior and encouraging children to identify with the French-speaking Cameroonians portrayed in the role plays. Through participation in these guided repetition routines, children took on the ways of speaking and acting that were congruent with idealized identities as members of the Cameroonian nation-state.

Paugh's (2001, 2005) research in Dominica describes how Patwa, a once-disdained French-based creole spoken in rural areas, has been seized upon by some intellectuals as a symbol of the nation's distinct cultural identity and become the focus of revitalization efforts. Nevertheless, the official national language (and the language of education, business, and the urban elite) is English. Paugh's analysis of classroom languages practices demonstrated how children's use of Patwa was corrected to English and an English-only policy remained in force, with the exception of Creole Day, when everyone was supposed to speak the vernacular as part of an islandwide cultural celebration. Paugh concluded that such practices were reinforcing language ideologies through which English had come to index membership in the national (and international) community beyond the village as well as desirable social values such as modernity and progress, thus contributing to an ongoing process of language shift to English. On the other hand, attempts to revalue Patwa and to position it as an emblem of an imagined Dominican identity were largely rejected by villagers, who associated the language with a purely local (and often stigmatized) identity. This dichotomy was also reflected in children's code choices during pretend play (Paugh, 2005), as children enacted roles such as schoolteacher in English, while switching to Patwa for roles such as farmer.

SOCIALIZATION OF IMMIGRANTS

Socialization of New Citizens

While the discourses of multiculturalism have largely replaced the melting pot metaphor in the rhetoric surrounding education of immigrants, recent ethnographic research has revealed that ideologies of assimilation still hold sway in many classrooms. For example, in their critical ethnography of an elementary school coping with a recent influx of Spanish-speaking immigrant children, Garza and Crawford (2005) explored the "contradictory missions of affirming diversity and promoting assimilation" (p. 600) that arose as the school sought to maintain high standardized test scores by bringing immigrant children up to grade-level performance standards as quickly as possible. Integrating classroom observations and interviews with teachers and school administrators, the authors argued that despite the school's stated intent to honor cultural diversity, school policies and classroom practices effectively marginalized Spanish-speaking children and defined academic success and community membership in terms of English language proficiency, thus promoting an agenda of linguistic assimilation. They further argued that through these practices, immigrant children were socialized into an ideology of *hegemonic multiculturalism*, defined as the appropriation of the rhetoric of multiculturalism to obscure an underlying assimilationist agenda.

Resnik, Sabar, and Shapira (2001) explored similar issues in Israel, another country where ideologies of assimilation (or what Israelis call *klitat aliyah*, "absorption of immigrants") have long dominated. In this multiple case study of fourth- to eighth-grade immigrants from the former Soviet Union, the authors identified a tension between two models of absorption: the assimilationist model, in which immigrants were expected to exchange their former cultural practices and political identification for Israeli ones, and the integration model, which allowed for a multicultural society and sought to gradually adapt newcomers to local cultural practices without the expectation that they would completely abandon their cultural identities. Similar to Garza and Crawford (2005), Resnik et al. found that teachers' stated support for an integration model contrasted with school and classroom practices that ignored the immigrants' Russian cultural backgrounds and sought to socialize them into Israeli norms. However, they also found that the immigrant students resisted this assimilation, in part because they viewed Russian culture as equal to or, in some cases, superior to that of Israel. This situation led to what the authors called a *semipermeable enclave model* of absorption in which immigrant students acquired sufficient language and social skills to function in Israeli society yet remained culturally isolated.

A closely related study is Golden's (2001) ethnographic research in an *ulpan* (Hebrew class) for adult immigrants to Israel from the former Soviet Union. While Golden's stated focus is on what the socialization process reveals about Israeli concepts of national identity rather than on the outcomes of this process, her analysis of teacher-student interactions provided a thought-provoking depiction of a second language classroom as a site for acculturation. Golden's major claim is that classroom practices treated the students (well-educated adults) like children, reflecting assumptions that newcomers to Israel should be emptied of their past memories and experiences and reborn into new identities. In addition, while the teacher repeatedly emphasized that students, as members of a democratic society, had the freedom to express their own opinions, on certain political or cultural matters they were expected to speak as Israelis and to adopt an appropriate Israeli perspective. Students, however, were resistant to this all-encompassing ethnonational view of Israeli citizenship; while acknowledging proficiency in Hebrew as necessary for full participation in Israeli society, they claimed the right to remain culturally Russian.

Also worthy of note is Griswold's (2007) recent dissertation research examining language socialization in a citizenship class in southern California. Although language instruction was not an official component of the class, Griswold found that the teacher frequently, albeit selectively, corrected students' linguistic errors. Her detailed analysis of classroom correction routines demonstrated how students were being socialized into an understanding of the centrality of English language competence in performing an identity as a (potential) American citizen and into using the language to demonstrate knowledge of American history and government in ways congruent with community practices (e.g., describing the colors of the flag as "red, white, and blue" rather than "blue, red, and white"). However, in line with the stated mission of the class to prepare students for their upcoming naturalization interviews, the definition of citizenship being coconstructed through these interactions reflected the very narrow concerns of the naturalization test (see Kunan, 2009). That is, rather than socializing students into the acts and stances associated with being American citizens, the class was socializing them into the acts and stances associated with being successful applicants for American citizenship.

Socialization into Immigrant Identities in the Classroom

Another issue that has emerged in several recent second language socialization studies concerns how immigrant students are identified in the classroom and how they take up or contest these ascribed identities (Duff, 2002; García Sánchez, 2009; Harklau, 2000, 2003; Talmy, 2008, 2009a, 2009b). A common finding of this work is that rather than socializing students into membership in a national community, classroom practices may deny them such membership by identifying them as outsiders, thus socializing both immigrant students and their local classmates into exclusionary notions of national identity.

Duff's (2002) study in a high school social studies class in Canada illustrates the challenges and contradictions inherent in attempts to balance two competing values: respect for cultural diversity and inclusion. In an effort to socialize her immigrant students into participation in the valued classroom discourse practice of whole-class discussions, the teacher frequently called on them to speak as representatives of what was characterized as "their culture" and to provide an alternative to the Canadian perspectives of other students. The minimal answers (or silence) given in response to these elicitations were interpreted as evidence of these students' resistance to these ascribed identities as others as well as a reluctance to further mark their difference through their nonnative English. Yet their silence also isolated and stigmatized them in the eyes of the other students. Duff concluded that through these practices teacher and students were co-constructing difference that worked against achievement of a classroom environment of respect and inclusion.

Both Harklau (2000, 2003) and Talmy (2008, 2009a, 2009b) have examined how identities as English as a second language (ESL) students were constructed within classrooms and how these identities positioned students relative to local and national communities. Harklau's ethnographic case study following the progress of four immigrant students in the United States as they transitioned from high school to community college focused on the contrasting *representations*—defined as "the images, archetypes, or even stereotypes of identity" (2000, p. 37)—assigned to these students in these two settings. In high school, they were what Harklau (2003, p. 87) referred to as "Ellis Island immigrants", hardworking strivers who overcame challenges to succeed in America. This representation, which recognized them as members (albeit peripheral members) of the national community and gave them a place in a traditional American national story, was readily taken up and performed by the students through practices such as writing inspirational essays on their immigration experience. However, these same students resisted the representations imposed upon them in community college ESL classes, where they were included among an undifferentiated group of international students who required socialization into American cultural and academic practices (despite the fact that the immigrant students were long-term residents with considerable cultural knowledge) and who were expected to write about "their" cultures (about which they had few memories and limited experience). These essentializing representations positioned these students as foreigners and denied the heterogeneity of their experiences and their own self-identification as legitimate members of the American community in which they had spent much of their lives.

Talmy's research in a high school ESL class in Hawai'i (2008, 2009a, 2009b) similarly described the resistance of those whom he called *oldtimer students* (i.e., long-term residents) to the stigmatized ESL identity assigned to them by the school that represented them as newly arrived Others who were culturally and linguistically deficient. However, in this case resistance took the form of construction of an alternative form of identification that Talmy labeled *Local ESL*, which was framed around the cultural and social practices of an established Local community in Hawai'i made up of Hawai'ian-born Asians and Pacific Islanders. Through a variety of practices, including not doing homework, disengaging from class activities, and speaking Hawai'i Pidgin rather than Standard English, these students disaffiliated themselves from both the school-sanctioned *good ESL student* identity and the newcomer ESL students and instead claimed full membership in a locally defined community of practice. At the same time, however, Talmy noted that by ensuring poor academic outcomes, these same practices served to keep these students in the very ESL classes they disdained.

García Sánchez (2009) took up this issue from a European perspective in her dissertation on language socialization of Moroccan immigrant children in Spain. The integration of Moroccan immigrants into Spanish society has been complicated by perceptions that they are both a threat to Spanish identity (e.g., they are non-Christians with radically different cultural practices) and to national security (through associations with the terrorist bombings in Madrid in 2004 as well as historical associations with the Moors who once controlled Spanish territory). García Sánchez's observations in a middle school classroom revealed how these negative perceptions impacted classroom interaction even in a school environment in which tolerance and inclusion were promoted and racial slurs and harassment were punished. For example, local Spanish children frequently singled out the Moroccan immigrant children as targets for tattletaling (*accusar*) and directives that characterized their behavior as outside the norms of acceptability, a characterization with which other local students as well as teachers often aligned. Moreover, school practices meant to be inclusive, such as Interculturality Day, emphasized differences rather than commonalities and implied that culture was something exotic and alien that only minority children had. García Sánchez concluded that by highlighting the ways in which Moroccan students failed to conform to expected Spanish cultural norms and behaviors, these practices were socializing Moroccan students into marginalized identities as others.

REIMAGINING THE NATION: SOCIALIZATION INTO NEW FORMS OF NATIONAL IDENTITY

Alterations in the political landscape brought about by events such as the collapse of the Soviet Union or shifting patterns of immigration can lead to changes in the composition of a national community and in how membership in that community is defined. Two recent language socialization studies conducted in post-Cold War Europe have examined the evolving conceptualizations of national identity being constructed in high school history classes in postunification Berlin (Vogel, 2008, Vogel-Langer, 2008) and fifth-grade language and literature classrooms in Ukraine (Friedman, 2006, 2010).

One of the major findings of Vogel-Langer's (2008) study was the fact that an ostensibly new unified German national identity was in fact grounded in the practices and ideologies of the politically dominant group, the former West Germans. For example, in classrooms in the former East Berlin, routines such as greeting sequences, which in the preunification period had been characterized by a high degree of formality and strict teacher control, had been relaxed or had disappeared altogether in accordance with the classroom norms and democratic values associated with the former West Germany. Students were also increasingly likely to associate a unified German identity with speaking Standard German in accordance with dominant West German language ideologies, while the local Berlin dialect had come to index an undesirable East German identity. Interestingly, however, Vogel-Langer found that these shifts in orientation were primarily driven by students, not teachers. East German teachers did not problematize or correct students' use of Berlin dialect in class, and the teachers sometimes used it themselves. Moreover, while East German teachers occasionally attempted to make relevant students' identities as East Germans through pronoun usage linking them to a supposedly shared East German past, students tended to resist such identification (Vogel, 2008). Similar to the situation described by Duff (1995, 1996) in her language socialization study of English immersion high school classrooms in postcommunist Hungary, teachers and students in these Berlin classrooms were engaged in a process of bidirectional socialization (Ochs, 1988) that inverted the expected expert-novice relationship, a phenomenon that may be characteristic of societies in the midst of rapid political and social transformation.

A similar process of national reimagining is occurring in Ukraine (Friedman, 2006, 2010), where the term *Ukrainian*, which once referred to an ethnic category with membership determined by descent, is being redefined as a civic category based on citizenship, encompassing all of the country's multiethnic and multilingual population. Nevertheless, the definition of Ukrainian being co-constructed in the classroom drew heavily upon traditional emblems of Ukrainian ethnolinguistic identity, in particular, the Ukrainian language, which has long been subordinate to Russian. In addition to teaching the mechanics of good grammar and spelling, teachers in the two classrooms engaged students in a variety of activities designed to socialize them into language ideologies that positioned Ukrainian as a pure and beautiful language and part of the children's linguistic and cultural heritage, even though not all of them were ethnic Ukrainians or spoke the language at home. Of particular significance were error correction routines that targeted children's mixing of Ukrainian and Russian, a common practice among Ukrainian-Russian bilinguals that is nevertheless widely condemned as a relic of past linguistic oppression and an impediment to establishment of Ukrainian as a national language distinct from Russian (Friedman, 2010). In addition, through activities such as recitation of poetry or whole-class discussions about what makes language beautiful, teachers encouraged children to evaluate language and language usage based on aesthetic criteria. Through their participation in such activities and routines, children were socialized into the ways of speaking and valuing language in ways congruent with dominant Ukrainian language ideologies and into speaking the language correctly and beautifully as a sign of pride in their language and nation.

Outside of a European context, Sandel (2003) used interviews with three generations of Taiwanese to explore the impact of evolving notions of language and national identity on school and home language socialization practices in Taiwan. In the past, government policy had strictly prohibited use of any language other than the national language (Mandarin Chinese) in schools as part of its promotion of a Chinese national identity, leading to large-scale language shift away from local vernaculars such as Tai-gi (Taiwanese) and Hakka. However, the growing political power of the local Taiwanese population (i.e., residents other than those descended from post-1949 immigrants from Mainland China), resulted in a revaluation of these vernaculars and to school policies promoting Mandarin-vernacular bilingualism in the 1990s. Sandel's analysis suggested that these macro-level shifts were accompanied by a growing tendency among his respondents to promote their children's proficiency in the vernacular through home socialization practices, as well as a trend toward assertion of a distinct Taiwanese identity indexed through that vernacular. While the study's reliance on interviews rather than actual observations or recordings of caregiver–child interaction somewhat limits the claims it can make regarding the ultimate effect of school language policies on home socialization practices, it nevertheless offers an intriguing glimpse of the interconnections between changing attitudes toward use of local vernaculars in schools and the emergence of alternative forms of political identification.

Another country in which definitions of citizenship are being redefined is Australia, where an influx of immigrants from Asia over the past two decades is challenging traditional exclusionist notions of national identity that limited the designation Australian to *descendents* of white Europeans. Lotherington (2003) examined this process through an analysis of the multiple literacy practices of immigrant high school students from Southeast Asia whose school had recently instituted courses in Khmer and Vietnamese literacy. Although such classes might be seen as legitimating non-English languages within the educational system and promoting a more multicultural vision of Australia, Lotherington found that the school still defined literacy as English language literacy, with literacy in other languages positioned as an optional extra; that is, multicultural competence had not yet been incorporated into core understandings of what it means to be Australian. While these results are intriguing, the published study lacks the detailed analysis of literacy-focused interactions in either the school or the community that would clarify how such practices were socializing students into identification as members or outsiders in the Australian national community.

NATIONS WITHIN NATIONS: SOCIALIZATION OF MINORITY POLITICAL IDENTITIES WITHIN THE NATION-STATE

While the belief that political units are ideally linguistically and culturally homogeneous remains widespread (e.g., Blommaert & Verschueren, 1998), the presence of ethnolinguistically defined nations within larger nation-states is a common phenomenon, especially in Europe. In settings in which control of the educational system has been decentralized, it becomes possible for locally controlled minority language schools or other institutions to promote a sense of ethnonational identification alongside, or in opposition to, identification with the nation-state.

Jaffe's (1993, 1996, 1999, 2003) long-term ethnographic research on Corsica has provided much insight into how the language ideologies of nationalist political movements can shape everyday language use and language attitudes. Her microlevel analysis of literacy instruction in a bilingual (Corsican-French) classroom (2003) described a situation in which a desire to impart Corsican language literacy skills existed alongside a desire to promote the language as an emblem of cultural and national identity. However, due to language shift, few of the children in this classroom had a high level of Corsican language proficiency, a fact that the teacher wanted to avoid calling attention to, as it would call into question the children's right to claim a linguistically defined Corsican identity. The resulting Corsican literacy practices, which included collaborative construction of texts (an activity dominated by a few linguistically proficient students) and recall and recitation of previously constructed texts, as well as the teacher's use of the first person plural (e.g., what "we" wrote) allowed for varied levels of student participation and transferred "symbolic ownership and competence" (p. 218) of the text and the language to all of the children, thus allowing (and encouraging) them to identify as

Corsican.

In a study conducted in high schools in the Basque country of Spain, Echeverria (2003) explored the dichotomy between ideologies of language and national identity promoted through Basque-medium schooling and more nuanced forms of identification expressed by students. Drawing primarily on analysis of textbooks along with a limited consideration of classroom talk, Echeverria found that teachers were attempting to socialize students into ideologies that associated Basque identity with speaking Basque. However, interviews with students revealed alternative ways of conceptualizing a Basque identity, such as being born in the Basque country, as well as claims of a hybrid Basque-Spanish identity. These results raise important questions about making direct connections between the goals and outcomes of school socialization, although further analysis of classroom interactions, in particular, the implicit (as well as explicit) ways that teachers used classroom practices to link Basque identity to speaking Basque and students' responses to such linkages, would be informative.

LANGUAGE SOCIALIZATION INTO TRANSNATIONAL IDENTITIES

As evidenced from this survey, educational institutions have tended to presume that the community into which newcomers are to be socialized coincides with the boundaries of a nation or nation-state. However, the increasing flow of people, commodities, and ideas across national borders that has characterized recent history has been accompanied by a shift in focus among social scientists from conventional notions of a territorially defined community of shared cultural norms to the study of borderlands and transnationalism. While the term *borderlands* originally referred to the territory on either side of the Mexican-U.S. border and the social practices and forms of cultural and political identification that metaphorically crossed this border, more recently it has also been used to refer to other border areas of the world (Alvarez, 1995). The related concept of *transnationalism* refers to "processes that are anchored in and transcend one or more nation-states" (Kearney, 1995, p. 548). The essence of both concepts is the assumption that the boundaries of community may extend across national borders and that these communities may partake of multiple cultural and linguistic practices.

What distinguishes research on borderlands and transnationalism from that on heritage language or cultural maintenance within immigrant communities (see He, this issue) is not so much the phenomenon being studied as the analytical lens through which it is being viewed. In other words, rather than asking how immigrant children are socialized into a cultural identity as (for example) Mexican, research on borderlands or transnationalism seeks to understand how supposedly bounded and discrete national identities are blended and transformed into new forms of identification. With this in mind, the survey that follows will be limited to those studies in which the concept of borderlands or transnationalism has been explicitly evoked by the researcher as an analytical framework.

For the most part, language socialization research in the borderlands has focused on settings outside of public education, although it has implications for understandings of identity as they are formulated within classrooms. The most extensive studies thus far are González's (2001) thoughtful account focusing on Mexican-origin mothers and children in Tucson and Schecter and Bayley's (2002) multiple case study of Mexican-descent families in California and Texas. While both studies focused primarily on caregiver-child socialization in the home and its effect on language and cultural identity maintenance, González also drew connections and contrasts between the multilayered forms of identification being socialized through these home interactional practices and the bounded and discrete American and Mexican identities that characterized schooling on both sides of the border. In particular, she proposed that home language practices, such as use of both English and Spanish and the adoption of school discursive practices during homework sessions, aimed to socialize children into a transformed Mexican identity that honored and preserved the children's cultural roots while at the same time incorporating certain practices of the dominant American society in which they lived.

Baquedano-López's (2001) study of language socialization and transnational identities examined narrative practices during *doctrina* (catechism) classes in a Catholic parish in Los Angeles with a large number of Mexican immigrants. Her analysis focused on the process through which the teacher and students collaboratively retold a version of the narrative of *Nuestra Señora de Guadalupe*, which tells the story of a Mexican Indian peasant who had a vision of the Virgin Mary in 1531. Using a variety of strategies, such as highlighting the children's

Mexican origins and describing the Virgin as being "a little dark (*morenita*) like us" (p. 353), the teacher engaged the children in co-constructing an inclusive community of Mexicans that transcended both time and space and linked the children's current lived experience as immigrants in Los Angeles to a long-ago event in Mexico.

The Internet has also been proposed as site for both the maintenance of ethnic, national, and linguistic identities by diasporic communities across national borders as well as the creation of new forms of transnational identification (see Lam, 2008). Lam's work on second language socialization and identity formation in virtual communities (2003, 2004) has been at the forefront of language socialization research in this area. Her case study of second language and literacy socialization of two Chinese immigrant teenage girls (2004) contrasted the practices in which these girls participated during school ESL classes with those in a bilingual Chinese-English chatroom based in Hong Kong that both girls frequented. Participation in this online community, whose members were primarily Chinese emigrants in a variety of countries along with bilingual Hong Kong Chinese, required proficiency in hybrid language practices involving code switching between Cantonese-influenced English and romanized Cantonese (i.e., Cantonese written in Latin letters). Lam argued that participation in these hybrid language practices was socializing the girls into identities as "bilingual Chinese emigrants" (p. 59) distinct from both English-speaking (Chinese) Americans and Cantonese-speaking Chinese and was providing alternative identities as English speakers that challenged the native-speaker models promoted through the school.

CONCLUSION

The language socialization research surveyed here is part of a growing body of ethnographic work that has enriched understandings of the role of everyday classroom practices in large-scale political projects such as acculturation and nation building. The findings that have emerged thus far have challenged assumptions of a simple or straightforward process of school-directed identity formation and revealed the complexities and contradictions inherent in this process.

One finding that has emerged across multiple studies is a dichotomy between discourses of inclusion and diversity that have become the norm in education and the explicit and implicit messages being conveyed through everyday classroom interaction. The persistence of narrow, exclusionary definitions of national community surface in the way that various languages or cultural practices are positioned in the classroom and belie claims that new multicultural visions of the nation are replacing the traditional homogeneous ideal. Indeed, as many of these studies have shown, the very celebration of multiculturalism may work against inclusion of newcomers who are perceived as occupying racial or cultural categories that are incompatible with a nation's vision of itself and how national membership is conceived. In this regard it is worth remembering a core principle of school language socialization studies that classrooms do not exist in a vacuum, but are situated within a web of cultural, social, and ideological beliefs and practices that shape both classroom routines and the way that these routines are interpreted. By contextualizing classroom interaction within an environment shaped by multiple local and national political and social forces, these language socialization studies have provided insight into how such forces affect patterns of classroom socialization and how these patterns may in turn affect how individual students are identified and come to identity themselves within a national (or transnational) community.

At the same time, however, this work has also confirmed the observation that the ideal of the nation as culturally and linguistically homogeneous is at odds with the multiplicity of cultural and linguistic practices actually employed by the people within its borders (e.g., Blommaert & Verschueren, 1998). In particular, these studies have documented many instances of student resistance to essentialized or exclusionary models of political identity as well as the emergence and assertion of alternative forms of political identification, such as separate cultural identities within the nation-state or transnational identities. In so doing, they have highlighted the importance of students' agency in their own socialization and the potential for language socialization to be a mechanism for social transformation as well as social reproduction (Garrett & Baquedano-López, 2002), even as they have shown the limits of such agency in engendering social or education change (e.g., Talmy, 2008, 2009a, 2009b).

Nevertheless, language socialization research focusing on the formation of political identities has thus far been fairly limited, leaving much scope for future work. For example, although there is a growing body of research on second language socialization of immigrant students (e.g., see Watson-Gegeo, 2004; Zuengler &

Cole, 2005), little of this work has directly taken up the issue of how language classrooms are socializing newcomers into the ideologies and subjectivities associated with speaking the national language. In addition, given that mid- to late childhood has been identified as a crucial period for identity formation (e.g., Kroger, 2004), the growing number of studies on the socialization of older children and adolescents (many of which have been reviewed here) represents a promising trend in language socialization research that should be further developed. Finally, more attention needs to be paid to Kulick and Schieffelin's dictum (cited at the beginning of this article) that language socialization studies should "demonstrate the acquisition (or not) of particular linguistic and cultural practices over time and across contexts" (2004, p. 350). A shortcoming of many of these studies is that, while providing a rich description of classroom interaction and its potential as a context for socialization, they often fail to provide sufficient evidence regarding how (or whether) the language learning, language ideologies, or political identities being promoted in the classroom are taken up, rejected, or modified by students. Although most of the studies reviewed here were longitudinal, there is a need for longer-term or follow-up research to investigate students' performance of political identities over time and across contexts both inside and outside of the classroom. By drawing upon its methodological strengths, the language socialization approach has the potential to make a major contribution to the study of classrooms as sites for the construction of both belonging and difference within national communities.

NOTES

1 See, for example, Anderson's (1991) definition of the nation as "an imagined *political* community—and imagined as both inherently limited and *sovereign*" (p. 6, my italics).

2 By *national language* I refer here to languages that either through official decree (e.g., French in Cameroon) or by convention (English in the United States) are thought to represent the nation, regardless of how widely those languages are actually spoken within the national community.

REFERENCES

Alvarez, R. R., Jr. (1995). The Mexican-US border: The making of an anthropology of borderlands. *Annual Review of Anthropology*, *24*, 447–470.

Anderson, B. R. (1991). *Imagined communities: Reflections on the origin and spread of nationalism* (2nd ed.). London: Verso.

Augsburger, D. (2004). *Language socialization and shift in an isthmus Zapotec community of Mexico.* Unpublished doctoral dissertation, University of Pennsylvania.

Baquedano-López, P. (2001). Creating social identities through *doctrina* narratives. In A. Duranti (Ed.), *Linguistic anthropology: A reader* (pp. 343–358). Malden, MA: Blackwell.

Baquedano-López, P., & Kattan, S. (2007). Growing up in a multilingual community: Insights from language socialization. In P. Auer & L. Wei (Eds.), *Handbook of multilingualism and multilingual communication* (pp. 59–100). Berlin, Germany: Mouton de Gruyter.

Bayley, R., & Schecter, S. (Eds.). (2003). *Language socialization in bilingual and multilingual societies.* Clevedon, UK: Multilingual Matters.

Blommaert, J., & Verschueren, J. (1998). The role of language in European nationalist ideologies. In B. B. Schieffelin, K. A. Woodward, & P. V. Kroskrity (Eds.), *Language ideologies: Practice and theory* (pp. 189–210). New York: Oxford University Press.

Dewey, J. (1966). *Democracy and education.* New York: Free Press. (Original work published 1916)

Duff, P. (1995). An ethnography of communication in immersion classrooms in Hungary. *TESOL Quarterly*, *29*, 505–537.

Duff, P. (1996). Different languages, different practices. Socialization of discourse competence in dual-language school classrooms in Hungary. In K. Bailey & D. Nunan (Eds.), *Voices from the language classroom: Qualitative research in second language acquisition* (pp. 407–433). New York: Cambridge University Press.

Duff, P. (2002). The discursive co-construction of knowledge, identity, and difference. An ethnography of communication in the high school mainstream. *Applied Linguistics*, *23*, 289–322.

Echeverria, B. (2003). Schooling, language, and ethnic identity in the Basque Autonomous Community. *Anthropology and Education Quarterly*, *34*, 351–372.

Fellin, L. (2001). *Language ideologies, language socialization, and language revival in an Italian Alpine community.* Unpublished doctoral dissertation, University of Arizona.

Friedman, D. (2006). *(Re)imagining the nation: Language socialization in Ukrainian classrooms.* Unpublished doctoral dissertation, University of California, Los Angeles.

Friedman, D. (2010). Speaking correctly: Error correction as a language socialization practice in a Ukrainian classroom. *Applied Linguistics*, *31*, 346–367.

García Sánchez, I. M. (2009). *Moroccan immigrant children in a time of surveillance: Navigating sameness and difference in contemporary Spain.* Unpublished doctoral dissertation, University of California, Los Angeles.

Garrett, P. B. (2006). Language socialization. In K. Brown (Ed.), *Encyclopedia of language and linguistics* (2nd ed., Vol. 6, pp. 604–613). Amsterdam: Elsevier.

Garrett, P. B., & Baquedano-López, P. (2002). Language socialization: Reproduction and continuity, transformation and change. *Annual Review of Anthropology, 31,* 339–361.

Garza, A. V., & Crawford, L. (2005). Hegemonic multiculturalism: English immersion, ideology, and subtractive schooling. *Bilingual Research Journal, 29,* 599–619.

Gellner, E. (1983). *Nations and nationalism.* Ithaca, NY: Cornell University Press.

Golden, D. (2001). "Now, like real Israelis, let's stand up and sing" : Teaching the national language to Russian newcomers in Israel. *Anthropology and Education Quarterly, 32,* 52–79.

González, N. (2001). *I am my language: Discourses of women and children in the borderlands.* Tucson: University of Arizona Press.

Griswold, O. V. (2007). *Becoming a United States citizen: Second language socialization in adult citizenship classrooms.* Unpublished doctoral dissertation, University of California, Los Angeles.

Harklau, L. (2000). From the "good kids" to the "worst" : Representations of English language learners across educational settings. *TESOL Quarterly, 34,* 35–57.

Harklau, L. (2003). Representational practice and multi-modal communication in U.S. high schools: Implications for adolescent immigrants. In R. Bayley & S. Schecter (Eds.), *Language socialization in bilingual and multilingual societies* (pp. 83–97). Clevedon, UK: Multilingual Matters.

Howard, K. (2003). *Language socialization in a northern Thai bilingual community.* Unpublished doctoral dissertation, University of California, Los Angeles.

Howard, K. (2004). Socializing respect at school in northern Thailand. *Working Papers in Educational Linguistics, 20,* 1–30.

Howard, K. M. (2009). "When meeting *Khun* teacher, each time we should show respect" : Standardizing respect and politeness in a northern Thai classroom. *Linguistics and Education, 20,* 254–272.

Jaffe, A. (1993). Obligation, error and authenticity: Competing cultural principles in the teaching of Corsican. *Journal of Linguistic Anthropology, 3,* 99–114.

Jaffe, A. (1996). The second annual Corsican spelling contest: Orthography and ideology. *American Ethnologist, 23,* 816–835.

Jaffe, A. (1999). *Ideologies in action: Language politics on Corsica.* Berlin, Germany/ New York: Mouton de Gruyter.

Jaffe, A. (2003). Talk around text: Literacy practices, cultural identity and authority in a Corsican bilingual classroom. *International Journal of Bilingual Education and Bilingualism, 6,* 202–220.

Kearney, M. (1995). The local and the global: The anthropology of globalization and transnationalism. *Annual Review of Anthropology, 24,* 547–565.

Kroger, J. (2004). *Identity in adolescence: The balance between self and other.* New York: Routledge.

Kulick, D., & Schieffelin, B. B. (2004). Language socialization. In A. Duranti (Ed.), *A companion to linguistic anthropology.* (pp. 349–368). Malden, MA: Blackwell.

Kunan, A. J. (2009). Politics and legislation in citizenship testing in the United States. *Annual Review of Applied Linguistics, 29,* 37–48.

Lam, W. S. E. (2003). *Second language literacy and identity formation on the Internet: The case of Chinese immigrant youth in the U.S.* Unpublished doctoral dissertation, University of California, Berkeley.

Lam, W. S. E. (2004). Second language socialization in a bilingual chat room: Global and local considerations. *Language Learning and Technology, 8,* 44–65.

Lam, W. S. E. (2008). Language socialization in online communities. In P. A. Duff & N. H. Hornberger (Eds.), *Encyclopedia of language and education: Vol. 8. Language socialization* (2nd ed., pp. 301–311). New York: Springer.

Langman, J. (2002). Mother-tongue education versus bilingual education: Shifting ideologies and policies in the Republic of Slovakia. *International Journal of the Sociology of Language, 154,* 47–64.

Levinson, B. A. U. (2005). Citizenship, identity, democracy: Engaging the political in the anthropology of education. *Anthropology and Education Quarterly, 36,* 329–340.

Lotherington, H. (2003). Multiliteracies in Springvale: Negotiating language, culture and identity in suburban Melbourne. In R. Bayley & S. Schecter (Eds.), *Language socialization in bilingual and multilingual societies* (pp. 200–217). Clevedon, UK: Multilingual Matters.

Mitchell, K. (2001). Education for democratic citizenship: Transnationalism, multiculturalism, and the limits of liberalism. *Harvard Educational Review, 71,* 51–78.

Moore, L. (2004). *Learning languages by heart: Second language socialization in a Fulbe community.* Unpublished doctoral dissertation, University of California, Los Angeles.

Moore, L. (2006). Learning by heart in Qur'anic and public schools in northern Cameroon. *Social Analysis,* 50, 109–126.

Ochs, E. (1988). *Culture and language development.* Cambridge, UK: Cambridge University Press.

Ochs, E. (1992). Indexing gender. In A. Duranti & C. Godwin (Eds.), *Rethinking context* (pp. 335–358). New York: Cambridge University Press.

Ochs, E. (1993). Constructing social identity: A language socialization perspective. *Research on Language and Social Interaction, 26,* 287–306.

Ochs, E. (1996). Linguistic resources for socializing humanity. In J. J. Gumperz & S. C.

Levinson (Eds.), *Rethinking linguistic relativity* (pp. 407–437). Cambridge, UK: Cambridge University Press.

Ochs, E. (2002). Becoming a speaker of culture. In C. Kramsch (Ed.), *Language socialization and language acquisition: Ecological perspectives* (pp. 99–120). New York: Continuum Press.

Olneck, M. (2004). Immigrants and education. In J. A. Banks & C. A. McGee Banks (Eds.), *Handbook of research on multicultural education* (pp. 310–331). San Francisco, CA: Jossey-Banks.

Paugh, A. (2001). *"Creole day is every day": Language socialization, shift, and ideologies in Dominica, West Indies*. Unpublished doctoral dissertation, New York University.

Paugh, A. (2005). Multilingual play: Children's code-switching, role play, and agency in Dominica, West Indies. *Language in Society*, *34*, 63–86.

Resnik, J., Sabar, N., & Shapira, R. (2001). Absorption of CIS immigrants into Israeli schools: A semipermeable enclave model. *Anthropology and Education Quarterly*, *32*, 424–436.

Sandel, T. T. (2003). Linguistic capital in Taiwan: The KMT's Mandarin language policy and its perceived impact on language practices of bilingual Mandarin and Tai-gi speakers. *Language in Society*, *32*, 523–551.

Schecter, S. R., & Bayley, R. (2002). *Language as cultural practice: Mexicanos en el norte*. Mahwah, NJ: Erlbaum.

Schieffelin, B. B. (1990). *The give and take of everyday life: Language socialization of Kaluli children*. New York: Cambridge University Press.

Schieffelin, B. B., & Ochs, E. (1986). Language socialization. *Annual Review of Anthropology*, *15*, 163–191.

Talmy, S. (2008). The cultural productions of the ESL student at Tradewinds High: Contingency, multidirectionality, and identity in L2 socialization. *Applied Linguistics*, *29*, 619–644.

Talmy, S. (2009a). A very important lesson: Respect and the socialization of order(s) in high school ESL. *Linguistics and Education*, *20*, 235–253.

Talmy, S. (2009b). Forever FOB?: Resisting and reproducing the Other in high school ESL. In A. Reyes & A. Lo (Eds.), *Beyond yellow English: Toward a linguistic anthropology of Asian Pacific America* (pp. 347–365). New York: Oxford University Press.

Vogel, A. (2008). Negotiating German identities in classroom interaction: An analysis of pronoun use. In D. Backman & A. Sakalauskaite (Eds.), *Ossi Wessi* (pp. 143–170). Newcastle, UK: Cambridge Scholars.

Vogel-Langer, A. (2008). *Becoming one nation: Explorations into language use and identity formation of German's post- and preunification generations*. Saarbruecken, Germany: VDM Verlag Dr. Mueller.

Watson-Gegeo, K. A. (2004). Mind, language, and epistemology: Toward a language socialization paradigm for SLA. *Modern Language Journal, 88*, 331–350.

Weber, E. (1976). *Peasants into Frenchmen: The modernization of rural France, 1870–1914.* Stanford, CA: Stanford University Press.

Woolard, K. A., & Schieffelin, B. B. (1994). Language ideology. *Annual Review of Anthropology, 23*, 55–82.

Zuengler, J., & Cole, K. (2005). Language socialization and second language learning. In E. Hinkel (Ed.), *Handbook of research in second language teaching and learning* (pp. 301–316). Mahwah, NJ: Erlbaum.

Language Socialization in the Workplace

Celia Roberts

This survey article looks first at the changing demands of the workplace in a globalized economy. The new work order creates a new word order, and the workforce has become a "wordforce" (Heller, in press) with new genres of language and communication. These changes have taken place at a time when global flows of people, from less wealthy and secure societies to more wealthy and secure ones, have created multilingual workplaces. Both sets of changes challenge the traditional notion of second language socialization, and this is the focus of the next section. The workplace represents a complex, dynamic setting where migrants experience a double socialization: into the hybrid discourses of the workplace, which all newcomers experience, and into the specific language and cultural practices that realize these discourses. The new language requirements of the workplace produce for migrant workers and professionals a "linguistic penalty" (Roberts & Campbell, 2006) since the communicative demands of the selection process may be greater than those of the job itself. The last section of the article is concerned with language socialization in multilingual settings where language socialization into the dominant language is only part of the story. There is a contrast between the low status multilingualism of migrant workers, and staff in globalized and international organizations who are being socialized into new lingua franca interaction. The article concludes with an example of how the complex linguistic and technical environment of a high-tech multilingual company produces radically different conditions for language socialization which challenge how this notion can be used in the 21st century.

INTRODUCTION

The notion of the workplace as a site where language socialization takes place is becoming increasingly complex and contested. The reasons for this include the way in which boundaries between work and other aspects of social life become problematic, the changing nature of work itself, and the continuing changes in the communicative environment at work. What counts as a workplace or a location for preparing for work is not easy to define. The boundaries between education and work are no longer patrolled by time, with a period of formal education leading seamlessly to work. People move back from work to education, do internships as part of formal education, and on- and off-site training and continuous professional development are routine (Duff, 2008; Vickers, 2007). Similarly, the home is often now the workplace as teleworking and training become common. Also, working parents socialize their children into work practices in their narratives of what happened at the office (Paugh, 2005). Language socialization in the workplace is, therefore, a combination of both formal and informal learning (Scollon & Scollon, 1995) and cannot be readily separated off from the professional socialization and training that takes place outside of the formal, physical workplace.

Work itself has also radically changed. The collapse of much traditional manufacturing in western societies, the "new work order" (Gee, Hull, & Lankshear, 1996; Hull, 1997), and new technologies have had a paradoxical effect on our understanding of the workplace as a key site for language socialization. On the one hand, the new work order has led to a "new word order" (Farrell, 2001, p. 57; Iedema, & Scheeres, 2003). The workforce has become a "wordforce" (Heller, in press) which manufactures talk and texts. Communications has become the most demanded competence in an increasingly competence-driven world (Matthewman, 1996). On the other hand, the new technologies that have helped to create the new work order have refocused linguists on the multimodality of everyday activities. Language interacts with the texts and materialities of these new technologies which themselves facilitate new forms of language (Goodwin, 1995; Heath & vom Lehn, 2008; Kleifgen, 2001).

Changes in the nature of work itself have occurred at much the same time as global flows of people have transformed employment. While the physical location of some workplaces has led to a particular ethnolinguistic group tending to be employed over others, in large urban centers, many organizations are characterized by "superdiversity" (Vertoveç, 2007, p. 1024) where no single ethnic group stands out but where employees are from many different backgrounds. Along with new technologies, globalization challenges traditional notions of community as homogeneous or geographically placed. A more dynamic view of community as heterogeneous and plural better represents living and working in the city. Similarly recent theorizing about space, language, and culture has raised questions about language choice and mix (Blommaert, Collins, & Slembrouck, 2005a). Rather than language practices being determined unproblematically by specific domains, with, for example, a particular language used in one domain rather than another, they are highly situated and dependent upon the context of the particular interaction and the mutual resources of the speakers (Blommaert, 2007; Blommaert, Collins, & Slembrouck, 2005b; Duff, 2005). So within a workplace, there may be a constant tension between "interactional regimes" (Blommaert et al., 2005b, p. 208) and the more creative and hybrid language practices of individuals in particular contexts.

Current theories on language and globalization (Blommaert et al., 2005a) also raise questions about the notion of language socialization in the workplace. The foundational studies on language socialization took place in small-scale societies where the notion of a community was relatively stable. The young child or novice gradually learned how to use language and learned through language how to conduct themselves within this relatively homogeneous community. More recent research has extended these studies to include the life span and complex, heterogeneous societies where the idea of single, fixed communities and a set of established linguistic standards and practices no longer obtain (Garrett & Baquedano-López, 2002). The originators of language socialization theory, Ochs and Schieffelin (1983; Schieffelin & Ochs, 1986) have themselves played a leading role in criticizing any static notion of socialization into a community, the stereotypes such research can produce, and the possible underplaying of more general or universal practices. For example, Ochs wrote the following:

> Language socialization research is aware that generalizations of this sort have several undesirable effects: for one thing, cultures are essentialized, and variation in communicative practices within communities is underemphasized.... Our accounts also seem like fixed cameos, members and communities enslaved by convention and frozen in time rather than

fluid and changing over a course of a generation, a life and even a single encounter.... [W]e have tended to over-emphasize the unique communicative configurations of particular communities and underspecify over-arching, possible universal, communicative and social practices that may facilitate socialization into multiple communities and transnational life worlds (Ochs, 2000, p. 231).

Ochs also stressed that socialization is a two-way street with more or less experienced members learning from each other. This more dynamic and transformative notion of language socialization, along with responses to Ochs's critique, are illustrated in the following examples.

Despite the expansion of studies on lifelong and "lifewide language socialization" (Duff, 2008, p. 258), there is still only a rather meagre trickle of workplace and professional socialization research. In Garrett and Baquedano-López's (2002) introduction to their review, looking back in 2002 over the previous 16 years, only 5 of the 48 studies they referenced related to workplace and professional socialization. One reason for this is that the methodology used in such studies is hard to carry out in workplaces. The core methodological features are that the research is ethnographic, holistic, longitudinal, and based on naturally occurring data. Such studies also require evidence of learning, both in terms of cognition and social interaction. Even in longitudinal studies, research on the shop floor or the office cannot readily capture the changes in how activities are accomplished over time. Another factor is that access to workplaces to carry out ethnographic studies is not easy to obtain, often because researchers are assumed to be either spies or troublemakers. Thus, many studies of language use in the workplace are connected to language and cultural training, since this may be the only way in which employers are willing to offer their organization as a field site for research. Teachers can act as ethnographers, collecting data from the workplace to produce research-based teaching materials.

Given the paucity of relevant research in the workplace, this review takes a rather elastic definition of language socialization research so that the workplace theme can be adequately discussed. It includes studies of socialization in formal off-site research examples of socialization based on ethnographic interviews rather than naturally occurring data. It also includes examples of second language use where the environment creates conditions for socialization, even though there is no systematic evidence collected of language learning taking place over time.

THE WORKPLACE AS A SITE OF SOCIALIZATION

The "interactional regimes" (Blommaert et al., 2005b) of the workplace make it a site where everyone at some stage is new to the environment and has to be socialized into its particular linguistic and cultural environment. This socialization can be seen as consisting of three parts: corporate or institutional discourses, professional discourses, and the social or personal aspects of the workplace (Roberts & Sarangi, 1999). The communities of practice model (Lave & Wenger, 1991; Wenger, 1998) have traced the gradual process of becoming a full participant in the workplace where there is not only one overarching community of practice but also multiple local communities depending on the particular sites of engagement that employees are subject to or contribute to creating.

Corporate discourses differ (and are dynamic) in different parts of the world but since virtually all management training resources are produced in the West (Jack, 2009; Poncini, 2003), this hegemonic discourse is what Scollon and Scollon (1995) have called "the Utilitarian Discourse System" (p. 107). It is empirical, deductive, individualistic, egalitarian, and institutionally sanctioned. New employees are inducted either formally or informally into the unique forms of text and talk, and the particular way things are done and categorized in any one institution (Iedema, 2003; Mawer, 1999).

Socialization into professional discourse occurs in formal training contexts both outside the workplace and within it (Roberts & Sarangi, 1999). Several studies have charted the processes of shaping a professional identity through acquiring new discourses and values in healthcare, scientific, legal, and vocational settings. Erickson (1999), in medicine, and Arakelian (2009), in nursing, documented how relative novices learn to be professional learners in the workplace. Hobbs (2004) analyzed how progress (treatment) notes are used in medical socialization. Mertz (2007) studied the novice law student socialization through Socratic dialogue and the reworking of legal texts in different contexts. Similarly, Jacoby (1998) looked at how adults master new registers and genres in the process of becoming physicists, and Vickers (2007) documented the processes of becoming a core member of an engineering team through observation, scaffolding, ridicule, and opportunities to talk through design processes.

In a very different setting, the African American cosmetology school, Jacobs-Huey (2003) charted how students become so-called hair experts. Like the student lawyers in Mertz's (2007) study, role-play is a key method for developing the scripts of the new profession and being evaluated on their competence in using them. One element of these scripts is the use of metaphors and proverbs socializing the apprentices "into shared moral ideologies and behaviour" (Jacobs-Huey, 2003, p. 294). Another element is the use of *metacommunication*, the talk about talk, when a student breaches the prescribed linguistic code. So despite the constant changes in workplace practices noted in the following paragraphs, the apprenticeship model of learning to become expert remains, and notions of what constitutes professionalism continue to be relatively stable, as part of the so-called *habitus* of a particular profession (Bourdieu, 1991).

The third aspect of workplace socialization relates to the personal and social discourses at work. As language work (talk and text as institutionalized tasks in the workplace) takes on an increasingly central role, the interrelationship of professional and personal or social discourses becomes ever more key. This has always been the case with the caring professions, but now that talk is work in call centers, shop floor team meetings, and workplace training sessions, the presentation of self is part of most people's working skills and requires an assertive persona that is by no means a cultural universal (Katz, 2000; see later in this article for how this plays out in terms of power and inequality). The Wellington Language in the Workplace project in New Zealand has made a particular study of politeness and humor in the relational work done within the contexts of power in organizational life (Holmes, 2005; Holmes & Stubbe, 2003; Daly, Holmes, Newton, & Stubbe, 2004; see also, in Australia, Willing, 1997). Workplace studies in Sweden (Gunnarsson, 2009) have shown how migrant workers and professionals have learned to use humor and developed high levels of pragmatic competence in this area. This has involved not only a linguistic view of appropriateness but also adaption to the flattened hierarchies of the Swedish workplace (Andersson, 2009; Nelson & Andersson, 2005, as cited in Gunnarsson, 2009).

The informal socialization of office workers (Li, 2000) and care workers (Duff, Wong, & Early, 2000) illustrate the significance of pragmatic and social skills in the necessary face work of daily interactions in the workplace. Li's case study traced the experience of a Chinese woman, Ming, from the employment preparation course into the workplace as a filing clerk in a U.S. medical equipment company. It was only in the workplace that her "indirect communicative style" (p. 67), particularly realized in how she made requests, brought along from her early socialization and work experience in China, changed to a more assertive style as she faced up to the unacceptable behavior of local American office workers. This longitudinal study goes beyond the pragmatics of making requests to wider issues of self-presentation and identity. It also explored the mix of the "new American way" of requesting: "directly, truthful and things a little bit sweeter," as Ming noted in her diary (p. 75) with the inductive way of making requests from her early habitus. Her new assertiveness, in which she requested coworkers to be more polite, exemplifies the transformative nature of language socialization in which the so-called novices become experts in managing the local politics of the office and contribute to changing the communicative environment.

In their study of migrant workers training to become long-term resident care aides, Duff et al. (2000) described a similar gap between formal training and informal socialization in the workplace. The more formal and technically specific focus in the English language training program did not prepare the trainees for the emotional labor of communicating with residents with a wide range of English language competence (including no English at all) and often with mental and linguistic abilities impaired by the aging process. Affective, personal, and social modes of talk and bodily language were more important in the healthcare aide jobs than accurate English grammar or medical terms.

These three aspects of workplace language socialization—corporate, professional, and social or personal—interact to produce new identities with new ways of being, feeling, and articulating the self in new moral worlds. These changes have always been central to the study of language socialization. In the workplace these identities are collaborative achievements (Ochs, 1993) within organizations, in professional socialization, and in the context of gendered migration (Holmes, 2006; Katz, 2000; Gunnarsson, 2009).

THE "NEW WORK ORDER"

While some aspects of working life remain stable, the globalized economy and working practices produced by the rapid expansion of new technologies has led to a "new work order" (Gee et al., 1996). This order is supported by the discourses of what have become known as "new capitalism" or "fast capitalism." The need to constantly change products and customize them to survive in the globalized marketplace has led to a restructuring of the workplace, which, in turn, has created new language and literacy demands that affect even the low-paid worker. These demands arise from an increased use of technologies, more multitasking at all levels, more flexibility required of workers as hierarchical structures are flattened, and, generally, a more "textualised workplace" (Iedema & Scheeres, 2003, p. 336) in which there is increasing reliance on written instructions and Web-based materials, so both new and well-established employees have had to be socialized into these new practices (Hull, 1997). Many studies of workplaces have shown how routine activities are mediated by digital technologies (Goodwin, 1995; Heath & vom Lehn, 2008; Hindmarsh, Heath, & Fraser, 2006; Lemke, 2002; Suchman, 1992).

The new work order has created a "new word order" (Farrell, 2001) or "word-force" (Heller, in press). There are new work genres, and new work and professional identities are constructed and negotiated through talk on the shop floor (Hull, 1997; Iedema & Scheeres, 2003; Kleifgen, 2001); in health settings (Cook-Gumperz & Messerman, 1999; Greatbatch, Luff, Heath, & Campion, 1993); and in call centers (Budach, Roy, & Heller, 2003; Cameron, 2000; Friginal, 2009a, 2009b; Heller 2002; Roy, 2003) where there is a constant tension between the highly routinized scripts of interaction and the emotional labor of dealing on a daily basis with often irate or frustrated customers and being expected to adapt to their style of communicating.

The globalized economy is paralleled by the global movements of people. "Superdiversity" (Vertoveç, 2007) is the norm in most large cities, and few places in the world remain untouched by migration or the effects of the diaspora, as the studies by Li (2000) and Duff et al. (2000) described earlier show. Global flows of people to more wealthy and secure societies have created workplaces where staff are bilingual or often multilingual. However, the dominant language of the nation state produces and enforces a linguistic capital that serves to maintain and reproduce linguistic and ethnic inequalities. Migration and mobility create the need for "double socialization" (Li, 2000, p. 61) into the workplace. So, in addition to the socialization processes that all new employees face, relative newcomers are expected to learn to participate in the linguistic and cultural practices of work in a new country.

The extensive literature on workplace language and cultural awareness training demonstrates the amount of retraining and more formal socialization expected of the migrant and international worker and professional (Belfiore, 1993; G. Bell, 2003; J. Bell, 1995; Goldstein, 1993; Grünhage-Monetti, Halewijn, & Holland, 2003; Hawthorne, 1997; Holmes, 2000; Mawer, 1999; O'Neill & Gish, 2001; Roberts, Davies, & Jupp, 1992). Some of this training has been questioned as being too narrow (Goldstein, 1997) or not sufficiently critical of the positioning of migrant workers within the new work order (Farrell, 2000). Some of these evaluation studies of language training take a wider and more ethnographic perspective, seeing the "workplace as the curriculum" (Mawer, 1999). However, few of them are framed by theories of second language socialization or examine the "exposure to similar communicative experiences in institutionalized networks of relationships" that contribute to the production of "shared culture and shared inferential practices" (Gumperz, 1997, p. 15).

This "double socialization" and the shift to language work in the new work order produce new regimes of inequality that, despite the relative stability of some work practices, as noted earlier, make language socialization in the workplace problematic. First, as McCall (2003) discussed, there is a linguistically divided labor market, similar in many ways to the traditional two-tier labor market. Many low-paid, so-called entry-level jobs are insecure, isolated, in poor and noisy conditions, and organized into ethnic work units (Campbell & Roberts, 2007; Goldstein, 1997; Gunnarsson, 2009; Roberts et al., 1992; Waldinger & Lichter, 2003). These are often the only jobs that minority ethnic workers, particularly relatively new arrivals, whatever their educational background, can obtain. Under these conditions, there is little opportunity to be socialized into the dominant language. Indeed, as McCall (2003) argued, those areas where there is relatively little talk, or certainly little talk in the majority language of the organization, are the areas where there is little power: "In the workplace power is exercised precisely in those areas where language is most intense" (p. 249). Goldstein's study of female Portuguese factory workers in Toronto illustrated how the assembly line workers chose to speak Portuguese on the line to assert their ethnic solidarity and so both in terms of place and language were isolated from the "intense" areas of English language work. Even non-Portuguese-speaking migrant workers were socialized into speaking Portuguese on the assembly lines (Goldstein, 1997).

Second, unlike the usually supportive conditions for early language socialization, second language socialization in the workplace often occurs in a relatively hostile environment (Katz, 2000; Li, 2000; Mawer, 1999; Roberts et al., 1992). Misunderstandings, racist comments, and the deliberate noncontact of some groups in relation to others both limit opportunities for socialization and actively construct resistances to it. However, some recent studies present an alternative view (Andersson, 2009; Duff et al., 2000, described earlier). Andersson's study in a Swedish hospital setting documented the use of communication strategies and humor and found that the local Swedish staff were patient listeners. Even when second language speakers had to use several communication strategies as they struggled to convey their intent, the local staff allowed them to finish their turn at talk.

Third, the language and literacy demands of the new work order, and its associated ideologies, can serve to exclude bilingual and multilingual workers even when they are considered expert speakers of the dominant language in their country of origin or in the multilingual community in which they grew up or now reside (Blommaert, 2007). Expertise, Blommaert argued, is relative. A speaker's use of English perceived as expert in, for example, Nigeria or the Philippines is downgraded to limited or inappropriate in the specific contexts and genres of the workplace in the new country. Hull (1997) and Katz (2000) described the linguistic and performance demands of multilingual workers in high-tech Silicon Valley companies in California. A similarly assertive stance was required of linguistic minority nurses retraining in the United Kingdom whose English was expert in their own country but rated as inappropriate in British hospitals (Arakelian, 2009).

Several studies in Canada have shown how speakers of English or French who were considered experts, linguistically, within their own communities can be disadvantaged by dominant norms and workplace ideologies. In their studies of francophone novice nurses in Quebec, Parks and Maguire (1999) found that the nursing reports and care plans they had been taught to produce were different from the conventional practices in both French- and English-speaking hospitals. Bilingual call workers in French Ontario also found they were excluded from the better-paid bilingual jobs because of the commodification, standardization, and codification of the dominant language, French. The ideology of a pure standard French, which was the stated call centers' requirement, excluded local vernacular French speakers from the better-paid bilingual worker jobs. Their French did not meet this new standard of bilingualism, and so, despite being bilingual, they were hired as English monolingual speakers (Roy, 2003; Budach et al., 2003). The effect of globalization in the new international call centers has local, exclusionary repercussions, even for bilingual and multilingual speakers and shows that there is a linguistic marketplace (Bourdieu, 1991; McCall, 2003) that determines what counts as linguistic capital and sets the standards for language socialization.

THE "LINGUISTIC PENALTY"

The call center studies in Canada and the United Kingdom document how the corporate discourses of the new work order impose a "linguistic penalty" (Roberts & Campbell, 2006, p. 1) on those who do not meet their standards of language and communicative competence. Early work on gatekeeping encounters in linguistically diverse societies established the gap between the sociolinguistic demands of the selection and assessment processes and those of the workplace (Brindley, 1994; Gumperz, Jupp, & Roberts, 1979; Mawer & Field, 1995; McNamara, 1997; Roberts et al., 1992). More recently, equal opportunity commitments and the widespread use of competency-based criteria in recruitment and training have done little to narrow the gap. The socialization required to be successful in the selection interview or assessment outstrips the language and interactional demands of the job or assesses language and communication skills that are not relevant to the job (Roberts & Campbell, 2006). On the analogy of the ethnic penalty, which describes the discrimination experienced by black and minority ethnic groups (Heath & Cheung, 2007), there is a linguistic penalty that excludes on the basis of language. (Other research suggests that the selection interview does not assess accurately for the interactional demands of the job, e.g., Friginal, 2009a, but this is outside the scope of this article.)

A recent study has shown that job interviews for low-paid, entry-level jobs in the United Kingdom require an astute performance by candidates that combines blending institutional, professional, and personal modes of discourse with a standard narrative structure (Campbell & Roberts, 2007; Roberts & Campbell, 2006). Candidates' responses also have to be what Iedema (2003) termed *bureaucratically processable.* In other words, they have to "fit their stories into boxes" (Roberts & Campbell, 2005, p. 45). The formal language socialization through language training and work preparation courses is far removed from the competency-based interview, which itself is distant from those areas of work, away from the language-intense areas, where linguistic minorities and relatively new arrivals are routinely positioned. Language socialization for entry into reasonably secure, if low-paid, work is a bigger hurdle than language socialization within the workplace itself.

A follow-up study (Roberts, Campbell, & Robinson, 2008) looked at the role of promotion interviews in contributing to what Phillips (2003) has called the snowy peaks of senior management: the fact that most companies had only white majority group members at the top. This study showed that the gradual process of socialization into management discourses was essential to success at the promotion interview. Access to informal interactional networks helped those from minorities to be socialized into what Roberts et al. (2008) called *talking like a manager.* However, there were tensions and struggles for those considering promotion since they were expected to be "authentic" members of the shop floor community. Going for promotion was seen as a double betrayal of this community and of their own ethnic group. So language socialization for promotion to management in this mosaic of affiliations and tensions is not a straightforward matter of gradual participation in a new community of practice.

Socialization into the competences of the promotion interview depended upon learning its communicative and rhetorical styles. The overriding orientation was to the self as a project, always self-aware and self-reflecting for the benefit of the organization the candidate aspired to be a manager in. Candidates born and educated abroad were less likely to produce this self, a synthesis of the utilitarian discourse of claims and evidence with euphemized feelings and informality. This group of candidates tended to be judged as either too emotional or too impersonal, relying on a generalized assertive style that did not blend the hybrid discourses of the selection interview.

Studies carried out on licensing and membership examinations for international medical graduates form part of a wider literature on this group (Erickson & Rittenburg, 1987; Spike, 2006). These studies of high-stakes gatekeeping encounters involving well-qualified professionals represent challenges that are broadly similar, in terms of communicative and rhetorical styles, to the job interviews for low-paid work (McNamara, 1997; Sarangi & Roberts, 2002). Mistica, Baldwin, Cordella, and Musgrave (2008) discussed how the communication skills of interacting with patients and conveying medical information accurately in simulated consultations correlated with overall final grades in the Australian context. Such simulations are widely used in health contexts for assessments. Whereas role-play and simulations are used in educational contexts as part of professional socialization, as discussed earlier, when used for assessment and selection they raise some awkward questions. Simulation requires several abilities in addition to communicative and rhetorical competences: the ability to manage both the outer performance and inner psychological experience of being assessed; the ability to manage the frame ambiguity of both the consultation and the assessment (Seale, Butler, Hutchby, Kinnersley, & Rollnick, 2007); and for international medical graduates, the "double consciousness" (E. L. Bell, 1990, p. 461) of compartmentalizing the personal and private spheres of their life and yet using personal qualities such as empathy in the consultation. These studies of the linguistic penalty in access to training, employment, and promotion show that language socialization into and in the workplace is problematic. There are different versions of the self required at different stages of the employment process as well as resistances and tensions within the apprenticeship period.

SOCIALIZATION INTO THE MULTILINGUAL WORKPLACE

The double socialization into a workplace officially dominated by the state or majority language implies that learning the practices of the workplace would go hand in hand with majority language socialization. However, studies have shown that for many workers, contact was most frequent either with those who shared a first language other than that of the majority or with speakers with very different styles and varieties of this majority language (Clyne, 1994, 2003; Day, 1992; Duff et al., 2000; Goldstein, 1997; Jupp, Roberts, & Cook-Gumperz, 1982). Since workplace language policies, work teams, and the linguistic backgrounds of those employed are all dependent on economic and structural factors, the communicative environment rarely remains stable. This raises the question of what linguistic communities of practice newcomers are socialized into, the extent to which such communities change over time, and the sociopolitical realities on the ground that cause these changes. For example, in a food factory in a small town in the United Kingdom, successive groups of workers, first from Pakistan, then Kurdish workers from Iraq and Turkey, and more recently from Eastern Europe, as well as the company's restructuring meant that changes in the linguistic makeup of the food-processing lines outstripped the opportunities for socialization into English, the official language and the language of opportunity, or indeed into any one language of the processing line (Roberts et al., 2008).

Although the globalized economy and the rhetoric of multilingualism used in corporate discourse would appear to imply that those who are multilingual are assets to the organization, the evidence is rather mixed. The literature suggests that there is a persistent gap between the official rhetoric of institutions and the policies on the ground and the linguistic ideology that underpins both of them, either explicitly or implicitly. Heller and Roy have shown that the so-called purity of the standard French required in call centers was at odds with the celebratory rhetoric around local vernacular French (Heller, 2002; Roy, 2003).Similarly, Duchêne (2009) described the commodification of multilingualism in a call center. His ongoing work in a Swiss international airport has shown the structuring work that linguistic ideologies do in positioning workers with the wrong kind of multilingualism. The neoliberal discourse that promotes the hiring of those with multilingual resources does not work through into status and pay. Even baggage handlers are doing language work. They are listed as interpreters and translators and expected to do language work as part of their duties. However, there is no recognition of this in terms of salary or official status (Duchêne). In such contexts, unofficial language policy and language socialization tend to reinforce unequal boundaries between different types of language workers and the languages they speak. The use of a language other than the state or majority languages, while functional and indeed of direct benefit to the organization, does not grant its user any more power than if they were monolinguals.

Other studies of socialization into the multilingual workplace are in contexts where bilingualism, multilingualism, and lingua franca usage (Firth, 1996) are ratified as functional and statusful practices; for example, international business negotiations and the interaction between what are termed *bilingual professionals* (Day & Wagner, 2007). These contexts contrast in several ways with workplaces discussed earlier. Firstly, they are not ethnically and linguistically stratified but relate to activities where participants have more or less equal status or valued skills, such as the international professional sportswoman or man in the Netherlands (Kellerman et al., 2005). Second, they are not tied to a particular geographic area. Third, and arising from the first two, language socialization in these contexts is a matter of choice dependent on the particular activity (Day & Wagner, 2007). Choices relate to choice of linguistic code both for the whole activity and in code-switching within it (Mondada, 2004; Poncini, 2003; Rasmussen & Wagner, 2002) to create a new "bilingual interactional order" (Day & Wagner; Mondada, p. 19). This order is not created in terms of difficulties or deficiencies in communication but as a pragmatic response to the functional requirements of the workplace event.

Studies of the use of English as a lingua franca in international domains demonstrate a similar defocusing of the problematics of language differences. Firth (1995, 1996) showed that interactants, in Ochs's (2000) terms, rely on "overarching, possible universal, communicative and social practices" (p. 232), which underplay cultural differences, play up orderliness across these differences and so "facilitate socialization into multiple communities and transnational life worlds" (Ochs, 2000; p. 232). Similarly, other lingua franca studies have shown how the pragmatic norms of the speakers' first language give way to new more informal norms (Rasmussen, 1998; Wagner, 1995), suggestive of a new "lingua franca interaction" (Day & Wagner, 2007, p. 398).

CONCLUSION

Micro-interactional studies like these document the complex and dynamic use of strategic choices in language code and style shifting, which suggest that, as workplaces become increasingly multilingual, so also will the process of language socialization. The study of a multilingual circuit-board manufacturing plant in California's Silicon Valley (Kleifgen, 2001) highlighted many of the themes in this overview and will be used, by way of a conclusion, to draw them together. In particular, Kleifgen's micro-interactional analysis confirmed the highly situated and creative use of language that is part of the linguistic environment of such high-tech multilingual work spaces (Kleifgen; Kleifgen & Frenz-Belkin, 1997).

This high-tech manufacturing plant is structured around natural teams in which workers are encouraged to organize their own work teams and use their shared language and cultural understanding to meet the production demands of the company. The data example analyzed was of a problem-solving task involving a Vietnamese supervisor and a machine operator. Kleifgen (2001) documented how they used what she termed a stripped-down version of Vietnamese, together with some code-switching into English to accomplish the troubleshooting task. This was not a simplified or pidginized version of Vietnamese but one influenced by American English styles of talking. The conventional Vietnamese personal references and honorifics were replaced by a more direct mode of talk that produced a symmetrical interaction to accomplish the task. As a solution to the problem was reached, the supervisor shifted back to forms that indexed more asymmetry, but this was done by using more directives rather than Vietnamese obligatory address systems. In this way, the interactants drew on language and interactional norms from two contrasting communicative systems to develop "a creative hybrid, showing remarkable social and linguistic adaption to the norms and constraints of the American workplace" (Kleifgen, p. 302).

This study illustrates many of the themes of this overview of language socialization in the workplace, even though it is a snapshot of language use rather than a longitudinal study of learning. It shows the changing and transformative potential of language use and the communicative environment (Garrett & Baquedano-López, 2002). Language socialization in multilingual workplaces can produce creative, hybrid interaction, new bilingual interactional orders, and changes in the behavior of majority speakers. These changes relate to changing cultural conventions and habitus and new identities and not just to linguistic competence. Another theme of Kleifgen's (2001) study relates to how language socialization is not only about acquiring new language but also about how and when to use different languages and styles in the microchoices and fleeting interpretive moments of interaction.

The Silicon Valley company exemplifies the new work order with its flattened hierarchies and where language socialization is in part mediated by the new technologies. The study also implicitly raises questions about the relationship between face work, language choice, and contexts of power: the extent to which ethnic work units are locally supportive and in the interests of management, but also present fewer opportunities of socialization into the language and territories of power within the workplace.

This overview also reflects the current mix of old and new conditions for language socialization. In some settings, multilingualism is a recognized professional asset; in others, it is exploited without giving additional status and remuneration. In many contexts where monolingual policy and practices are enforced, language socialization into the majority language is the only route to more secure and well-paid work. And in these settings, the linguistic penalty experienced by many migrant workers is greater in gaining access to work than it is in the workplace itself.

The overarching context of the workplace determines the conditions for language socialization and the form it takes. Corporate and institutional priorities, ideologies and structures, the values and practices of different professions, and the particular social climate of the local work group construct these conditions and their dynamics. Language socialization, together with the individual agency of workers and apprentice professionals, is the consequence of these conditions. But what it will consist of in terms of language mix, switch, and shift within multimodal practices remains still relatively uncharted research territory. Future research will need to map this territory, with micro-analysis of the local contexts of production, as well as more long-term studies of what constitutes language socialization in the complex communicative environments and requirements of the 21st-century workplace.

REFERENCES

Andersson, H. (2009). *Intercultural communication at a Swedish hospital: Case studies of second language speakers in the workplace.* Unpublished doctoral dissertation, University of Uppsala, Uppsala, Sweden.

Arakelian, C. (2009). Professional training: Creating intercultural space in multi-ethnic workplaces. In A. Feng, M. Byram, & M. Fleming (Eds.), *Becoming interculturally competent through education and training* (pp. 174–192). Bristol, UK: Multilingual Matters.

Belfiore, M. (1993.) The changing world of work. *TESL Talk*, *21*, 2–20.

Bell, E. L. (1990). The bicultural life experience of career-oriented black women [Special issue: The Career and Life Experiences of Black Professionals]. *Journal of Organizational Behaviour*, *11*, 459–477.

Bell, G. (2003). Back to school: Learning practices in a job retraining programme. In R. Bayley & S. Schecter, (Eds.), *Language socialization in bilingual and multilingual societies* (pp. 251 – 268). Bristol, UK: Multilingual Matters.

Bell, J. (1995). Canadian experiences of training linguistically diverse populations for the workplace. *Australian Review of Applied Linguistics*, *18*, 35–51.

Blommaert, J., Collins, J., & Slembrouck, S. (2005a). Spaces of multilingualism. *Language and Communication*, *25*, 197–216.

Blommaert, J., Collins, J., & Slembrouck, S. (2005b). Polycentricity and interactional regimes in "global neighborhoods". *Ethnography*, *6*, 205–235.

Blommaert, J. (2007). Sociolinguistics and discourse analysis: Orders of indexicality and polycentricity. *Journal of Multicultural Discourses*, *2*, 115–130.

Brindley, G. (1994). Competency-based assessment in second language programmes: Some issues and questions. *Prospect*, *9*, 41–55.

Bourdieu, P. (1991). *Language and symbolic power.* Cambridge, UK: Polity.

Budach, G., Roy, S., & Heller, M. (2003). Community and commodity in French Ontario. *Language and Society*, *32*, 603–627.

Cameron, D. (2000). *Good to talk? Living and working in a communication culture.* London: Sage.

Campbell, S., & Roberts, C. (2007). Migration, ethnicity, and competing discourses in the job interview: Synthesizing the institutional and the personal. *Discourse and Society*, *18*, 243–272.

Clyne, M. (1994). *Intercultural communication at work: Cultural values in discourse.* Cambridge, UK: Cambridge University Press.

Clyne, M. (2003). *The dynamics of language contact.* Cambridge, UK: Cambridge University Press.

Cook-Gumperz, J., & Messerman, L. (1999). Local identities and institutional practices: Constructing the record of professional collaboration. In S. Sarangi & C. Roberts (Eds.), *Talk, work and institutional order* (pp. 145–182). Berlin, Germany: Mouton de Gruyter.

Daly, N., Holmes, J., Newton, J., & Stubbe, M. (2004). Expletives as solidarity signals in FTAs on the factory floor. *Journal of Pragmatics*, *36*, 945–964.

Day, D. (1992). Communication in a multicultural workplace: Procedural matters. In H. Crischel (Ed.), *Intercultural Communication: Proceedings of the 17th International L.A.U.D. Symposium.* Duisburg, Germany: University of Duisburg.

Day, D., & Wagner, J. (2007). Bilingual professionals. In P. Auer & L. Wei (Eds.), *Handbook of multilingualism and multilingual communication* (pp. 390–404). Berlin, Germany: Mouton de Gruyter.

Duchêne, A. (2009). Marketing, management and performance: Multilingualism as a commodity in a foreign call centre. *Language Policy, 8*, 27–50.

Duff, P. (2005). Thinking globally about English and new literacies: Multilingual socialization at work. In J. Anderson, M. Kendrick, T. Rogers, & S. Smythe (Eds.), *Portraits of literacy across families, communities, and schools* (pp. 341–362). Mahwah, NJ: Erlbaum.

Duff, P. (2008). Language socialization, higher education and work. In P. A. Duff & N. H. Hornberger (Eds.), *Encyclopedia of language and education* (Vol. 8., pp. 257–270). New York: Springer.

Duff, P., Wong, P., & Early, M. (2000). Learning language for work and life: The linguistic socialization of immigrant Canadians seeking careers in health care. *Canadian Modern Language Review, 57*, 9–57.

Erickson, F. (1999). Appropriation of voice and presentation of self as a fellow physician: Aspects of a discourse of apprenticeship in medicine. In S. Sarangi & C. Roberts (Eds.), *Talk, work and institutional order* (pp. 109–144). Berlin, Germany: Mouton de Gruyter.

Erickson, F., & Rittenburg, W. (1987). Topic control and person control: A thorny problem for foreign physicians in interaction with American patients. *Discourse Processes, 10*, 401–415.

Farrell, L. (2000). Ways of doing, ways of being: Language, education and "working" identities. *Language and Education, 14*, 18–36.

Farrell, L. (2001). The "new word order": workplace education and the textual practice of globalisation. *Pedagogy, Culture, and Society, 9*, 57–74.

Firth, A. (1995). Talking for a change: Commodity negotiating by telephone. In A. Firth (Ed.), *The discourse of negotiation: Studies of language in the workplace* (183–222). Oxford, UK: Pergamon.

Firth, A. (1996). The discursive accomplishment of normality: On "lingua franca" English and conversation analysis. *Pragmatics, 26*, 237–258.

Friginal, E. (2009a). *The language of outsourced call centers: A corpus-based study of cross-cultural interaction.* Amsterdam: John Benjamins.

Friginal, E. (2009b). Threats to the sustainability of the outsourced call center industry in the Philippines. *Language Policy, 8*, 51–68.

Garrett, P., & Baquedano-López, P. (2002). Language socialization: Reproduction and continuity, transformation and change. *Annual Review of Anthropology, 31*, 339–361.

Gee, J., Hull, G., & Lankshear, C. (1996). *The new work order: Behind the language of the new capitalism.* Sydney, Australia: Allen and Unwin.

Goldstein, T. (1993). The ESL community and the changing world of work. *TESL Talk, 21*,

56–64.

Goldstein, T. (1997). *Two languages at work: Bilingual life on the production floor.* Berlin, Germany: Mouton de Gruyter.

Goodwin, C. (1995). Seeing in depth. *Social Studies of Science, 25,* 237–274.

Greatbatch, D., Luff, P., Heath, C., & Campion, P. (1993). Interpersonal communication and the human-computer interaction. *Interacting with Computers, 5,* 193–216.

Grünhage-Monetti, M., Halewijn, E., & Holland, C. (2003). *Odysseus: Second language in the workplace.* Strasbourg, France: Council of Europe.

Gumperz, J. (1997). A discussion with John J. Gumperz. In S. Eerdmans, C. Previgagno, & P. Thibault (Eds.), *Discussing communication analysis 1: John Gumperz* (pp. 6–23). Lausanne, Switzerland: Beta Press.

Gumperz, J., Jupp, T., & Roberts, C. (1979). *Crosstalk.* London: National Centre for Industrial Language Training.

Gunnarsson, B. (2009). *Professional discourse.* London: Continuum.

Hawthorne, L. (1997). Defining the target domain: What language skills are required for engineers and nurses? *Melbourne Papers in Language Testing, 6,* 5–20.

Heath, A., & Cheung, S. (2007). *Ethnic penalties in the labour market: Employers and discrimination.* Sheffield, UK: Department of Work and Pensions.

Heath, C., & vom Lehn, D. (2008). Construing interactivity: Enhancing engagement with new technologies in science centres and museums. *Social Studies of Science, 38,* 63–96.

Heller, M. (2002). Globalization and the commodification of bilingualism in Canada. In D. Block & D. Cameron (Eds.), *Globalization and language teaching* (pp. 47–63). London: Routledge.

Heller, M. (in press). Language as a resource in the globalized new economy. In N. Coupland (Ed.), *Handbook of language and globalization.* Oxford, UK: Blackwell.

Hindmarsh, J., Heath, C., & Fraser, M. (2006). (Im)materiality, virtual reality, and interaction: Grounding the "virtual" in studies of technology in action. *Sociological Review, 54*(4), 794–816.

Hobbs, P. (2004). The role of progress notes in the professional socialization of medical residents. *Journal of Pragmatics, 36,* 1579–1607.

Holmes, J. (2000). Talking English 9 to 5: Challenges for ESOL learners at work. *International Journal of Applied Linguistics, 10,* 125–140.

Holmes, J. (2005). Story-telling at work: A complex discursive resource for integrating personal, professional, and social identities. *Discourse Studies, 7,* 671–700.

Holmes, J. (2006). *Gendered talk at work: Constructing gender identity through workplace discourse.* Malden, MA: Blackwell.

Holmes, J., & Stubbe, M. (2003). *Power and politeness in the workplace: A sociolinguistic analysis of talk at work.* London: Pearson Education.

Hull, G. (Ed.). (1997). *Changing work, changing workers: Critical perspectives on language, literacy and skills.* Albany, NY: SUNY Press.

Iedema, R. (2003). *Discourses of post-bureaucratic organisation.* Amsterdam: John Benjamins.

Iedema, R., & Scheeres, H. (2003). From doing to talking work: Renegotiating knowing, doing, and talking. *Applied Linguistics, 24*, 316–337.

Jack, G. (2009). A critical perspective on teaching intercultural competence in a management department. In A. Feng, M. Byram, & M. Fleming (Eds.), *Becoming interculturally competent through education and training* (pp. 95–114). Bristol, UK: Multilingual Matters.

Jacobs-Huey, L. (2003). "Ladies are seen not heard" : Language socialization in a southern, African American cosmetology school. *Anthropology and Education Quarterly, 34*, 277–299.

Jacoby, S. (1998). *Science as performance: Socializing scientific discourse through the conference talk rehearsal.* Unpublished doctoral dissertation, University of California, Los Angeles.

Jupp, T., Roberts, C., & Cook-Gumperz, J. (1982). Language and disadvantage: The hidden process. In J. Gumperz (Ed.), *Language and social identity* (pp. 232–256). Cambridge, UK: Cambridge University Press.

Katz, M. (2000). Workplace language teaching and the intercultural construction of ideologies of competence. *Canadian Modern Language Review, 57*, 144–172.

Kellerman, E., Van Der Haagen, M., & Koonen, H. (2005). "Feet speak louder than the tongue" : A preliminary analysis of language provisions for foreign footballers in the Netherlands. In M. Long (Ed.), *Second language needs analysis* (pp. 200–224). Cambridge, UK: Cambridge University Press.

Kleifgen, J. (2001). Assembling talk: Social alignments in the workplace. *Research on Language and Social Interaction, 34*, 279–308.

Kleifgen, J., & Frenz-Belkin, P. (1997). Assembling knowledge. *Research on Language and Social Interaction, 30*, 157–192.

Lave, J., & Wenger, E. (1991). *Situated learning: Legitimate peripheral participation.* Cambridge, UK: Cambridge University Press.

Lemke, J. (2002). Travels in hypermodality. *Visual Communication, 3*, 299–325.

Li, D. (2000). The pragmatics of making requests in the L2 workplace. *Canadian Modern Language Review, 57*, 58–87.

Matthewman, J. (1996). Trends and developments in the use of competency frameworks. *Competency, 4*, 2–11.

Mawer, G. (1999). *Language and literacy in workplace education: Learning at work.* London:

Longman.

Mawer, G., & Field, L. (1995). *One size fits some! Competency training and non-English speaking background people.* Canberra, Australia: AGPS.

McCall, C. (2003). Language dynamics in the bi- and multilingual workplace. In R. Bayley & S. Schecter (Eds.), *Language socialization in bilingual and multilingual societies* (pp. 235–250). Bristol, UK: Multilingual Matters.

McNamara, T. (1997). Problematizing content validity: The Occupational English Test (OET) as a measure of medical communication. *Melbourne Papers in Language Testing, 6,* 19–43.

Mertz, E. (2007). *The language of law: Learning to think like a lawyer.* Oxford, UK: Oxford University Press.

Mistica, M., Baldwin, T., Cordella, M., & Musgrave, S. (2008). Applying discourse analysis and data mining methods to spoken OSCE assessments. In *The 22nd International Conference on Computational Linguistics: Vol. 1. Proceedings of the conference,* October (pp. 577–584). University of Melbourne, University of Melbourne Press, Australia.

Mondada, L. (2004). Ways of "doing being plurilingual" in international work meetings. In R. Gardner & J. Wagner (Eds.), *Second language conversations* (pp. 27–60). London: Continuum.

Ochs, E., & Schieffelin, B. (1983). *Acquisition of conversational competence.* London: Routledge.

Ochs, E. (1993). Constructing social identity: A language socialization perspective. *Research on Language and Social Interaction, 26,* 287–306.

Ochs, E. (2000). Socialization. *Journal of Linguistic Anthropology, 9,* 230–233.

O'Neill, S., & Gish, A. (2001). *Apprentices' and trainees' English language and literacy skills in workplace learning and performance: Employer and employee opinion.* Leabrook, Australia: National Centre for Vocational Education Research.

Parks, S., & Maguire, M. (1999). Coping with on-the-job writing skills in ESL: A constructivist-semiotic perspective. *Language Learning, 49,* 143–175.

Paugh, A. (2005). Learning about work at dinner time: Language socialization in dual-earning American families. *Discourse and Society, 16,* 55–78.

Phillips, T. (2003). *Speaking at J. P. Morgan's leadership day, 2003.* Retrieved November 25, 2003, from http://www.cre.gov.uk

Poncini, G. (2003). Multicultural business meetings and the role of languages other than English. *Journal of Intercultural Studies, 24,* 17–32.

Rasmussen, G. (1998). The use of address forms in intercultural business conversation. *Revue de Semantique et Pragmatique, 3,* 57–72.

Rasmussen, G., & Wagner, J. (2002). Language choice in international telephone conversations. In K. Luke & T. Pavlidou (Eds.), *Telephone calls. Unity and diversity in conversational structure across languages and cultures* (pp. 111-131). Amsterdam: John Benjamins.

Roberts, C., Davies, E., & Jupp, T. (1992). *Language and discrimination: A study of communication in multi-ethnic workplaces.* London: Longman.

Roberts, C., & Campbell, S. (2005). Fitting stories into boxes: Rhetorical and textual constraints on candidates' performances in British job interviews. *Journal of Applied Linguistics, 2,* 45-73.

Roberts, C., & Campbell, S. (2006). *Talk on trial: Job interviews, language, and ethnicity.* Retrieved from Department for Work & Pensions Web site: http://www.dwp.gov.uk/asd/asd5/rrs2006.asp#talkontrial.

Roberts, C., Campbell, S., & Robinson, Y. (2008). *Talking like a manager: Promotion interviews, language, and ethnicity.*

Roberts, C., & Sarangi, S. (1999). Hybridity in gatekeeping discourse: Issues of practical relevance for the researcher. In S. Sarangi & C. Roberts (Eds.), *Talk, work and institutional order* (pp. 473-504). Berlin, Germany: Mouton de Gruyter.

Roy, S. (2003). Bilingualism and standardization in a Canadian call center: Challenges for a linguistic minority community. In R. Bayley & S. Schecter (Eds.), *Language socialization in bilingual and multilingual societies* (pp. 269-285). Bristol, UK: Multilingual Matters.

Sarangi, S., & Roberts, C. (2002). Discoursal (mis)alignments in professional gatekeeping encounters. In C. Kramsch (Ed.), *Language acquisition and language socialization: Ecological perspectives* (pp. 197-227). New York: Continuum.

Schieffelin, B., & Ochs, E. (Eds.). (1986). *Language socialisation across cultures.* Cambridge, UK: Cambridge University Press.

Scollon, R., & Scollon, S. (1995). *Intercultural communication.* Oxford, UK: Basil Blackwell.

Seale, C., Butler, C., Hutchby, I., Kinnersley, P., & Rollnick, S. (2007). Negotiating frame ambiguity: A study of simulated encounters in medical education. *Communication and Medicine, 4,* 177-188.

Spike, N. (2006). International medical graduates: The Australian perspective. *Academic Medicine, 81,* 842-846.

Suchman, L. (1992). Technologies of accountability: Of lizards and airplanes. In G. Button (Ed.), *Technology in working order: Studies of work interaction and technology* (pp. 113-126). London: Routledge.

Vertoveç, S. (2007). Superdiversity and its implications. *Ethnic and Racial Studies, 30,* 1024-1054.

Vickers, C. (2007). Second language socialization through team interaction among electrical and computing engineering students. *Modern Language Journal, 91,* 621-640.

Wagner, J. (1995). Negotiating activity in technical problem solving. In A. Firth (Ed.), *The discourse of negotiation: Studies of language in the workplace* (pp. 223–246). Oxford, UK: Pergamon.

Waldinger, R., & Lichter, M. (2003). *How the other half works: Immigration and the social organization of labor.* Berkeley, CA: University of California Press.

Wenger, E. (1998). *Communities of practice: Learning, meaning, and identity.* Cambridge, UK: Cambridge University Press.

Willing, K. (1997). Modality in task-orientated discourses: The role of subjectivity in "getting the job done." *Prospect, 12,* 33–42.

SECTION D: LINGUISTIC THEORY AND SECOND LANGUAGE ACQUISITION

Semantic Theory and Second Language Acquisition

Roumyana Slabakova

The article identifies four different types of meaning situated in different modules of language. Such a modular view of language architecture suggests that there may be differential difficulties of acquisition for the different modules. It is argued that second language (L2) acquisition of meaning involves acquiring interpretive mismatches at the first and second language (L1-L2) syntax-semantics interfaces. In acquiring meaning, learners face two types of learning situations. One situation where the sentence syntax presents less difficulty but different pieces of functional morphology subsume different primitives of meaning is dubbed simple syntax-complex semantics. Another type of learning situation is exemplified in less frequent, dispreferred, or syntactically complex sentences where the sentential semantics offers no mismatch; these are labeled complex syntax-simple semantics. Studies representative of these learning situations are reviewed. The issues of importance of explicit instruction with respect to interpretive properties and the effect of the native language are addressed. Studies looking at acquisition of language-specific discourse properties and universal pragmatics are also reviewed. These representative studies and numerous other studies on the L2 acquisition of meaning point to no visible barrier to ultimate success in the acquisition of semantics and pragmatics.

INTRODUCTION: TYPES OF MEANING

Few people start learning an L2 for the exotic sounds or for the elegant sentence structure that they detect in it. Meaning is what we are all after. We would all like to understand and to be able to convey thoughts and feelings and observations in another language the way we do in our native language. Ever since Aristotle, linguists have considered language to be the pairing of form (sound or written strings) and meaning. In this article, I examine the road to meaning, that is, how we get to understand and convey meaning in an L2, and where the pitfalls to that may lie. I begin by distinguishing among several types of meanings: lexical, grammatical, semantic, and pragmatic. Next, I situate them in the language architecture.

For many people, when they think of learning a foreign language, semantics describes predominantly what meanings are encoded in the foreign words. For example, the English *cat* is *gatto* in Italian; both words denote *a small furry animal*. Semantics, however, involves much more than word meaning. Lexical meanings are stored in our mental lexicon, while sentential semantics is compositional, that is, it is calculated by combining the meanings of all the words in a sentence and taking their order into account. Take, for example, the English sentence *Cats were exterminated in a cataclysm*. Depending on the context, it may mean that *a number of cats* were exterminated in a specific tragic event in the past, but it can also mean (untruthfully) that *all cats* were affected by a cataclysm and are now extinct, like dinosaurs. Of these two meaning of *cats*, only the first is available for the equivalent Italian sentence *Gatti sono stati sterminati da un cataclisma*, while the second is not (Longobardi, 2001, among others). Although *cats* and *gatti* have the same word meaning in both languages, when used in speech, they give rise to two sentence meanings in English, but only one sentence meaning in Italian. This difference is captured and explained by the rules for calculating sentence meaning in the two languages, which is the research focus of (phrasal) semantics.

Grammatical meaning also comes into consideration in calculating sentential meaning. Consider the two sentences *Jane eats sushi* and *Jane ate sushi*. They contain two identical lexical items (*Jane, sushi*), and the third, the verbal form, encodes a grammatical difference in tense and aspect. We understand that a present habitual (but not an ongoing) event is meant by the first utterance, while a past habitual event or a past completed event is a possible reading of the second. Grammatical meanings are mostly encoded in inflectional morphology (*-ed* for past simple,*-s* for third-person singular present simple, etc.).

A fourth type of meaning, known as pragmatic meaning, depends on context consideration and knowledge of the world. It is the object of investigation of linguistic pragmatics. Scalar implicatures are a good example of the dissociation between semantic (or logical) and pragmatic meaning. Consider the following example of a well-known pragmatic inference. When we hear the sentence *Some professors are smart*, we actually understand that the speaker wants to say *Not all professors are smart*. Notice that the meaning *not all* is not encoded by the speaker's utterance, nor is it part of what the speaker has said. Rather, that interpretation is an assumption inferentially derived by the hearer on the basis of what the speaker has said. Logically speaking, *some means some and possibly all*. For pragmatic felicity, however, *some* means *some but not all*. The rationale goes like this: If the speaker wanted to say that *some and possibly all* professors are smart, she would have uttered *all professors are smart*, being maximally informative. Since she did not, she must really mean *not all* professors are smart. Understatements of this sort in human speech are regulated by Gricean maxims and, more specifically, the maxim of quantity: Make your contribution as informative as is required; do not make your contribution more informative than is required (Grice, 1989). Lexical items that induce such calculations are arranged on a scale: <*some, most, all*>, <*start, finish*>, and so on, where uttering the lower-placed item implies that the higher placed item is not true.

When learning an L2, speakers are faced with four different acquisition tasks regarding meaning: First, they have to learn the lexical items of the target language, that is, map the linguistic form and lexical meaning one by one. This is certainly a laborious task. Second, learning the functional morphology is qualitatively

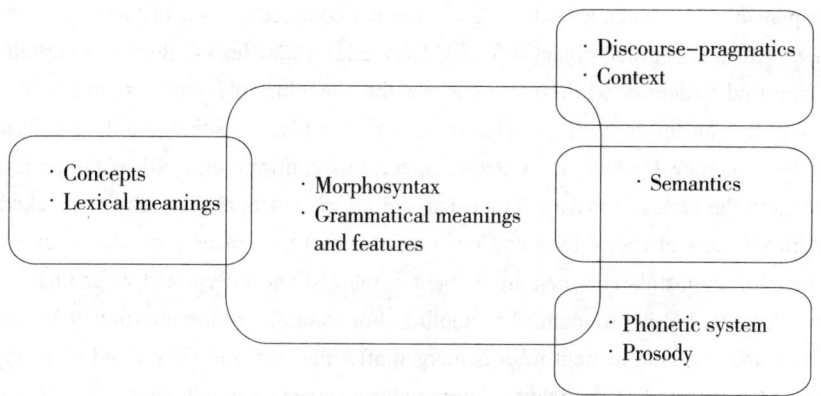

Fig. 1. Modular design of the language faculty, following Reinhart (2006).

different: Abstracting away from irregular morphology, once a speaker learns that *-ed* in English encodes a past habit or a past completed event, she can apply this knowledge to all English regular verbs. Third and fourth are sentential and pragmatic meanings, which are calculated using universal mechanisms of human language. Once the lexical and grammatical meanings are learned, sentential and pragmatic meanings come for free and do not constitute a barrier for acquisition. I will explain these statements based on current assumptions of the language architecture in the next section.

LANGUAGE ARCHITECTURE AND TYPES OF MEANINGS

It is important to review current proposals for the language architecture in order to clarify our assumptions on types of meanings, modularity, and learning tasks in L2 acquisition. I assume a widely accepted model of the grammar following Reinhart (2006), illustrated in Figure 1 and explained below.

What is to be learned and what comes for free, keeping in mind the language architecture in Figure 1 above? In producing a sentence, all the requisite lexical items are drawn from the mental lexicon into the computational system (the morphosyntax box). The latter can be imagined as a working space where operations such as select, merge, and agree combine lexical items into phrases, and then into bigger phrases until a sentence tree is complete. The operation select is responsible for a category selecting a particular complement, for instance, the verb *read* selects a nominal object *a book*. *Merge* adds a new lexical item to a partially composed structure, while *agree* ensures the checking of features such that two categories on the tree are in agreement, for example, the subject and verb form in the sentence *He knows*. Syntactic operations continue until all of the lexical items in the lexical array are exhausted and all grammatical features are checked. Both visible and invisible operations (movements) take place here. A movement operation is postulated when an element is merged and interpreted in one part of the structure but is pronounced in another: For example, in the question *What did you read?*, the complement *what* is merged after the verb and interpreted as asking about the object of reading, but we pronounce it sentence-initially.

Universal principles and language-specific parameters reside in this computational system. The latter are reflected in the features of the grammatical morphemes also residing in the morphosyntax box. The complete syntactic object (the tree) is then passed on by means of a spell-out procedure to the phonetic system for pronunciation and to the semantic system for interpretation. Context, for example, the discourse-pragmatics of the message or the dialogue, also impacts semantic processes and interacts with the computational system. A reverse mechanism of building a syntactic tree in the syntactic module and sending it for interpretation to the semantic module is proposed for comprehension.

The key ideas here are compositionality (building up structure from building blocks: lexical and grammatical morphemes) and a matching procedure between syntactic structure and interpretation. Next, I elaborate on this matching procedure, or interface, between syntax and semantics. Fairly uncontroversially, syntactic structure needs to be correlated with semantic structure for a form-meaning mapping; however, this correlation is not always trivial (Jackendoff, 2002). The syntactic processor works with objects like syntactic trees, their constituents, and relations: noun phrases, verb phrases, grammatical features, and so forth. The semantic processor operates with events and states, agents and patients, individuals and propositions. For example, in the sentence *The teacher ate the apple*, *the teacher* is a noun phrase in subject position in the syntax, but an agent in the semantics. The operations at the interface are limited precisely to those structures that need to be correlated, and they do not see other structures and operations (like case-marking) that would have no relevance to the other module.

When two languages come into play, this computation gets even more complicated. That is why it is crucial to identify how languages differ and how we learn meanings in an L1 and L2. Within a formalist framework such as minimalism (Chomsky, 1995) or Jackendoff's (2002) parallel architecture, Universal Grammar (UG) makes available universal principles common to all languages and a finite number of grammatical meanings and word order options. Children learning their native language fix these parametric options based on the input they are exposed to.

The central question for L2 researchers then is: How much of semantic or conceptual structure is part of Universal Grammar, and how much of it may be parameterized? Jackendoff (2002) argued that the basic architecture and contents of conceptual structure are universal and innate, while languages differ in their syntactic strategies for expressing phrasal semantics. Different linguistic forms assemble and map different natural groupings of meanings. There are numerous instances of mismatches at the syntax-semantics interface. For example, while the English past progressive tense signifies an ongoing event in the past, Spanish imperfect can have both an ongoing and a habitual interpretation. The English simple past tense, on the other hand, has a onetime finished event interpretation and a habitual interpretation, while the Spanish preterit has only the former. Thus, the same semantic primitive meanings (ongoing, habitual, and onetime finished event), which have to be expressed in every language and are therefore part of universal conceptual structure, are distributed over different pieces of functional morphology. What hosts most of the language variation in meaning, then, is the syntax-semantics interface.

Context-dependent meanings are calculated at the interface between syntax and discourse/pragmatics. For example, topic and focus (roughly, old and new information) are universal categories and all languages have to reflect them in one way or another. But some languages use intonation, other languages use clitic doubling or movement of certain phrases, and many others can use a mix of both strategies to mark topic and focus. Thus, the grammatical meanings of old and new information can be calculated at two different interfaces: at the syntax-phonetics/phonology interface and the syntax-discourse interface, or both.

To recapitulate our assumptions, linguistic meaning has its own combinatorial structure and is not simply read off the syntax. The operations at the form-meaning interfaces are nontrivial computations. Linguistic computations at all levels of structure are universal. When learning an L2, however, a speaker may be confronted with different mappings between units of meaning and units of morphosyntactic structure. Syntax and phonetics/phonology, syntax and discourse, and semantics and pragmatics also interface in a nontrivial, but universal, way.

TWO LEARNING SITUATIONS AT THE SYNTAX-SEMANTICS INTERFACE

Recent studies on the L2 acquisition of interpretive properties have looked mainly at two types of learning tasks. In one type, the properties to be learned demonstrate quite complex syntax, in the sense that sentences involve less frequent constructions (e.g., French double genitives[1] in Dekydtspotter, Sprouse, &

Anderson, 1997; French discontinuous *wh*-phrases[2] in Dekydtspotter & Sprouse, 2001; French quantifiers at a distance[3] in Dekydtspotter, Sprouse, & Thyre, 1999/2000; Dutch and German scrambling[4] in Unsworth, 2005; Hopp, 2007). The native speakers in these experiments very often show far lower acceptance rates than we are used to seeing in the L2 literature. In many cases, alternative ways of articulating the same message exist, making the tested constructions dispreferred. (This in itself may explain the fact that learners sometimes have higher rates of acceptance than native speakers.) In most cases, the properties under scrutiny present the poverty of the stimulus situations to the learner, in the sense that no positive evidence exists for them in the linguistic input. However, at the syntax-semantics interface, these same properties do not present much difficulty, as there are no mismatches. This learning situation can be dubbed *complex syntax-simple semantics*. If learners have acquired the relevant functional lexicon item and have constructed the right sentence representation, the presence or absence of semantic interpretation follows in a straightforward way without any more stipulations. In most cases, learners demonstrate that a contrast exists in their grammar between the allowed and the disallowed interpretations.

In another type of learning situation, the syntactic structure presents less difficulty to the learners. Quite often, these studies deal with properties related to truth-conditional meanings of common morphological forms, like the preterit and imperfect tenses in Spanish-English interlanguage (Montrul & Slabakova, 2002), progressive tenses in Japanese-English interlanguage (Gabriele, 2005), and bare verb meaning in Bulgarian-English interlanguage (Slabakova, 2003). Not surprisingly, native speakers in these experiments show the regular range of accuracy found in studies of L2 acquisition (80–90%). The learning challenges lie, however, at the syntax-semantics interface. Learners have to figure out what morphological forms are mapped onto what meanings in the target language, since there is no one-to-one correspondence at the syntax-semantics interface. Somewhat simplistically, I dub this learning situation *simple syntax-complex semantics*. Results at all levels of proficiency from beginner to near-native point to the conclusion that knowledge of this type of semantic mismatch emerges gradually but surely. Next, I discuss some studies representative of the two learning situations.

As an example of the complex syntax-simple semantics learning situation, I examine tense-dependent interpretations of discontinuous quantifiers, as studied by Dekydtspotter and Sprouse (2001). The semantic knowledge to be acquired involves the speech-time versus past time construal of adjectival restrictions of quantifiers. Consider the French sentence in (1).

(1) *Qui de célèbre fumait au bistro dans les année 60?*
 Who of famous smoked in the bar in the 60s?
 "Which famous person smoked in bars in the 60s?"

A possible answer to this question may involve a present and a past celebrity. On the other hand, it is impossible to answer the discontinuous interrogative constituent as in (2) with a present celebrity. Only someone who was a celebrity in the past is the appropriate answer.

(2) *Qui fumait de célèbre au bistro dans les année 60?*
 Who smoked of famous in the bar in the 60s?
 "Which famous person smoked in bars in the 60s?"

Without going into analysis of details, the two interpretations depend on where the adjectival phrase *de célèbre* is interpreted in the structure: below or above the tense operator. What kind of knowledge must an L2 learner have in order to be aware of both interpretations in the case of continuous *wh*-constituents but only one interpretation in the case of discontinuous ones? First, knowledge of overt *wh*-movement is required. It relies on properties of *wh*-words encoded in the functional lexicon, but such knowledge can be transferred from the native language in English-French interlanguage, since both English and French exhibit *wh*-movement. Second, knowledge that discontinuous interrogatives are allowed in French is necessary. This property is not taught in French classrooms (Dekydtspotter & Sprouse, 2001) but was given to the participants in the experiment in the form of the test sentences (assuming they believe that the researchers did not trick them into judging ungrammatical sentences). Third, the (not taught) language-specific knowledge that French allows the *wh*-word *qui* (*who*) to have an adjectival restriction at all is necessary, while English *who famous* and *who of famous* are not legitimate strings. Most importantly, however, what Dekydtspotter and Sprouse labeled *the universal deductive procedure* is indispensable for reaching the interpretive knowledge. The authors made a convincing case for the interpretations not being learnable on the basis of input alone and not transferable from English.

The task of the participants was to read a paragraph-length context in English matched with a test sentence in French. After the test sentence, the participants had to answer whether that was the correct answer to the question. The results show that past-time readings were preferred for continuous and discontinuous interrogatives by natives and learners alike. In this respect, learners followed the native pattern. It is knowledge of the missing interpretation, namely, the speech-time reading (in example 2, someone who is a celebrity at present) with discontinuous constituents that is crucial in answering the research question of this study. Both intermediate and advanced learners demonstrated a statistically significant difference in their acceptance of the available and the unavailable interpretations. In other words, they reliably treated the two constructions differently. Learners were capable of successfully combining the properties related to the French functional lexicon—the availability of *wh*-movement and discontinuous interrogatives—with the universal meaning-calculating algorithm. Even not very proficient L2 learners, in this case learners with as little as three semesters of exposure to French, manifested knowledge depending on this universal algorithm. It is no small achievement on the part of the learners that even with dispreferred strings or interpretations and under severe poverty of the stimulus, they manage to exhibit the contrasts we expect based on the respective syntactic structures and the universal meaning computation procedure.

To illustrate the simple syntax-complex semantics learning situation, we take a look at an aspectual mismatch. The linguistic properties whose acquisition Slabakova (2003) investigated have to do with grammatical aspect. English differs from German, Romance, and Slavic with respect to the semantics of the present tense. The hachure sign # signifies that this interpretation is not available.

(3) a. *She eats an apple right now.   #Ongoing event
    b. She is eating an apple right now. Ongoing event
    c. She eats an apple (every day).   Habitual series of complete events

Furthermore, the English bare infinitive denotes not only the processual part of an event but includes the completion of that event.

(4) a. I saw Mary cross the street. (completion entailed)
    b. I saw Mary crossing the street. (no completion entailed)

In trying to explain the facts illustrated in (4), many researchers have noticed that English verbal morphology is impoverished (Bennett & Partee, 1972). The experimental study adopts Giorgi and Pianesi's (1997) proposal. English verbs, they argued, are "naked" forms that can express several verbal values, such as the bare infinitive, the first and second person singular, and the first, second, and third person plural. Giorgi and Pianesi proposed that verbs are categorically disambiguated in English by being marked in the lexicon with the aspectual feature [+perf], standing for perfective. Thus, children acquiring English can distinguish verbal forms from nominals, whose feature bundle will exclude the feature [+perf]. In Romance, Slavic, and other Germanic languages, on the other hand, all verbal forms have to be inflected for person, number, and tense. Thus, nouns and verbs cannot have the same forms, unlike English, in which zero-derivation abounds. The Bulgarian verb, for example, is associated with typical verbal features as [+V, person, number], and it is recognizable and learnable as a verb because of these features. Bulgarian verbs are therefore not associated with a [+perf] feature. Consequently, Bulgarian equivalents to bare infinitives do not entail completion of the event, as (5) illustrates.

(5) Ivan vidja Maria da presiča ulicata. (no completion entailed)
    Ivan saw Maria to cross street-DET
    "John saw Mary crossing the street."

Thus, Bulgarian and English exhibit a contrast in the present viewpoint aspect. It follows that the Bulgarian equivalent to the bare verb does not have to check the feature [+perf] because the verbal root does not carry this feature from the lexicon. In the acquisition of English by Bulgarian native speakers, then, the learning task is to notice the trigger of this property: The fact that English inflectional morphology is highly impoverished, lacking many person-number-tense verb endings. The property itself, if Giorgi and Pianesi (1997) were correct, is the [+perf] feature that is attached to English eventive verbs in the lexicon. Knowledge of this property will entail knowledge of four different interpretive facts:

(a) bare verb forms denote a completed event; (b) present tense has only habitual interpretation; (c) the progressive affix is needed for ongoing interpretation of eventive verbs; (d) states in the progressive denote temporary states. This is a syntax-semantics mismatch that relates a minimal difference between languages—the presence or absence of a feature in the lexicon—to various and superficially not connected interpretive properties. All of the properties are not attested in the native language of the learners. Even more importantly, of the four semantic properties just enumerated, the second, third, and fourth are introduced, discussed, and drilled in language classrooms. The first one, however, is not explicitly taught.

The learners in this study were typical classroom instructed learners of low, high intermediate, and advanced proficiency. All participants took a production task to ascertain knowledge of inflectional morphology and a truth value judgment task with a story in their native language and a test sentence in English; they had to indicate whether the test sentence was a good description of the story.

Results on the acquisition of all four semantic properties pattern the same way. On the three instructed properties (habitual interpretation of the present, progressive needed for ongoing interpretation, and states in the progressive denote temporary states), the advanced learners were highly accurate. Intermediate learners were more accurate on the habitual present than on ongoing progressive. Recall that the simple present in Bulgarian has both a habitual and an ongoing interpretation, so the progressive tense is a new form-meaning mapping for them. Advanced learners had no problem with the meaning of the progressive tense. Thus initial first language (L1) transfer and subsequent morphological acquisition were clearly attested in the data.

On the crucial knowledge that an English bare verb denotes a complete event, and consequently is incompatible with an incomplete event story, advanced learners were even more accurate than native speakers. They rejected the unavailable meaning 87% of the time. Even more importantly, all learner groups were quite accurate in attributing a complete interpretation to the bare verb, a property that cannot transfer from the L1, as example (5) indicates. Individual accuracy showed that more than half of individual learners had acquired successfully every aspect of the taught properties. Importantly, 44% to 72% of individuals in different proficiency groups were successful on the mappings of the untaught property.

After establishing that it is possible to acquire semantic properties in the

L2 that are not manifested in the native language, let us now turn to the impact of the instruction variable. Slabakova (2003) reported that extensive scrutiny of the instruction materials and discussions with the instructors ascertained that the present simple and progressive tense meanings are explicitly taught and drilled from the beginning of classroom instruction. On the other hand, the closed denotation of bare verb forms is not taught, and the Bulgarian teachers are not consciously aware of it. Is it the case that instruction is a significant variable and learners were more accurate on the taught than on untaught properties? The short answer is no. All groups performed equally well on all conditions. The theoretical implication of this finding is that all semantic effects of learning the trigger (English verbs are morphologically impoverished) and the related property ([+perf] feature attached to verbs in the lexicon) appear to be engaged at the same time. Even untaught syntax-semantics mismatches are learnable to a nativelike level.

Finally, in this section I summarize some research on what has been argued to be a true semantic parameter: the article choice parameter. The learning situation can still be described as involving a simple syntax-complex semantics; however, understanding how the discourse affects article choice is crucial for correct usage, too. As is well known, speakers of a language without articles (e.g., Japanese, Chinese, Korean, and Russian) have a hard time using articles correctly in English. A number of experimental studies (e.g., Huebner, 1983; Robertson, 2000, among many others) have identified two types of errors these learners make: They either omit articles altogether or use them in inappropriate contexts. A series of recent studies, reported on in Ionin (2003); Ionin, Ko, and Wexler (2004); and Ionin, Zubizarreta, and Maldonado (2008) provide a principled, parameter-based explanation of learner article interpretation and use. Definiteness and specificity are semantic features; both are part of the conceptual arsenal of language. They are also discourse-related since they rely on the knowledge of the speaker and the hearer in a communication situation. By using a definite nominal phrase, a speaker refers to a uniquely identified individual in the mind of the speaker and the hearer. Definiteness is morphologically encoded by *the*; indefiniteness by *a(n)* for singular count nouns and by zero article for plural nouns. Uniqueness can be established by either prior mention or shared knowledge. Specificity, on the other hand, also reflects the property of uniqueness (an object or person being singled-out in the situation), but only in the mind of the speaker, not of the hearer. A specific nominal phrase has to be noteworthy in some discourse-related way. Specificity is not marked morphologically in standard English; that is, nominal phrases can be specific or not, as the examples in (6) illustrate for indefinites.

(6) a. Jill wants to marry a Canadian. She is going to present him to her family at Christmas. (indefinite specific)
    b. Jill wants to marry a Canadian, but she has not met one yet. (indefinite nonspecific)

When speakers of a language without articles have to acquire articles in English, their learning task is to map the semantic feature definiteness onto its morphological expression *the*, and the lack of it to *a(n)* or zero article. Note that in article-less languages definiteness is established through context and other linguistic means such as demonstrative pronouns but does not have dedicated morphology. Thus, it is not the semantic feature definiteness that is new to the learners, just its morphological expression is. The two semantic features, specificity and definiteness, are somewhat close in meaning, having to do with establishing uniqueness of an object in the discourse. It is not inconceivable, then, for learners to use both features in semantically bootstrapping themselves into the morphology. However, Ionin (2003) and Ionin et al. (2004) went one step further and propose the article choice parameter as in (7), a principled explanation of how languages choose which feature their articles reflect.

(7) A language that has two articles distinguishes them as follows:
  - The definiteness setting: Articles are distinguished on the basis of definiteness (exemplified in English).
  - The specificity setting: Articles are distinguished on the basis of specificity (exemplified in Samoan).

Cross-linguistic evidence for this semantic parameter comes mainly from Samoan, a language that purportedly uses the article *le* with specific nominal phrases and the article *se* with nonspecific ones, regardless of definiteness. Based on the article choice parameter, Ionin et al. (2004) predicted that learners of English from articleless languages will fluctuate between the different settings of the UG-supplied semantic parameter until the input leads them to the target value (definiteness). Their native language will not aid them in this choice since it distinguishes both features, but none of them morphologically. Importantly, they will overuse *a* in nonspecific contexts and *the* in specific contexts. These predictions are subsumed under the fluctuation hypothesis.

Ionin et al. (2004) tested beginning, intermediate, and advanced learners of English with Russian or Korean as their native languages. They employed a forced-choice elicitation task and a production task. Results indicate that when the target article is *the*, learners incorrectly use *a* with 8% of the specific NPs but with 33% of the nonspecific NPs. Similarly, when the target article is indefinite, learners incorrectly chose *the* 36% of the time with specific NPs but only 7% with nonspecific NPs. Thus learners' behavior is not random; their choice of article is significantly affected by the specificity of the nominal phrase. In the process of acquiring the morphological expressions of definiteness, they may sometimes map nonspecific definite NPs onto *a*, and specific indefinite NPs onto *the*. In other words, they fluctuate between the definiteness and the specificity value of the article choice parameter. The predictions of the fluctuation hypothesis are supported indeed.

However, individual results reveal a more complex picture. Of the 25 intermediate and advanced Russian-native learners, only 5 had acquired the definiteness, target-like English pattern. Two participants demonstrated the opposite (specificity) setting of the parameter and 8 fluctuated between definiteness and specificity. Furthermore, there were 3 learners who only heeded specificity with either indefinite or definite NPs but not both. Finally, 7 learners showed a truly miscellaneous pattern, unpredicted by the fluctuation hypothesis. In addition, Ionin et al. (2004) production results revealed that learners overused *the* with specific indefinites, but did not overuse *a* with nonspecific definites. In conclusion, the article choice parameter and the related fluctuation prediction is a principled explanation of learners' ostensibly erratic, but actually predictable article choice. It is an eminently testable hypothesis. Moreover, as more English L2 groups are being tested from different languages without articles, some interesting variation is being uncovered. For example, the presence of classifiers in Chinese (which are only used with indefinite NPs) may be aiding the learners in acquiring English articles, while the presence of demonstrative pronouns (which are specificity and deixis markers) is not aiding Polish (Tryzna, 2009) and Russian learners in a similar way. However, the main conclusion remains that, even though the learners cannot transfer any morphology knowledge from their native languages, the universal semantics helps them to bootstrap themselves into language-specific morphological expressions of definiteness.

In this section, three studies illustrative of two types of learning situations were reviewed. These are representative of a range of recent studies on the L2 acquisition of the syntax-semantics interface (for an extensive review, see Slabakova, 2006, 2008). In the next section, I turn to acquisition at the syntax-discourse interface.

THE SYNTAX-DISCOURSE INTERFACE

The syntax-discourse interface may be qualitatively different from the syntax-semantics interface. There is a growing body of research suggesting that external interface properties, those that are at the interface of linguistic modules and other cognitive systems such as syntax-discourse, are especially difficult to acquire and cause developmental delays for L1-L2 learners. On the other hand, internal interface properties, those that are at the interface of different linguistic modules such as syntax and semantics are acquired more fluidly and faster (Tsimpli & Sorace 2006, White, 2009). The most well-researched property at the syntax-discourse interface is the null subject parameter, since it involves both syntactic and pragmatic constraints (Belletti, Bennati, & Sorace, 2007; Rothman, 2009, among many others) I will compare here two studies that investigate another property: clitic doubling. Clitic doubling in Bulgarian (a syntactic property) is sensitive to which argument is topic (old information, based on the current discourse). Topics are clitic-doubled whether they are fronted as in (8A) or in situ as in (8B).

(8) Q: Has anybody seen Ivan?
    A: Ivan go vidja Maria.   O-Cl_{obj}-V-S
    Ivan him-cl saw Maria
    B: Maria go   vidja Ivan   S-Cl_{obj}-V-O
    Maria him-cl saw Ivan
    C: #Ivan vidja Maria   #O-V-S

"Maria saw Ivan."

In Spanish, a very similar construction is known as clitic-left dislocation (CLLD)[5] : A fronted topic is doubled by a clitic, but only when that fronted object is specific:

(9) El libro, lo lei
 the book, it-cl read-1sg
 "The book, I read."
(10) *Un libro, lo lei
 a book, it-cl read-1sg
 "A book, I read."

Valenzuela (2006) studied knowledge of this semantic-pragmatic constraint in the interlanguage grammar of near-native speakers of Spanish with English as their native language. She employed an oral grammaticality judgment (GJ) task, an oral sentence selection task, and a written sentence completion task, all targeting knowledge of the same property. Oral presentation of the experimental stimuli is crucial in such studies, as the intonation should include a pause between the fronted object and the rest of the sentence, but not a very long pause (Valenzuela, 2006). Results of all three tasks indicate that near-native speakers are not distinguishing between specific and nonspecific topic constructions to the same degree as the monolingual controls. However, the differences are really a matter of degree, as all the choices of the near-natives are in the right direction. It is also notable that about 30% of individual learners demonstrate the target contrast in their L2 grammars.

Ivanov (2009) also studied knowledge of clitic doubling as a marker of topicality, but he compared it to knowledge of the fact that the clitic is ungrammatical when it doubles focused constituents. He employed a GJ task and a context-sentence evaluation task: a situation described in English and a short dialogue in Bulgarian where the participants had to evaluate four different word order and clitic combinations (fronted object versus object in situ, presence versus absence of a clitic) on a scale from 1 (totally unacceptable) to 5 (perfectly acceptable). Test items were presented both written and aurally. Fourteen intermediate and 10 advanced learners of Bulgarian as well as 15 native Bulgarian controls participated in the experiment.

Recall that knowledge of clitic doubling in these learners' interlanguage cannot come from English since English lacks clitics. The discourse requirements are not taught in Bulgarian classrooms but they are extremely frequent in everyday informal Bulgarian. Intermediate learners as a group were not sensitive to the discourse properties of clitic doubling, although on the whole they were aware of their syntactic properties. All advanced learners exhibited knowledge of syntactic as well as the discourse requirements of clitic doubling, and 9 out of 24 learners (37.5%) were statistically indistinguishable from native speakers in recognizing the pragmatic constraints. The results of this study demonstrate that complex properties at the syntax-pragmatics interface are not impossible to acquire.

While the jury is still out on L2 acquisition at the syntax-discourse interface, some studies indicate that there is extended optionality and variability in the acquisition of different types of interface properties while other studies point to complete and successful acquisition. It is essential in the future to expand the range of properties and languages that we investigate at this interface so that we get a better picture of the underlying reasons for the variability.

THE SEMANTICS-PRAGMATICS INTERFACE

Finally, I review some recent work on the acquisition of properties on the interface between semantics and pragmatics. Work on L2 acquisition of such properties is in its very early stages, but there is already a considerable body of findings on the child knowledge of such properties. To remind the reader, a scalar implicature is the additional (not all) meaning calculated over and above the literal meaning in sentences such as *Some professors are smart*. Since their computation mechanism is universal, the learning task in L2 acquisition involves transferring this purportedly universal mechanism from the L1. Therefore, we expect L2 learners to be accurate in scalar implicature derivation once they know the scalar lexical items, but that processing resources may have an impact on accuracy and speed.

Slabakova (in press) tested knowledge of scalar implicatures by 23 English native speakers, 30 Korean native speakers, and 30 advanced and 20 intermediate Korean learners of English. The two native speaker groups were intended to ascertain that the scalar implicature calculation mechanism is indeed universal. In

Experiment 1, subjects read eight universally true sentences (*All elephants have trunks*), eight sentences infelicitous with *some* (*Some elephants have trunks*), eight sentences felicitous with *some* (*Some books have color pictures*), 8 sentences false with *all* (*All books have color pictures*), and eight absurd fillers (*All/some garages sing*). If the participants agreed with the sentences such as *Some elephants have trunks*, the answer was coded as logical; if they rejected the sentences as not fully informative since all elephants have trunks, the answer was coded as pragmatic.

The results confirmed that English and Korean adult native speakers give about 60% logical answers and 40% pragmatic answers. In addition, individual results revealed that these participants fell roughly into two groups: people who consistently gave logical answers and people who consistently chose pragmatically felicitous answers. Importantly, Korean learners of English attributed more pragmatic interpretations to scalar implicatures without context (around 60%) than they did in their native Korean, and significantly more than English native speakers. When asked to judge sentences with *some* in context, they offered pragmatic judgments around 90% of the times (Experiment 2). These findings suggest that L2 learners observe Gricean maxims even at an intermediate level of attainment, and probably right after they learn the scalar lexical terms. Much more research on properties at the semantics-pragmatics interface is necessary before we come to any solid conclusions. However, it is safe to say at this point that the first findings point to no real difficulty at this interface.

CONCLUSION

The acquisition of meaning is arguably the most important task of the L2 learner. Linguists distinguish between lexical, grammatical, semantic, and discourse-pragmatic meanings, situated in different modules of the language architecture. By definition, lexical and grammatical meanings capture language variation. Mapping of forms to lexical and grammatical meanings constitutes the main task, and the hardest part, of language acquisition. The remaining two meanings, sentential and discourse-pragmatic, are calculated using universal computation mechanisms. It was illustrated that universal semantic meanings (e.g., specificity) affect the morphological mapping of closely related meanings (e.g., definiteness, Ionin et al., 2004). It was argued that once the inflectional morphology is learned, learners are aware of all its semantic consequences (Dekydtspotter & Sprouse, 2001), no matter whether the properties are taught or untaught (Slabakova, 2003). Even at the syntax-discourse interface, acquisition of properties unavailable from the L1 is possible (Ivanov, 2009; Valenzuela, 2006). At the semantics-pragmatics interface, L2 learners transfer universal properties like Gricean maxims (Slabakova, in press). It follows that in order to acquire meaning in an L2, the learner has to go through the inflectional morphology, and hence, morphology is the bottleneck of acquisition (Slabakova, 2008). Phrasal and linguistic pragmatic meaning comes for free!

In the future, it will be profitable to dig deeper into meaning-form mismatches across languages and factor in the effect of the different surface realizations of the same meaning. For example, as discussed earlier, all languages mark topic and focus, also known as theme and rheme, old and new information. If the L1 marks topic and focus with lexical means only, is it harder to learn a language that marks them through intonation, or through word order changes and regular morphology like clitics? A specific case of a L1-L2 form-meaning mismatch is the case when a language (e.g., English) marks a meaning, say, past time, through a regular morpheme such as *-ed*, while another language (e.g., Vietnamese, Thai) indexes time through various adverbials and discourse. The prediction is that it will be much harder to acquire a qualitatively different way of denoting a grammatical meaning as compared to just mapping it to another piece of morphology. Going even deeper into form-meaning mappings, we should point out that one form-one meaning mappings are extremely rare in practice. In this article, I have mentioned the past tense morpheme in English as a carrier of the past time meaning. However, as Lardiere (2007) convincingly argued, there is no such thing as a plus or minus past feature reflected in past tense marking. The latter can also mark eventive perfect aspect (*Paul walked the dog*), counterfactuality (*If I bought this, I'd be sorry*), politeness or distance (*I was wondering ...*), or even lack of tense in sequence of tense situations (in *Roger said that he disagreed with her analysis*, the disagreement may still be going on). Which of those many meanings of the *-ed* morphology are learned first, and which are learned through more extensive exposure? Answers to these and other intriguing research questions will bring more detail into the bigger picture, permit new generalizations, and enhance our understanding of how we acquire meaning in an L2 language.

NOTES

1 Nominal phrases that contain two arguments marked by prepositions as in:

Les preuves brilliants du théorème du professeur
"the brilliant proofs of the theorem of the professor"

2 See example in (1) below.

3 This is a construction in which a quantifiers such as the equivalent of *many* is pronounced in another position, away from the nominal it quantifies over, in this case "gold coins":

Il a	*beaucoup*	*trouvé*	*de pièce d'or.*
he has	many	found	gold coins

"He found many gold coins."

4 Scrambling is an optional movement of nominal phrases to positions different from those of the neutral word order of the sentence.

5 Valenzuela (2006) specifically claimed that examples such as these in (9) are not hanging topics but true CLLD, and the comma is indicative of a short pause, not a long pause as in hanging topic. She provided numerous tests to distinguish between the two constructions.

REFERENCES

Belletti, A., Bennati, E., & Sorace, A. (2007). Theoretical and developmental issues in the syntax of subjects: Evidence from near-native Italian. *Natural Language and Linguistic Theory*, 25, 657–689.

Bennett, M., & Partee, B. (1972). *Toward the logic of tense and aspect in English*. Santa Monica, CA: System Development Corporation.

Chomsky, N. (1995). *The minimalist program*. Cambridge, MA: MIT Press.

Dekydtspotter, L., Sprouse, R., & Anderson, B. (1997). The interpretive interface in L2 acquisition: The process-result distinction in English-French interlanguage grammars. *Language Acquisition*, 6, 297–332.

Dekydtspotter, L., Sprouse, R., & Thyre, R. (1999/2000). The interpretation of quantification at a distance in English-French interlanguage: Domain-specificity and second language acquisition. *Language Acquisition, 8*, 265–320.

Dekydtspotter, L., & Sprouse, R. (2001). Mental design and (second) language epistemology: Adjectival restrictions of *wh*-quantifiers and tense in English-French interlanguage. *Second Language Research, 17*, 1–35.

Gabriele, A. (2005). *The acquisition of aspect in a second language: A bidirectional study of learners of English and Japanese.* Unpublished doctoral dissertation, City University of New York.

Giorgi, A., & Pianesi, F. (1997). *Tense and aspect: From semantics to morphosyntax.* Oxford, UK: Oxford University Press.

Grice, P. (1989). *Studies in the way of words.* Cambridge, MA: Harvard University Press.

Hopp, H. (2007). Ultimate attainment at the interfaces in second language acquisition: Grammar and processing (Doctoral dissertation, University of Groningen, Netherlands). Groningen *Dissertations in Linguistics (GRODIL), 65.*

Huebner, T. (1983). *A longitudinal analysis of the acquisition of English.* Ann Arbor, MI: Karoma.

Ionin, T. (2003). *Article semantics in second language acquisition.* Unpublished doctoral dissertation, MIT, Cambridge, MA.

Ionin, T., Ko, H., & Wexler, K. (2004). Article semantics in L2 acquisition: The role of specificity. *Language Acquisition, 12*, 3–69.

Ionin, T., Zubizarreta, M. L., & Maldonado, S. B. (2008). Sources of linguistic knowledge in the second language acquisition of English articles. *Lingua, 118*, 554–576.

Ivanov, I. (2009, March). *Pragmatic effects of clitic doubling in L2 Bulgarian: A test case for the Interface Hypothesis.* Paper presented at the Generative Approaches to Second Language Acquisition (GASLA) 10 conference, Urbana-Champaign, IL.

Jackendoff, R. (2002). *Foundations of language.* Oxford, UK: Oxford University Press.

Lardiere, D. (2007). *Ultimate attainment in second language acquisition: A case study.* Mahwah, NJ: Lawrence Erlbaum Associates.

Longobardi, G. (2001). How comparative is semantics? A unified parametric theory of bare nouns and proper names. *Natural Language Semantics, 9*, 335–369.

Montrul, S., & Slabakova, R. (2002). Acquiring morphosyntactic and semantic properties of preterite and imperfect tenses in L2 Spanish. In A.-T. Perez-Leroux & J. Liceras (Eds.), *The acquisition of Spanish morphosyntax: The L1-L2 connection* (pp. 113–149). Dordrecht, Netherlands: Kluwer.

Reinhart, T. (2006). *Interface strategies.* Cambridge, MA: MIT Press.

Robertson, D. (2000). Variability in the use of the English article system by Chinese learners of English. *Second Language Research, 16*, 135–172.

Rothman, J. (2009). Pragmatic deficits with syntactic consequences? L2 pronominal subjects and the syntax-pragmatic interface. *Journal of Pragmatics, 41*, 951–973.

Slabakova, R. (2003). Semantic evidence for functional categories in interlanguage grammars. *Second Language Research, 19*, 42–75.

Slabakova, R. (2006). Is there a critical period for the acquisition of semantics. *Second Language Research, 22*, 302–338.

Slabakova, R. (in press). Scalar implicatures in L2 acquisition. *Lingua.*

Slabakova, R. (2008). *Meaning in the second language.* Berlin, Germany: Mouton de Gruyter.

Tryzna, M. (2009). Questioning the validity of the Article Choice Parameter and the Fluctuation Hypothesis: Evidence from L2 English article use by L1 Polish and L1 Mandarin Chinese Speakers. In M. del P. García Mayo & R. Hawkins (Eds.), *Second language acquisition of articles: Empirical findings and theoretical implications* (pp. 67–86). Amsterdam: John Benjamins.

Tsimpli, I. M., & Sorace, A. (2006). Differentiating interfaces: L2 performance in syntax-semantics and syntax-discourse phenomena. In D. Bamman, T. Magnitskaia, & C. Zaller (Eds.), *Proceedings of the 30th annual Boston University Conference on Language Development* (pp. 653–664). Somerville, MA: Cascadilla Press.

Valenzuela, E. (2006). L2 end state grammars and incomplete acquisition of Spanish CLLD constructions. In R. Slabakova, S. Montrul, & P. Prevost (Eds.), *Inquiries in linguistic development* (pp. 283–304). Amsterdam: John Benjamins.

Unsworth, S. (2005). *Child L2, adult L2, child L1: Differences and similarities. A study on the acquisition of direct object scrambling in Dutch.* PhD dissertation, Utrecht University. Published by LOT, Trans 10, 3512 JK Utrecht, the Netherlands.

White, L. (2009). Grammatical theory: Interfaces and L2 knowledge. In W. C. Ritchie & T. K. Bhatia (Eds.), *The new handbook of second language acquisition.* Leeds, UK: Emerald.

Second Language Acquisition and Syntactic Theory in the 21st Century

Juana M. Liceras

Syntactic theory has played a role in second language acquisition (SLA) research since the early 1980s, when the principles and parameters model of generative grammar was implemented. However, it was the so-called functional parameterization hypothesis together with the debate on whether second language learners activated new features or switched their value that led to detailed and in-depth analyses of the syntactic properties of many different nonnative grammars. In the last 10 years, with the minimalist program as background, these analyses have diverted more and more from looking at those syntactic properties that argued for or against the various versions of the UG-access versus non-UG-access debate (UG for Universal Grammar) and have more recently delved into the status of nonnative grammars in the cognitive science field. Thus, using features (i.e., gender, case, verb, and determiner) as the basic units and paying special attention to the quality of input as well as to processing principles and constraints, nonnative grammars have been compared to the language contact paradigms that underlie subsequent bilingualism, child SLA, creole formation, and diachronic change. Taking Chomsky's I-language/E-language construct as the framework, this article provides a review of these recent developments in SLA research.

INTRODUCTION

The early version of Chomsky's minimalist program (Chomsky, 1995), which was developed in the last years of the 20th century, as well as the subsequent versions (Chomsky, 2001, 2007, 2008), and, most importantly, one of the core constructs of this program, formal features, have set the pace for the formalist research in second language acquisition (SLA) that has been conducted in this century. Notwithstanding, the constructs and categories that were central to the previous model, the government and binding model (Chomsky, 1981), and its acquisition counterpart, the principles and parameters model (Chomsky, 1986; Chomsky & Lasnik, 1993), continue to be at the core of the present research. This is so not only because many of the learnability issues that they raised have not been resolved, but also because they have been incorporated into the minimalist program.

FEATURE SELECTION AND FEATURE CHECKING

In Chomsky (1970), the four categories noun (N), verb (V), preposition (P), and adjective (A) were defined as combinations of the two features [+/–N] and [+/–V], as follows: N = [+N, –V]; V = [–N, +V], P = [–N, –V], A = [+N, +V]. In later work (Chomsky, 1986), the main role of features was to project functional categories such as the determiner phrase (DP), the inflectional/tense phrase (IP/TP) or the complementizer phrase (CP). In minimalist theory (e.g., Chomsky, 1993, 1995), it is proposed that the content of functional categories is defined by bundles of features. Features also have a crucial role in the operations merge, agree, and move. While these operations are assumed to belong to Universal Grammar (UG) and to be innate, not all features are activated or organized in the same way in all languages. Therefore, it is how learners activate and organize the features of the target language, as well as how they make them interact with the operations merge, agree, and move, that may be problematic for the second language (L2) learner. In other words, in order to acquire the grammar of a given language, the L2 learner has to combine elements from the target lexicon to form a derivation by means of the structure-building operation merge. The L2 learner also has to determine how agree establishes relations of syntactic dependency by means of features, as well as when and how move displaces an element (the goal) from its canonical position to have a feature checked or valued by the element that has the corresponding feature (the probe).

In the last decade, a substantial amount of research on SLA has dealt with whether and how L2 learners activate features which are not present in the first language (L1) and whether these learners make the appropriate use of those features for feature checking, agreement, and movement purposes.

PARAMETERS, FUNCTIONAL CATEGORIES, AND FEATURES

We cannot talk about features without referring to functional categories and parameters (Liceras, 1997, 2007, 2009). Features are the units that make up functional categories and features are the locus of parametrization, since the presence or absence of a feature or its value in a given functional category defines the parametric options for the various languages. Features were already present in the interlanguage descriptions provided by those researchers who pioneered the adoption of the extended standard theory (Chomsky, 1977) and the government and binding model (Chomsky, 1981) to the analysis of nonnative systems (e.g., Flynn, 1983; Liceras, 1983, 1986; Mazurkevich, 1984; White, 1985). Features were also relevant in the generative accounts of how L2 learners project functional categories (Eubank, 1996; Schwartz & Sprouse, 1996; Vainikka & Young-Scholten, 1996; Zobl & Liceras, 1994, among others). However, it is with the minimalist program that formal syntactic features became the center of learnability theory, the reason being that they are conceptualized as the elementary building units of linguistic structure. Drawing on a physics-based metaphor, Adger (2003) defined features as the "atoms" of language while Liceras, Zobl, and Goodluck (2008) linked features to biological rather than to inorganic systems and defined them as the so-called DNA (base pairs) of human language that, as bundles, constitute the so-called genes (the functional categories) that determine the structure of particular languages.

While the inventory of formal features is available to all human beings, not all features are activated in any given language. This implies that the functional categories of natural languages (i.e., the DP, the IP/TP, or the CP) may not be made up of the exact same bundle of features, either because some are not activated or because their combinations are different. For instance, the presence of the feature Q in the CP (or the EPP feature, explained next, associated with it) is responsible for the fronting of wh-words in interrogatives in languages such as English or Spanish, while its absence in Chinese or Japanese accounts for the lack fronting of wh-words in the latter languages. Thus the presence/absence of the feature Q (or the EPP associated with it) can be said to parametrically differentiate languages such as English and Spanish from languages such as Chinese and Japanese. EPP stands for *extended projection principle*, a principle proposed within the government and binding model of grammar (Chomsky, 1981), according to which all sentences have to have subjects, though in some cases (as in the case of pro-drop or null subject languages) they can be implicit. In recent minimalist analyses, EPP has been used to refer to a feature which is bundled with other features to trigger movement. In other words, it has somehow taken over the role of the [+/–strong] value of features.[1]

Another example of how parameters, functional categories, and features are interrelated is the so-called null subject parameter. In the minimalist analysis proposed by Alexiadou and Anagnostopoulou (1998), languages are parameterized depending on whether the EPP is satisfied via merge or via move. *Merge* is the structure-building operation that combines elements from the lexicon to form a derivation, while *move* is the operation that displaces elements from their canonical positions to bring them into a local relationship. According to Alexiadou and Anagnostopoulou, in Spanish and Italian, the bound morphemes such as *-mos* in *canta-mos* (*we sing*), which merge with the verbal root to satisfy the EPP, are the actual personal pronouns. In other words, these bound morphemes have the feature [+D], the categorial feature that gives them the status of a determiner, which means that no overt personal pronoun is needed. In fact, when the strong personal pronoun *nosotros* (*we*) is used in Spanish, it has a pragmatic value (i.e., emphasis, contrast). In English, rather than merging with the verb, the obligatory subject *we* is moved to the specifier of the TP to satisfy the EPP and no null subject is allowed. Thus, the feature [+D] located in the functional category TP determines the parametric option to which a given type of language belongs (Liceras, Fernández Fuertes, & Pérez-Tattam, 2008; Liceras, Fernández Fuertes, & Alba de la Fuente, in press).

THE I-LANGUAGE/E-LANGUAGE DICHOTOMY REVISITED: LANGUAGE ACQUISITION AND LANGUAGE CONTACT

The field of SLA began to occupy a relevant place within the cognitive science field in the late 1970s and early 80s with the adoption of the Chomskian view of language acquisition, the development of the interlanguage hypothesis, and the call for analyzing nonnative systems as natural languages (e.g., Adjémian, 1976,

Corder, 1967; Selinker, 1972). Notwithstanding, there are two new developments that have played a very important role in bringing together the analysis of primary language acquisition, child and adult nonprimary language acquisition, the pidgin-creole continuum, and diachronic change. First, the field of SLA has adopted the new Chomskian linguistic models, specifically the principles and parameters model (Chomsky, 1981, 1986; Chomsky & Lasnik, 1993) and the minimalist program (Chomsky, 1995, 2001). Second, the prominent role of functional categories and features with Chomsky's I-language/E-language dichotomy (Chomsky, 1986) in the background has guided the comparative analyses of these systems. The reason why the I-language/E-language dichotomy has had an implicit role is that the primary data used in the projection of an I-language (language competence) undergo changes that pertain to the E-language domain (language usage). Thus, the individual and internal knowledge of language as represented in the speaker's mind, the I-language, is different from the external performance data, the E-language, which constitutes the primary linguistic data to which the child is exposed. In other words, the child, guided by UG, projects an I-language, which is a reflection of his or her competence. This, in principle, should be the case for the acquisition of any natural language. However, there are ways in which the acquisition of the various systems listed earlier (the primary language of the monolingual, the two primary languages of the simultaneous bilingual, and the second or third language of the child or the adult) may differ. One is the previous representation of language in the learners' brains together with the processing mechanisms that deal with actual input. The other is the different types of input that learners may be exposed to. Because the initial state in terms of competence (UG versus UG plus a L1, various L1s, or L2s) and the processing of input may differ depending on whether we are dealing with children or adults, the way in which the primary linguistic data is dealt with may be different. Also, because it is as E-language that the effects of language change and language contact are available to the learner, the primary linguistic data, and consequently the triggers available in the input, may also differ in the case of different language contact situations (i.e., bilingual L1 acquisition, nonprimary language acquisition in formal versus natural settings, or the special language contact situations that lead to the development of pidgin and creole systems).

ON THE NATURE OF NONNATIVE GRAMMARS: ARE INTERLANGUAGES I-LANGUAGES?

Put in terms of features, if adults learning a language do not activate the input features in the same way children do (be it because they are not sensitive to the same triggers or because the L1 and other L2s act as the initial state), they may create a different I-language. The question is, can we still say that the L2 system qualifies as being an I-language? In Liceras (1996), the answer was no because the various properties of a given parameter are set locally and individually, not as a result of changing a feature or the value of a feature in a given functional category. However, in Liceras (2007), it is argued that as long as the nonnative system contains the features and feature distribution of any given natural language, the nonprimary system qualifies as an I-language. This implies that a nonnative language is an I-language even if the various options of a parameter are not implemented as in the target (primary) language. Thus, in minimalist terms, it is the operations of the computational system (merge, agree, and move) and the implementation of features (the activation of the feature [gender] in the case of the Spanish determiner or the assignment of the feature [+D] to the Spanish verbal agreement markers) that result in an I-language. Mechanisms such as parameter setting (how parameters are fixed), feature activation or feature organization, which may be dependent on processing principles, may certainly be different from those which led to the creation of the primary system. However, the individual and internal representation of the nonprimary language in the L2 speaker's mind will still be an I-language. In other words, according to this latter view, while primary and nonprimary language acquisition may be different, and while the role of the adult and the child in the formation of the pidgin and the creole may be different too, the systems that we are to analyze are I-languages and therefore mental representations of the speaker's knowledge. Consequently, even if primary and nonprimary language acquisition differ with respect to something such as the proposed deficits in the activation of features argued for by the so-called failed functional features hypothesis (Hawkins & Chan, 1997; Hawkins & Hattori, 2006), Adjémian's (1976) assertion that interlanguages are natural languages still holds in that L2 systems (interlanguages) are I-languages. In terms of the pidgin—creole continuum, and in spite of the tenets of the language bioprogram hypothesis (Bickerton, 1984, 1996,

1999), according to which only children can create a creole language, this latter interpretation of the I-language/E-language dichotomy holds for both pidgin and creole systems. Namely, pidgins, in the same way as interlanguages, are I-languages because the operations merge, agree, and move are involved in the projection of their structure. This is so in spite of the fact that their functional categories may not contain the same features or feature combinations that are found in the corresponding creole and native (primary) languages.

BEYOND PARAMETERS AND FUNCTIONAL CATEGORIES: THE PROMINENT ROLE OF FEATURES

As we have seen in the previous section, features do not exist in isolation, which means that the learnability issues discussed in terms of features are always related to one or several functional categories and may be parameterized. Nonetheless, the innate view of language acquisition as a selective or deductive process that leads the learner to identify the categories of the input relevant for the projection of the I-language has evolved from taking principles and parameters as the pivotal categories, to concentrating on functional categories and finally, to present the prominent role of features. Features offer the researcher a more refined tool to compare languages and to identify learnability issues, but as has already been pointed out (Lardiere, 2009; Liceras, Zobl, et al., 2008; White, 2009), they also raise a great deal of unresolved problems. In spite of these problems, nowadays the logical and developmental problems of both primary and nonprimary language acquisition are mainly dealt with from the perspective of features. One of the most recent developments has been the investigation of the different ways in which features may be combined or assembled and the problems this may create for the L2 learner. Relevant examples are found in Lardiere's (2008) comparison of English and Chinese or in Valenzuela's (2008) comparison of English and Spanish.

Lardiere (2008, 2009) argued that definiteness and number form a union in Chinese, whereas in English, the number feature is independent of definiteness. This, according to Lardiere, accounts for the fact that her participant continued to have problems with the assignment of plural markers to English indefinite nouns. In other words, feature assembly has been identified as a potential candidate for fossilization.

Valenzuela (2008) showed that while both Spanish and English have contrastive left dislocation, a construction where topic preposing is dependent on the presence of a null anaphoric operator, only Spanish has clitic left dislocation, a construction where the topicalized element is coindexed with an agreement clitic in the IP. This construction requires that the topicalized constituent bears the feature [+specific]. This means that English learners of Spanish have to identify the [+specific] feature associated with the clitic left dislocation construction.

In the forthcoming sections we review recent developments in L2 research from three different perspectives. First, we look at how formal features have been used to compare adult SLA with child second language acquisition (L2A) and first language acquisition (L1A) and to investigate degrees of native-like attainment. Second, we review the studies that have compared native and nonnative systems with pidgin and creole languages. We finally look at the studies where L2 development is compared to diachronic change.

SECOND LANGUAGE ACQUISITION AND BILINGUALISM: THE ROLE OF FORMAL FEATURES

Besides feature selection or incomplete specification and feature organization or feature assembly, the relevant learnability issues that have been formulated around formal features have dealt with their strength, hierarchical accessibility, interpretability, and valuation.

In relation to feature strength, Leung (2008) investigated whether Chinese speakers with English L2 were able to activate the strength value responsible for verb movement in their third language (L3) French. She concluded that adult L2 learners are able to instantiate the feature strength value that is responsible for verb movement in French but is neither present in the L2 nor in the L1 grammar.

With respect to hierarchical accessibility, Radford (2008) raised the question of whether all features are equally accessible. To the best of our knowledge, the hierarchy that Radford proposed based on L1 acquisition data (mood > EPP > person > number > tense) has not been tested against L2 acquisition data. Testing this hierarchy against L2 acquisition data will imply taking into consideration feature interpretability and the role of the L1.

Features have also been divided according to their interpretability (Adger, 2003). Interpretable features such as cardinality or definiteness make a semantic contribution to interpretation. Uninterpretable features such as case or gender do not make such a contribution and have to be checked and eliminated for the derivation of a sentence to converge (achieve grammaticality). Interpretable features are checked, but they are not eliminated because they interface with the semantic-conceptual system of the mind.

The [+/−interpretable] contrast has also been taken up by L1 and L2 acquisition researchers (Bel, 2001; Díaz, Bel, & Bekiou, 2008; Hulk & Müller, 2000; Sorace, 2003; Tsimpli, 2001, among others). For instance, Tsimpli and Dimitrakopoulou (2007) and Tsimpli and Mastropavlou (2008) claimed that uninterpretable features are problematic for adult L2 learners, while interpretable features are not. This, according to these authors, accounted for the fact that (a) the acceptability rate of subject and direct object resumptive pronouns by Greek learners of English was determined by the interpretability of the features instantiated, and (b) Russian and Turkish L2 learners of Greek have fewer problems acquiring the indefinite article than the definite article because only the indefinite article has a [−definite] interpretable feature. These facts are attributed to critical period effects on the adults' representational system. In other words, the learners' competence differs from that of native speakers in relation to the activation of uninterpretable features. Along similar lines, the position taken by the proponents of the failed functional features hypothesis (e.g., Hawkins & Chan, 1997; Hawkins & Franceschina, 2004; Hawkins & Hattori, 2006; Hawkins et al., 2008, among others) is that while an uninterpretable feature selected by both the L1 and the L2 is always available to the adult learners, uninterpretable features selected by the L2 but not present in the L1 will create a representational deficit for these learners.

Platzack (2008), using data from the acquisition of verb second (V2) phenomena in Swedish, claimed that uninterpretable features such as EPP, which is responsible for moving elements from their canonical positions, are problematic for L2 learners due to critical period effects. However, for Platzack, those critical period effects resulted in a mere performance deficit rather than a competence deficit.

According to more recent developments in the minimalist program (Chomsky,

2001; Hornstein, Nunes, & Grohmann, 2005; Pesetsky & Torrego, 2007; Radford, 2004), rather than being divided into the [+interpretable] and [–interpretable] subsets, the inventory of features is represented in pairs so that all features have an interpretable and an uninterpretable counterpart. This implies that while person and number features on the subject DP are interpretable, these same features are uninterpretable (make no semantic contribution) on TP, where they are realized as agreement markers. Uninterpretable features are still eliminated, but it is via the valuation by their interpretable counterparts. Therefore, under this framework, the question is whether adult L2 learners have representational problems with the valuation procedure. Jakubowicz and Roulet (2008) argued that this is not the case for children with specific language impairment (SLI). They based their assertion on the dissociation between comprehension and production found in the experimental tasks administered to these children. The dissociation was interpreted as evidence that the problems SLI children encounter with gender agreement morphology are the result of a production (interface) deficit.[2] However, according to Liceras, Zobl, et al. (2008), the reinterpretation of existing adult SLA (Guillelmon & Grosjean, 2001) and SLI data (Clahsen, Bartke, & Göllner, 1997) in terms of valuation show that both types of speakers exhibit a form of impairment to the computations involved in agree.

As we will see in the next section, recent developments in the investigation of the role played by the various properties of features in SLA have run parallel to developments in the investigation of whether adult SLA resembles child SLA or L1A.

CHILD SECOND LANGUAGE ACQUISITION AT THE L1-ADULT L2 CROSSROADS

The discussion that took place in the late 1970s and early 80s with respect to whether the order of acquisition of morphemes by child L2 learners was similar to that of adult L2 learners or to that to L1 learners (Van Naerssen, 1980, 1981, 1986) has been revisited in light of the recent developments in syntactic theory. Presently, there is no agreement as to where child L2 acquisition stands with respect to L1A and adult SLA. While some researchers (e.g., Schwartz, 2004) claim that child L2 is like child L1 in the domain of morphology, and both are distinct from adult L2, others (e.g., Meisel, 2008) argue that child L2 resembles adult L2 in the domain of morphology. Schwartz (2004) based her claim on a review of the child L2 literature that provides evidence for the role of the L1 in the acquisition of L2 syntax by children, an influence that resembles adult SLA. Meisel's (2008) conclusion was based on the analysis of the development of verbal morphology in 3- to 4-year-old L1 German children learning French as a L2 at the *Lycée Français de Hambourg*. The children were interviewed over 2 years upon their entering the *Ecole Maternelle* (preschool). This author argued that some aspects of the development of the inflectional morphology in the children's French more closely resemble the morphological development of adult L2 French than that of L1 French.

Najmi (2009), using data from a 4-year-old child native speaker of Arabic learning English as an L2, showed the constructions this child used provide evidence that she has assembled all features related to functional categories. This child's data contained complex and embedded wh-questions and relative clauses, which makes her different from Haznedar's (2003) child, who did not show evidence of having projected CP until rather late. Also, unlike Haznedar's child, who had a high rate of missing auxiliaries, Najmi's child used auxiliaries and copula *be* (as well as modals) productively from the beginning. What these two children share is their failure to use proper verbal inflections. However, Najmi argued that since the child used other constructions that showed that her English grammar had the relevant functional categories, the morphological errors were performance errors; in other words, those errors were instances of missing inflection, as in Prévost and White (2000). In fact, not only Najmi's study but most studies of child SLA before the age of 5 (Grondin & White, 1996; Haznedar, 2001, 2003; Lakshmanan & Selinker, 1994) show that functional features and functional categories are available from the very early stages, which, from a continuity approach (no prefunctional stage), implies that child SLA is like L1A.

The foregoing conclusion is not shared by all researchers. For instance, in a recent study where Mobaraki, Vainikka, and Young-Scholten (2008) investigated the acquisition of L2 English by two Farsi-speaking children in a natural setting, it was claimed that L2 children start just with a verb phrase (VP) as adult L2 learners do (Vainikka & Young-Scholten, 1996). These authors based their assertion on the lack of case distinctions in the use of English pronouns, the frequent omission of copula with nonnominative pronominal subjects and the fact that even after 3 months of constant exposure to English, the two children continued to produce head-final VPs in their L2 English. This suggests that in the early stage of L2 acquisition, the VP headedness is transferred from the learner's native language. These two children are different in that they started acquiring English at the age of 7 to 8, not at the age of 4 to 5.

This is an important difference because in child L2 research (Meisel, 2008; Schwartz, 2004; Haznedar & Gavruseva, 2008), as well as in research on ultimate attainment (e.g., DeKeyser, 2000; Herschensohn, 2007; Johnson & Newport, 1989, 1991; among others), it is specifically stated that L2 children who begin learning a L2 before age 5 are different from older children and from adult L2 learners in the acquisition of morphosyntax. However, there are also differences among the 4- to 5-year-old group of children, since the L2 English morphosyntax in Najmi's (2009) child seems to develop much faster than that of Haznedar's (1997, 2001) child. Thus, if age 5 is the limit, why is it that there were rather relevant differences between Haznedar's and Najmi's children that cannot be accounted for on the basis of their different L1 (Turkish and Arabic, respectively)? Najmi (2009) offered two possible explanations. One is that his child had more exposure to English input and had systematic instruction in the target language at the day care (preschool) center that she attended. This did not seem to be the case with Haznedar's child. The other possible explanation would be to attribute the different development of these two children's L2 English to individual differences, an issue that is systematically dealt with in the acquisition literature. What the children in all these studies share is the fact that there is transfer from their L1. For instance, Haznedar's (1997, 2001) child and Mobaraki et al.'s (2008) children transferred the head-final VPs from Turkish and Farsi respectively, while Najmi's child transferred the resumptive pronoun strategy from her L1 Arabic.

As for the debate on whether child SLA resembles child L1A or adult SLA in the domain of syntax and/or morphology (Meisel, 2008; Schwartz, 2004), Najmi (2009) specifically argued that child SLA is different from both L1A and adult SLA in both the morphological and the syntactic domains. Thus, what the data from the reviewed studies show is that quality and quantity of input, age and individual differences, the L1s involved, and specific constructions have to be taken into account before definite conclusions can be reached.

Adult SLA has not only been investigated at the child SLA/L1A crossroads but also in relation to the so-called heritage speaker's language.[3] This comparison is interesting because it has led researchers to reconsider what the initial state and the ultimate attainment of a bilingual speaker may be and also to refine concepts such as near-native and native-like speaker.

THE BILINGUAL, THE NEAR-NATIVE, AND THE NATIVE-LIKE SPEAKER

It is not my intention to discuss the concepts of near-native and/or native-like speaker in relation to the main topic of this article, which is the SLA of syntax, since this could not be achieved without taking into consideration at least the literature on the critical period and on ultimate attainment. Because heritage speakers' language systems differ from the immigrant and the nonimmigrant native systems (Liceras & Senn, 2009; Senn, 2008) in ways that resemble the differences attributed to L2 learners, what I would like to address is whether this fact has implications for adhering to the view that ILs are I-languages or, alternatively, for adhering to the view that ILs are not I-languages.

Heritage speakers' competence has been measured using the same spontaneous and experimental data used to determine adult L2 competence. In the review carried out by Montrul (2008), she concluded that, as is the case with L2 learners, heritage speakers may end up with incomplete knowledge of the target language because of the reduced degree and consistency of exposure to primary linguistic data (the E-language) and their motivation. However, in terms of age of exposure and mode (naturalistic setting), heritage speakers have more in common with L1 learners than with L2 learners. In fact, heritage speakers have advantages over L2 learners that may be related to their childhood exposure to the target. However, these advantages seem to be selective in terms of the areas of grammar, the types of tasks, the degree of proficiency and the use of the language by the various speakers. Montrul (2008) stated that in spite of the advantages that heritage speakers have over L2 speakers, there was not enough experimental data to determine whether the incomplete grammars of heritage speakers are fundamentally different from the incomplete grammars of the L2 speakers or whether or not the so-called fundamental difference hypothesis (Bley-Vroman, 1989; Epstein, Flynn, & Martohardjono, 1996; Liceras, 1996, 2003) applies to heritage speakers.

In Liceras (1996, 2003) the fundamental difference hypothesis was interpreted in terms of how feature selection determines parameter setting, but not in relation to the UG principles that led to the acquisition of a L2. Thus, it was argued that nonnative languages are different from native languages in that parameters are not set in a similar way. As I have indicated earlier, if one follows Chomsky's (1986) direct relationship between the properties of parameters and I-language, ILs may not be instances of I-languages because they may not implement all the properties of a given parameter. However, in minimalist terms, if it is the operations of the computational system (merge, agree, and move) and the implementation of features that result in an I-language, ILs are instances of I-languages. In other words, the requirement is not that features be activated (or organized) as in child L1A but that the grammar of the output system be made up of bundles of features that form functional categories in a given natural language. This implies that when compared to a target, there may be I-languages where none or only some specific properties of a parametric option may be set in a target-like way or that functional categories may be underspecified. In other words, the fundamental difference hypothesis holds in relation to the subjects' sensitivity to the triggers of the E-language (primary linguistic data is processed differently in L1A and adult SLA) but does not hold in relation to the I-language (the structure of L1 and L2 systems and the representation of those systems in the respective speakers' minds is not qualitatively different).

Going back to the comparison of heritage speakers and L2 learners, I would like to point out that the differences will again pertain to the E-language because if the heritage speakers' initial contact with the primary linguistic data occurs when they are born, they will process the input as L1 speakers do. However, the type of input they will be exposed to will probably differ from that of their parents (the immigrant population) and the native speakers of the language in the country where it is a majority language (Liceras & Senn, 2009; Senn, 2008). The input they will be exposed to will also be different from the one their parents were exposed to because the immigrant speech may have suffered from attrition with respect to the majority usage of the same language. Thus, in parallel with the situation of child SLA, which seems to differ from both L1A and adult SLA, heritage languages may differ from both the corresponding native languages and the corresponding ILs. However, under this view, heritage languages, as well as the pidgin and creole languages, are I-languages.

SLA AND THE PIDGIN/CREOLE CONTINUUM: THE FORMAL FEATURES CONNECTION

The comparison of SLA with L1A, diachronic change, and the pidgin/creole continuum has taken rather different forms. In the case of L1A and SLA, whether the comparison was meant to argue for or against the similarity of the two processes, research has been carried out in a rather systematic way (e.g., Bley-Vroman, 1989; Ellis, 1994; Unsworth & Schwartz, 2006). The comparison with creole formation reached a peak when the process of L2 acquisition was conceptualized as a pidginization (Schumman, 1978) or a nativization (Andersen, 1983) process. Then, for the last two decades of the 20th century, it became almost a nonissue for the field of L2 studies. However, this century has seen a revival of the dialogue between acquisitionists and creolists (e.g., Becker & Veenstra, 2003; Lefebvre, White, & Jourdan, 2006).

FEATURE ACTIVATION AND THE LANGUAGE BIOPROGRAM HYPOTHESIS

The activation of features in the type of language contact that manifests itself as code-mixing has served as ground for investigating possible commonalities and differences between the SLA and the pidginization-creolization processes (Liceras, Martínez, Pérez-Tattam, Perales, & Fernández Fuertes, 2006). Drawing a parallel with Pesetsky and Torrego's (2001) proposal concerning the relationship between nominative case (nominative case is a T feature on D) and agreement (phi) (agreement is a D feature on T), Liceras et al. (2006) assumed that gender is an N feature on D and gender agreement is a D feature on N. Based on this dichotomy, the authors made a number of predictions about how the native and nonnative mental representation of these features determines the directionality of code mixing (which language contributes the functional or the lexical category as in *la door* versus *the puerta*). Specifically, Liceras et al. (2006) argued that the grammatical features spell-out hypothesis (Liceras, Fernández Fuertes, Perales, Pérez-Tattam, & Spradlin, 2008; Liceras, Spradlin, & Fernández Fuertes, 2005)— the preference shown by children to select the language whose functional category displays the most grammaticalized feature—accounts for the code-mixing options selected by L1 children and adult native speakers. Namely, it accounts for the fact that only the adult native speakers (but not the nonnative speakers) favor the gender-matching options (*la door* instead of *el door* because *door* bears the gender feature [+feminine] in Spanish), also known as the "analogical criterion." Liceras et al. (2006) attributed this to the fact that adult L2 learners do not process and internalize formal abstract features from input in the same way that children do (Liceras, 2003). Thus, in the spirit of Bickerton (1984, 1996, 1999), Liceras et al. (2006) maintained that adults do not create language and that this explains why adult nonnative systems and pidgins may share a number of properties, as initially proposed by Schumann (1978) and Andersen (1983) and recently discussed by DeGraff (1999) and Winford (2003), among others.

As for the masculine as default option, Liceras et al. (2006) argued that it can be taken as a diagnostic for the role of bilingualism in creole formation, in that it is the bilingual speakers who incorporate this underspecified or unspecified option of the lexifier language (the superstratum or, if we compare this process to L2 acquisition, the actual L2 target) into the creole system. In fact, the creoles with a Romance lexifier always display the masculine (under-specified) form. If a creole is created via L1 acquisition and children are not in contact with a lexifier language that has gender features, they have no reason to incorporate gender features into that creole. However, if the creole speakers grow up in a bilingual situation (creole and lexifier), they would choose the lexifier language's determiner to activate the gender feature. But, as they become adult bilinguals, they will keep the two systems separate and will make default choices in their potential mixed production. Furthermore, since gender related to [–animacy] is a highly formal feature that only acts as a noun classifier, it may never make it into a creole system. In other words, unlike elements such as the TMA (tense/mood/aspect) markers or even case, gender related to [–animacy] does not play any role in terms of theta-roles (agent, theme, benefactive).

RELEXIFICATION IN L2 ACQUISITION AND CREOLE GENESIS

Taking a totally different approach to Bickerton's, for whom, as we have seen earlier, creole genesis is an instance of L1A, Lefebvre (1998) argued that creole genesis is a particular case of SLA within a context of limited access to the superstratum language (the L2). Central to this view of creole genesis is the process of relexification (Lefebvre, 1998; Lefebvre & Lumsden, 1989). Relexification consists of relabeling lexical items from the L1 using a phonetic string from the L2 but keeping the L1 semantic and syntactic properties. An example of relexification provided by Lefebvre (1998) is the formation of the Haitian creole determiner. This determiner has very different syntactic and semantic properties from that of the superstratum language, the French determiner. Lefebvre argued that while the source of the phonological form of the Haitian creole [+definite] determiner is French deictic *là*, the syntactic and semantic properties are those of Fongbe, the substratum language. In fact, unlike the French [+definite] determiner, both the Haitian creole and the Fongbe [+definite] determiner are postnominal, identify old and new information, are not used with generic and mass nouns, do not have partitive value, and can have a relative clause separating the head noun from the determiner.

In an attempt to determine whether instances of relexification were present in her participant's L2 English idiolect, where English would represent the superstratum and Mandarin and Hokkien the substratum, Lardiere (2006) analyzed the status of several different constructions and concluded that the relexification hypothesis cannot account for the English idiolect of her participant, Patty. This author suggested that unlimited access to the target language community, like the one Patty has had, makes it possible to go beyond relexification and acquire many of the semantic and syntactic properties of the target grammar. However, Lardiere (2006) also pointed out that even with unlimited access, Patty's English idiolect was far from target-like, especially in the domain of inflectional morphology. This characteristic of Patty's English is not compatible with the relexification hypothesis because the relabeling mechanism links to relexification, as we saw in the case of the Haitian creole determiner, proceeds on the basis of free morphemes (French deictic *là* is the source), and the resulting creole is an isolating language. Since Patty's mother tongues (Mandarin and Hokkien) are isolating, the relexification hypothesis would lead us to expect an isolating English dialect as a result. However, Patty's problems with inflectional morphology do not provide any evidence for the relexification hypothesis. This leads us to the issue of how and at which point in the development of a nonnative system the L1 plays a role. A hypothesis intended to account for the interaction between the L1 and the L2 grammars is the competing grammars hypothesis, which was formulated to explain why, in the process of diachronic change, individual speakers' grammars displayed two options of a given parameter.

SECOND LANGUAGE DEVELOPMENT AND DIACHRONIC CHANGE: PARAMETERS, GRAMMATICALIZATION, AND FEATURES

SLA research refers only occasionally to parallels between diachronic change and developmental change (Liceras, 1985; Montrul, 1997; Zobl, 1979), in spite of the fact that syntactic optionality (Sorace, 2003), one of the most relevant characteristics of adult L2 acquisition, is a well-documented aspect of historical change. Other characteristics of change in SLA such as gradualness and incrementalism in parametric shifts are also attested for one type of historical change. These parallels between SLA and diachronic change are worth exploring since, in the case of SLA, they have been interpreted as instances of representational impairment (Beck, 1998; Meisel, 1997). Since it seems an unquestionable fact that impairment cannot account for historical change, the question then arises whether mechanisms or processes operative in diachronic parametric change may be operative in L2 development.

OPTIONALITY AND THE COMPETING GRAMMAR HYPOTHESIS

Kroch (1994, 2001) formulated the competing grammar hypothesis (CGH) to account for unstable periods of time where more than one parametric option was available for individual speakers (i.e., diglossia), as well as for the gradual and incremental nature of the process of diachronic change. Zobl and Liceras (2005, 2006) argued that the process of SLA is comparable to the process of diachronic change in that the properties associated with a given parameter are acquired in a piecemeal fashion. They further proposed that the CGH should be seen as an alternative framework for the study of SLA that relies mainly on the comparison between the L1A and the SLA processes. Zobl and Liceras have shown that four diachronic changes that occurred in an orderly manner in the history of English are acquired by Dutch learners of English in approximately the same order as the diachronic change occurred. The changes were: (a) OV to VO order as in *ate the strawberries* versus *the strawberries ate;* (b) I final to I medial as in that **John the strawberries eaten has* versus *that John has eaten the strawberries;* (c) loss of V2 phenomena as in **yesterday ate John the strawberries* versus *yesterday John ate the strawberries;* and (d) loss of verb raising as in **John eats not the strawberries* versus *John doesn't eat the strawberries*. Since the status of these properties in modern Dutch grammar is the same as the one they had in Old English, Zobl and Liceras concluded that the comparison between SLA and diachronic change is worth exploring.

Perales and Liceras (2009) investigated the relationship between the evolution of object clitics from Old to Modern Spanish and the acquisition of Spanish clitics by English speakers.

The evolution of clitics in the history of Spanish has been analyzed as an instance of grammaticalization. According to Fontana (1993, 1994, 1997), from the 12th to the 16th century Spanish clitics underwent a reanalysis from maximal projections (XPs) to heads ($X°$). As maximal projections, Old Spanish clitics could occupy a postverbal position with inflected verbs, they could be separated from the verb by intervening categories such as adverbs or nouns (the so-called interpolation phenomenon) and were in complementary distribution with strong pronouns (clitic doubling was not possible). These three properties, which are not possible in Modern Spanish, were not lost abruptly but coexisted with the Modern Spanish grammatical options in the mind of the speakers for five centuries until the $X°$ option replaced the XP option.

The process of acquisition of Spanish clitic pronouns by English speakers implies going from a system that has full pronouns to one that has categorial clitics. English pronouns may be phonologically reduced (*I love' im*), but this does not have consequences for the syntax. Categorial clitics can only have the verb as their host. If these clitics are agreement markers (as is the case with Spanish), clitic doubling (the co-occurrence of the clitic before the inflected verb and the presence of the corresponding overt pronoun in its canonical position) is possible. Under a feature-based analysis, the process of acquiring Spanish clitics by English speakers implies changing the [–phonological] [+XP] features of English pronouns to the [+phonological] [–XP] features of Spanish pronouns. Based on the results of a cross-sectional study consisting of a grammaticality judgment task, Perales and Liceras (2009) concluded that English learners of Spanish accept clitic configurations that are not found in the target language but that are found in a previous stage of diachronic development. They also found that not all properties of clitics were equally problematic for the L2 learners. In fact, interpolation and verb-clitic order, the two properties related to the phonological status of clitics, were less problematic than the properties related to the syntactic status (clitic doubling). The authors concluded that in spite of the fact that the CGH is compatible with the L2 data, there are differences in the way competition is implemented in diachronic change and in L2 development.

CONCLUSION AND DIRECTIONS FOR FUTURE RESEARCH

Even though there are many unresolved issues surrounding the nature and the status of features, there are obvious advantages to using them as constructs to investigate language contact in general and SLA in particular, since they allow us to identify phenomena that had not been recognized in previous frameworks and also to formulate novel research questions. Specifically, we have suggested that features are useful tools to analyze the output of all language contact situations as instances of I-languages. Notwithstanding, as Liceras, Zobl, et al. (2008) suggested, there are a number of unresolved issues related to features that cognitive theory and syntactic theory have to address; among them, I would like to highlight the following:

(1) Establishing what the inventory of features is and how they are to be defined. For instance, should we keep strength as a feature value, or should we add EPP-type features to define the operations triggered by features?

(2) Determining what the relationship is between the intrinsic grammatical content of features and their role in triggering structure-building operations such as the specifier of DP created by the presence of the D feature on tense in English.

(3) Determining how features are to be classified. Chomsky's (1995) intro-

duction of the distinction between interpretable features (required for semantic interpretation) and uninterpretable features (required for formal reasons) brought with it the problem of deciding whether a particular feature should be regarded as one or the other. Furthermore, since in recent work (Pesetsky & Torrego, 2007) the notion of *uninterpretable* has been separated from semantic-conceptual interpretability, will the next minimalist step be to admit nothing but interpretable features?

(4) Establishing what the possible relationship is between features. For instance, we need to determine whether there should be some structure or hierarchy within feature bundles (Travis, 2008) so that mood is higher (i.e., developmentally primary) than person and number, and tense is last, as suggested by Radford (2008).

To conclude, I point very briefly to two different ways of addressing the relationship between the principles and parameters model and the minimalist program and the so-called acquisition paradox, since these two ways are significant to the linguistic discussions surrounding the acquisition of L2 syntax.

With respect to the relationship between the principles and parameters model and the minimalist program, we have, on the one hand, Roberts and Roussou (2003) and Liceras (2009), who placed, without any rupture, the minimalist program within a parameterized view of language. Lardiere (2008, 2009), on the other hand, took a confrontational view toward parameter setting, a metaphor that she considered highly insufficient to account for language acquisition, specifically in relation to the feature selection mechanism that underlies parameter setting. She argued that the emphasis should be put on how features are assembled with regard to specific lexical items. The virtues and shortcomings of Lardiere's proposal have been extensively discussed in the commentaries to Lardiere's article included in *Second Language Research*, Volume 25, Number 2, 2009.

The acquisition paradox results from the deterministic view of the language acquisition process that characterizes the Chomskian model and emerges from the assumption that the child always sets the parameters as the adult generation did. If this were the case, languages would not change (Niyogi & Berwick, 1995). But the issue is not to set parameters correctly, as if we were dealing with prescriptive grammar, but to set parameters in accordance with triggers. Here, I suggest, is where the concept of E-language has an important role in acquisition, since it accommodates language contact and input variability in a way that leads the child to interpret triggers differently from his or her ancestors so that a different I-language may be created. While adult L2 learners may interpret input triggers differently from child L2 learners or L1 learners, they will nonetheless create an I-language and may also, provided a language community is created (the generation that creates a pidgin or the immigrant community where heritage speakers acquire their language), contribute to language change.

NOTES

1 In fact, for Pesetsky and Torrego (2001), the EPP feature is a property of a feature, or a "subfeature of a feature" (p. 359). However, as Travis (2008) pointed out, even though EPP is usually associated to other features to produce movement, it represents an improvement with respect to the [+/-strong] concept because it is independent and can be separated from the other features.

2 In the minimalist program (Chomsky, 1995; Marantz, 1995), the language system does not have a level of surface structure but a point called spell-out. At this point the generalize transformations of the computational system are no longer active, and the derivation splits into two different interface levels, the phonological (PF) interface and the interpretive (LF) interface. The interfaces are conceptualized as performance systems. If a structure does not meet the interface conditions of these two levels, the result is an ungrammatical sentence (it cannot be pronounced or provided a semantic interpretation). One important interface condition is the elimination of features prior to their visibility at any of the two interface levels. Thus, formal features—or morphological features as Chomsky calls them—play a role in the computational system of language, but play no role at the PF or LF interfaces.

3 According to Valdés (2000), a heritage speaker is a bilingual speaker who grew up in a household where a nonofficial language was spoken (i.e., the child of a Mexican family in the United States). It may also refer to an individual who speaks or understands a heritage language or who is a heritage language–English bilingual.

REFERENCES

Adger, D. (2003). *Core syntax: A minimalist approach.* Oxford, UK: Oxford University Press.

Adjémian, C. (1976). On the nature of interlanguage systems. *Language Learning, 26,* 297–320.

Alexiadou, A., & Anagnostopoulou, E. (1998). Parametrizing AGR: Word order, V-movement and EPP-checking. *Natural Language and Linguistic Theory, 16,* 491–539.

Andersen, R. (1983). *Pidginization and creolization as language acquisition.* Rowley, MA: Newbury House.

Beck, M.-L. (1998). L2 acquisition and obligatory head movement. *Studies in Second Language Acquisition, 29,* 311–348.

Becker, A., & Veenstra, T. (2003). The survival of inflectional morphology in French-related creoles. *Studies in Second Language Acquisition, 25,* 283–306.

Bel, A. (2001). *Teoria lingüística i adquisició del llenguatge: anàlisi comparada dels trets morfològics en catalài en castellà*[Linguistic theory and language acquisition: A comparative analysis of morphological features in Catalan and Castilian Spanish]. Barcelona: Institut d'Estudis Catalans [Barcelona: Institute for Catalan Studies].

Bickerton, D. (1984). The language bioprogram hypothesis. *Behavioral and Brain Sciences, 7,* 173–188.

Bickerton, D. (1996). A dim monocular view of Universal Grammar access. Commentary to S. Epstein, S. Flynn, & G. Martohardjono. Second language acquisition: Theoretical and experimental issues in contemporary research. *Behavioral and Brain Sciences, 19,* 716–717.

Bickerton, D. (1999). How to acquire language without positive evidence: What acquisitionists can learn from creoles. In M. DeGraff (Ed.), *Language creation and language change: Creolization, diachrony and development.* Cambridge, MA: MIT Press.

Bley-Vroman, R. (1989). What is the logical problem of foreign language learning? In S. Gass & J. Schachter (Eds.), *Linguistic perspectives on second language acquisition* (pp. 41–68). Cambridge, UK: Cambridge University Press.

Chomsky, N. (1970). Remarks on nominalization. In R. Jacobs & P. Rosenbaum (Eds.), *Readings in English transformational grammar* (pp. 184–221). Waltham, MA: Ginn-Blaisdell.

Chomsky, N. (1977). On wh-movement. In P. Culicover, T. Wasow, & A. Akmajian (Eds.), *Formal syntax* (pp. 71–132). New York: Academic Press.

Chomsky, N.(1981). *Lectures on government and binding.* Dordrecht, Netherlands: Foris.

Chomsky, N. (1986). *Knowledge of language: Its nature, origin, and use.* New York: Praeger.

Chomsky, N. (1993). A minimalist program for linguistic theory. In K. Hale & S. J. Keyser (Eds.), *The view from Building 20. Essays in linguistics in honor of Sylvain Bromberger* (pp. 1–52). Cambridge, MA: MIT Press.

Chomsky, N. (1995). *The minimalist program.* Cambridge, MA: MIT Press.

Chomsky, N. (2001). Derivation by phase. In J. Kenstowicz (Ed.), *Ken Hale: A life in language* (pp. 1–52). Cambridge, MA: MIT Press.

Chomsky, N. (2007). Approaching UG from below. In U. Sauerland & H.-M. Gärtner (Eds.), + *recursion = language? Chomsky's minimalism and the view from syntax-semantics*, (pp.1–29). Berlin, Germany: Mouton de Gruyter.

Chomsky, N. (2008). On phases. In R. Freidin, C. P. Otero, & M. L. Zubizarreta (Eds.), *Linguistic theory: Essays in honor of Jean-Roger Vergnaud* (pp. 133–166). Cambridge, MA: MIT Press.

Chomsky, N., & Lasnik, H. (1993). The theory of principles and parameters. In A. Jacobs, W. von Stechow, & T. Vennemann (Eds.), *Syntax. An international handbook of contemporary research* (pp. 506–569). Berlin, Germany: Mouton de Gruyter.

Clahsen, H., Bartke, S., & Göllner, S. (1997). Formal features in impaired grammars: A comparison of English and German SLI children. *Journal of Neurolinguistics, 10,* 151–171.

Corder, S. P. (1967). The significance of learners' errors. *IRAL, 4,* 161–170.

DeGraff, M. (1999). *Language creation and language change: Creolization, diachrony and development.* Cambridge, MA: MIT Press.

DeKeyser, R. M. (2000). The robustness of critical period effects in second language acquisition. *SSLA, 22,* 499–533.

Díaz, L., Bel, A., & Bekiou, K. (2008). Interpretable and uninterpretable features in the acquisition of Spanish past tenses. In J. M. Liceras, H. Zobl, & H. Goodluck (Eds.), *The role of formal features in second language acquisition* (pp. 484–512). New York: Erlbaum.

Ellis, R. (1994). *The study of second language acquisition.* Oxford, UK: Oxford University Press.

Epstein, S., Flynn, S., & Martohardjono, G. (1996). Second language acquisition: Theoretical and experimental issues in contemporary research. *Behavioral and Brain Sciences, 19,* 677–758.

Eubank, L. (1996). Negation in early German-English interlanguage: More valueless features in the L2 initial stage. *Second Language Research. 12,* 73–106.

Flynn, S. (1983). *A study of the effects of principal branching direction in second language acquisition: The generalization of a parameter of Universal Grammar from first to second language acquisition,* Unpublished doctoral dissertation. Cornell University, Ithaca, NY.

Fontana, J. (1993). *Phase structure and the syntax of clitics in the history of Spanish.* Unpublished doctoral dissertation. University of Pennsylvania, Philadelphia.

Fontana, J. (1994). A variationist account of the development of the Spanish clitic system. In K. Beals (Ed.), *Papers from the 13th regional meeting of the Chicago Linguistic Society: Vol. 2. The parasession on variation in linguistic theory* (pp. 87–100). Chicago: Chicago Linguistic Society.

Fontana, J. (1997). On the integration of second position phenomena. In A. VanKemenade &

N. Vincent (Eds.), *Parameters of morphosyntactic change* (pp. 207–249). Cambridge, UK: Cambridge University Press.

Grondin, N., & White, L. (1996). Functional categories in child L2 acquisition of French. *Language Acquisition*, 5, 1–34.

Guillelmon, D., & Grosjean, F. (2001). The gender marking effect in spoken word recognition: The case of bilinguals. *Memory and Cognition*, 29, 503–511.

Hawkins, R., Casillas, G., Hattori, H., Hawthorne, J., Husted, R., Lozano, C., et al. (2008). The semantic effects of verb raising and its consequences in second language grammars. In J. M. Liceras, H. Zobl, & H. Goodluck (Eds.), *The role of formal features in second language acquisition* (pp. 328–351). New York: Erlbaum.

Hawkins, R., & Chan, Y.-H. C. (1997). The partial availability of Universal Grammar in second language acquisition: The failed functional features hypothesis. *Second Language Research*, 13, 187–226.

Hawkins, R., & Franceschina, F. (2004). Explaining the acquisition and non-acquisition of determiner-noun gender concord in French and Spanish. In J. Paradis & P. Prévost (Eds.), *The acquisition of French in different contexts* (pp. 175–205). Amsterdam: John Benjamins.

Hawkins, R., & Hattori, H. (2006). Interpretation of English multiple wh-questions by Japanese speakers: A missing uninterpretable feature account. *Second Language Research*, 22, 260–301.

Haznedar, B. (1997). *Child second language acquisition of English: A longitudinal case study of a Turkish-speaking child.* Unpublished doctoral dissertation, University of Durham, UK.

Haznedar, B. (2001). The acquisition of the IP system in child L2 English. *Studies in Second Language Acquisition*, 23, 1–39.

Haznedar, B. (2003). The status of functional categories in child second language acquisition: Evidence from the acquisition of CP. *Second Language Research*, 19, 1–41.

Haznedar, B., & Gavruseva, E. (2008). *Current trends in child second language acquisition: A generative perspective.* Amsterdam: John Benjamins.

Herschensohn, J. (2007). *Language development and age.* Cambridge, UK: Cambridge University Press.

Hornstein, N., Nunes, J., & Grohmann, K. H. (2005). *Understanding minimalism.* Cambridge, UK: Cambridge University Press.

Hulk, A., & Müller, N. (2000). Cross-linguistic influence at the interface between syntax and pragmatics. *Bilingualism: Language and Cognition*, 3, 227–244.

Jakubowicz, C., & Roulet, L. (2008). Narrow syntax or interface deficit? Gender agreement in French. In J. M. Liceras, H. Zobl, & H. Goodluck (Eds.), *The role of formal features in second language acquisition* (pp. 184–225). New York: Erlbaum.

Johnson, J. S., & Newport, E. L. (1989). Critical period effects in second language learning.

Cognitive Psychology, 21, 60–99.

Johnson, J. S., & Newport, E. L. (1991). Critical period effects on universal properties. *Cognition, 39*, 215–258.

Kroch, A. (1994). Morphosyntactic variation. In K. Beals (Ed.), *Papers from the 13th Regional Meeting of the Chicago Linguistic Society: Vol. 2. The parasession on variation and linguistic theory* (pp. 180–201). Chicago: Chicago Linguistic Society.

Kroch, A. (2001). Syntactic change. In M. Baltin & C. Collins (Eds.), *The handbook of contemporary syntactic theory* (pp. 699–729). Oxford, UK: Blackwell.

Lakshmanan, U., & Selinker, L. (1994). The status of CP and the tensed complementizer *that* in the developing L2 grammars of English. *Second Language Research, 10*, 25–48.

Lardiere, D. (2006). Comparing creole genesis with SLA in unlimited-access contexts: Going beyond relexification. In C. Lefebvre, L. White, & Ch. Jourdan (Eds.), *L2 acquisition and creole genesis: Dialogues* (pp. 401–427). Amsterdam and Philadelphia: John Benjamins.

Lardiere, D. (2008). Feature assembly in second language acquisition. In J. M. Liceras, H. Zobl, & H. Goodluck (Eds.), *The role of formal features in second language acquisition* (pp. 106–140). New York: Erlbaum.

Lardiere, D. (2009). Some thoughts on the contrastive analysis of features in second language acquisition. *Second Language Research, 25*, 173–227.

Lefebvre, D. (1998). *Creole genesis and the acquisition of grammar: The case of Haitian creole.* Cambridge, UK: Cambridge University Press.

Lefebvre, C., & Lumsden, J. (1989). Les langues créoles et la théorie linguistique [Creole languages and linguistic theory]. *Revue Canadienne de Linguistique, 34*, 319–337.

Lefebvre, C., White, L., & Jourdan, C. (2006). *L2 acquisition and creole genesis. Dialogues.* Amsterdam: John Benjamins.

Leung, Y.-K. I. (2008). The verbal functional domain in L2A and L3A: Tense and agreement in Cantonese-English-French interlanguage. In J. M. Liceras, H. Zobl, & H. Goodluck (Eds.), *The role of formal features in second language acquisition* (pp. 378–403). New York: Erlbaum.

Liceras, J. M. (1983). *Markedness, contrastive analysis and the acquisition of Spanish as a second language.* Unpublished doctoral dissertation, University of Toronto, Ontario, Canada.

Liceras, J. M. (1985). The value of clitics in non-native Spanish. *Second Language Research, 1*, 4–36.

Liceras, J. M. (1986). *Linguistic theory and second language acquisition: The Spanish non-native grammar of English speakers.* Tubingen: Gunter Narr.

Liceras, J. M. (1996). To "grow" and what to "grow" : that is one question. Commentary to Epstein, Flynn, & Martohardjono, Second language acquisition: Theoretical and experimental issues in contemporary research. *Behavioral and Brain Sciences, 19*, 734.

Liceras, J. M. (1997). The now and then of L2 growing pains. Views on the acquisition and use of a second language. In L. Díaz Rodríguez & C. Pérez Vidal (Eds.), *EUROSLA '97 Proceedings* (pp. 65–85). Barcelona: Universitat Pompeu Fabra.

Liceras, J. M. (2003). Monosyllabic place holders in early child language and the L1/L2 "Fundamental Difference Hypothesis." In P. Kempchinsky & C.-L. Piñeiros (Eds.), *Theory, practice and acquisition: Papers from the sixth Hispanic linguistics symposium and the fifth conference on the acquisition of Spanish and Portuguese* (pp. 258–283). October 2002. Somerville: Cascadilla Press.

Liceras, J. M. (2007). La adquisición de lenguas segundas y la encrucijada Lengua-I(interna) / Lengua-E(xterna) en la adquisición, el cambio diacrónico y la formación de criollos [Second language acquisition at the I(nternal)-language/E(xternal)-language crossroads in acquisition, diachronic change and creole formation]. In R. Mairal, et al. (Eds.), *Actas del XXIV Congreso Internacional de AESLA. Aprendizaje de lenguas, uso del lenguaje y modelación cognitiva: perspectivas aplicadas entre disciplinas* [Proceedings of the 24th International Congress of AESLA. Language learning, language use and cognitive modelling: Applied perspectives across disciplines]. (pp. 67–90). Madrid: UNED.

Liceras, J. M. (2009). On parameters, functional categories and features ... and why the trees shouldn't prevent us from seeing the forest. *Second Language Research, 25*(2), 279–289.

Liceras, J. M., Fernández Fuertes, R., & Pérez-Tattam, R. (2008). Null and overt subjects in the developing grammars (L1 English/L1 Spanish) of two bilingual twins. In C. Pérez-Vidal, M. Juan Garau, & A. Bel (Eds.), *A portrait of the young in the new multilingual Spain* (pp. 111–134). Clevedon, UK: Multilingual Matters.

Liceras, J. M., Fernández Fuertes, R., Perales, S., Pérez-Tattam, R., & Spradlin, K. T. (2008). Gender and gender agreement in the bilingual native and the non-native grammar: A view from child and adult functional-lexical mixings. *Lingua, 118*, 827–851.

Liceras, J. M., Fernández Fuertes, R., & Alba de la Fuente, A. (in press). Overt subjects and copula omission in the Spanish and the English grammar of English-Spanish bilinguals: On the locus and directionality of interlinguistic influence. *First Language*.

Liceras, J. M., Martínez, C., Pérez-Tattam, R., Perales, S., & Fernández Fuertes, R. (2006). L2 acquisition as a process of creolization: Insights from child and adult code-mixing. In C. Lefebvre, L. White, & C. Jourdan (Eds.), *L2 acquisition and creole genesis: Dialogues* (pp. 113–144). Amsterdam and Philadelphia: John Benjamins.

Liceras, J. M., & Senn, C. (2009). Linguistic theory and the analysis of minority languages: Native, immigrant and heritage Spanish. *Lengua y Migración, 1*, 39–74.

Liceras, J. M., Spradlin, K. T., Fernández Fuertes, R. (2005). Bilingual early functional-lexical mixing and the activation of formal features. *International Journal of Bilingualism, 9*, 227–252.

Liceras, J. M., Zobl, H., & Goodluck, H. (2008). Introduction. In J. M. Liceras, H. Zobl, & H. Goodluck (Eds.), *The role of formal features in second language acquisition* (pp. 1–19). New York: Erlbaum.

Marantz, A. (1995). The minimalist program. In G. Webelbuth (Ed.), *Government and binding theory and the minimalist program* (pp. 349–382). Oxford, UK: Blackwell.

Mazurkevich, I. (1984). The acquisition of the dative alternation by second language learners and linguistic theory. *Language Learning, 34*, 91–109.

Meisel, J. (1997). The acquisition of the syntax of negation in French and German: Contrasting first and second language development. *Second Language Research, 13*, 227–263.

Meisel, J. (2008). Second language acquisition or successive first language acquisition. In B. Haznedar & E. Gavruseva (Eds.), *Current trends in child second language acquisition: A generative perspective* (pp. 55–80). Amsterdam: John Benjamins.

Mobaraki, M., Vainikka, A., & Young-Scholten, M. (2008). The status of subjects in early child L2 English. In B. Haznedar & E. Gavruseva (Eds.), *Current trends in child second language acquisition: A generative perspective* (pp. 209–235). Amsterdam: John Benjamins.

Montrul, S. (1997). On the parallels between diachronic change and interlanguage grammars: The L2 acquisition of the Spanish dative system. *Spanish Applied Linguistics, 1*, 87–113.

Montrul, S. (2008). *Incomplete acquisition in bilingualism. Re-examining the age factor.* Amsterdam: John Benjamins.

Najmi, A. (2009). *Clause structure in the development of child L2 English of L1 Arabic.* Unpublished doctoral dissertation, University of Ottawa, Ontario, Canada.

Niyogi, P., & Berwick, R. C. (1995). *The logical problem of language change* (Tech. Rep.) Cambridge, MA: MIT, AI Lab.

Perales, S., & Liceras, J. M. (2009, March). *Unexpected constructions in SLA: A diachronic approach.* Paper presented at the 10th Generative Approaches to Second Language Acquisition Conference (GASLA 10), University of Illinois at Urbana-Champaign.

Pesetsky, D., & Torrego, E. (2001). T to C movement: Causes and consequences. In M. Kenstowicz (Ed.), *Ken Hale: A life in language* (pp. 355–426). Cambridge, MA: MIT Press.

Pesetsky, D., & Torrego, E. (2007). The syntax of valuation and the interpretability of features. In S. Karimi, V. Samiian, & W. Wilkins (Eds.), *Phrasal and clausal architecture. Syntactic derivation and interpretation* (pp. 262–294). Amsterdam: John Benjamins.

Platzack, C. (2008). Uninterpretable features and EPP: A minimalist account of language buildup and breakdown. In J. M. Liceras, H. Zobl, & H. Goodluck (Eds.), *The role of formal features in second language acquisition* (pp. 48–80). New York: Erlbaum.

Prévost, P., & White, L. (2000). Missing surface inflection or impairment in second language acquisition? Evidence from tense and agreement. *Second Language Research, 16*, 103–133.

Radford, A. (2004). *Minimalist syntax: Exploring the structure of English.* Cambridge, UK:

Cambridge University Press.

Radford, A. (2008). Feature correlations in nominative case marking in L1, L2 and native English. In J. M. Liceras, H. Zobl, & H. Goodluck (Eds.), *The role of formal features in second language acquisition* (pp. 82–104). New York: Erlbaum.

Roberts, I., & Roussou, A. (2003). *Syntactic change. A minimalist approach to grammaticalization.* Cambridge, UK: Cambridge University Press.

Schumann, J. (1978). *The pidginization process: A model for second language acquisition.* Rowley, MA: Newbury House.

Schwartz, B. (2004). Why child L2 acquisition. In J. V. Kampen & S. Baauw (Eds.), *The Proceedings of GALA 2003. LOT Occasional Series* (pp. 47–66). Utrecht University, Netherlands.

Schwartz, B., & Sprouse, R. (1996). L2 cognitive states and the full transfer/full access model. *Second Language Research, 12*, 40–72.

Selinker, L. (1972). Interlanguage. *IRAL, 3*, 209–231.

Senn, C. (2008). *Reasuntivos y doblado del clítico: En torno a la caracterización del término 'casi nativo.'* Unpublished doctoral dissertation, University of Ottawa, Ontario, Canada.

Sorace, A. (2003). Near-nativeness. In M. Long & C. Doughty (Eds.), *Handbook of second language acquisition* (pp. 130–152). Oxford, UK: Blackwell.

Travis, L. (2008). The role of features in syntactic theory and language variation. In J. M. Liceras, H. Zobl, & H. Goodluck (Eds.), *The role of formal features in second language acquisition* (pp. 22–47). New York: Erlbaum.

Tsimpli, I.-M. (2001). LF-interpretability and language development: A study of verbal and nominal features in Greek normally developing and SLI children. *Brain and Language, 77*, 432–448.

Tsimpli, I.-M., & Dimitrakopoulou, M. (2007). The interpretability hypothesis: Evidence from wh-interrogatives in second language acquisition. *Second Language Research, 23*, 215–242.

Tsimpli, I.-M., & Mastropavlou, M. (2008). Feature interpretability in L2 acquisition and SLI: Greek clitics and determiners. In J. M. Liceras, H. Zobl, & H. Goodluck (Eds.), *The role of formal features in second language acquisition* (pp. 142–183). New York: Erlbaum.

Unsworth, S., & Schwartz, B. (2006). *Paths of development in L1 and L2 acquisition.* Amsterdam: John Benjamins.

Vainikka, A., & Young-Scholten, M. (1996). Gradual development of L2 phrase structure. *Second Language Research, 12*, 7–39.

Van Naerssen, M. (1980). How similar are Spanish as a first language and Spanish as a second language? In R. Scarcella & S. D. Krashen (Eds.), *Research in second language acquisition* (pp. 146–154). Rowley, MA: Newbury House.

Van Naerssen, M. (1981). *Generalizing second language acquisition hypotheses across lan-*

guages: A test case in Spanish as a second language. Unpublished doctoral dissertation, University of Southern California, Los Angeles.

Van Naerssen, M. (1986). Hipótesis sobre la adquisición de una segunda lengua: Consideraciones inter-lenguaje; comprobación en el español [Second language acquisition hypotheses: Interlinguistic approaches. Evidence from Spanish]. In J. Meisel (Ed.), *Adquisición del lenguaje / Aquisiçao da linguagem* [Language acquisition]. Frankfurt: M. Kaus-Dieter Vervuert.

Valdés, G. (2000). AATSP Professional Development Series Handbook for Teachers K-16, Vol. I: Spanish for Native Speakers (pp. 1–20). New York: Harcourt College Publishers.

Valenzuela, E. (2008). On CP positions in L2 Spanish. In J. M. Liceras, H. Zobl, & H. Goodluck (Eds.), *The role of formal features in second language acquisition* (pp. 534–558). New York: Erlbaum.

White, L. (1985). The "pro-drop" parameter in adult second language acquisition. *Language Learning, 35*, 47–61.

White, L. (2009). Some questions about feature reassembly. *Second Language Research, 25*, 343–348.

Winford, D. (2003). *An introduction to contact linguistics*. Oxford, UK: Blackwell.

Zobl, H. (1979). Systems of verb classification and cohesion of verb—complement relations as structural conditions of interference in a child's L2 development. *Working Papers in Bilingualism, 18*, 25–63.

Zobl, H., & Liceras, J. M. (1994). Functional categories and acquisition orders. *Language Learning, 44*, 159–180.

Zobl, H., & Liceras, J. M. (2005). Accounting for optionality in nonnative grammars: Parametric change in diachrony and L2 development as instances of internalized diglossia. In L. Dekydtspotter, Rex A. Sprouse, and Audrey Liljestrand (Eds.), *Proceedings of the seventh Generative Approaches to Second Language Acquisition conference (GASLA 2004)* (pp. 283–291). April 2004. Somerville, MA: Cascadilla Proceedings Project.

Zobl, H., & Liceras, J. M. (2006). Competing grammars and parametric shifts in second language acquisition and the history of English and Spanish. In D. Bamman, T. Magnitskaia, & C. Zaller (Eds.), *Proceedings of the 30th Boston University Conference on Language Development (BUCLD)*, (pp.713–724). November 2005. Somerville, MA: Cascadilla Press.

AUTHOR NOTE

This research was funded by the Social Sciences and Humanities Research Council of Canada (SSHRC #410–2004–2034).

Usage-Based Approaches to Language and Their Applications to Second Language Learning

Andrea Tyler

Over the past 20 years, many in the field of second language learning and pedagogy have become familiar with models of language that emphasize its communicative nature. These models are often referred to as usage-based because they emphasize the notion that actual language use is a primary shaper of linguistic form. Supporters of these models also argue that making meaning, that is, the use to which language is put, is central to how language is configured. Usage-based models share several other underlying assumptions as well. While these usage models have a number of ideas in common, several distinct approaches have emerged. They often use similar terms, such as cognition and metaphor, but the precise interpretations can vary from model to model. The overall result is that without extensive reading, it is not always clear just how these models differ and what unique insights each offer. This article attempts to address this situation by examining three major usage-based models—systemic functional linguistics, discourse functionalism, and cognitive linguistics. First, the common, underlying tenets shared by the three models are discussed. Second, an overview of the unique tenets and concerns of each approach is presented in order to distinguish key differences among them. Within the discussion of each approach, I also discuss various attempts to apply the model to issues in second language learning.

INTRODUCTION

The term *usage-based* provides a useful prism through which to view a group of linguistic models that emphasize the notion that actual language use is a primary shaper of linguistic form and the foundation for language learning. This article examines three usage-based approaches: systemic functional linguistics (SFL), discourse functionalism, and cognitive linguistics (CL), and their applications to second language (L2) learning issues.[1] Although usage-based models of language have tended to be more or less on the fringes of mainstream L2 endeavors in the past, ideas from these approaches have begun to receive attention from L2 researchers and teachers. In terms of a theory-language learning connection, SFL, especially as it has evolved in Australia, is probably the most well established of these models. By the mid-1980s, many L2 researchers and language teaching professionals in the United States had begun turning from formal, highly abstract generative models of language to more communicative and contextualized approaches. These researchers drew on work from a range of sociolinguistically influenced research, including what I term the discourse functionalists, such as Wallace Chafe, Scott Delancy, Talmy Givón, Paul Hopper, Sandra Thompson, and Russell Tomlin. More recently, with advances in cognitive psychology (such as the development of our knowledge of schema and prototype effects) and frequency-based analyses of language learning (e.g., Ellis, 2008a, 2008b), CL has begun to garner attention. In this article, I identify the common underlying tenets shared by usage-based approaches to language. Then I explore in more depth the three distinct approaches. Within the discussion of each approach, I touch on various attempts to apply the model to issues in L2 learning. Since CL has recently generated substantial interest and is the newest on the L2 scene and probably the least familiar, I devote substantial attention to it.

COMMON UNDERLYING TENETS

The central idea in usage-based models is that a user's language emerges as a result of exposure to numerous *usage events* (Kemmer & Barlow, 2000), that is, situated instances of the language user understanding or producing language to convey particular meaning in a specific communicative situation. When a speaker engages in communication, it is assumed that she is attempting to achieve specific interactional goals using intentionally chosen linguistic strategies aimed at members of her speech community. Tying usage events to particular speech communities reflects the understanding that actual language use is culturally and contextually embedded.

All usage-based approaches adhere to five key tenets: (a) The primary purpose of language is communicative; communicative use shapes language itself. As Tomasello (2003) argued in relation to first language learning, "language structure emerges from language use" (p. 5). (b) Natural language always occurs in context, and the user's choices in crafting an utterance are influenced by an array of contextual factors. Context itself is a complex construct that transcends a compositional approach in which additional dimensions can simply be added without recognizing subtle, interacting linguistic reflexes that occur in relation to multidimensional context. For instance, all usage-based models have recognized the audience or the participants in an interaction as a major aspect of context (for genre, see Martin & Rose, 2008; for listener expectation, see Chafe, 1994; for "ground," see Langacker, 1987, 1991b; Taylor, 2004). Subtle changes in the relationship between the speaker and the audience result in changes in the speaker's language choices. (c) Language is learned. Patterns of usage, including collocational information (at the level of grammatical patterns as well as the word level) and frequency information, are held to be central to the learning of the system. This tenet entails a rejection of a separate language module with a preestablished grammatical configuration that is activated or triggered by exposure to salient language data. (d) Meaning is not housed solely in lexical items. Grammatical patterns are meaningful in and of themselves (e.g., Givón, 2001; Langacker, 2008a; Martin, 2002). (e) Language can be accurately and fully accounted for through a monostratal model, that is, all syntactic patterns can be accounted for without assuming two (or more) levels, such as deep structure and surface structure. Alternative syntactic patterns, such as active versus passive, are separate, meaningful patterns, not transforms of each other. (See Zyzik, 2009, for further discussion of usage-based approaches, especially on the importance of input frequency.)

SYSTEMIC FUNCTIONAL LINGUISTICS

SFL began with the work of M. A. K. Halliday in the 1970s, largely in response to more formal, structuralist approaches that discounted the centrality of communication and context in shaping language. The main goal of Halliday's model has been to account for culturally situated linguistic communication that is understood as a transmitter not only of propositional information but also of larger cultural values, and as a tool for getting things done (e.g., Byrnes, 2009; Halliday, 1994). In this model, language is inextricably bound to human social behavior, culture making, and culture transmittal, including transmission of status and power relations.[2] A central goal is to understand how ordinary language as it is used in everyday practice transmits systematic patterns of culture. (Halliday, 1978; Halliday & Matthiessen, 2004).

Much of more recent SFL work views language through the filter of genre (Martin, 2002, 2009). Genre is understood as a specific text type, aimed at a narrowly specified audience (e.g., scientific academics) with specific communicative goals (e.g., persuading, informing) in particular formats (e.g., scientific journals). The emphasis is on analyzing text produced by speakers and writers as they communicate in a given genre. Thus, SFL clearly situates all analysis in a defined sociocultural context. Every language has numerous genres, and every genre is language specific. Each genre is held to utilize slightly different, conventionalized patterns of linguistic resources, and the patterned occurrence of these linguistic bundles determines whether a text represents an appropriate example of that genre.

Below the overarching level of genre, SFL posits a tripartite division of context: (a) *field*, which concerns what is being talked about and what is going on in terms of the social activity of a situation; (b) *tenor*, which refers to how social roles and relations are being enacted; and (c) *mode*, which relates to the opportunities and constraints on deployment of linguistic resources associated with the situated text, including resources and constraints inherent in spoken versus written discourse (e.g., Byrnes, 2009; Halliday & Matthiessen, 2004; Martin, 2009). For example, consider how these three contextual elements might play out in an article about the battle of Gettysburg written for an academic journal: The information about the battle (and argumentation concerning its import to the Civil War) as well as the components of description (informing) and persuasion (presenting an opinion and attempting to convince the audience it is an opinion worth considering) would represent the field; the positioning of the author as an academic authority on the subject communicating to an informed readership who share similar expectations about how such information and argumentation is presented would represent the tenor; and the expectations and stylistic constraints of the academic journal would represent the mode. Each of these dimensions of context is in turn related to a *metafunction*, described in the following paragraph, which is realized in terms of specific aspects of linguistic expression. Of the three usage-based approaches, SFL has developed the most delineated constructs concerning how specific aspects of context relate to the linguistic realizations found in a situated text (e.g., Martin, 2002, 2009; Martin & Rose, 2008).

In terms of actual linguistic expression, the deployment of various linguistic resources or patterns is argued to enact three different communicative metafunctions, all of which exist simultaneously and interactively in any text: *ideational*, what is being done and what the text is about or what meaning the text is expressing; *interpersonal*, linguistic cues indicating speaker stance and relationship to audience; and *textual*, or what makes a stretch of language hang together as a coherent whole and how participants are tracked through the discourse, information flow, and so on. (The constructs of theme/rheme are classic examples of the textual metafunction; e.g., Halliday, 1978; Halliday & Matthiessen, 1999; Martin & Rose, 2008).

SFL represents linguistic patterning as involving networks of closed systems of options offered by the particular language for the purpose of communication. These are the systematic bundles of linguistic forms associated with the field, tenor, and mode of each genre.[3] Halliday clearly saw meaning as the shaper of language: "[I]n a systemic grammar every category (i.e., theoretical concept) is based on meaning: it has a semantic, as well as a formal, lexicogrammatical reactance" (Halliday & Matthiessen, 1999, pp. 3–4). Choice of lexicogrammatical form is understood as a meaning-making choice. The focus is on identifying linguistic patterns that are typically employed to create a situated, coherent text (as perceived by the intended audience) that matches a particular communicative context (defined in terms of genre with specifically defined audience and register). Although audience and audience expectation have been identified as part of tenor and the interpersonal dimension, the emphasis has been on meaning being primarily a property of the text itself rather than deriving through dynamic interpretation and inferencing on the part of the listener.

Halliday believed that the form of language is explicable almost solely in terms of communicative function; he rejected "the psychological or physiological" as motivating factors (Halliday & Matthiessen, 1999, p. 7). Indeed, he stated, "Instead of explaining language by reference to cognitive processes, we explain cognition by reference to linguistic processes" (p. 7). An example of this focus is his definition of theme/rheme; theme is simply seen as the departure point of the sentence. The speaker's choice of theme is primarily related to the textual metafunction, which has to do with information flow and how the speaker chooses to lay out the message. Importantly, the analysis of theme/rheme does not address underlying cognitive or neuro-physical motivations. Halliday's almost exclusive concern with language as a social-cultural phenomenon and disregard for cognitive and physical-neural dimensions is an important factor that sets SFL apart from discourse functionalism and CL.

Halliday's analysis of the passive is tied to his understanding of theme and reflects his belief in the unimportance of cognitive motivation. He has noted that English speakers have an awareness of the meaning expressed when something is in first position and, moreover, that theme is usually associated with the actor role unless there is good reason not to do so. He further noted that the passive allows the speaker to disassociate theme from actor in order to change focus or omit the actor, but his analysis offered no explicit discussion of general cognitive motivation for these choices.

The emphasis on using genre as the filter through which to analyze syntax has tended to lead SFL linguists away from general descriptions of grammatical constructions as they are used to communicate across a range of text types. The close ties between narrow context and the situatedness of linguistic choices are another factor that distinguishes SFL from CL. It should be noted that a relatively new development in SFL has involved close analysis of the discourse of multiple areas and an increased understanding of generic structures and intertextual relations among various genres (Martin, 2002).

The majority of the applications of SFL to issues in L2 have come from the work of Halliday's followers in Australia. In Australian educational linguistics, genres have been defined as "staged, goal-oriented social processes" (Martin, 1999, p. 127). Fuller understanding of the linguistic and discourse patterns generally employed within a particular genre has served as the basis for genre-based instruction that addresses the notion that genres unfold in stages and that experienced readers or listeners are likely to experience a sense of frustration or negative evaluation when phases do not unfold as expected. Christie (2006) also emphasized the importance to L2 teachers of the knowledge about language (KAL), including knowledge of grammar (as long as grammar is understood in terms of making appropriate grammatical choice in order to create effective, situated meaning) as an important result of genre-based teaching. Research into *field*, or the particular activity that is being accomplished through discourse, has explored several kinds of school and workplace discourse, including the areas of mathematics, science, geography, history, and English for academic purposes (see Martin, 2009, for a fuller discussion). In general, there has been a recent shift to analyze longer texts as a series of smaller genre complexes that unfold in stages (see Christie, 1999; Martin, 2009, for classroom discourse). These insights have been used to teach both L2 written discourse and spoken discourse. For overviews of application of genre to L2, see Byrnes (2006, 2009).

In the United States, Byrnes and her colleagues (e.g., Byrnes, 2009; Byrnes, Maxim, & Norris, in press) have successfully developed a genre-based curriculum for advanced learners of German as a foreign language. The focus is on close reading of genre-defined texts and analysis of the situated choices writers make in order to create meaning. Thus, the reading-writing-speaking connections are of central concern. The close reading involves intensive analysis of genre-based usage of lexicon, grammatical choices, and rhetorical structure in reading and writing. Texts are presented as "models for the meaning-making resources available in the language system; texts are instances of linguistically construed cultural situations that themselves are reflective of the entire cultural system" (Byrnes et al., in press). Schleppegrell and her colleagues have also applied SFL to issue in L2 writing (e.g., Achugar, Schleppegrell, & Oteíza, 2007; Schleppegrell, 2004, 2008; Schleppegrell, Greer & Taylor, 2008). Colombi (2009) has used concepts from SFL in her work with heritage language learners.

Both in theory and in application, SFL has a strong tendency to focus on the surface patterns of the text, such as use of nominalizations, hypotactic versus paratactic sentence structure, amount of pronoun usage, ellipsis, lexical repetition, and semantic networking. While recognizing audience expectation and participants as part of culturally situated context, the assumption seems to be that, for the most part, meaning exists in the text (Halliday, 1994, 2002; Halliday & Hasan, 1976; Hoey, 1991). Issues such as linguistic elements underspecifying the intended interpretation, the importance of inferencing, and the use of background knowledge in both the interpretation and production of discourse are not addressed. This lack of emphasis on the listener as an active creator of meaning, as well as lack of emphasis on human cognition (such as human category formation, organization of memory, and use of background knowledge) as central to shaping language and to meaning making, have been key distinctions between SFL and the other two usage-based approaches considered here.

DISCOURSE FUNCTIONALISM

While SFL represents a model of language clearly distinguishable from discourse functionalists and CL, these last two are more appropriately seen as models located on a continuum. Historically, the two approaches have exerted considerable influence over each other, and some of the same scholars have been associated with both (e.g., Wallace Chafe and Paul Hopper).

The discourse functionalists have sought to develop a relatively detailed description of grammar that attends closely to the relationships among grammar, discourse, and the producers of the discourse. Grammar usage is seen through the lens of discourse and meaningful speaker choice. Their understanding of the discourse producers also includes an explicit recognition of the cognitive dimension, in addition to the social-cultural. For instance, Chafe's (1994, 2005, 2007) explanation of English speakers' choice of determiners is largely based on the role of memory (including information retrievable from schema-based knowledge) and attention. In his analysis of spoken English, Chafe (2001) noted that language is produced in relatively short intonation units, which he hypothesized are constrained by the *one new idea per unit* constraint, which is in turn tied to short-term memory and processing constraints.

Although there are a number of important researchers associated with discourse functionalism, here I will focus on Givón's contributions as representative of the approach. Givón (e.g., 1995, 2001) recognized the importance of discourse context, although he has not developed a formalism for the connections between context and grammar as found in SFL. In distinction from SFL, in considering context, he does not recognize genre as an overarching construct which is central to understanding the connection between syntax and meaning. In further contrast to SFL, he has argued for the importance of taking more than just the social-cultural-communicative dimensions into account in order to fully understand why language is as it is. Givón (2001) has taken what might be understood as a broadly biological approach to functionalism. He argued that biologists long ago recognized that they could not adequately understand a particular part of an organism, for instance, the human heart, without understanding how it functioned within the organism as a whole. On analogy, he has argued that it is impossible to adequately understand language (or any particular formal structure found in language) without understanding how language functions in terms of the purposeful social and communication activities that its producers use it to perform. Moreover, language cannot be understood apart from the full human organism itself. At a more specific level, Givón looks to general cognitive processes as important in shaping language. He sees cognition and the brain (including issues of language processing), as well as communication and social interaction, as some of the central, natural parameters that shape language (Givón, 1995, 2001). A good example of integrating cognitive motivation into his explanation of grammar is his discussion of an animacy hierarchy and its relation to thematic roles. In terms of cognitive saliency rooted in evolution and survival, humans are especially concerned with their own actions and the forces that impinge upon them; this is reflected in sentence structure and thematic roles. At the most basic level, agents are usually animate, preferably human; patients or themes are more likely to be inanimate. Nonanimate forces, such as earthquakes, which affect humans in ways that are similar to animate beings, are less typical but possible agents.

Givón's (1995, 2001) analysis of iconicity, or the notion that a resemblance exists between the shape of language and the concepts being represented, also illustrates his inclusion of the cognitive dimension as an important factor in determining the structure of language. He noted that formalists tend to dismiss iconicity in language as untenable because of the tremendous morphosyntactic variation found across languages. One of the seeming problems with iconicity has been the basic claim that word order essentially corresponds to the order of thought. On the face of it, this claim appears false, given that languages demonstrate many word orders, while human conceptualization or thought order is presumably universal. Givón has argued that the existence of competing pragmatic and communicative principles accounts for the variation. For instance, he argued that the universal principle of focused elements coming first (or iconically, the information the speaker finds most pressing coming at the beginning of the sentence) is often in competition with the well-documented principle of given information coming at the beginning of the sentence (iconically, starting with what is known). Competition between these two communicative and cognitive forces accounts for certain patterns of variation. Givón explained the failure to find obvious iconic universals, such as a single word order for all languages, by drawing on the notion that humans represent complex biological systems that have evolved and adapted to multiple, often competing pressures over time. Because of the complexity of the process of evolutionary development in response to multiple forces, simple one-to-one relationships between form and function are rare. He further argued that if one views iconicity at a more abstract level and takes competing forces into account, iconicity can be seen as a fundamental force shaping language. Note that Givón's explanation of the speaker's choice of what information comes at the beginning of a sentence was essentially a reanalysis of theme/rheme. Givón's attribution of speaker choice being influenced by cognitive principles contrasts with SFL.

While firmly arguing for meaning, discourse, communicative, and cognitive motivations as the genesis of grammar, Givón did not reject formal grammatical structure as a reality of language. He argued that competing motivations (communicative, cognitive, social-cultural, etc.) often lead to a situation in which grammar becomes established as a conventionalized system (e.g., 2001). In terms of analysis of specific grammatical constructions, Givón's work on the role of passive versus active is representative. Having analyzed multiple instances of discourse in several languages, Givón argued that passive accomplishes several functions: (a) de-emphasizes the agent, (b) places focus on the theme/patient, (c) allows for continued focus on a topical participant that may not be agentive, and (d) tends to make the action more static.

Taking a strong comparative linguistic typological approach, many of his studies consider the frequency distribution of features in different languages, striking a balance between what is common across languages and their individual characteristics. In distinction from SFL, discourse functionalism focuses on syntax as coding meaning in a way that is generalizable across discourse contexts rather than concentrating on the typical syntactic patterns that co-occur in a particular genre. Discourse functional analyses do not focus on issues such as patterns of ellipsis or tendency to use nominalizations in a particular text type.[4]

We turn now to applications of discourse functionalists to issues in second language learning and teaching. Setting aside work which focuses on speech acts, it is probably fair to say that a majority of discourse applications to issues in L2 learning have been influenced by discourse functionalists. Celce-Murcia (2002) acknowledged the important contributions of Givón in her discussion of teaching L2 grammar from a discourse/functional perspective. Tomlin's (1994, 1997) influential red fish/blue fish experiments, which demonstrated that native English speakers' use of active constructions when the focus is on the agent and passive when the focus in on the patient grew out of Givón's analysis. This understanding of active versus passive has been widely accepted by L2 discourse analysts (e.g., Celce-Murcia & Larsen-Freeman, 1999; Celce-Murcia & Olshtain, 2005; Larsen-Freeman, 2002; McCarthy & Carter, 2002). Many studies by Celce-Murcia (e.g., 2002) and her students have analyzed speaker choice between competing constructions, such as used *to* versus *would*, in naturally occurring discourse; these studies assumed that speaker choice in lexical constructions and syntax has a general communicative meaning across a wide range of text types. Carter, Hughes, and McCarthy (2000) provided analysis of numerous grammatical patterns, from aspectual choices to use of relative clauses, in terms of general communicative functions. They pointed out a range of text types as good sources of naturally occurring uses of a particular pattern, but did not tie the pattern to a particular genre. For instance, their discussion of modal usage included analysis of newspaper horoscopes and print advertisements, two quite different genres.

COGNITIVE LINGUISTICS

CL inherits many basic assumptions from discourse functionalism. For instance, there has been general recognition of the importance of discourse-level phenomena, although relatively little discourse analysis has actually been carried out by cognitive linguists. As Sanders & Spooren (2005), in their review of the discourse-CL connection, noted, "At the moment, the cognitive linguistic study of discourse is still more of a promising challenge to linguists and students of discourse, rather than a well-established part of everyday cognitive linguistic practice" (p. 917).[5] (Exceptions to this trend include the work by, e.g., Cameron, 2008; Dancygier,

2008; Moder, 2004, 2008). CL also recognizes the role of iconicity, particularly as it relates to metonymy and some aspects of primary metaphor.

What sets CL apart from the discourse functionalist approach is its primary commitment to developing a model of language that reflects human neural-physical architecture and human interaction with the social-physical world. By extension, CL assumes that reflexes of the same neuro-cognitive principles should operate in multiple areas of language. This is what Lakoff (1990) termed the "generalization commitment" (p. 39). Thus, it is of theoretical import for CL that we find occurrences of polysemy in lexical items, such as *give* (Newman, 1996); functional morphemes, such as tense markers (Tyler & Evans, 2001) and *-er* (Panther & Thornburg, 2001); and grammatical constructions (Goldberg, 1995). Moreover, CL pays a great deal of attention to evidence from psychology and neuroscience (e.g., Coventry & Garrod, 2004; Coventry & Guijarro-Fuentes, 2008; Gibbs, 2006; Taylor, 2003; von Stutterheim, 2003) concerning human category formation, memory capacity and the role of input frequency in automaticity (e.g., Bybee, 2003, 2006; Schmid, 2007) and in first language acquisition (e.g. Tomasello, 2003; Lieven & Tomasello, 2008). Tomasello (2003) also argued for a unique genetic endowment involving joint attention and ability to develop a theory of the mind as essential social components required for symbolic communication and hence language.

CL is deeply rooted in the notion of embodied meaning (e.g., Gibbs, 1994, 2006; Lakoff, 1987; Lakoff & Johnson, 1999; Langacker, 1987, 1991b). Cognition itself is understood as being shaped by humans' unique neural and physical architecture in interaction with the social-spatial-physical environment. Consider one aspect of humans' unique physical architecture, its consequences for human conceptualization of the world, and one of its reflexes in language: Humans stand on their hind legs. This means that beginning in infancy, humans are acutely aware of balance, the force of gravity, and the salience of being "up" for being able to see more, grasp objects more freely, move more quickly, and so on. Being able to stand upright makes "up-down" and resistance to gravity meaningful to humans in ways they are simply not to, say, snakes or hummingbirds. Standing, the quintessential human experience of upness and resistance to gravity, figures into many metaphors that have to do with persistence and self-esteem, for example, *stand up for yourself, stand for something you believe in, this aggression will not stand*. Grady (2007) argued that a primary metaphor found in many languages is "persistence is remaining erect." The salience of up versus down for humans and its reflex in language was well documented in Lakoff and Johnson's (1980) study on orientation metaphors.

In terms of human perceptual systems, since the Gestalt psychologists, it has been established that the human visual system is configured such that, when viewing a spatial array, humans tend to focus on smaller, more mobile entities (focus) that are located in terms of larger, more stable entities (ground). CL has emphasized that this aspect of the human visual system is reflected in language (Talmy, 2000a,b), as in the prepositional system (*The **bike** is by the **school***) in which the smaller, more moveable "bike" is the focus and located in relation to the larger, less mobile "school" (the ground). Consider the oddness of the sentence? *The **school** is by the **bike***, in which the focus/ground relationship is reversed. Talmy (2000a) argued that figure/ground relations account for many patterns of clause ordering in complex sentences. Langacker (1987, 1991b) also argued that the focus/ground relation is ubiquitous in larger language structures, for example, the sentential subject acts as the focus element in relation to the predicate, which acts as the ground.

Basic human interactions with the physical and social world provide a foundation for human conceptual and cognitive representations which are in turn reflected in language. Humans use their understanding of the external, physical world as a framework for representing internal phenomena—emotions, self-reflective concepts, and more abstract concepts. The physical underpinning for conceptualization is reflected throughout language. In other words, humans regularly think and talk about internal phenomena in terms of the external, sociophysical. This is central to conceptual metaphor theory, one of the constructs most closely associated with CL (e.g., Grady, 1997, 1999, 2007; Lakoff & Johnson, 1980, 1999). Within CL, metaphor is understood as a ubiquitous part of thought and language. Rejecting the traditional analysis that metaphor is based solely on resemblance, Grady has argued that much of metaphor is based in fundamental human experiences of the world in which two independent phenomena repeatedly co-occur, such that they become closely associated in memory. Once this association has been established, humans appear to think about the more abstract phenomena in terms of the more concrete. A straightforward example is the everyday observation that as more liquid is added to a container, there is a simultaneous rise in the level of the liquid. This ubiquitous observation leads to a tight mental association between the concepts of "amount" and vertical elevation, that is, "up-down." As a result, we think and talk about an increase in amount in terms of an increase in vertical elevation (Grady, 1999; Lakoff & Johnson, 1999), as in *The price of potatoes is up/rising* or *Executive compensation remains elevated*. Grady (1999) termed this type of metaphor *primary metaphor*, which is based on experiential correlation. After examining more than 20 languages, many of which are not historically related, Grady (1999) argued that the primary metaphor, "more is up," (p. 87) along with a dozen other primary metaphors, appears to be universal. CL's emphasis on cognition and embodied meaning allows exploration of many linguistic phenomena which are of no theoretical import to SFL nor discourse functionalists, such as recurring instances of the same cognitive processes at different levels of language, metaphor, and polysemy.

CL maintains that the multiple, rich, interacting cognitive capacities of humans are sufficient to account for language. In the general area of classification and organization of memory, some of the key cognitive capacities include humans' incredibly well developed abilities at classifying, pattern finding, and a huge, highly structured memory capacity. See Taylor (2003, 2004) for a detailed discussion of categorization and CL. Humans are particularly adept at forming categories, that is, at perceiving similarities over several specific instances of entities or events which may differ substantially in terms of surface manifestations (e.g., a wide range of entities are perceived as chairs even though they differ in terms of shape [a desk chair versus a bean bag chair], materials [wood versus soft fabric], and numerous other physical properties). Moreover, human memory is richly patterned and networked. Work by Rosch and her colleagues (e.g., Rosch, E. & C. Mervis, 1975) has established that one key aspect of human categorization (and hence memory structuring) involves centrality or prototype effects and radial categories. Radial categories are organized around a set of attributes abstracted from best exemplars of the category (this is the central prototype); other entities that are perceived to resemble the prototype in important ways (including how humans interact with an entity or how a type of event affects humans) are part of the category but understood to be less good examples. The classic case is that for English speakers from North American the general attributes of a small songbird, such as a robin, represent a prototypical bird while penguins and ostriches represent less good exemplars. Goldberg (1995) argued that the same principles of categorization and centrality effects apply to syntactic constructions and the particular verbs that occur in the construction. For instance, in the double object construction (Subj-X Verb Obj-Y Obj-Z), the central meaning is *X caused Y to receive Z*, and the verb that most closely matches this meaning is *give*. Corpus analyses have revealed that *give* is the most commonly occurring verb in the double object construction. Thus a sentence such as *Yun **gave** Hiro the paper* represents a prototypical instance of the construction. A sentence such as *Mari willed Miko her house* can be explained through systematic principles of extension, but is a less central exemplar of the construction, as it does not entail physical transfer of an entity from one participant to another. Goldberg further argued that the predominance of *give* in the double object construction in motherese provides the young child an anchor for learning the meaning of the construction. First, the most central case is learned; extended uses are gradually added to the child's repertoire as they encounter adult use of less prototypical verbs, such as *bake* or *fax* in the construction.

Another component of category formation is the ability to recognize patterns and perceive resemblances among varied entities, events, and even attributes that are simultaneously understood as different. This is the heart of conceptual metaphor, conceptualizing one entity in terms of another. When we say a person is a twig, we are reflecting our ability to see a resemblance between the fleshless structure of a tree branch and a human with exposed bone structure due to very little body fat. Goldberg (1995, 2006) argued that syntactic constructions can also be extended metaphorically. For instance, *Lou told Chris a story* is analyzed as a metaphoric extension of the double object construction; the acceptability of verbs of communication in this construction is accounted for by the conduit metaphor for communication (Reddy, 1993), by which English speakers perceive a similarity between exchanging information and exchanging physical entities.

Memory is also organized in terms of flexible, dynamic schemas that involve abstract, hierarchical generalizations built up over a number of specific instances; both specific instances and the abstracted generalizations are represented in memory. Psychologists have represented schemas in various ways from scripts for specific types of recurring sociocultural events, such as going to a restaurant, to development of abstract concepts such as *hot*, to knowledge of the general rhetorical structure and language of fairy tales. The point is that human memory is richly, systematically patterned. Moreover, any one entity or event or experience can be part of multiple schemas, thus memory is massively interconnected and redundant. Humans use established, schematic patterns to help interpret and organize new information. Richly structured, massively interconnected memory has numerous reflexes in language. Langacker (e.g., 1987, 2008a) has argued that our knowledge of sentence structures is schematic, with some representations of a particular pattern being quite specific and lexically (and phonetically) filled in while others are highly abstract and general. In other words, humans have both vast lists of sentences stored in memory (including information about the contexts in which the sentences occurred) and generalizations or "templates" representing abstract sentential structure. Crucially, these templates are not represented as being disconnected from meaning. For example, a template for an active, transitive sentence might be represented as something like [Subject-X Verb Object-Y] connected to a general meaning of [X-Actor/Initiator causes some effect on Y-Patient]. The argument that syntactic patterns are best understood as high-level schematic abstractions is also at the heart of construction grammar, Adele Goldberg's particular take on syntax (Goldberg, 1995, 2006). Humans can tap into the schema at whatever level of abstractness is most useful at the moment. Words are argued to act as under-specified prompts into encyclopedia memory (Evans & Green, 2006; Langacker, 1987, 1991b; Taylor, 2004). Langacker (e.g., 1987, 1991a, 2008a) and cognitive linguists generally argue against strict divisions between lexical items and syntactic patterns, as well as strict divisions between semantics and pragmatics. Fauconnier and Turner (2002) argued that many linguistic forms are best understood as prompts from the speaker to the listener to access pertinent schemas and construct particular relational configuration among concepts, such as analogy, role and identity, causality, and so forth. The general claim, then, is that words and the syntactic patterns in which they occur always underdetermine the rich interpretation regularly assigned to any utterance. Thus, humans' well-developed inferencing abilities, in conjunction with richly structured memory, are also seen as a central part of how language works.

Part of the ability to form schema is importantly connected to humans' large memory capacity and sensitivity to linguistic input and input frequency. In fact, studies of frequency effects (e.g., Bybee, 2003, 2006; Bybee & Moder, 1983; Ellis, 2002a, 2002b, 2008a,b) have shown that humans are quite sensitive to the frequency with which they have encountered words and the constructions in which words are encountered, down to evidencing reaction time sensitivity to how likely they are to hear a verb in the present tense versus the past tense. The growing body of evidence amassed by Tomasello (e.g., 2003) and his colleagues (e.g., Lieven & Tomasello, 2008) indicates that first language learning is item-based and frequency driven. Their work shows that young children are highly attuned to the specific exemplars of language in the input and the context in which they are used. For instance, children appear to constrain their use of a particular verb heard in an intransitive construction to intransitive use until they also hear that verb used in a transitive construction, even though they use other verbs in transitive constructions (Tomasello & Brooks, 1998). As we have seen, Goldberg (1995) exploited sensitivity to frequency in her explanation of the co-occurrence of particular verbs in syntactic constructions. SFL and discourse functionalism also assume that input is central to learning language and the shape language takes. However, CL's commitment to putting established cognitive processes at the center of the theory and its dedicated explorations of exemplar based learning, abstraction over numerous instances, and automaticity as a result of entrenchment (based primarily on input frequency) sets it apart from the other two approaches.[6]

Cognitive linguists exploit findings from psychology indicating that concepts deriving from human interaction with the social-physical world, such as the spatial relations coded by prepositions or our conceptualization of a horse, crucially involve sensory-motor imagery. CL has argued concepts are better represented as being gestaltlike and schematic in nature, rather than represented as linguistic propositions or semantic feature bundles (e.g., Langacker, 1987). A tremendous amount of psychological evidence exists demonstrating sensory images are an essential part of human conceptualization. One simple example is the vast reaction time literature documenting the effect of imageability on how quickly readers process words.

The connections between spatial conceptualization and language have provided powerful theoretical insights (e.g., Langacker, 1987; Talmy, 2000a,b). Talmy extended notions of spatial boundedness, which derive largely from visual perception, to explanations of mass versus count nouns as well as aspect. One particularly important aspect of spatial conceptualization is the human ability to conceptualize an event or state as a spatial scene. A related facet involves humans' ability to manipulate their perspective on a scene, that is, humans have the ability to construe or view a single scene from several perspectives. The ability to conceptually construe a scene from multiple perspectives has many reflexes in language. One central reflex is the various syntactic constructions found in language that convey similar propositional content but provide a different speaker stance or perspective, such as the active construction which puts the focus on the agent versus the passive construction that defocuses the agent and instead puts focus on the patient/theme. Note that Givón's analyses recognize general principles of cognitive processing, such as the tendency to start with what is given because this provides the listener with a shared reference point, but makes no reference to the human perceptual system and its effect on cognition, which is in turn reflected in language.

Talmy (2000a) also discovered cross-linguistic typologies involving differences in how individual languages "divide up" their conceptualization of a spatial scene. He argued that while all humans see the same elements in a motion scene, for example, they all see the participants, the manner in which they move and the path of their motion, different speech communities have developed distinct, conventionalized patterns of packaging the information. Perhaps the most well known is the packaging difference between a satellite framed language (like English in which manner is often incorporated into the motion verb and path indicated by a separate particle construction, as in the sentence *The woman strolled into the room*) versus a verb-framed language (such as Spanish, in which motion and path tend to be conflated and manner expressed in a separate phrase, as in the sentence *The woman entered the room strolling*). This distinction has been a major focus of Slobin's (1996a, 1996b, 2003, 2009) cross-linguistic studies and his theory of thinking for speaking.

Applying CL to issues in L2 research and learning is still in its infancy. Although a handful of books and overview articles have been dedicated to the connection, the majority of the work has focused on potential insights rather than reporting on classroom applications or experiments (Achard & Niemeier, 2004; Boers & Lindstromberg, 2008; De Knop & De Rycker, 2008; Pütz, Niemeier, & Dirven, 2001b; Langacker, 2008b; Robinson & Ellis, 2008; Tyler, Kim, & Takada, 2008; Verspoor & Tyler, 2009). Even though the body of applied work is relatively small, space limitations allow for just a brief mention of some of the applications of CL. As I noted earlier, CL conceptualizes lexical items, phrases and morphosyntax on a continuum rather than as distinct components of language. As an organizational device, I will discuss the applications by dividing the studies into two main areas: vocabulary and morphosyntax. This should not be taken as an indication of a theoretical divide between the lexicon and morphosyntax.

Vocabulary teaching, broadly defined, has been the area of L2 learning to which CL has been most frequently applied. This is probably due to the fact that some of the central, unique constructs from CL, such as conceptual metaphor theory, polysemy networks, and embodied meaning, are particularly useful in explaining some of the most difficult aspects of word meaning. The volume edited by Boers and Lindstromberg (2008) presented recent empirical findings on the applications of metaphor and metonymy in teaching general vocabulary, idioms, figurative language, and phrasal verbs. MacArthur and Littlemore (2008) and Walker (2008) presented effect-of-instruction studies based on CL in conjunction with corpus-based instruction. In general, the findings over the past 10 years indicate that alerting subjects to L2 patterns of metaphor and metonymy (and how they relate to semantic networks) is often effective in increasing learners' ability to learn and retain new words. For instance, Boers & Lindstromberg (2006) found that having students consider salient consequences of *up-down* led to an increased ability to interpret and retain unfamiliar metaphoric uses of verbs such as *soar*, *skyrocket*, and *plunge* (such as *My spirits soared*), as well as phrases and idioms. See also Boers, Eyckmans, and Stengers (2007) and Littlemore & Low (2006).

A number of insights have emerged from analyses that combine metaphor theory with the notions of prototype effects and polysemy networks, for example, Csabi (2004), for teaching the distinction between *hold* versus *keep* and their multiple meanings by using the metaphor "possessing is holding" (p. 234); Lowie & Verspoor (2004), for teaching English prepositions; Rudzka-Ostyn (2003), for teaching phrasal verbs; and Verspoor & Lowie (2003), for teaching multiple senses of polysemous words. Tyler and her colleagues (reported in Tyler, 2008b) have successfully used Tyler & Evans's (2001, 2003, 2004) analysis of the semantics of English prepositions (which draws heavily on polysemy networks, metaphoric extension, and embodied meaning), in effects-of-instruction experiments to teach the many meanings of *over.*

Metaphoric extension and embodied experience are central to Sweetser's (1990) analysis of the multiple meanings associated with all English modals (i.e., the social world-speech act or root meaning versus the logical reasoning or epistemic meaning). For example, *You should take a sweater* (social) ver-sus *That should be Eve at the door* (reasoning). Sweetser's basic analysis was that the meaning of the modals is based in force dynamics.[7] Understanding of physical forces that affect forward motion have been extended first to the social world and then to the world of reasoning. Tyler converted Sweetser's descriptions of the various types of force dynamics associated with each modal into a set of simple figures, depicting various forces as being internal or external to a mover. In a series of experiments, Tyler and her colleagues (reported in Tyler, 2008a, 2008b) found that subjects receiving instruction on the semantics of modals from a CL perspective used modals in a more nativelike way than subjects who were in an input flood situation but did not receive a CL explanation.

A number of studies have successfully applied CL insights to aspects of learning L2 morphology. Hamrick and Attardo (in press) exploited Talmy's analysis of boundedness, in conjunction with prototype theory, to successfully teach learners of Italian appropriate auxiliary selection in the *passato prossimo*. Niemeier (2008) also used boundedness to create teaching materials for English progressive aspect, as well as mass-count distinction. Huong (2005) drew on boundedness in the explaining mass-count distinctions in English nouns in relation to learning the English article system. Drawing on the primary metaphors "here is now/there is then" and "physical closeness is control," Tyler and Evans (2001) created pedagogical materials that systematically explained unusual uses of English past and present tenses, such as the use of past tense to indicate politeness, as in *I **was** wondering if you'd like to have lunch*, where the wondering is clearly taking place in the moment of speaking. Using notions of semantic extension and polysemy, Liamkina (2006, 2008) carried out a longitudinal study examining advanced foreign-language German learners' mastery of the multiple meanings and uses of German dative. Those who received explanations based on prototype theory and polysemy networks outperformed those receiving a traditional approach. Panther and Thornburg (2001) created a systematic, pedagogically oriented account of Englisher nominals, drawing on conceptual schema theory, prototypes, and conceptual metaphor.

Complex syntactic points have also been addressed. Cadierno (2008) reviewed several studies that focused on learning motion verb constructions; these studies applied Talmy's verb-framed/satellite-framed analysis, as well as Slobin's (1996b) insights on thinking for speaking. The concept of construal has been fruitfully applied by several researchers. Achard (e.g., 2008) investigated naturally occurring uses of definite and partitive articles in French. He argued that a speaker's choice between the two was a matter of construal and conventionalized cultural schemas; he successfully applied that analysis to L2 instruction. See Verspoor and Tyler (2009) and Achard and Niemeier (2004) for discussion of other applications of construal to language teaching.

Recall that CL argues that syntax itself is meaningful and that syntactic pat-terns are templates abstracted over many instances of utterances. Moreover, there are no derivations or transformations of a more basic syntactic pattern to a second, derived pattern. Thus, Goldberg represented the double object construction (Subj-X Verb Obj-Y Obj-Z) as meaning *X caused Y to receive Z*, as in *Hiro gave Yun the book*. This construction contrasts with the caused-motion construction (Subj-X Verb-Obj Y Oblique object Z) which means X caused Y to move to Z, as in *Lissa threw the football to Mike*. A few studies demonstrating the usefulness of Goldberg's construction grammar (Goldberg, 1995, 2006) in L2 learning are beginning to emerge: Mellow (2006) for teaching relative clause constructions; Manzanares and Rojo Lopez (2008) for double object constructions; Strauss, Lee, and Ahn (2006) for Korean completive constructions.

CONCLUSION

All three approaches—SFL, discourse functionalism, and CL—share a number of tenets that place them in a usage-based paradigm. At the same time, each has its own distinctive approach to language. Perhaps the most salient difference among the three involves the conceptualization of the key factors that shape language. SFL draws almost exclusively on social-communicative factors in its analyses; discourse functionalism recognizes the social-communicative functions, while adding general principles of cognitive processing; and CL prioritizes the salience of human neurophysical anatomy and human interaction with the physical world.

NOTES

1 The usage-based approaches discussed in this article have also been labeled as functional, broadly defined, as they all adhere to the notion that any language system is intimately related to and derives from how language is actually used, as opposed to formalist approaches which argue that language is the result of a genetically endowed, predetermined set of linguistic-specific principles. However, the traditional understanding of functionalism focuses on the communicative function as *the* prime language shaper. Some analysts (e.g., Butler, 2006) have questioned whether CL, with its strong emphasis on the neuro-cognition and embodied experiences, falls outside the traditional understanding of a functional approach.

2 This focus on cultural transmission has influenced the area of critical discourse analysis, language and power, and language and identity.

3 Butler (1989) stated, "Perhaps the single most important feature running through Halliday's work is the formalisation of paradigmatic patterning as systems and giving the category of system the central role in grammar" (p. 6).

4 Tannen (1989) in *Speaking Voices* did examine lexical repetition, but her analysis argued for repetition of phrases in conversation as both a rapport-building strategy and as reflecting online cognitive production and processing constraints.

5 Fauconnier (1997) and Fauconnier and Turner (2002) have developed a cognitive model of discourse through the theory of mental spaces and blending. This theory attempts to model how humans create and interpret unfolding discourse through setting up temporary *mental spaces*. Certain linguistic elements, such as tense marking and conjunctions, have been identified as "space builders," for example, instructions to the listener or reader to establish a new mental space. Recently, Dancygier (2008) has extended mental space theory to account for shifts in viewpoint in narratives. However, the majority of work done in mental space theory does not examine how particular grammatical constructions or larger rhetorical patterns work in discourse.

6 Frequency effects in both first and second language learning are an extremely complex phenomenon. Frequency effects interact with multiple factors such as saliency, learned attending, whether or not a lexical item is a basic level term, and discourse effects, just to mention a few. It is far beyond the scope of this

article to even begin to adequately address the issue. The reader is directed to the many works of Joan Bybee, Nick Ellis, and Michael Tomasello for fuller discussion.

7 Sweetser based her analysis on Talmy's (2000a) original analysis of force dynamics and modals.

REFERENCES

Achard, M. (2008). Teaching construal: Cognitive pedagogical grammar. In P. Robinson & N. C. Ellis (Eds.), *Handbook of cognitive linguistics and second language acquisition* (pp. 432–455). New York: Routledge.

Achard, M., & Niemeier, S. (Eds.). (2004). *Cognitive linguistics, second language acquisition, and foreign language teaching.* Berlin, Germany: Mouton de Gruyter.

Achugar, M., Schleppegrell, M. J., & Oteíza, T. (2007). Engaging teachers in language analysis: A functional linguistics approach to reflective literacy. *English Teaching: Practice and Critique, 6,* 8–24.

Boers, F., & Lindstromberg, S. (2006). Cognitive linguistic applications in second language or foreign language instruction: Rationale, proposals, and evaluation. In G. Kristiansen, M. Achard, R. Dirven, & F. Ruiz de Mendoza (Eds.), *Cognitive linguistics: Current applications and future perspectives* (pp. 305–355). Berlin, Germany: Mouton de Gruyter.

Boers, F., & Lindstromberg, S. (Eds.). (2008). *Cognitive linguistic approaches to teaching vocabulary and phraseology.* Berlin, Germany: Mouton De Gruyter.

Boers, F., Eyckmans, J., & Stengers, H. (2007). Presenting figurative idioms with a touch of etymology: More than mere mnemonics? *Language Teaching Research, 11,* 43–62.

Butler, C. S. (1989). Systemic models: Unity, diversity and change. *Word, 40,* 1–35.

Butler, C. S. (2006). Functionalist theories of language. In K. Brown (Ed.), *The encyclopedia of language and linguistics* (Vol. 4, pp. 696–704). Oxford, UK: Elsevier.

Bybee, J. (2003). Mechanisms in change in grammaticalization: The role of repetition. In R. Janda & B. Joseph (Eds.), *Handbook of historical linguistics* (pp. 602–623). Oxford, UK: Blackwell.

Bybee, J. (2006). *Frequency of use and the organization of language.* Oxford, UK: Oxford University Press.

Bybee, J., & Moder, C. (1983). Morphological classes as natural categories. *Language, 59,* 251–270.

Byrnes, H. (2006). A semiotic perspective on culture and foreign language teaching: Implications for collegiate materials development. In V. Galloway & B. Cothran (Eds.), *Language and culture out of bounds: Discipline-blurred perspectives on the foreign language classroom* (pp. 37–66). Boston, MA: Heinle Thomson.

Byrnes, H. (2009). Systemic-functional reflections on instructed foreign language acquisition as meaning-making: An introduction. *Linguistics and Education, 20*, 1–9.

Byrnes, H., Maxim, H., & Norris, J. (in press). *Realizing advanced FL writing development in collegiate education: Curricular design, pedagogy, assessment.* London: Continuum.

Cadierno, T. (2008). Learning to talk about motion in a foreign language. In P. Robinson & N. C. Ellis (Eds.), *Handbook of cognitive linguistics and second language acquisition* (pp. 239–275). New York: Routledge.

Cameron, L. (2008). A discourse approach to metaphor: Explaining systematic metaphors for literacy processes in a school discourse community. In A. Tyler, Y. Kim, & M. Takada (Eds.), *Language in the context of use: Discourse and cognitive approaches to language* (pp. 321–338). Berlin, Germany: Mouton de Gruyter.

Carter, R., Hughes, R., & McCarthy, M. (2000). *Exploring language in context.* Cambridge, UK: Cambridge University Press.

Celce-Murcia, M. (2002). Why it makes sense to teach grammar in context and through discourse. In E. Hinkle & S. Fotos (Eds.), *New perspectives on grammar teaching in second language classrooms* (pp. 119–134). Mahwah, NJ: Erlbaum.

Celce-Murcia, M., & Larsen-Freeman, D. (1999). *The grammar book: An ESL/EFL teacher's course.* Boston, MA: Heinle & Heinle.

Celce-Murcia, M., & Olshtain, E. (2005). Discourse based approaches: A new framework for second language teaching and learning. In E. Hinkle (Ed.), *Handbook of research in second language teaching and learning* (pp. 729–741). New York: Routledge.

Chafe, W. (1994). *Discourse, consciousness, and time: The flow and displacement of conscious experience in speaking and writing.* Chicago: Chicago University Press.

Chafe, W. (2001). The analysis of discourse flow. In D. Schiffrin, D. Tannen, & H. E. Hamilton (Eds.), *The handbook of discourse analysis* (pp. 673–687). Oxford, UK: Blackwell.

Chafe, W. (2005). The relation of grammar to thought. In C. S. Butler, M. de los Ángeles Gómez-González, & S. M. Doval-Suàrez (Eds.), *The dynamics of language use: Functional and contrastive perspectives* (pp. 55–75). Amsterdam: John Benjamins.

Chafe, W. (2007). Language and consciousness. In P. D. Zelazo, M. Moscovitch, & E. Thompson (Eds.), *Cambridge handbook of consciousness* (pp. 355–373). Cambridge, UK: Cambridge University Press.

Christie, F. (2006). Literacy teaching and current debates over reading. In R. Whittaker, M. O'Donnell, & A. McCabe (Eds.), *Language and literacy: Functional approaches* (pp. 45–65). London: Continuum.

Colombi, M. C. (2009). A systemic functional approach to teaching Spanish for heritage speakers in the United States. *Linguistics and Education, 20*, 39–49.

Coventry, K., & Garrod, S. (2004). *Saying, seeing and acting: The psychological semantics of spatial prepositions. Essays in cognitive psychology series.* New York: Psychology Press.

Coventry, K., & Guijarro-Fuentes, P. (2008). Spatial language learning and functional geometry. In P. Robinson & N. C. Ellis (Eds.), *Handbook of cognitive linguistics and second language acquisition* (pp. 114–138). London: Routledge.

Csabi, S. (2004). A cognitive linguistic view of polysemy in English and its implications for teaching. In M. Achard & S. Niemeier (Eds.), *Cognitive linguistics, second language acquisition, and foreign language teaching* (pp. 233–256). Berlin, Germany: Mouton de Gruyter.

Dancygier, B. (2008). Personal pronouns, blending, and narrative viewpoint. In A. Tyler, Y. Kim, & M. Takada (Eds.), *Language in the context of use: Discourse and cognitive approaches to language* (pp. 167–183). Berlin, Germany: Mouton de Gruyter.

De Knop, S., & De Rycker, T. (Eds.). (2008). *Cognitive approaches to pedagogical grammar.* Berlin, Germany: Mouton de Gruyter.

De Knop, S., Boers, F., & De Rycker, T. (Eds.). (in press). *Applications of cognitive linguistics: Exploring the lexis-grammar continuum in second language pedagogy.* Berlin, Germany: Mouton de Gruyter.

Ellis, N. C. (2002a). Frequency effects in language processing: A review with implications for theories of implicit and explicit language acquisition. *Studies in Second Language Acquisition, 24,* 143–188.

Ellis, N. C. (2002b). Reflections on frequency effects in language processing. *Studies in Second Language Acquisition, 24,* 297–339.

Ellis, N. C. (2008a). Usage-based and form-focused SLA: The implicit and explicit learning of constructions. In A. Tyler, Y. Kim, & M. Takada (Eds.), *Language in the context of use: Discourse and cognitive approaches to language* (pp. 93–121). Berlin, Germany: Mouton de Gruyter.

Ellis, N. C. (2008b) Usage-based and form-focused language acquisition: The associative learning of constructions, learned attention and the limited L2 end state. In P. Robinson & N. C. Ellis (Eds.), *Handbook of cognitive linguistics and second language acquisition* (pp. 372–406). London: Routledge.

Evans, V., & Green, M. (2006). *Cognitive linguistics: An introduction.* Edinburgh, UK: Edinburgh University Press.

Fauconnier, G. (1997). *Mappings in thought and language.* Cambridge, UK: Cambridge University Press.

Fauconnier, G., & Turner, M. (2002). *The way we think: Conceptual blending and the mind's hidden complexities.* New York: Basic Books.

Gibbs, R. W. (1994). *The poetics of mind: Figurative thought, language, and understanding.* Cambridge, UK: Cambridge University Press.

Gibbs, R. W. (2006). *Embodiment and cognitive science.* Cambridge, UK: Cambridge University Press.
Givón, T. (1995). *Functionalism and grammar.* Amsterdam: John Benjamins.
Givón, T. (2001). *Syntax*: An introduction. Amsterdam: John Benjamins.
Goldberg, A. E. (1995). *Constructions: A construction grammar approach to argument structure.* Chicago: Chicago University Press.
Goldberg, A. E. (2006). *Constructions at work: The nature of generalization in language.* Oxford, UK: Oxford University Press.
Grady, J. (1997). Theories are buildings revisited. *Cognitive Linguistics, 8,* 267–290.
Grady, J. (1999). A typology of motivation for conceptual metaphor: Correlation vs. resemblance. In R. W. Gibbs & G. Steen (Eds.), *Metaphor in cognitive linguistics* (pp. 79–100). Amsterdam: John Benjamins.
Grady, J. (2007). Metaphor. In D. Geeraertz & H. Cuyckens (Eds.), *The Oxford handbook of cognitive linguistics* (pp. 188–213). Oxford, UK: Oxford University Press.
Halliday, M. A. K. (1994). *An introduction to functional grammar.* London: Edward Arnold.
Halliday, M. A. K. (1978). *Language as social semiotic: The social interpretation of language and meaning.* London: Edward Arnold.
Halliday, M. A. K. (2002). Spoken and written modes of meaning. In J. Webster (Ed.), *On grammar* (pp. 323–351). London: Continuum Press.
Halliday, M. A. K., & Hasan, R. (1976). *Cohesion in English.* London: Longman.
Halliday, M. A. K., & Matthiessen, C. M. (1999). *Construing experience through meaning: A language-based approach to cognition.* London: Cassell.
Halliday, M. A. K., & Matthiessen, C. M. (2004). *An introduction to functional grammar.* London: Edward Arnold.
Hamrick, P., & Attardo, S. (in press). Evaluating applied cognitive linguistics in Italian L2 instruction: Towards a pedagogical cognitive grammar. In S. De Knop, F. Boers, & T. De Rycker (Eds.), *Applications of cognitive linguistics: Exploring the lexis-grammar continuum in second language pedagogy.* Berlin, Germany: Mouton de Gruyter.
Hoey, M. (1991). *Patterns of lexis.* Oxford, UK: Oxford University Press.
Huong, N. T. (2005). *Vietnamese learners mastering English articles.* Unpublished doctoral dissertation, University of Groningen, Netherlands.
Kemmer, S., & Barlow, M. (2000). Introduction: A usage-based conception of language. In M. Barlow & S. Kemmer (Eds.), *Usage-based models of language* (pp. vii–xxviii). Stanford, CA: CSLI.
Lakoff, G. (1987). *Women, fire, and dangerous things: What categories reveal about the mind.* Chicago: University of Chicago Press.
Lakoff, G. (1990). The invariance hypothesis: Is abstract reason based on image schemas?

Cognitive Linguistics,1, 39–74.
Lakoff, G., & Johnson, M. (1980). *Metaphors we live by.* Chicago: University of Chicago Press.
Lakoff, G., & Johnson, M. (1999). *Philosophy in the flesh.* New York: Basic Books.
Langacker, R. W. (1987). *Foundations of cognitive grammar: Vol. I. Theoretical prerequisites.* Stanford, CA: Stanford University Press.
Langacker, R. W. (1991a). *Concept, image, and symbol: The cognitive basis of grammar.* Berlin, Germany and New York: Mouton de Gruyter.
Langacker, R. W. (1991b). *Foundations of cognitive grammar: Vol. II. Descriptive application.* Stanford, CA: Stanford University Press.
Langacker, R. W. (2008a). *Cognitive grammar: A basic introduction.* Oxford, UK: Oxford University Press.
Langacker, R. W. (2008b). Cognitive grammar as a basis for language instruction. In P. Robinson & N. C. Ellis (Eds.), *Handbook of cognitive linguistics and second language acquisition* (pp. 66–88). New York: Routledge.
Larsen-Freeman, D. (2002). The grammar of choice. In E. Hinkle & S. Fotos (Eds.), *New perspectives on grammar teaching in second language classrooms* (pp. 103–118). Mahwah, NJ: Erlbaum.
Liamkina, O. A. (2006). The role of explicit meaning-based instruction in foreign language pedagogy: Applications of cognitive linguistics to teaching the German dative case to advanced learners. *Dissertation Abstracts International, 66*(10), 3627. (UMI No. AAT 3193301).
Liamkina, O. A. (2008). Making dative a case for semantic analysis: Differences in use between native and non-native speakers of German. In A. Tyler, Y. Kim, & M. Takada (Eds.), *Language in the context of use: Discourse and cognitive approaches to language* (pp. 145–166). Berlin, Germany: Mouton de Gruyter.
Lieven, E., & Tomasello, M. (2008). Children's first language acquisition from a usage-based perspective. In P. Robinson & N. C. Ellis (Eds.), *Handbook of cognitive linguistics and second language acquisition* (pp. 168–198). New York: Routledge.
Littlemore, J., & Low, G. (2006). Metaphoric competence, second language learning, and communicative language ability. *Applied Linguistics, 27*, 268–294.
Lowie, W., & Verspoor, M. (2004). Input versus transfer?—The role of frequency and similarity in the acquisition of L2 prepositions. In M. Achard & S. Niemeier (Eds.), *Cognitive linguistics, second language acquisition, and foreign language teaching* (pp. 77–94). Berlin, Germany: Mouton de Gruyter.
MacArthur, F., & Littlemore, J. (2008). A discovery approach to figurative language learning with the use of corpora. In F. Boers & S. Lindstromberg (Eds.), *Cognitive linguistic approaches to teaching vocabulary and phraseology* (pp. 159–188). Berlin, Germany:

Mouton De Gruyter.

Manzanares, J. V., & Rojo Lopez, A. M. (2008). What can language learners tell us about constructions? In S. De Knop & T. De Rycker (Eds.), *Cognitive approaches to pedagogical grammar* (pp. 197–230). Berlin, Germany: Mouton de Gruyter.

Martin, J. R. (1999). Mentoring semogenesis: "Genre-based" literacy pedagogy. In F. Christie (Ed.), *Pedagogy and the shaping of consciousness: Linguistic and social processes* (pp. 123–155). London: Cassell.

Martin, J. R. (2001). From little things big things grow: Ecogenesis in school geography. In R. Coe, L. Lingard, & T. Teslenko (Eds.), *The rhetoric and ideology of genre: Strategies for stability and change* (pp. 253–271). Cresskill, NJ: Hampton Press.

Martin, J. R. (2002). Meaning beyond the clause: SFL perspectives. *Annual Review of Applied Linguistics, 22*, 52–74.

Martin, J. R. (2009). Genre and language learning: A social semiotic perspective. *Linguistics and Education, 20*, 10–21.

Martin, J. R., & Rose, D. (2008). *Genre relations: Mapping culture.* London: Equinox.

McCarthy, M., & Carter, R. (2002). Ten criteria for a spoken grammar. In E. Hinkle & S. Fotos (Eds.), *New perspectives on grammar teaching in second language classrooms* (pp. 51–76). Mahwah, NJ: Erlbaum.

Mellow, J. D. (2006). The emergence of second language syntax: A case study of the acquisition of relative clauses. *Applied Linguistics, 27*, 645–670.

Moder, C. L. (2004). Ice box moms and hockey dads: Context and the mapping of N-N metaphorical expressions. In M. Achard & S. Kemmer (Eds.), *Language, culture and mind* (109–121). Stanford, CA: CSLI.

Moder, C. L. (2008). It's like making a soup: Metaphors and similes in spoken news discourse. In A. Tyler, Y. Kim, & M. Takada (Eds.), *Language in the context of use: Discourse and cognitive approaches to language* (pp. 301–320). Berlin, Germany: Mouton de Gruyter.

Newman, J. (1996). *Give: A cognitive linguistic study.* New York: Mouton de Gruyter.

Niemeier, S. (2008). The notion of boundedness/unboundedness in the foreign language classroom. In F. Boers & S. Lindstromberg (Eds.), *Cognitive linguistic approaches to teaching vocabulary and phraseology* (pp. 309–327). Berlin, Germany: Mouton de Gruyter.

Panther, K., & Thornburg, L. (2001). A conceptual analysis of English *-er* nominals. In M. Pütz, S. Niemeier, & R. Dirven (Eds.), *Applied cognitive linguistics II: Language pedagogy* (pp. 149–200). Berlin, Germany: Mouton de Gruyter.

Pütz, M., Niemeier, S., & Dirven, R. (Eds.). (2001). *Applied cognitive linguistics I: Theory and language acquisition.* Berlin, Germany: Mouton De Gruyter.

Pütz, M., Niemeier, S., & Dirven, R. (Eds.). (2001). *Applied cognitive linguistics II: Language pedagogy.* Berlin, Germany: Mouton De Gruyter.

Reddy, M. (1993). The conduit metaphor: A case of frame conflict in our language about language. In A. Ortony (Ed.), *Metaphor and thought* (pp. 164–201). Cambridge, UK: Cambridge University Press.

Robinson, P., & Ellis, N. C. (Eds.). (2008). *Handbook of cognitive linguistics and second language acquisition.* New York: Routledge.

Rosch, E., & Mervis, C. (1975). Cognitive representations of semantic categories. *Journal of Experimental Psychology: General, 104,* 382–439.

Rudzka-Ostyn, B. (2003). *Word power: Phrasal verbs and compounds: A cognitive approach.* Berlin, Germany: Mouton De Gruyter.

Sanders, T., & Spooren, W. (2005). Discourse and text structure. In D. Geeraertz & H. Cuyckens (Eds.), *The Oxford handbook of cognitive linguistics* (pp. 916–937). Oxford, UK: Oxford University Press.

Schleppegrell, M. J. (2004). *The language of schooling: A functional linguistics perspective.* Mahwah, NJ: Erlbaum.

Schleppegrell, M. J. (2008). Grammar, the sentence, and traditions of linguistic analysis. In Charles Bazerman (Ed.), *Handbook of writing research* (pp. 549–564). Mahwah, NJ: Erlbaum.

Schleppegrell, M. J., Greer, S., & Taylor, S. (2008). Literacy in history: Language and meaning. *Australian Journal of Language and Literacy, 31,* 174–187.

Schmid, H. (2007). Entrenchment, salience and basic levels. In D. Geeraerts & H. Cuyckens (Eds.), *The Oxford handbook of cognitive linguistics* (pp. 117–138). Oxford, UK: Oxford University Press.

Slobin, D. I. (1996a). Two ways to travel: Verbs of motion in English and Spanish. In M. Shibatani & S. A. Thompson (Eds.), *Grammatical constructions: Their form and meaning* (pp. 195–220). Oxford, UK: Clarendon Press.

Slobin, D. I. (1996b). From "thought and language" to "thinking for speaking." In J. Gumperz & S. Levinson (Eds.), *Rethinking linguistic relativity. Studies in the social and cultural foundations of language, No. 17* (pp. 70–96). Cambridge, UK: Cambridge University Press.

Slobin, D. I. (2003). Language and thought online: Cognitive consequences of linguistic relativity. In D. Gentner & S. Goldin-Meadow (Eds.), *Language in mind: Advances in the investigation of language and thought* (pp. 157–191). Cambridge, MA: MIT Press.

Slobin, D. I. (2009). Relations between paths of motion and paths of vision: A crosslinguistic and developmental exploration. In V. M. Gathercole (Ed.), *Routes to language: Studies in honor of Melissa Bowerman* (pp. 197–221). New York: Psychology Press.

Strauss, S., Lee, J., & Ahn, K. (2006). Applying conceptual grammar to advanced-level language teaching: The case of two completive constructions in Korean. *Modern Language*

Journal, 90, 185–209.

Sweetser, E. (1990). *From etymology to pragmatics: Metaphorical and cultural aspects of semantic structure*. Cambridge, UK: Cambridge University Press.

Talmy, L. (2000a). *Toward a cognitive semantics: Vol. I. Concept structuring systems*. Cambridge, MA: MIT Press.

Talmy, L. (2000b). *Toward a cognitive semantics: Vol. II. Typology and process in concept structuring*. Cambridge, MA: MIT Press.

Tannen, D. (1989). *Talking voices: Repetition, dialogue, and imagery in conversational discourse*. Cambridge, UK: Cambridge University Press.

Taylor, J. R. (2003). *Linguistic categorization*. Oxford, UK: Oxford University Press.

Taylor, J. R. (2004). *Cognitive grammar*. Oxford, UK: Oxford University Press.

Tomasello, M. (2003). *Constructing a language: A usage-based theory of language acquisition*. Cambridge, MA: Harvard University Press.

Tomasello, M., & Brooks, P. (1998). Young children's earliest transitive and intransitive constructions. *Cognitive Linguistics, 9*, 379–395.

Tomlin, R. (1994). Functional grammar, pedagogical grammars, and communicative language teaching. In T. Odlin (Ed.) *Perspectives on pedagogical grammar* (pp. 140–178). Cambridge, UK: Cambridge University Press.

Tomlin, R. (1997). Mapping conceptual representations into linguistic representations: The role of attention in grammar. In J. Nuyts & E. Pederson (Eds.), *Language and conceptualization* (pp. 162–189). Cambridge, UK: Cambridge University Press.

Tyler, A. (2008a). Cognitive linguistics and second language instruction. In P. Robinson & N. C. Ellis (Eds.), *Handbook of cognitive linguistics and second language acquisition* (pp. 456–488). London: Routledge.

Tyler, A. (2008b). Applied cognitive linguistics: Putting linguistics back into second language learning. In M. Pü tz (Ed.), *Cognitive approaches to second/foreign language processing: Theory and pedagogy* (pp. 904–923). Essen, Germany: LAUD.

Tyler, A., & Evans, V. (2001). The relation between experience, conceptual structure and meaning: Non-temporal uses of tense and language teaching. In M. Pü tz, R. Dirven, & S. Niemeier (Eds.), *Applied cognitive linguistics I: Theory and language acquisition* (pp. 63–105). Berlin, Germany: Mouton de Gruyter.

Tyler, A., & Evans, V. (2003). *The semantics of English prepositions: Spatial scenes, embodied meaning and cognition*. Cambridge, UK: Cambridge University Press.

Tyler, A., & Evans, V. (2004). Applying cognitive linguistics to pedagogical grammar: The case of over. In M. Achard & S. Neimeier (Eds.), *Cognitive linguistics, second language acquisition, and foreign language teaching* (pp. 257–280). Berlin, Germany: Mouton de Gruyter.

Tyler, A., Kim, Y., & Takada, M. (Eds.). (2008). *Language in the context of use: Discourse and cognitive approaches to language.* Berlin, Germany: Mouton de Gruyter.

Verspoor, M., & Lowie, W. (2003). Making sense of polysemous words. *Language Learning, 53*, 547–586.

Verspoor, M., & Tyler, A. (2009). The role of cognitive linguistics in second language research. In W. Ritchie & T. K. Bhatia (Eds.), *The new handbook of second language acquisition* (pp. 160–177). Oxford, UK: Emerald.

von Stutterheim, C. (2003). Linguistic structures and information organisation: The case of very advanced learners. In S. Foster-Cohen (Ed.), *EUROSLA Yearbook 3* (pp. 183–206). Amsterdam: John Benjamins.

Walker, C. (2008). Factors which influence the process of collocation. In F. Boers & S. Lindstromberg (Eds.), *Cognitive linguistic approaches to teaching vocabulary and phraseology* (pp. 291–308). Berlin, Germany: Mouton De Gruyter.

Zyzik, E. (2009). The role of input revisited: Nativist and usage-based models. *L2 Journal, 1,* 42–61.

CONTRIBUTOR BIODATA

Jeffrey Bale is an assistant professor of second language education at Michigan State University. He coordinates the world languages teacher preparation program in the Department of Teacher Education and is an affiliate of MSU's Literacy Achievement Research Center. He received his doctorate from Arizona State University, specializing in language education policy analysis. His academic work builds on nearly 10 years as a classroom teacher of English as a second language and German. His research interests include sociohistorical and comparative perspectives on language education policy. Recent publications can be found in *Language Policy* and the *International Multilingual Research Journal*.

Melissa A. Bowles is an assistant professor of Spanish and second language acquisition at the University of Illinois at Urbana-Champaign. Her research focuses on instructed (classroom) second language acquisition and introspective methods of data collection in SLA. Her forthcoming book, *The Think-Aloud Controversy in Language Acquisition Research* (Routledge) presents an in-depth analysis of verbal reports as they have been used in language research.

Patricia A. Duff is a professor of language and literacy education at the University of British Columbia and the director of the Centre for Research in Chinese Language and Literacy Education. Her research, teaching, and publications, including three books, deal primarily with language socialization across bilingual and multilingual settings; qualitative research methods and generalizability in applied linguistics (especially case study and ethnography); issues in the teaching and learning of English, Mandarin, and other international languages; the integration of second language learners in high schools, universities, and society; multilingualism and work; and sociocultural, sociolinguistic, and sociopolitical aspects of language(s) in education.

Paola E. Dussias is an associate professor of Spanish, linguistics, and psychology at the Pennsylvania State University. Her research takes a cross-disciplinary approach to bilingual sentence processing. Using a variety of behavioral methods, ranging from off-line questionnaires to eye-tracking methods during reading and spoken language comprehension, she examines the way that second language readers and listeners negotiate the presence of two languages in a single mind. Her work has appeared in journals such as *Bilingualism, Language and Cognition, The International Journal of Bilingualism, Studies in Second Language Acquisition,* and *Second Language Research,* as well as in a number of edited volumes.

Debra A. Friedman is an assistant professor in the Department of Linguistics and Germanic, Slavic, Asian, and African Languages at Michigan State University, where she teaches courses in second language pedagogy, language socialization, and qualitative research methods. She specializes in the application of discourse analysis and language socialization approaches to the study of language classroom interaction, with a focus on the sociocultural, political, and ideological aspects of second language education and language education policy.

Agnes Weiyun He is an associate professor of applied linguistics and Asian studies at Stony Brook University. She is the author of *Reconstructing Institutions: Language Use in Academic Counseling Encounters* (Greenwood, 1998), co-editor of *Talking and Testing: Discourse Approaches to the Assessment of Oral Proficiency* (John Benjamins, 1998) and the primary editor of *Chinese as a Heritage Language: Fostering Rooted World Citizenry* (University of Hawaii Press, 2008). Her work has been funded by the Spencer Foundation, the National Academy of Education, and the U.S. Department of Education.

Kimi Kondo-Brown is an associate professor in the Department of East Asian Languages and Literatures at the University of Hawaii at Manoa. She is also the interim associate dean of the College of Languages, Linguistics, and Literature. Her research focuses on language education, pedagogy, and assessment. In addition to numerous book chapters and articles in journals such as *Modern Language Journal, Language Learning, Language Testing,* and *Foreign Language Annals,* she recently published three edited books including *Teaching Chinese, Japanese, and Korean Heritage Language Students: Curriculum Needs, Materials, and Assessment* (with J. D. Brown, LEA/Taylor & Francis, 2008).

Juana M. Liceras is a professor in the Department of Modern Languages and the Department of Linguistics at the University of Ottawa and the director of the Language Acquisition Research Laboratory (http://aix1.uottawa.ca/~lalab/). She is a member of the editorial boards of several periodicals, among them *Second Language Research*, *Revista Española de Lingüística Aplicada*, and *Lengua y Migración*. Her research interests and publications deal with the relationship between linguistic theory and language acquisition, and language acquisition and diachronic change, as well as comparative grammar, bilingualism, and language contact.

Silvina Montrul is an associate professor of Spanish, linguistics, and second language acquisition at the University of Illinois at Urbana-Champaign. She is author of *The Acquisition of Spanish* (Benjamins, 2004) and *Incomplete Acquisition in Bilingualism* (Benjamins, 2008), as well as numerous articles in journals such as *Bilingualism: Language and Cognition*, *The International Journal of Bilingualism*, *Language Learning*, *The Heritage Language Journal*, *Studies in Second Language Acquisition*, *Language Acquisition*, and *Second Language Research*. Her research focuses on linguistic and psycholinguistic approaches to adult second language acquisition and bilingualism, in particular syntax, semantics, and morphology. She also has expertise in language loss and retention in minority language-speaking bilinguals.

Frederick L. Oswald is an associate professor of industrial and organizational psychology at Rice University. His research takes place in educational, organizational, and military settings, and deals with measuring, modeling, and predicting performance outcomes with psychological measures (personality, motivation, knowledge, experience, and ability). His methodological work in meta-analysis, multilevel modeling, and structural equation modeling serves this end. He publishes and serves on the editorial boards for several major organization research journals including *Journal of Applied Psychology*, *International Journal of Selection and Assessment*, *Journal of Management*, and *Organizational Research Methods*.

Luke Plonsky is a Ph.D. student in second language studies at Michigan State University, where he teaches Spanish, ESL, and introductory courses on second language acquisition and pedagogy. His research has employed meta-analysis and corpus techniques to investigate topics such as L2 strategy instruction and acquisition of tense and aspect in Spanish. Recent and forthcoming publications appear in *Studies in Second Language Acquisition*, *Foreign Language Annals*, and *Applied Language Learning*. He is currently editing (with Maren Schierloh) the conference proceedings of the 2009 Second Language Research Forum.

Celia Roberts is a professor of applied linguistics at King's College, London. She is a co-author of several books in the areas of intercultural communication and second language socialization (*Language and Discrimination*, Longman, 1992; *Achieving Understanding*, Longman, 1996); the field of urban discourse (*Talk, Work, and Institutional Order*, Mouton, 1999); and the field of language and cultural learning (*Language Learners as Ethnographers*, Multilingual Matters, 2001). Over the last 10 years, she has undertaken research on effective practice in ESOL, in doctor-patient communication in linguistically diverse settings, and in job interviews and ethnolinguistic disadvantage.

Roumyana Slabakova is an associate professor of linguistics at the University of Iowa. Her primary area of expertise is the second language acquisition of tense and aspect, and the mapping of inflectional morphology to meaning. She has done experimental research on various properties at the syntax-semantics and the syntax-discourse/pragmatics interfaces. She is the author of two monographs, *Aspect in the Second Language* (Benjamins) and *Meaning in the Second Language* (de Gruyter). Her bottleneck hypothesis proposes that there is no critical period for the acquisition of meaning, but that inflectional morphology is the real bottleneck of the second language acquisition process.

Steven Talmy is an assistant professor in the Department of Language and Literacy Education at the University of British Columbia. His academic interests include critical analyses of discourse, K–12 ESL, the sociology of ESL education, resistance to second language learning, and qualitative research methods. He is co-editor (with Keith Richards) of the 2010 special issue of *Applied Linguistics* entitled "Qualitative Interviews in Applied Linguistics: Discursive Perspectives."

Andrea Tyler is a professor of linguistics at Georgetown University. Her research focuses on the interaction between linguistic theory, especially cognitive linguistics and discourse analysis, and issues in second language learning. She is the co-author of *The Semantics of English Prepositions: Spatial Scenes, Embodied Meaning and Cognition* and *U.S. Legal Discourse: Legal English for Foreign LLMs*. She has co-edited two volumes focusing on discourse, cognitive linguistics, and language learning. Her work has appeared in such journals as *Applied Linguistics, Cognition, Language, Language and Memory, Journal of Pragmatics, Studies in Second Language Acquisition, TESOL Quarterly*, and *Text*.

图书在版编目(CIP)数据

剑桥应用语言学年度评论.2010:应用语言学专题＝Annual Review of Applied Linguistics 2010·A Survey of Selected Topics in Applied Linguistics:英文/(美)查伦·波利奥(Charlene Polio)主编.—北京:商务印书馆,2016
(剑桥应用语言学年度评论)
ISBN 978-7-100-12626-7

Ⅰ.①剑… Ⅱ.①查… Ⅲ.①应用语言学—研究—英文 Ⅳ.①H08

中国版本图书馆 CIP 数据核字(2016)第 240751 号

所有权利保留。
未经许可,不得以任何方式使用。

剑桥应用语言学年度评论 2010·应用语言学专题
Annual Review of Applied Linguistics 2010·
A Survey of Selected Topics in Applied Linguistics
主编 〔美〕Charlene Polio
导读 郑 萱

商 务 印 书 馆 出 版
(北京王府井大街36号 邮政编码100710)
商 务 印 书 馆 发 行
北京市松源印刷有限公司印刷
ISBN 978-7-100-12626-7

2016年12月第1版　　开本 880×1230　1/32
2016年12月北京第1次印刷　印张 14
定价:42.00元